FRENCH AND FRANCOPHONE STUDIES

Women's Writing in Twenty-First-Century France

Series Editors

Hanna Diamond (University of Bath)
Claire Gorrara (Cardiff University)

Editorial Board

Ronan le Coadic (Université Rennes 2)
Nicola Cooper (Swansea University)
Colin Davis (Royal Holloway, University of London)
Didier Francfort (Université Nancy 2)
Sharif Gemie (University of South Wales)
H. R. Kedward (Sussex University)
Margaret Majumdar (University of Portsmouth)
Nicholas Parsons (Cardiff University)
Max Silverman (University of Leeds)

FRENCH AND FRANCOPHONE STUDIES

Women's Writing in Twenty-First-Century France

Life as Literature

EDITED BY

AMALEENA DAMLÉ AND GILL RYE

UNIVERSITY OF WALES PRESS

© The Contributors, 2013
Reprinted 2014 (US distribution) and 2015

All rights reserved. No part of this book may be reproduced in any material form (including photocopying or storing it in any medium by electronic means and whether or not transiently or incidentally to some other use of this publication) without the written permission of the copyright owner except in accordance with the provisions of the Copyright, Designs and Patents Act 1988. Applications for the copyright owner's written permission to reproduce any part of this publication should be addressed to The University of Wales Press, 10 Columbus Walk, Brigantine Place, Cardiff CF10 4UP.

www.uwp.co.uk

British Library CIP
A catalogue record for this book is available from the British Library.

ISBN   978-1-78316-206-2
e-ISBN 978-0-7083-2589-6

The rights of the Contributors to be identified as authors of this work have been asserted in accordance with sections 77, 78 and 79 of the Copyright, Designs and Patents Act 1988.

Printed by CPI Antony Rowe, Chippenham, Wiltshire

In memoriam
Elizabeth Fallaize

Contents

Acknowledgements		xiii
List of illustrations		xv
Notes on contributors		xvii

Part One: Women's Writing in Twenty-First-Century France: Trends and Issues

Chapter 1:	Women's Writing in Twenty-First-Century France: Introduction *Amaleena Damlé and Gill Rye*	3
Chapter 2:	What 'Passes'?: French Women Writers and Translation into English *Lynn Penrod*	17
Chapter 3:	What Women Read: Contemporary Women's Writing and the Best-seller *Diana Holmes*	30

Part Two: Society, Culture, Family

Chapter 4:	Vichy, Jews, *Enfants Cachés*: French Women Writers Look Back *Lucille Cairns*	47
Chapter 5:	Wives and Daughters in Literary Works Representing the *Harkis* *Susan Ireland*	60
Chapter 6:	(Not) Seeing Things: Marie NDiaye, (Negative) Hallucination and 'Blank' *Métissage* *Andrew Asibong*	73

Chapter 7:	Rediscovering the Absent Father, a Question of Recognition: Despentes, Tardieu *Lori Saint-Martin*	87
Chapter 8:	Babykillers: Véronique Olmi and Laurence Tardieu on Motherhood *Natalie Edwards*	98

Part Three: Body, Life, Text

Chapter 9:	The Becoming of Anorexia and Text in Amélie Nothomb's *Robert des noms propres* and Delphine de Vigan's *Jours sans faim* *Amaleena Damlé*	113
Chapter 10:	The Human-Animal in Ananda Devi's Texts: Towards an Ethics of Hybridity? *Ashwiny O. Kistnareddy*	127
Chapter 11:	Embodiment, Environment and the Reinvention of Self in Nina Bouraoui's Life-Writing *Helen Vassallo*	141
Chapter 12:	Irreverent Revelations: Women's Confessional Practices of the Extreme Contemporary *Barbara Havercroft*	154
Chapter 13:	Contamination Anxiety in Annie Ernaux's Twenty-First-Century Texts *Simon Kemp*	168

Part Four: Experiments, Interfaces, Aesthetics

Chapter 14:	Experience and Experiment in the Work of Marie Darrieussecq *Helena Chadderton*	183
Chapter 15:	Interfaces: Verbal/Visual Experiment in New Women's Writing in French *Shirley Jordan*	196
Chapter 16:	'Autofiction + x = ?': Chloé Delaume's Experimental Self-Representations *Deborah B. Gaensbauer*	212

Chapter 17:	Beyond Antoinette Fouque (*Il y a deux sexes*) and Beyond Virginie Despentes (*King Kong théorie*)? Anne Garréta's Sphinxes *Owen Heathcote*	225
Chapter 18:	Amélie the Aesthete: Art and Politics in the World of Amélie Nothomb *Anna Kemp*	237
Conclusion	*Amaleena Damlé and Gill Rye*	251
Works Cited		253
Index		275

Series Editors' Preface

This series showcases the work of new and established scholars working within the fields of French and francophone studies. It publishes introductory texts aimed at a student readership, as well as research-orientated monographs at the cutting edge of their discipline area. The series aims to highlight shifting patterns of research in French and francophone studies, to re-evaluate traditional representations of French and francophone identities and to encourage the exchange of ideas and perspectives across a wide range of discipline areas. The emphasis throughout the series will be on the ways in which French and francophone communities across the world are evolving into the twenty-first century.

Hanna Diamond and Claire Gorrara

Acknowledgements

We are very grateful to Girton College, Cambridge and the Faculty of Modern and Medieval Languages at the University of Cambridge for their support in bringing this book to fruition. We should also like to thank the Cassal Trust Fund, administered by the School of Advanced Study, University of London, the French Embassy in London and the Institute of Germanic & Romance Studies, University of London, for their earlier contributions to our project.

List of illustrations

Figure 14.1 'Learning to write', Marie Darrieussecq, *Le Pays* (2005). By kind permission of P.O.L.

Figure 14.2 'La Transfrontalière', Marie Darrieussecq, *Le Pays* (2005). By kind permission of P.O.L.

Figure 15.1 *L'Usage de la photo*, 'a register of excess' (2005), © Annie Ernaux and Marc Marie, reproduced by kind permission.

Figure 15.2 *L'Épouvante l'émerveillement*, 'inflammatory marking', Béatrix Beck (illustrations by Gaël Davrinche), © Les Éditions du Chemin de fer, 2010.

Figure 15.3 *Version live*, 'daughter/mother identification', Sigolène Prébois, © P.O.L., 2010.

Figure 15.4 *Version live*, 'drawing as tending', Sigolène Prébois, © P.O.L., 2010.

Notes on contributors

Andrew Asibong is Senior Lecturer in the Department of European Cultures and Languages at Birkbeck, University of London, where he is also co-director of the research centre Birkbeck Research in Aesthetics of Kinship and Community (BRAKC). His research focuses on the radical reconfiguration of subjectivity and inter-subjective modes of relationality in the contemporary arts, drawing especially on fantastical or pseudo-fantastical films and fictions, mainly psychoanalytic forms of psychotherapy, and the ethics and politics of class and stigma. He has published articles on the writers Jacques Stephen Alexis, Marie Chauvet, Marie Darrieussecq, Mohammed Dib, Hervé Guibert and Marie NDiaye, and on the filmmakers Pedro Almodóvar, Gregg Araki, Claire Denis, Georges Franju, François Ozon and Alain Resnais. He is the author of *François Ozon* (2008) and co-editor (with Shirley Jordan) of *Marie NDiaye: l'étrangeté à l'œuvre* (2009). He is currently preparing a monograph entitled *Marie NDiaye: Blankness and Recognition*.

Lucille Cairns is Professor of French at Durham University. She is the author of numerous articles and chapters, both on French women's writing and filmmaking and on male and female homosexuality in French literature and film, as well as of five sole-authored monographs: *Marie Cardinal: Motherhood and Creativity* (1992), *Privileged Pariahdom: Homosexuality in the Novels of Dominique Fernandez* (1996), *Lesbian Desire in Post-1968 French Literature* (2002), *Sapphism on Screen: Lesbian Desire in French and Francophone Cinema* (2006) and *Post-War Jewish Women's Writing in French* (2011). She is also sole editor of *Gay and Lesbian Cultures in France* (2002). She was President of the Association of University Professors and Heads of French from 2007–10, and is currently the national representative for French Studies on the Executive Committee of the University Council of Modern Languages. In 2009, she was made a Chevalier dans l'Ordre des Palmes Académiques by the French government.

In 2011, she became a member of REF 2014 sub-panel 28 (Modern Languages and Linguistics). In 2011, the Agence Nationale de la Recherche appointed her Vice-President of the *Laboratoires d'excellence* scheme for the Humanities jury and, in 2012, she became President of the ANR's new Humanities scheme of grant awards.

Helena Chadderton is Lecturer in French at the University of Hull. She is the author of *Marie Darrieussecq's Textual Worlds: Self, Society and Language* (2012), as well as several articles on Darrieussecq. More broadly her research topics include contemporary fiction, women's writing, narrative theory, stylistics, the relationship between text, self and society, and the development of politically committed literature in a postmodern world.

Amaleena Damlé is Research Fellow in French at Girton College, Cambridge. Her research interests lie in intersections between modern and contemporary thought and literature, with a particular emphasis on gender and sexuality. Her monograph – *The Becoming of the Body: Contemporary Women's Writing in French* – is forthcoming in 2014. The book considers articulations of female corporeality and transformation in contemporary works by four female authors, in dialogue with Deleuzian philosophy and recent (post)feminist and queer thought. She is also working on a new book project that looks at notions of love, desire and ethics in modern and contemporary French culture, and is co-editing, with Gill Rye, two further volumes of articles on women's writing in French. She has written articles on Nina Bouraoui, Marie Darrieussecq, Ananda Devi and Amélie Nothomb, and is the co-editor of *The Beautiful and the Monstrous: Essays in French Literature, Thought and Culture* (2010).

Natalie Edwards is Lecturer in French Studies and member of the Fay Gale Centre for Research on Gender at the University of Adelaide. She specialises in contemporary women's writing and autobiography. Her book *Shifting Subjects: Plural Subjectivity in Francophone Women's Autobiography* was published in 2011. She co-edited with Christopher Hogarth *This Self Which Is Not One: Francophone Women's Life Writing* (2010) and *Gender and Displacement: 'Home' in Contemporary Francophone Women's Autobiography* (2008). She also co-edited with Amy Hubbell and Ann Miller *Textual/Visual Selves: Art, Photography and Performance in French Autobiography* (2011).

She is currently working on a book on representations of voluntarily childless women in French literature and film.

Deborah B. Gaensbauer is Professor in the Department of Modern and Classical Languages at Regis University. Her current research focuses on trauma narrative and autofiction in works by contemporary French and francophone women writers. Recent publications include essays on Maryse Condé, Marie NDiaye and Elsa Triolet. Her essay, 'Juste une petite mise en scène de la problématique: citational construction of an autofictional voice in Chloé Delaume's *Éden matin midi et soir*', is forthcoming in *Women in French Studies*.

Barbara Havercroft is Professor in the Department of French and at the Centre for Comparative Literature at the University of Toronto. She has published extensively on contemporary French and Quebec autobiographical writings (especially by women authors), on the literary encounter between feminism and postmodernism, on the theories of enunciation, on the theory and writing of trauma, and on the 'extreme contemporary' in French literature. She is also the co-founder and co-director of the research group GRELFA (Groupe de recherche et d'étude sur la littérature française d'aujourd'hui) at the University of Toronto. Her recent book publications include *Vies en récit: formes littéraires et médiatiques et la biographie et de l'autobiographie* (co-edited, 2007) and *Le Roman français de l'extrême contemporain: écritures, engagements, énonciations* (co-edited, 2010). She is currently working on a book project entitled '*Unspeakable Wounds': Personal Trauma in Contemporary Women's Autobiographical Writings* and is co-editing, with Bruno Blanckeman, a volume entitled *Narrations d'un nouveau siècle: romans et récits français (2001–2011)* (forthcoming, 2013).

Owen Heathcote is Honorary Visiting Reader in Modern French Studies at the University of Bradford. He researches on the relationship between violence, gender and representation in French literature and film and has published widely on such writers as Balzac, Cardinal, Chawaf, Duras, Guibert, Guyotat, Hyvrard and Wittig. He is a co-editor of *Negotiating Boundaries? Identities, Sexualities, Diversities* (2007) and the author of *Balzac and Violence: Representing History, Space, Sexuality and Death in* La Comédie humaine (2009). He is currently writing a book on masculinity and violence in the work of Éric Jourdan.

Diana Holmes is Professor of French at the University of Leeds, where she teaches twentieth- and twenty-first-century French literature and film. She has published widely on women's writing in France from late nineteenth to twenty-first centuries, including monographs on *Colette* (1991), *French Women Writers 1848–1994* (1996), *Rachilde: Decadence, Gender and the Woman Writer* (2001) and *Romance and Readership in Twentieth-Century France: Love Stories* (2006). She co-edited (with Carrie Tarr) *A 'Belle Epoque'? Women in French Society and Culture 1890–1914* (2005) and (with John Gaffney) *Stardom in Postwar France* (2007). Her second research field is cinema: she co-edits the Manchester University Press series *French Film Directors* and co-authored the volume on Truffaut. Her current research is on popular fiction and the pleasures of reading, and includes a recent special issue of *French Cultural Studies: Story-Telling in Contemporary French Fiction: le 'prêt-à-penser' and Reading Pleasure* (co-edited with David Platten, 2010), and a forthcoming book *Imagining the Popular in Contemporary French Culture*, co-edited with David Looseley, in which she has written the chapter on the popular novel. She is working on a book *Reclaiming the Middlebrow: Women, Stories and the Hierarchy of Culture in France since the Belle Époque*.

Susan Ireland is Orville and Mary Patterson Routt Professor of Literature at Grinnell College. Her research interests include contemporary French fiction, Quebec women writers, the Algerian novel and the literature of immigration in France and Quebec. She is an editor of *The Feminist Encyclopedia of French Literature* (1999) and, with Patrice Proulx, of *Immigrant Narratives in Contemporary France* (2001) and *Textualizing the Immigrant Experience in Contemporary Quebec* (2004). She has also published articles in journals such as *L'Esprit Créateur, Québec Studies, World Literature Today* and *Nottingham French Studies*.

Shirley Jordan is Professor of French Literature and Visual Culture at Queen Mary University of London. She has published on twentieth- and twenty-first-century art and art criticism, on photography (including photobiography and contemporary city photography), on new women's writing in French and on experimental self-narrative across media. She has written chapters and articles on Marie Darrieussecq, Marie NDiaye, Christine Angot, Lorette Nobécourt, Virginie Despentes, Annie Ernaux, Amélie Nothomb, Sophie Calle and Agnès Varda. She has also written on the art critical texts of Nathalie Heinich. Recent publications include *Contemporary French Women's Writing* (2004) and the co-edited volumes *Marie NDiaye: l'étrangeté à l'œuvre* (2009); *Watch This Space: Women's Conceptualisations of Space in Contemporary French Film and Visual Art* (2011); and *Space, Place and Landscape: New Women's Writing in French* (2011). Current projects include the monograph *Private Lives, Public Display: Intimacy and Excess in French Women's Self-Narrative Experiment* (forthcoming), a further monograph on the poetics of inhospitality in Marie NDiaye and a co-edited volume on contemporary city photography.

Anna Kemp is Lecturer in French at Queen Mary University of London. She has worked on French and francophone writing by women and its relationship to feminist discourses. Her first book *Voices and Veils: Feminism and Islam in French Women's Writing and Activism* was published in 2010. She has also published articles on the figure of the *beurette*, and on the work of contemporary writers including Amélie Nothomb and Nina Bouraoui. She is currently investigating fantasies of self-creation in twentieth- and twenty-first-century art and literature.

Simon Kemp is Fellow of Somerville College, Oxford. He has published extensively on Marie Darrieussecq, including 'Darrieussecq's mind' in *French Studies* (2008) and 'Homeland: voyageurs et patrie dans les romans de Marie Darrieussecq' in *Nomadismes des romancières contemporaines de langue française*, edited by Anne Simon and Audrey Lasserre (2008). His most recent monograph is *French Fiction into the Twenty-First Century: The Return to the Story* (2010). The book focuses in particular on the work of Annie Ernaux, exploring how her life story is cast in different lights by her diary extracts and retrospective narratives, and Darrieussecq, examining how she adapts stream-of-consciousness techniques in her work. His current project is a cultural history of consciousness in modern French literature, analysing how writers since Proust have represented the mind in their fiction.

Ashwiny O. Kistnareddy is an independent researcher and teacher of French and Spanish. In 2010, she completed an M.Phil. thesis on 'Hybridity in Ananda Devi's novels' at the University of Nottingham. She has given a number of papers at national and international conferences, and has published several articles on Devi's work, including 'Représenter l'altérité: le corps grotesque dans l'œuvre romanesque d'Ananda Devi' (2011), 'Interrogating identity: psychological dislocations in Ananda Devi's novels' (2011), as well as the forthcoming 'Rebelles, meurtrières et prostituées dans les romans d'Ananda Devi' and 'Almost white but not quite: a comparative reading of Ferblanc's hybridity in Ananda Devi's *Soupir*'. Her broader research interests include corporeality, language, femininity, exile, memory and nostalgia, hybridity, identity and madness.

Lynn Penrod is Professor of French in the Department of Modern Languages and Cultural Studies at the University of Alberta in Edmonton. Her research and teaching focus on twentieth-century French literature (J. M. G. Le Clézio, Michel Tournier), women writing in French (Hélène Cixous, Annie Ernaux, George Sand, Christiane Rochefort, Simone de Beauvoir), French children's literature, literary translation, and the interrelationships between literature and law. Author or co-author of four books and numerous articles in scholarly journals, her most recent publications include 'Just pottering around: impersonation and translation and the case of *Harry Potter*', in *TranscUlturAl* (2010), and 'Ethical sentiments and the role of literature in the jurisprudence seminar', in *Forum on Public Policy* (2010). A chapter on using law as a teaching tool in studying George Sand's *Indiana* is forthcoming in the MLA *Approaches to Teaching* series in 2012.

Gill Rye is Professor Emerita and Associate Fellow at the Institute of Germanic & Romance Studies, University of London, where she is Director of the cross-cultural Centre for the Study of Contemporary Women's Writing. Since 2000, she has also convened the Contemporary Women's Writing in French seminar. Her book publications include *Reading for Change* (2001), *Narratives of Mothering* (2009), *Women's Writing in Contemporary France* (co-edited with Michael Worton, 2002), *'When familiar meanings dissolve ...: Essays in French Studies in Memory of Malcolm Bowie* (co-edited with Naomi Segal, 2011), and two more volumes on twenty-first-century women's writing in France (co-edited with Amaleena Damlé). She has also edited or co-edited special issues of *Paragraph*, *Journal of Romance Studies*, *Dalhousie French Studies*, *L'Esprit Créateur* and *Nottingham French Studies*, with a special issue on Marie Darrieussecq (co-edited with Helena Chadderton) and an issue of *Forum for Modern Language Studies* forthcoming. She is currently also leading the AHRC-funded Motherhood in post-1968 European Literature Network.

Lori Saint-Martin is Professor in the Department of Literary Studies at the University of Quebec at Montreal (UQAM). A member of the Institut de recherches et d'études féministes at UQAM, where she has held various administrative positions, she has published two collections of short stories and over a dozen scholarly works on women's writing in Quebec, including *Le Nom de la mère: mères, filles et écriture dans la littérature québécoise au féminin* (1999) and *La Voyageuse et la prisonnière: Gabrielle Roy et la question des femmes* (2002). Her latest books are *Au-delà du nom: la question du père dans la littérature québécoise actuelle* (2010) and *Postures viriles: ce que dit la presse masculine* (2011), as well as two edited collections, *Les Pensées "post-": féminismes, genres et narration* (with Rosemarie Fournier-Guillemette and Moana Ladouceur, 2011) and *Entre pouvoir et plaisir: lectures contemporaines de l'érotisme* (with Rosemarie Fournier-Guillemette and Marie-Noëlle Huet, 2012). She is also the author of a novel, *Les Portes closes* (2013) and of a book of microfiction, *Mathématiques intimes* (2013). With Paul Gagné, she has translated more than sixty Canadian works of fiction and non-fiction into French, winning the Governor General's award in 2000 and 2007. In 2010, she received the Career Award for Excellence in Research from the Université du Québec network of universities.

Helen Vassallo is Senior Lecturer in French at the University of Exeter. Her primary research interests are in autobiography, illness narratives and legacies of conflict. She is the author of *Jeanne Hyvrard, Wounded Witness: The Body Politic and the Illness Narrative* (2007) and of *The Body Besieged: The Embodiment of Historical Memory in Nina Bouraoui and Leïla Sebbar* (2012). She has also published a number of articles on French and francophone women's life-writing, including 'Nous n'avions ni communauté ni confession: the alienation of "liberation" in *Le Jour où Nina Simone a cessé de chanter* (Darina

Al-Joundi, 2008)' in the *International Journal of Francophone Studies* (2012), 'Re-mapping Algeria(s) in France: Leïla Sebbar's *Mes Algéries en France* and *Journal de mes Algéries en France*', in *Modern and Contemporary France* (2011), and 'Impossible alterity? The pursuit of otherness in Nina Bouraoui's life writing', in the *International Journal of Francophone Studies* (2009). She has co-edited two volumes on alterity in francophone literature and culture, and was awarded a Certificate of Scholarly Merit for outstanding contribution in the field of Francophone Postcolonial Studies by the *International Journal of Francophone Studies* in 2010.

Part One
Women's Writing in Twenty-First-Century France: Trends and Issues

Chapter One
Women's Writing in Twenty-First-Century France: Introduction

AMALEENA DAMLÉ AND GILL RYE

At the beginning of the new millennium and into the second decade of the twenty-first century, women's writing in French continues to be a fertile field of study for both teaching and research in the UK, the US, Canada, Europe and beyond. The first texts of the so-called 'new generation' of young French writers of the 1990s – Christine Angot, Nina Bouraoui, Marie Darrieussecq, Virginie Despentes, Ananda Devi, Marie NDiaye, Marie Nimier, Lorette Nobécourt, Amélie Nothomb – have expanded into mature bodies of work, and some exciting new authors, worthy of wider interest, have come to the fore, such as Chloé Delaume, Claudie Gallay, Anna Gavalda, Véronique Olmi and Laurence Tardieu.[1] *Women's Writing in Twenty-First-Century France* takes stock of the first decade of the new century, identifying and exploring its key trends and issues. While some of the themes and literary techniques appearing in the 2000s expand upon what has gone before, others take altogether different directions and forge new ground.[2]

It might be thought no longer necessary in the third millennium to privilege the work of female writers. The point of much feminist literary analysis may well have been achieved and women authors are now arguably an integral part of the mainstream. Yet it is our (feminist) position that the study of writing by women offers crucial – and unparalleled – insights into women's lives, experiences and creativity, as well as into their perspectives on a range of issues. By means of overviews, comparisons and single-author or single-text readings, this collection of essays critically analyses the ways in which women writers are responding to and reflecting upon women's experiences in a rapidly changing world. As the title implies, and for reasons of coherence, the volume focuses on the work of authors who live and work in metropolitan France, rather than considering a wider body of literature written in French. It does, however, include the work of writers who have migrated, who are of mixed race, or who only partly live or work in the metropole, thus reflecting the composition of multicultural twenty-first-century France.

While the rationale behind this volume is to explore themes and strategies raised in writing, the two chapters immediately following our introduction relate in different ways to the interrelated and important issue of readership. Lynn Penrod's chapter reminds us of the role of translation in canon-formation. Likewise scholarly work: although, as editors and contributors, we do not claim to identify the classics of the future, it is nonetheless part of our aim to bring particular authors and works to the attention of a wider public. Diana Holmes's chapter focuses on popular, best-selling literature and, although there is some crossover between best-sellers and titles considered to be literary, her recognition of the success of middlebrow works in France is a salutary reminder that the experimental texts which often attract scholarly attention are not always commonly read by non-academic readers. As the chapters in this volume disclose, reading literature of all kinds encourages us to think, evaluate and imagine, and thus shapes our social and cultural values.

In the handful of years that precede and succeed the turn of any century, a charged atmosphere tends to prevail, on the one hand characterised by a sense of crisis and precarious hurtling towards uncertain futures, on the other curiously, inevitably, intermingled with hope, excitement and the opening out of new horizons. The vibrancy of this ambient turn-of-the-century flux gives rise to important critical debates and a rich seam of artistic endeavours that engage with the immediacy of the now and project themselves into realities to come. But it also provides an opportunity to look back, to take stock of the past, to reconsider our relationship to the historical events that have structured, and continue to inform, our political, social and cultural lives. This panoramic perspective can only have been magnified by our most recent turn of the century, the threshold into not only a new century but a new millennium.[3]

In this sense, the return to history that Colin Davis and Elizabeth Fallaize (2000: 13) identify in their consideration of French fiction in the 1980s is amplified in the twenty-first century. The legacy of the Second World War and the Algerian war of independence continue to be central themes in French literature more broadly, and they are increasingly being taken up in women's writing. This is a significant new development: since the explosion of published writing by women in France in the 1970s, authors have tended to focus on the creation of individual female voices (Cixous 1975; Cixous and Clément 1975), to explore female subjectivity and family relations through psychoanalytical perspectives (Cardinal 1975) or to harness the specificity of female experiences such as adolescence, sexuality, marriage and motherhood within sociocultural contexts (see, for example, the early work of Annie Ernaux), rather than to look back to collectively experienced historical events. However, as Nathalie Morello and Catherine Rodgers (2002: 36) observe, this recent return to history carries a particular gendered inflection in female-authored works, in which the historical is inextricably bound up with the personal. In the twenty-first century, new perspectives are being brought to bear on historical events and their intervention in private lives and personal identities. Lucille Cairns identifies in this volume an emerging body of work that voices the experiences of the wartime *enfant caché* (hidden child) in contemporary Jewish women's writing, that not only illuminates the socio-political implications of Vichy collaboration, genocide and exclusion, but also raises intimate questions about childhood, gender and trauma and, importantly, about testimony (see also Cairns 2011). Bearing witness to the past, as Shoshana Felman and Dori Laub's (1992) influential work has shown, enables the communication of traumatic experience and a healing process in which the reader participates.

What is particularly striking about this recent trend is the now relatively advanced age of authors producing first-hand accounts of this period in history and of their encrypted secrets of the past. This revisiting of past traumas after a prolonged period of time is also visible in another body of work, signalled by Susan Ireland in this volume, that speaks of the wounds borne by the *harkis*, the Algerians who worked for the French army during the war of independence, which have been until recently shrouded in silence. In such works, testimony is filtered through members of a new generation, who bear witness not only to their parents' untold stories, but to the impact on their families who carve out differently oriented, gendered accounts of the past. Testifying to historical events in the twenty-first century is thus opened out beyond the immediacy of the first-hand witness experience, mediated through time, memory and a sense of haunting that now carries through to future generations.[4]

Alongside this increasing tendency to revisit the past, women's writing in French in the first decade of the new millennium continues, in the vein of previous work by authors such as Cardinal, Ernaux, Danièle Sallenave, Leïla Sebbar, Paule Constant and Sylvie Germain in the 1970s, 1980s and 1990s, to be firmly committed to exploring the dynamics of its present social, political and economic realities. Over the last half of the twentieth century, French society has undergone massive social transformation and diversification, yet religion, race and immigration remain particularly charged areas in the twenty-first century, evidenced most recently by the killings in Toulouse which dominate the news at the time of writing. The roles that religious and cultural signs, symbols and clothing play in French society have been hotly debated over the past decade, culminating in the 2011 ban on Islamic face veils.[5] The twenty-first-century French state continues to pride itself on a secular stance, but one that may arguably eclipse the particularity of ethnic, cultural and religious identities and disavow deeply entrenched and deeply problematic attitudes towards difference and minority groups.[6] These embedded and often internalised attitudes towards difference are underscored in Andrew Asibong's contribution to this volume, where the staking out of racial identity in a short story by Marie NDiaye is complexly bound up with negotiating false selves, blank recognition and negative hallucination.

The French state's desire to uphold the republican logic of universalism that assumes all citizens to be the same and equal, and minimises the recognition of difference, has obvious implications for the questions of sexual difference with which this volume is particularly concerned. The relationship between universalism and equality with regard to women's position in society re-emerged with vigour in the French political sphere, with the *parité* (equality) debates of the late 1980s and 1990s (Célestin, DalMolin and Courtivron 2003). This led to a new equality law focused on representation in June 2000, less than a year after the introduction of the *Pacte civil de solidarité* (civil partnership) law, which arguably set the new millennium in France off on a path to rejuvenate existing gender and sexual politics. Feminism has gained a renewed sense of activity and activism, with groups such as Mix-cité, Les Sciences-Potiches se Rebellent, Les Pénélopes, Ni Putes, Ni Soumises and Chiennes de Garde leading the fights against economic and legal discrimination, harassment and violence against women. Such groups have also begun to integrate their work into broader issues, including domestic *parité*, as well as international concerns such as globalisation or the situation of women within fundamentalist cultures (Célestin, DalMolin and Courtivron 2003: 7). This would seem to suggest that French feminism in the twenty-first century has begun to address multilayered concerns and to engage with questions of composite identities. Yet issues such as domestic *parité* nonetheless still tend to be problematically inscribed within a heterosexist logic.

Gay and lesbian rights have increasingly come to the fore over the last decade in the French political sphere, and their visibility has perhaps been enabled by the election of the openly gay Bertrand Delanoë as mayor of Paris in 2001. But more political work is required to achieve equality and agency for individuals who identify in a spectrum of non-heterosexual positions, be they lesbian, gay, bisexual, trans-, queer or other, and to recognise the changing dynamics of relationships beyond heteronormative patterns of the couple and/or the family. Same-sex marriage has yet to be legalised, for example,[7] and until 2009 transexuality was still pathologised as an illness. Here French feminist theory and women's writing would seem to be advancing important work, forging new discourses that articulate a range of gendered positions and sexualities. Feminist and queer theorists in the English-speaking world who have formulated gender and sexuality through poststructuralist or postmodern perspectives may have taken longer to filter through to French feminism (evidenced by the fact that it took fifteen years before Judith Butler's otherwise hugely influential *Gender Trouble* (1990) was translated and published in France). Yet over the last decade, the influence of such thinkers (Butler; Grosz 1994; Braidotti 1994, 2002; Haraway 1991, 1996) can be discerned in the French context and would appear to be generating new French feminisms. Virginie Despentes's feminist manifesto, *King Kong théorie* (2006) (King Kong Theory), is a prime example here: rather than searching for authenticity or an arguably essentialist difference, in the manner of feminist manifestos of the 1970s, this text is more preoccupied with multilayering, diversity, hybridity and transgression.[8] Beyond the category of femininity, radically non-essentialist queer perspectives are mobilised in the work of authors such as Anne Garréta, for example, whose moves beyond conventional feminism are analysed in Owen Heathcote's contribution to this volume.

The family still occupies a prominent position in female-authored texts in the twenty-first century, with questions of mothering that reveal deep-seated assumptions about gender continuing to take centre stage. Yet, changing family practices (single-parent families, multiple family configurations post-divorce, single-sex parenting, group parenting), as well as new reproductive technologies (IVF, artificial insemination, surrogacy),[9] availability of contraception and abortion, and increased adoption possibilities, have all contributed to the reshaping of family patterns (Rye 2009a: 15–16). In particular they have allowed for new configurations of the sedimented relationship between femininity and mothering by creating opportunities for choice and control over mothering decisions. In twenty-first-century women's writing, narratives of mothering (Rye 2009a) have emerged which increasingly take on the mother's perspective rather than the previously dominant daughter's view, thus lending a further agency to motherhood. While some are concerned with the intimacy and positivity of the mother–child bond, others reveal more ambivalent attitudes and the darker side to mothering. Natalie Edwards's contribution to this volume highlights one extreme of this tendency in its consideration of fictional mothers who have committed infanticide and whose voices we carry an ethical injunction to hear for what they reveal about the desperate situations they find themselves in, but also for what might be disclosed about contemporary attitudes towards mothering and female identity.

However, in twenty-first-century women's writing, consideration of family relations is no longer entirely focused on the figure of the mother. Representations of fathers, as well as fathers as narrators, have come to the fore, as evidenced by Lori Saint-Martin's chapter in this volume. Such narratives often signal a desire to reconnect, from the father's or child's perspective, in a world where family relations are increasingly estranged. Elisabeth Roudinesco's (2002) polemical study of the family 'in disorder' analyses, through a variety of theoretical perspectives, the evolution of the concept of the family in the contemporary climate, tying familial estrangement into the demise of patriarchy and the rise of the feminine. While Roudinesco calls for the symbolic reinvention of the family, Marie-Claire Barnet astutely insists upon the plural form – families – that would adequately reflect the realities of new postmodern 'tribes' in twenty-first-century France, rather than reinstate the sacrosanct ideal of 'the' family (a concept which has arguably not been as stable in the past as Roudinesco wants to argue) (Barnet 2007: 13). In its engagement with different elements of family life beyond the ambivalent mother–daughter relationship, women's writing in the new millennium thus suggests that family might be productively viewed as an ongoing 'practice' rather than a unified, or unifying, construct.

In the twenty-first century, identity, too, is increasingly wrested away from unified, stable positions. Poststructuralist and postmodern perspectives have been viewed in the past with suspicion, as a fracturing of female specificity before it has been fully shored up (Irigaray 1977: 139). However, women writers in the third millennium are engaging in productive ways with the precarious nature of identity. Whether viewed through more conventional psychoanalytical paradigms, or through new interventions in critical thought, numerous studies on French women's writing have identified a focus on a subject that is somehow other than itself or uncanny (Asibong and Jordan 2009; Bragard and Ravi 2011; Connon 2010; Hutton 2009), a plural, shifting subject (Edwards and Hogarth 2010; Edwards 2011), a subject that hovers in in-between spaces (Caine 2003; Thumerel 2004), or a subject that 'becomes' (Damlé 2014, forthcoming). The wealth of literary texts and cultural criticism within postcolonial contexts in recent years has tremendously influenced writing more broadly, and has, as Simon Kemp (2010: 13) has suggested, altered the character of the French novel. This is particularly evidenced by the seepage of postcolonial vocabulary into cultural criticism, with metaphors of hybridity (Rye 2004), displacement (Edwards and Hogarth 2008) and nomadism (Lasserre and Simon 2008; Damlé 2011) evoking the idea that subjectivity, in the twenty-first-century climate of unprecedented globalisation and technological development, is always already deterritorialised, set apart and elsewhere. Hybrid, nomadic, displaced subjects are never at home, or entirely at ease, as Ashwiny O. Kistnareddy's contribution to this volume suggests in its analysis of different positions of hybridity in Ananda Devi's work. Yet, there is an increasing feeling in women's writing in French that this flux and displacement might open out more enticing, enabling glimpses into female embodied experience. Indeed alongside notions of deterritorialisation, there is also a sense that subjectivity might be *re*territorialised, within particular environments, that the very tissue of the self might be interwoven with place and space (see Barnet and Jordan 2010), as an embodied relation to and in the world. In an analysis of Nina Bouraoui's work, Helen Vassallo's chapter in this volume underscores this idea and explores the role that (life-)writing itself plays in the interweaving of the embodied self with her particular environment.

Such notions of embodiment signal the ways in which women's writing in the new millennium continues to challenge the Cartesian duality of mind and body, instead folding and enfolding mind and body into one another. Rather than representing a passive shell that encases identity, the body marks the point where the intimacy of the real touches the fabric of the symbolic, desire branches out towards the other, where boundaries are permeable and malleable. The complex negotiation of the body through the gaze of the other takes on ever-increasing pertinence and new meanings, however, in the contemporary 'hyperreal' climate, in which technological developments and a media-fuelled preoccupation with image reinforce visual and virtual means of representation and processes of signification. In such an environment, the possibilities for the appearance, reappearance but also the disappearance of the body are more boundless than ever before. The implications of the ensuing tension between embodiment and disembodiment in terms of gender, politics and representation can be seen in the increasing prevalence of anorexic experience in contemporary Western society, a concern that is raised in Amaleena Damlé's contribution to this volume. These articulations of disembodiment also point to ongoing anxieties about the body, its vulnerability and its mortality. In the 1970s and 1980s, authors such as Cixous, Chantal Chawaf, Annie Leclerc and Marie Redonnet sought to celebrate the rhythms and plenitude of the female body in writing. Yet, since the 1990s, illness, death and trauma have surfaced as corporeal themes that expose the darker side to female bodily experience (see Robson 2004), and reflect a wider trend of witnessing texts and 'wound culture' (Seltzer 1997). These elements are still very much present in the twenty-first century, in Ernaux's literature that revisits death and illness, in Ananda Devi's writing that considers abuse and suffering, in Despentes's work that exposes violence and rape. In the 1990s, the French cultural scene witnessed an explosion of female-authored texts in which desire and sex were presented in much more provocative and pornographic terms that contrast with the safer, affirmative spaces of female desire evoked by Cixous and others. From excessive desire in Alina Reyes, violence and viscerality in Despentes, Christine Angot's ongoing narratives of incest, Sophie Calle's invasions of privacy, to the catalogic enumeration of sexual acts in Catherine Millet or Catherine Cusset, the explicit exposure of female sexuality has been at the forefront of French culture (see Best and Crowley 2007). Though women's writing in the twenty-first century continues to highlight female desire, it appears to enable a spectrum of desiring positions, rather than focalise around one explicit pole. It is interesting to observe, for example, ten years after Millet's *La Vie sexuelle de Catherine M.* (2001) (*The Sexual Life of Catherine M.*), the publication of *L'Envie* (2011) (*Desire*) by Sophie Fontanel, an autofictional text that proffers chastity as a new form of sensual pleasure.[10] And between these two extremes, desire is multiply opened out in twenty-first-century women's writing, in a visible 'return to romance' (Holmes 2006) and to affective relations that is apparent in writing by, for example, Camille Laurens. Recent engagement with transgressive female desire would seem to nuance the previous decade's rather more detached provocations, taking the form of a more confessional and intimate, even if irreverent, exposure, as Barbara Havercroft's contribution to this volume evidences in its exploration of the work of Angot and Reyes. Where in twentieth-century women's writing lesbian desire is reinscribed beyond heterocentric configurations of sameness and difference (see Cairns 2002a and 2002b), the twenty-first century sees desire become a vital force in non-heteronormative contexts that collapses binary oppositions of homosexuality and heterosexuality (see Damlé 2014, forthcoming). If such articulations of desire go some way to destabilise sexual binaries, a great deal of women's writing nonetheless still (necessarily) insists on a – to some extent – recognisable female subject. In Anne Garréta's work, however, as Heathcote's contribution in this volume reveals, sexual subjectivity reaches beyond identifiable categories, becoming fluid and amorphous. Such elements in women's writing that reinscribe desire within queer contexts thus importantly disclose new modes of ethical engagement with the other in twenty-first-century sexual politics.

Creative innovation has been a hallmark of women's writing in French since Cixous's call for an avant-garde *écriture féminine* that might circumvent or 'deconstruct' masculine representation (Cixous 1975; Cixous and Clément 1975). However, new literary strategies wielded by women writers in the twenty-first century can be read alongside broader trends in French literature of the 'extreme contemporary', described by Warren Motte (2008: 15) as the undefined terrain of the now as it perpetually escapes from us (see also Havercroft, Michelucci and Riendeau 2010). The return to the story signalled by Davis and Fallaize (2000) is a notion that has been taken up in a great deal of literary criticism in recent years (S. Kemp 2010: 1–2), as indicating a move beyond the often opaque formal innovations of the *nouveaux romanciers*, the *Oulipo* and *Tel Quel*. Yet, as Simon Kemp points out, this return should neither suggest that the story was entirely absent from previous experimental literature, nor suppose that the new generation of writers has no suspicions about conventionally formal aspects such as plot, character and mimesis. The 'fables' of the novel that Motte discusses in literature of the extreme contemporary are fabular in the sense that they fable *themselves*. Alongside displaying a greater degree of narrativity, contemporary novels in some way self-reflexively draw attention to the status of the novel, its limits and its possibilities (Motte 2003: 6).[11]

In the work of women writers in the twenty-first century, this self-conscious approach to storytelling is often highlighted in the blurring of boundaries between the fantastic and the banal and can be seen in the writing of, for example, Darrieussecq, NDiaye and Nothomb (see Hutton 2009). Dislocations in narrative voice (Darrieussecq), or the intervention (and death) of the author as a character in the text (Nothomb) alert the reader to the status of the story *as a story* and to the machinations of storytelling. The death of the author of course provokes the birth of the reader who is often incited to participate actively rather than implicitly in the creative process, being offered the choice between different endings (Nothomb), or being invited to become a character and navigate the story from within (Delaume). In twenty-first-century's women's writing, literature and life are collapsed into one another, as Anna

Kemp's contribution to this volume reveals, opening out ways of existing otherwise and inhabiting, through art, the plural, and perhaps contradictory, positions of the self with which so many female authored-texts are concerned. Telling stories, and moreover reading stories, as Holmes suggests in this volume, thus becomes a way for female authors, characters and readers to be creatively and pleasurably suspended in the world.

Life-writing is a genre that has long been associated with female-authored works in their discernible emphasis on the intimate spaces of the self, and twenty-first-century women's writing is no exception. Since the 1980s and into the twenty-first century, Ernaux's social autobiographies, or autoethnographies, and *journaux extimes* have continued to blur – but also to reveal anxieties about – the boundaries between the public and the private, and as Simon Kemp analyses in this volume, between the writerly and the experiencing self. The blurred genre *par excellence*, autofiction, first coined by Serge Doubrovsky (1977), has been subject to renewed critical debate in recent years, as ever-increasing forms emerge which pose new challenges to the precise definition of this term (see Burgelin, Grell and Roche 2010; Colonna 2004; Havercroft and Sheringham 2012; Jeannelle 2009; Jeannelle, Viollet and Grell 2007; Oullette-Michalska 2007). But, as Jean-Louis Jeannelle points out, the compulsion to assign a definitive signification to autofiction would seem to undermine the very slipperiness of the genre, and its driving force which resides precisely in a readerly hesitation as to the exact status of the text. Indeed, as Jeannelle concludes, it is this slipperiness that imbues autofiction with its creative and critical possibility, stimulating fertile ground for productive disagreement (Jeannelle 2007: 33–6).

The autofictional genre seems to hold considerable appeal for a great many contemporary women writers (for example, Angot, Bouraoui, Cusset, Darrieussecq, Delaume, Laurens, Régine Robin), and several have produced theoretical accounts of autofiction in relation to their work (Burgelin, Grell and Roche 2010). In spite of this, and as Shirley Jordan (2013a) has noted, there has been a lack of critical approaches to autofiction that take gender into account or situate it within broader trends in women's (life-)writing. As Jordan aptly observes, autofiction provides women writers with the means to grapple with a range of experiences that have been central to evocations of female subjectivity. These include the splitting of the subject, self-conscious performance, mirroring or doubling, cultural hybridity, displacement and extremes of experience that resist easy articulation, from excessive desire to traumatic and painful experiences such as anorexia, rape or incest. If, for Doubrovsky (2007: 64), the practice of autofiction enables the reinvention, rather than the reproduction, of life experience, this would seem to be reflected in the concerns of female authors to recreate in art a plural subjectivity, a subjectivity that might be always already fictionalised, as Chloé Delaume (2010b: 109) suggests. The inflections of gender in the production, consumption and interrelation of female-authored autofictional works seems a vital critical avenue and it will be fascinating to see how this trend develops in years to come in new creative practices and critical discourses in thinking about the relationships between self and text, life and literature.

Some of the most innovative and exciting creative leaps in recent women's writing in French have involved not only the blurring of distinctions within the broader definition of literature, but an opening out of the literary text beyond linguistic confines. Helena Chadderton's contribution to this volume shows how Darrieussecq pushes language to its limits, playing with sound, layout and arrhythmic, elliptical syntax to creative immersive texts that challenge the senses to capture the nature of experience all the while metatextually signalling that impossibility. The relationship between word and image in the communication of experience has contributed to what Shirley Jordan terms a visual swell in women's writing in the twenty-first century. Authors such as Ernaux, Laurens and NDiaye have all recently incorporated photographic texts into their writing, raising a host of questions about the possibilities and limitations of these different forms of representation, and what they might reveal or conceal about the self, in particular with regard to memory and notions of the real. Jordan's contribution to this volume also indicates that the graphic novel, which draws on comic-strip book techniques that might conventionally be associated with action-driven, male-centred, plots, is increasingly being manipulated in female-authored works that deal with more difficult, intimate concerns, an area that is beginning to attract sustained critical attention (see Edwards, Hubbell and Miller 2011; Miller 2007). What these innovations appear to have in common is a desire for the literary text to tap into a broader range of sensory responses. This is particularly brought into a twenty-first-century context by writers such as Robin and, as discussed in Deborah B. Gaensbauer's contribution to this volume, Delaume, who engage with multimedia installations and the cyberworld endlessly to refashion the self, interfacing text with image, sound and the plane of the virtual. In a world of Facebook, Twitter and blogging, the processes of self-narrative are widely available on some level and an everyday practice for many. Through their engagement with the possibilities of virtual interaction, the textual innovations of Delaume and others highlight, within the particularity of our twenty-first-century world, the suspension into immediate contact with other selves, other lives and other forms of expression, the pleasures of identification and the dynamic spaces of exchange that the act of reading has always involved.[12]

As we can see, fascinating new elements are surfacing in the twenty-first century: hopeful themes – ethics, creativity, relations with the other – and textual and aesthetic experiments – written, visual and virtual. The volume thus not only demonstrates how women's writing is engaging with and intervening into contemporary issues in a changing socio-political, globalised and technological era. It also explores ways in which literary debates are in the process of being shaped. The chapters that follow chart that journey.

Notes

1 This is not to say that the writers cited began publishing in the decade in which they became well-known, especially to readers outside France – NDiaye and Devi first published in the 1980s, Olmi and Gavalda in the 1990s – but, rather, that they did not begin to attract substantial critical and scholarly attention until later.
2 See Fallaize 1993 for an invaluable introduction to 1970s and 1980s French women's writing to an English-speaking audience. On the 1990s generation of women authors, see Jordan 2004; Morello and Rodgers 2002; Rye and Worton 2002; Rye 2002, 2004, 2005; Sarrey Strack 2002.
3 See Cruickshank 2009 for an analysis of the aesthetics of crisis in French fiction at the turn of the millennium.
4 See Hirsch 1997 and 2012 for critical perspectives on family, trauma and second-generation testimony.
5 See A. Kemp 2010 for a discussion of Islam and feminism in French culture.
6 Literary critics in France have made their own intervention here, calling for a *littérature-monde en français* (world literature in French). Disillusioned with the notion of *francophonie*, which arguably relegated the work of non-metropolitan authors writing in French to the

margins, it calls for such works – in all their multiplicity and diversity – to be recognised within the mainstream of French literature. See *http://www.etonnants-voyageurs.com/spip.php?article1574*, and also Le Bris and Rouaud 2007. For a critical response, see Hargreaves, Forsdick and Murphy 2010.

7 At the end of 2012, a new French law was drafted authorising gay marriage and adoption for same-sex couples. It will be voted on early in 2013.

8 The example of Despentes here carries an obvious feminist agenda, and it must be acknowledged that feminist positions are not always so explicitly embraced in female-authored works – ambivalent or controversial attitudes towards feminism have been apparent since the 1990s in French women's writing, as Anna Kemp's chapter in this volume suggests (see also Jordan 2004). But this ambivalence may also evidence the extent to which feminist concerns have become either implicit (Morello and Rodgers 2002), or renegotiated within poststructuralist paradigms (Damlé 2011).

9 Surrogate motherhood is illegal in France, although it is practised, either unofficially or through arrangements overseas.

10 With thanks to Alice Blackhurst for drawing this text to our attention.

11 The recurrent notion of 'crisis' in respect of the French novel also arose in French literary criticism in the 2000s, see, for example, Baetens 1999; Dandrieu 2006; Rakocevic 2007.

12 On reading as a dynamic process, see, for example, Barthes 1984; Felman and Laub 1992; Pearce 1994 and 1997; Rye 2001; and Wilson 1996.

Chapter Two
What 'Passes'?: French Women Writers and Translation into English

LYNN PENROD

Beyond critical questions of women's writing within the formation of a literary canon (however that might be defined and however the concept has changed over the years), there remains the fundamental reality of translation, the reality of 'what passes'. Which texts by women writing in French have been, are, or will be translated into English? How are they chosen? By which criteria? How accessible are they even if chosen? And why does it matter?

The translational fates of already canonical writers from the twentieth century, such as Simone de Beauvoir or Marguerite Duras, or even later generation authors such as Annie Ernaux, Amélie Nothomb or Marie Darrieussecq, are often difficult to trace. Even using the limiting factor of translation from French into English alone, reliable data relating to currency of translation, availability of translation and readership of translated texts by these writers is often next to impossible to locate. Yet in addition to reaffirming one of the basic principles of Itamar Even-Zohar's (1990) polysystem theory, where translation becomes a significant factor within a cultural and literary structure, such data relate in critical ways to important questions concerning (a) editors' and publishers' choices of texts to translate; (b) the reception of translated authors and texts – both by academic readers (researchers, professors, students) and by the larger reading public (through numbers of copies sold, scope of international distribution and the like); (c) the adaptation of original text to media in other languages (film, television, internet); and (d) the inclusion within university course syllabi or the availability of translated texts in so-called pedagogical editions.

Looking back on French women writers who produced texts during the decade 2000–10 invites us both to review questions relevant to the history of translation from French to English of women writers in French and to suggest future directions where research and scholarship in translation will play a key role in the survival and growth of literary production by women. This chapter makes no claim to provide an inclusive overview of the current state of play regarding the translation from French into English of texts by French women writers. Nonetheless, it does aim to raise awareness of the critical importance of this area, which has until now often been neglected. Following an overview of the translation into English of women's writing in French prior to the first decade of the twenty-first century, I briefly discuss the importance of translation studies to the mobility of literary texts. Finally, I consider translation via a snapshot of the decade of 2000–10, suggesting areas where future collaborative work should be encouraged and supported, not only within the academy but within the larger world of the movement of texts through the international literary marketplace.

Translation into English of women's writing in French: a brief overview

Given the ability of the speed of the internet to update information today in an almost instantaneous fashion, material from the year 1984 may now seem to be steeped in ancient history. However, my starting point is a volume published by Garland in that year entitled *Women Writers in Translation: An Annotated Bibliography 1945–1982*, edited by Margery Resnick and Isabelle de Courtivron, at the time both professors at Boston's Massachusetts Institute of Technology (MIT) (Resnick in Spanish and Courtivron in French). They note in their preface that their project had its genesis in 1978 when the Division of Women's Studies in Language and Literature of the Modern Language Association (MLA) in the United States had organised a panel on translation to be presented at that year's annual meeting. In the editors' words:

> As the five panelists prepared materials for that meeting, it became clear that in each of our respective fields almost no information

regarding works in translation was available. No published bibliographies provided information on women writers that would expand the traditional canon by making accessible texts that had been overlooked because of scholarly conventions. (vii)

As a result of these findings, they enlisted colleagues 'dedicated to cross-cultural and multi-disciplinary feminist studies' (vii) in a collaborative endeavour to remedy the situation. It is interesting to note that, despite these observations, the situation today has not changed substantially, at least not in any sort of organised way. Although technology has allowed us much greater access to data relating to women writers, their publishers and editors, translators and/or translations are still often difficult to locate. The words of the editors of the 1984 bibliography could, indeed, in many cases be repeated by today's scholars as well. As they noted at that time:

> At the initial stage of this project, none of us imagined the breadth or the complexity of the problems to be encountered as the work unfolded [...] Much like the women writers who found little regard for their publications and like their translators whose work lacked support, we, as individual scholars, were beset by numerous problems [...] Our experience confirmed that although a large number of women are extremely interested in the field of translation, their activities are not respected or encouraged, either economically or professionally. In universities, little is done to encourage translation as thesis work or as valid scholarly work with a view to promotion. Few translation proposals receive grant awards [...] [T]ranslation is yet another volunteer activity, dependent on the good will of those committed to retrieving creative women from historical silence and absence. (vii)

Although it may appear that in the second decade of the twenty-first century we have moved beyond the retrieval of creative women from historical silence and absence noted by Resnick and Courtivron, we nonetheless continue to risk the silence and absence of French women writers if we simply consider the issue of translation as a 'given' in the literary landscape, which unfortunately is more often than not the case.

In the French section of the Garland bibliography, there are three separate sub-sections devoted to women's writing in French: France; Francophone Canada; and Other francophone countries (which include Algeria, Belgium, Guadeloupe, Haiti and Nigeria). Other sections of the volume are dedicated to English translations of women's writing in Brazil and Portugal; Austria, the Federal Republic of Germany, the German Democratic Republic and Switzerland; Italy; Japan; Russia; and Spain and Spanish America. The top ten French women writers available in English translation in the Resnick and Courtivron volume (number of texts annotated by collaborating contributors indicated in parentheses) include Colette (36), Marguerite Duras (17), Simone Weil (16), Françoise Sagan (13), George Sand (13), Juliette Benzoni (12), Françoise Mallet-Joris (12), Christine Arnothy (10), Zoë Oldenbourg (10) and Nathalie Sarraute (10). It should be noted that, even in 1984, only forty-one out of the seventy-three authors listed as translated into English were still alive and that twenty-three of the writers annotated in the 1984 volume had birth dates ranging from 1890 to 1925. Many of these writers have since died, and many have been forgotten (for the second time perhaps) and are unavailable in English translation, perhaps because the demand for their works is no longer there.

The range of genres included within the Garland bibliography is striking since it includes canonical texts by Sand, Colette and Beauvoir, but also popular works by writers such as Oldenbourg, Sagan and Benzoni, as well as non-fictional works by Weil and Mme de Sévigné's letters. The editors and their collaborators had selected 1945 as the 'start year' for English translation primarily because there was general agreement that accessibility of translations was a key element in their work. That is to say there were other women writers whose work may have existed in English translation but their translated texts were long since out of print or located only in remote archives. Given, too, that neither Internet research nor online searching of extensive databases like World Cat were possible in the late 1970s and early 1980s when this reference work was being prepared, one can only imagine the task facing the group forced to work with nothing but annual paper volumes of *Books in Print* and obliged to perform laborious and time-consuming research into publishers' catalogues, library catalogues and microfiche journal and newspaper records, in order to locate in-print English translations of works in French written by women. Even in jurisdictions where French and English may both have had official language status, translation of a literary work from one official language to another was not necessarily a *fait accompli* (as a cursory glance at the Resnick and Courtivron subsections on Canada and 'other' francophone countries readily demonstrates). Though the 1984 volume may now be considered obsolete, exploring this interesting text nonetheless gives us much to consider in terms of encouraging the work of literary translation to stay apace with contemporary literary production as well as maintaining access to important works of the past via translation.

Moving forward a decade to 1993, a text that continues to be a relevant starting point for many of those who teach French women's writing or who are interested in more recent developments on the French literary scene is Elizabeth Fallaize's *French Women's Writing: Recent Fiction*, an anthology of translated excerpts. Like Resnick and Courtivron, Fallaize, was obliged to set parameters for her selection of authors to include in 'recent fiction' as well as limitations on her list of authors, given the particular focus of the series in which her volume was published. Unlike the Garland volume, which was clearly meant to serve as a basic bibliographical reference guide, Fallaize's text was published in a series edited by Jo Campling at Macmillan called 'Women in society: a feminist list', whose stated objective was to commission and publish books that 'consolidate and advance feminist research and debate in key areas in a form suitable for students, academics and researchers but also accessible to a broader general readership'. As Fallaize explains in her introduction:

> A first constraint on choice is the difficulty of persuading French publishers to allow the translation of extracts; this inevitably affects choice in a rather arbitrary way. A less arbitrary and important consideration was my desire to make available writing which had not yet been translated and which deserves circulation outside the French-speaking world. For this reason none of the more institutionalised figures who are more widely read in English such as Duras, Sarraute, Wittig or Rochefort has been included, even though they themselves are not necessarily well known. A third and finally paramount consideration in my choice has been the fact that all the writers represented have consciously produced texts as women. (1–2)[1]

The Fallaize list, which is, of course, not intended to be a reference tool but, rather, an introduction in English to contemporary French fiction by women writers, includes the following authors: Marie Cardinal, Chantal Chawaf, Annie Ernaux, Claire Etcherelli, Jeanne Hyvrard, Annie Leclerc and Marie Redonnet. Either in her introductory material or in various notes about her primary choices, Fallaize also mentions the following writers: Christine Arnothy, Nicole Avril, Simone de Beauvoir, Emmanuèle Bernheim, Raphaëlle Billetdoux, Anne Bragance, Muriel Cerf, Hélène Cixous, Florence Delay, Hortense Dufour, Marguerite Duras, Jocelyne François, Anne Garréta, Sylvie Germain, Catherine Hermary-Vieille, Luce Irigaray, Annie Leclerc, Françoise Mallet-Joris, Michèle Perrein, Catherine Rihoit, Christiane Rochefort, Françoise Sagan, Danièle Sallenave, Nathalie Sarraute, Monique Wittig and Marguerite Yourcenar.

Fallaize's list includes several writers from the Garland top ten (Duras, Sagan, Mallet-Joris and Sarraute) or at least annotated in that volume (Cardinal, Chawaf, Etcherelli and Leclerc) as well as three completely new names: Ernaux, Hyvrard and Redonnet. At the time of writing in 2012, it is interesting to note that, of the three 1993 'newcomers', Ernaux is the only author to have had the majority of her oeuvre translated into English. Although several of Redonnet's works are also available in English translation (*Forever Valley* (1994a), *Rose Mellie Rose* (1994c), *Splendid Hotel* (1994d), *Candy Story* (1995), *Nevermore* (1996), *Understudies* (2005), for example), they are often difficult to obtain since their print runs are relatively low. And, whereas the work of Hyvrard experienced a surge of popularity among an academic audience in the early 1990s, translations into English did not necessarily keep pace; today *The Dead Girl in a Lace Dress* (1996a) and *Mother Death* (1988) (and from time to time *Waterweed in the Wash-Houses* (1996b)) are the only Hyvrard translations available and they are often located only in academic libraries. In brief, it suffices to say that the choice of text, the sequencing of the translations of selected texts and their ongoing availability in English translation continues to be widely variable.

A brief excursion into translation studies theory

It may seem unnecessary to remind academic researchers who specialise in the work of French women writers that most first-language English readers do not speak, understand, read or write French. There is thus a genuine necessity for many interested readers to approach French texts by women writers via translation. Indeed, one of my own first encounters with the problem of French to English translation, one that certainly transcended mere linguistic difficulty, centred on the reception of Hélène Cixous's work in North America. *The Newly-Born Woman*, the English translation of Cixous's *La Jeune Née* (1975) (written in collaboration with Catherine Clément) did not appear in English translation by Betsy Wing until 1986, when it was published by the University of Minnesota Press in its literary theory series. Along with Cixous's essay, 'Le rire de la Méduse' (1975) (translated as 'The laugh of the Medusa' by Keith and Paula Cohen in 1976), it created a whirlwind of interest among North American feminists, many of whom did or do not read French. The Wing translation is certainly not a bad one; in fact, even after twenty-five years, it is still readable and provides intelligible access to the translation difficulties emanating from the author's style. However, since Cixous's earliest texts (some of which remain untranslated even today) had presented such tremendous translation difficulties, not the least of which were heavy demands on readers' cultural literacy combined with Cixous's incredibly complex lexical and syntactical playfulness, the Wing translation was for a long time the only book-length work by Cixous in English to be found in many libraries. This absence of translation into English plus the 'lag' between original French text production and English translation publication, combined with the seemingly arbitrary appearance of translations of Cixous's work into English, that followed neither a particular chronological logic nor a pathway that retraced the writer's own evolving writing trajectory, began to have a curious effect on the way in which 'Cixous' was read in the United States in particular. Indeed, many anglophone North American feminists maintained a very out-of-date view of Cixous well into the 1990s, at a time when she herself had radically changed not only her style of writing (today's texts are much more accessible, and thus perhaps appear more rapidly in translation) but also her major preoccupations, including an increasing amount of work in theatre.

The Cixous example remains pertinent today because in reality the perception of what constitutes 'French literature' or 'Women's writing in France' from outside the French-speaking world is largely shaped by translation, constructed literally by 'what passes' from French into English. Where would English readers of women's writing in French be today without the efforts of the University of Nebraska's series on 'European women writers in translation', the MLA 'Texts in translation' series, the Feminist Press at CUNY or

The Women's Press in London – all of whom have provided support to the translation of women's texts into English and all of whom are under siege as the fate of the humanities as an area of academic scholarship and/or research funding or a centre of interest or business viability for publishers (even academic ones) continues face a grim future?

Sebnem Susam-Sarajeva's *Theories on the Move: Translation's Role in the Travels of Literary Theory*, published by Rodopi in 2006, focuses primarily on the travelling of literary theory through translation and is a text in which my own Cixous anecdote is illustrated in full. In brief, *Theories on the Move* centres on the problems of the translation of two influential theorists, Cixous and Roland Barthes, into two foreign languages and cultures, North America for Cixous and Turkey for Barthes. This gives rise to the rather amusing reference to a body of feminist literary theory Susam-Sarajeva calls the 'North American Cixous' and its literary theory counterpart in Turkey, which he refers to as the 'Turkish Barthes'. Even though this text focuses on the transcultural journeys of literary theory, it makes sense to extrapolate from Susam-Sarajeva's central argument that translation, lack thereof or time lag in translation can fundamentally alter the receiving culture's take on any literary theory or theorist. Thus, any concept of trend in literary production within a single language or culture (here, women's writing in France in the first decade of the twenty-first century) is fundamentally influenced by trends in translation.

Two quotations from Susam-Sarajeva illustrate what I intend here – the absolutely critical role that translation plays within the entire system of literary production as texts cross the liminal no-man's-land between languages and cultures. The first function of translation is to serve as a marker of textual migration, a kind of diagnostic tool that shows us that the text is 'on the move':

> Translation firstly plays an *indicative* role in the study of this migration. It allows insights into, and analysis of, the workings of a given system. The product and the process of translation – both the translated texts themselves and the translation practices – are shaped according to the local concerns in the receiving systems, to what is deemed urgent, important, and necessary [...] Translation indicates how the system views itself, what its needs and expectations are, and how it handles 'interferences' from other sources. Translation and translator patterns – such as text-selection, publication dates

of individual translations, translators' professional profiles and
agendas, selection of terms – together with the meta-discourse
accompanying translations reflect and reveal how the source texts
and authors are received in their new environments. (1)

Yet over and above the role translation has as a diagnostic tool in
studying the migration of text from one culture to another, translation also plays what Susam-Sarajeva describes as a formative role:

> [A]part from being just a symptom, translation also plays a *formative*
> role in the migration of literary and cultural theories. It shapes and
> transforms the images of writers and texts, influences the receiving
> system's attitudes towards importations, and contributes to the
> development of local (critical) discourses and terminologies. (2)

Of course, Susam-Sarajeva is much more concerned with the migration of theoretical concepts via translation than the mere fact of
translation of an individual text by an individual writer from one
language to another. However, in terms of both cultural literacy and
the ongoing globalisation of the literary marketplace, the importance of translation cannot be dismissed.

A decade of women's writing in France: trends and horizons 2000–2010

The conference which took place in October 2010 at the Institute
of Germanic & Romance Studies (IGRS), University of London, 'A
decade of women's writing in France: trends and horizons 2000–
2010', from which some of the chapters in this volume are drawn,
called for the discussion of works by women writers in France over the
course of the first decade of the twenty-first century. Celebrating the
tenth anniversary of the founding of the 'Contemporary women's
writing in French' seminar, the occasion was not only one of looking
back to a past decade of literary production but also an opportunity
for new women writers to be presented to a wider reading audience.
The number of different writers represented in presentations and
discussion either at plenary sessions or in smaller parallel panels
included some sixty-six authors, some of whom were discussed
more than once while others were introduced perhaps for the first
time to an international audience. These writers represented a
broad cross-section of literary production. Although fictional prose
works were predominant, other genres – from detective fiction and

theatre to poetry, memoir and children's literature – also had their place. The colloquium, then, provided a stimulating and provocative mixture of more widely read writers along with many new young writers who have only just begun their careers in the first decade of the twenty-first century.

For researchers and scholars in the field of women's writing in French who live and work in mainly anglophone territory – the United Kingdom, the United States, a large part of Canada, Australasia – translation into English does not often concern us personally. We have access to both versions, as do many of our French academic colleagues from the francophone world. Even our French colleagues who do not deal actively with English readily agree that a French author who has an important creative talent most certainly merits translation into other languages. It is not simply a question of translation into English, of course, but a question of translation per se and what that means in terms of cultural transfer among languages. Although translation issues do not necessarily arise when we approach our scholarly work on familiar writers or texts or when we encounter a new text or author for the first time, the future of many contemporary French women writers, and even of some writers who belong to the past, will continue to be largely dependent on their availability in translation. It is self-evident that their impact and influence will extend beyond the francophone world only if they are accessible to readers who do not read French.

Of the sixty-six authors discussed in panels during the three-day colloquium in 2010, the following constitute the top ten: Annie Ernaux (8 panels); Marie Darrieussecq (7); Christine Angot and Virginie Despentes (6 on each); Hélène Cixous, Catherine Millet and Marie NDiaye (5 on each); Camille Laurens, Marie Nimier and Amélie Nothomb (4 on each). Other authors receiving multiple presentations included Éliette Abécassis, Calixthe Beyala, Nina Bouraoui, Catherine Breillat, Ananda Devi, Alice Ferney, Nancy Huston, Linda Lê, Gisèle Pineau, Leïla Sebbar and Laurence Tardieu. Although Ernaux, Millet, Nothomb and Cixous are available in English translation (Millet with not many titles to her name, and Cixous's more recent rather than earlier work, with some exceptions), many of the others are not. There are important reasons that we care about these women writers (and although the focus of the conference was to discuss women writing in French principally domiciled in France, it is clear that all women writing in French merit inclusion). The translation gap should encourage us, indeed urge us, to negotiate with editors and publishers in order to facilitate their translation into English.

Of the top ten, the two that are currently most widely available in English translation (Ernaux and Nothomb) are also often included on the syllabi of university-level French literature courses as well as on women's studies or comparative literature syllabi, where works from French literature that may have a broader appeal are often taught in translation. Informal responses to my queries of why these particular writers appeal to teachers for these kinds of courses often cite the average length of text since both Ernaux and Nothomb tend to produce shorter texts that are more easily accessible, at least in linguistic terms, to those who either have French as a second (or third) language or who are monolingual English readers. Texts by these two writers are also often topical in terms of theme or focus, relating to issues of concern to women readers: body image, abortion, death of a parent, jealousy, relationships, parenting. The works of Darrieussecq are currently being translated and more widely distributed. Accordingly, the use of translated texts or French texts with at least some availability in English may see an increase in publications of English translations for these authors as well. Other popular choices for course syllabi include English translations of many of the shorter texts by Duras (*Moderato cantabile* (1960) or *The Lover* (1993), for example) and Beauvoir's *The Woman Destroyed* (1969). Expanding curricula in popular culture have also perhaps motivated a recent upsurge of translation in other genres: most of the detective novels of Fred Vargas are now available in English as are best-sellers by writers as different as Muriel Barbery and Nancy Huston. Sadly, however, many of the texts by writers omitted from Fallaize's 1993 volume because of their status as being 'institutionalised' and readily available at the time in English (Duras, Sarraute, Wittig and Rochefort) are no longer so easily accessible in English, apart from Duras.

Critical studies of contemporary women writers in French are being produced, however. A recent example is Warren Motte's *French Fiction Now: The French Novel in the Twenty-First Century*, published in 2008. Rather than solely focusing on women writers, though, Motte presents authors who, in his view, are committed to innovative practice. Considered as a companion piece to his 2003 volume entitled *Fables of the Novel: French Fiction Since 1990*, the more recent work 'proposes to report on [. . .] literary experimentation in its plurality and its variety, taking a series of "soundings" within the compass of innovative French fiction since 2001' (Motte 2008: back cover). Along with male authors Jean Echenoz, Christian Gailly, Gérard Gavarry and Patrick Lapeyre, Motte includes four chapters on women writers: 'Marie Redonnet's hospitality', 'Lydie Salvayre's literature', 'Hélène Lenoir's still life' and 'Christine Montalbetti's showdown'. This is, then, another interesting list to consider in terms of available English translations, since there is a tendency in literary criticism works like Motte's to assume a readership competent enough to read works in their original French.[2]

In terms of publications or academic research on the top ten authors at the 2010 conference in London, most are readily found on Google or Wikipedia (sometimes only in the French versions) and they are gradually making their way on to larger databases. Problems related to the expansion of the publication of English translations of women's writing in French are obviously related to the difficult situation of book publishing worldwide. The economic downturn has meant that once robust translation lists are now increasingly unable to fund translations, given that the profit line is simply not attractive enough. In the past, if one could not engage a commercial publisher to buy into a proposal to translate a text from French into English, one could at least sometimes find an academic publisher willing to do so; yet, today, these opportunities are fast disappearing as well. It is interesting to note, too, that as in Fallaize's volume, and as for many literary translators of women writers or publishers of translations, the focus is often on the novel or other kinds of fiction. It is perhaps a slightly different argument, but theatre translation is also an incredibly important strategy for the movement of text from one culture to another, and poetry, of course. And there are other questions that cry out for discussion and debate as well. What about bilingual texts? Is there a difference between translating a poem as opposed to an entire collection of poems? Where is the place for adaptation into other media? Film script, television scenario? Even today's quick search of World Cat shows us that the only readily available English translations by such a well-known author as Marie Cardinal are *The Words to Say It* (1984) and *Devotion and Disorder* (1991); for Claire Etcherelli, only *Elise, or The Real Life* (1969); for Christiane Rochefort, *Warrior's Rest* (1959).

This chapter may succeed only in raising more questions than it could even pretend to answer in relation to the English translation of women's writing in French over the course of the past decade and the issue of 'what passes'. Yet, in the very connected world of scholarly research today, it does seem that we could do a much better job of encouraging the movement of translated texts between one culture and another. There is an increasingly porous membrane separating literary translation and creative writing. The work of translation, the training of literary translators and the support for translation are in today's world of more importance than ever before.[3] Translations – creative, thoughtful translations – allow access to other worlds, other ways of thinking and being, other ways of feeling and understanding ourselves and others. When we work in two or three languages, we are blessed with a wider and deeper understanding and appreciation of the other, opening ourselves up as well. If we care about French women writers in the twenty-first century, we must never forget that they need to exist not only in French but in as many other languages as possible.

Notes

1   It is interesting to note that Fallaize later states: 'Nevertheless, I am happy to report that since my original set of choices some works from which I gave extracts have now been translated into English in full.' (25)
2   Like Fallaize, Motte also mentions women writing in French who interest him but for whom he simply has not the space to consider: Marie NDiaye, Anne Garréta, Olivia Rosenthal, Isabelle Lévesque, Danielle Mémoire, Linda Lê, Nathalie Quintane, Marie Darrieussecq, Maryline Desbiolles, Annie Ernaux, Caroline Lamarche, Amélie Nothomb, Emmanuèle Bernheim, Marie Cosnay and Anne Godard, 'to name just a few'. As Motte (2008: 13) writes: 'But clearly one cannot make room for everyone in a study such as this.'
3   The IGRS was actually awarded funding for training literary translators. The project has now moved to Birkbeck College, University of London. See *http://www.bbk.ac.uk/european/about-us/use-your-language-use-your-english.*

Chapter Three
What Women Read: Contemporary Women's Writing and the Best-seller

DIANA HOLMES

> What I'm suggesting here is that people bring similar questions to high and low art, that their pleasures and satisfactions are rooted in similar analytic issues, similar ways of relating what they see or hear to how they think or feel. The differences between high and low emerge because these questions are embedded in different historical and material circumstances and are therefore framed differently. (Frith 1998: 19)

Despite the proliferation of media through which stories may be told, the novel still represents a widely consumed medium for storytelling, in France as elsewhere.[1] Almost from its birth, and despite the heavy predominance of male authors, the novel genre has been associated with women: escapism, the indulgence of the imagination, the excessive enjoyment of vicarious emotion have been deemed *feminine* weaknesses since well before Emma Bovary. Although, prior to 1973, men in fact formed the majority of readers in France, more recent surveys of French cultural practices suggest that the reality now matches the general perception of fiction reading as a feminine occupation: in the twenty-first century women form a clear majority of readers across genres, with the feminisation of fiction reading particularly marked.[2] And, at least at the popular level, this gender shift is reflected in the success of women writers. Men may still dominate the lists of literary prizewinners and the literary columns of the 'serious' press,[3] but women novelists have certainly achieved parity on the best-seller lists. *Le Figaro*'s authoritative survey of the best-selling French novelists for 2010 showed a top ten made up of five male and five female authors: Marc Levy, Guillaume Musso, Eric-Emmanuel Schmitt, Michel Houellebecq and Maxime Chattam were the top-selling male writers; Katherine Pancol, Anna Gavalda, Tatiana de Rosnay, Fred Vargas and Amélie Nothomb balanced the list.[4] In the 2009 survey, women writers were in a majority of six to four, with Marie NDiaye's Prix Goncourt success *Trois femmes puissantes* (2009) (*Three Strong Women*) carrying her into the top ten, alongside Muriel Barbery with her unexpectedly popular *L'Élégance du hérisson* (2006) (*The Elegance of the Hedgehog*), republished in paperback in 2009. Barbery was replaced in 2010 by Tatiana de Rosnay thanks to the huge success of the latter's *Elle s'appelait Sarah* (2007b) (*Sarah's Key*).[5]

Popular best-sellers thus form a significant dimension of contemporary women's writing, and what I propose here is to extend the study of female-authored literature in twenty-first-century France in the direction of the popular. This chapter asks what pleasures are offered by the best-selling 'women's novel', and where such texts stand in relation to more 'serious' literary writing by women. I frame the argument with a brief account of certain common features identified across a wide corpus of best-selling novels, and a discussion of how these contrast with the textual qualities widely defined as authentically literary. For the sake of concision, and in order to avoid over-generalisation, I then focus the analysis of reading pleasure and its relationship to feminist values on a single, recent and very successful popular novel, Claudie Gallay's *Les Déferlantes* (2008) (*The Breakers*).

The genres of recent best-sellers in France are varied, from Marc Levy or Guillaume Musso's fantasy-tinged romances, to Fred Vargas's droll, warm-hearted and often crudite crime stories, to Rosnay's historical melodrama.[6] Despite their diversity, however, it is possible to discern certain strongly recurring characteristics, both formal and thematic, in the most popular of popular fictions, and thus to explore what it is that provides the pleasure and satisfaction of reading fiction, for a readership that is increasingly composed of women. The first thing to say is that the popular novel functions mimetically, using a language sufficiently transparent to draw the reader into a fictional world that seems 'real' and thus engage both curiosity about 'what happens next' and the reader's emotions. Most best-sellers are what Marie-Laure Ryan (2001) calls 'immersive' texts. As one typical reader put it on an online discussion forum about Anna Gavalda's novels: 'Je ne pouvais plus m'arrêter de lire tant je souhaitais connaître la fin [. . .] C'est un livre magnifique qui m'a fait vibrer, rire, pleurer . . . on ne peut rester insensible à cette histoire.'[7] Secondly, popular novels tend to propose an optimistic vision of the world, however dark some elements of plot, setting and character. Their optimism emerges not only (and not in every case) from a diegesis that stages human happiness or concludes with a happy ending. Rather, a sense of optimism arises from the shared attributes of narrative coherence and closure: the world represented may contain suffering and conflict, but it is a world that has a discoverable meaning and in which some kind of resolution is possible. Thirdly, many or even most of the novels that figure in annual 'top tens' deploy the familiar script of romance.[8] Some of the press commentaries on the feminisation of reading in France draw attention to the way that women (more than men) tend to find pleasure in the collective dimension of reading, through book clubs, online chat and the passing round of books among a group of friends.[9] As Janice Radway's seminal 1984 study of romance readers suggested, even though the pleasure of reading fiction resides partly in an assertion of the subject's freedom to escape the everyday and strike off independently into a more vital imaginary world, reading romance – the 'feminine' genre par excellence – can also provide an agreeable sense of collectivity, of being part of a like-minded community. Since Radway's study, the proliferation of dialogue between readers through online reviews, Facebook pages devoted to authors and other digital fora has further strengthened this dimension.

Mimetic realism, optimism and the genre of romance are all features that run directly counter to dominant definitions of the authentically literary, particularly in France. As Jean-Marie Schaeffer (1999: 24) argues, the 'soutien, de nos jours, apporté aux œuvres qui "subvertissent" leur fondement mimétique' contrasts with the 'condamnation de celles qui, au contraire, mettent en valeur les techniques imitatives'.[10] Most of the best-selling novels read and appreciated by the general reading public are thus greeted in France with critical disdain.[11] Feminist academics working in the domain of French literature, whether inside or outside France, inevitably share in this very French definition of all authentic art as intellectually restless and aesthetically challenging, but they also have good feminist reasons to suspect conventional modes of representation. Language used in such a way as to make verbal representation appear 'natural, immutable, unproblematic' (Radway 1991 [1984]: 191) may be assumed to discourage critical thinking and encourage an unreflective acceptance of the dominant discourse as simply reflecting 'the way things are'. Easy immersion in imaginary worlds seems to run counter to the type of reading that mobilises consciousness of real conflicts and inequalities. The narrative of romance in particular tends to represent dissatisfaction with one's life as open to resolution through personal relationships, and moreover ends, in its most traditional form, with a reaffirmation of heterosexual coupledom as the answer to a woman's problems. Thus a transparently written, immersive and upbeat popular novel with a strong element of romance tends to be deemed of little interest for the study of contemporary women's literature. The types of contemporary women's writing that have elicited critical analysis and scholarly debate are, rather, the more opaque and challenging texts that may only be read by a minority – and on the whole a highly educated minority – but that nonetheless constitute original interventions in important, ongoing debates: for example, how to write a life story in the face of postmodernity's challenges to any notion of a unified, coherent self? How to find authentic linguistic and narrative forms for experience, shaped as our imaginations are by powerful cultural myths?[12]

However, it is surely also the case that the study of women's writing needs to include the study of what most women read. As so much work in cultural studies has demonstrated – and it is significant that feminism has been woven into the fabric of Cultural Studies since the late 1970s and early 1980s[13] – to see popular fictions as simply a product of consumer capitalism, imposed on a manipulated public, fails to take account of the complexities and contradictions of any fictional text, as well as denying the reader any degree of agency. The model proposed by cultural studies scholarship is, rather, that of popular fiction as a changing repertoire of representations from which consumers select and with which they engage in order to make sense of their lives, to find 'a workable, if temporary sense of self' (McCracken 1998: 2), to rejoice in imagination's capacity to transcend everyday reality, to adopt alternative subjectivities. Thus feminist writers have proposed revisionary readings of the most widely consumed and derided 'women's' genres (romance, soaps), taking seriously the pleasures of audiences and questioning the assumption that the critic herself stands aloof from such pleasures. Here, one recent French best-seller serves as a specific yet representative case study for an analysis of what produces a page-turning, pleasurable read, and what vision of the world such a text implies.

Claudie Gallay's *Les Déferlantes* was a surprise word-of-mouth best-seller that passed the 300,000 mark soon after publication and remained one of France's top-selling novels throughout the following two years, winning the Grand Prix des Lectrices d'*Elle* for 2009.[14] Translated into seventeen languages, it is now being adapted for the cinema. *Les Déferlantes* was the author's sixth novel, the previous five having achieved respectable but unremarkable sales: there was something about this work that chimed with readers' desires. A substantial novel at over 500 pages, the text is divided into very short chapters (two to eight pages), and written with a spare, transparent simplicity that both makes for easy reading and is diegetically motivated, since the first-person narrator is a woman numbed by grief and wary of emotion. It is, as the critic of the online magazine *Esprits libres* put it, a 'bon roman populaire d'aujourd'hui'.[15] It displays the three recurring attributes of the popular novel as defined above: immersion of the reader in a highly dramatised fictional world, optimism (despite the novel's dark themes) and deployment of the romance narrative, interwoven with a mystery plot.

The reader's 'immersion' in the fictional world of *Les Déferlantes* is achieved in part through its vivid evocation of place. It is set on the Atlantic coast of Normandy, in the isolated village of La Hague and its still more isolated port, La Griffue, 'un endroit comme un bout du monde' (11).[16] The sea here is wild, even on rare sunlit days, and the violence of the elements and sense of remoteness are echoed in the inhabitants' rarely articulated but intense emotional lives, and in the narrator's lonely struggle to survive the death of her lover. It is mourning that has driven her to this desolately kindred place: 'c'est une affaire de peau, La Hague. Une affaire de sens.' (138)[17] Though a place that can be found on a map, a part of real France probably known to some readers, La Hague in the novel is 'fictionalised' through the intense coherence of its physical description and figurative meanings: the savage beauty of land and seascape transport the reader into fictional space. Like many of the *roman-feuilletons* (serialised popular novels) of the nineteenth century[18] (also a female genre in terms of readership and to some extent authorship), *Les Déferlantes* offers a portal that leads out of the everyday into a more extreme and colourful elsewhere, which nonetheless resonates through its metaphorical force with the reader's own emotional experience. The device of a powerfully imagined fictional geography is not common to all popular novels, but it is certainly one commonly employed 'route to pleasure', to use Radway's (1991: 10) term. It represents not only escapism, but also a heightened sense of the sheer quiddity of the material world, and of its possible concordance with human emotion.

The relationship of physical reality to emotional experience is thus anthropomorphic in precisely the way that Alain Robbe-Grillet, in his polemical attack on the mainstream novel, condemned as typical of an outdated, humanist realism[19] – but for most readers it remains absolutely central to reading pleasure. Not only are the seascapes and landscapes of *Les Déferlantes* savagely beautiful, providing the enjoyment that comes from imaginary travel, they are also one part of a dense if unflamboyant network of textual coherence in which most elements work simultaneously at a literal and figurative level. Thus in the opening pages of the novel, during a violent storm, the narrator is cut on the face by a sharp piece of metal whirled by the wind. The cut will gradually scar and finally heal, providing a physical correlative for her emotional trajectory. Paralleling the narrator's slow movement from utter desolation to cautious re-engagement with life, the text incorporates numerous further images of wounding and healing: one character, Morgane, keeps a rat she has rescued from starvation; another saves a wounded seagull. Stray cats and a wild horse that wanders into the village, starving and damaged, are taken in, cared for and recover. Central to the geography of La Hague, and to the plot, is a building that for many years served as a nurturing refuge for orphaned children. Though La Hague is the site of nature's violence and of much human pain, a dense weave of redemptive images echoes the plot's overall progression from numb sadness to hope.

This web of imagery operates with such familiar simplicity that its textual working scarcely demands analysis. If it represents a 'route to pleasure', it is because, first, it provides a heightened sense of the concordance and coherence of experience. Frank Kermode explains the joy of mimetic fictions by the human need to exercise a 'synthesising consciousness' and thus exorcise 'the merely successive character of events' (Kermode 1967: 56), to transform mere chronicity into a sense of time patterned towards an ending. It is not, as Robbe-Grillet's influential dismissal of mimetic fictions would imply, that the reader is duped or mystified by this process into believing in the world's total coherence but, rather, that fiction offers the pleasure of provisionally inhabiting a world of which sense can be made, a satisfying model of the reader's own attempts to render meaningful a complex, resistantly chaotic reality. And, secondly, the meaning affirmed by plot and corroborating images is an optimistic one, that affirms the power of human agency and the validity of hope.

Gallay's style is interesting too in this context. Popular writers are often patronised by French critics for their bland facility, for offering the reader too 'comfortable' a position.[20] In *Les Déferlantes* the simplicity of syntax and the semi-spoken register certainly make few demands on understanding, just as the very short chapters lend themselves to interrupted lives. But the narration also carries undertones of Duras's spare lyricism, and in its simplicity and ellipsis contains a jagged, syncopated note of pain and desolation:

> Sous la violence, les vagues noires s'emmêlaient comme des corps [...]
> Ces vagues, les déferlantes.
> Je les ai aimées.
> Elles m'on fait peur.
> Il faisait tellement nuit. (Gallay 2008: 19)[21]

The transparency of the writing facilitates absorption in the fictional world, but is also central to the novel's depiction of the bleak austerity of grief.

Realist, mimetic storytelling offers the pleasure of immersion in a world whose patterns of meaning are discernible and life affirming. But *Les Déferlantes*, like the majority of best-sellers written by and implicitly addressed to a predominantly female readership, also deploys the narrative structure and tropes of romance. The novel opens with the first encounter with the hero – 'La première fois que j'ai vu Lambert, c'était le jour de la grande tempête' (9) – marking his appearance as the vital catalyst of plot.[22] And Lambert rapidly displays the marks of the romantic hero: he is good looking ('plutôt beau gosse' (10)), and betrays beneath a taciturn exterior that capacity for emotional intimacy that will make him a satisfactory partner for the heroine ('Il y avait en lui une tendresse un peu brutale, une séduction gauche' (120)).²³ He is mysterious and, indeed, the enigma of his identity and sudden presence in La Hague will be central to the diegesis. As in so many mass-market romances, his desire for the heroine is unspoken and unrecognised for much of the text, but made apparent to the reader, if not the narrator, by involuntary signs and the perspicacity of secondary characters. Thus the final revelation of mutual love comes at once as a pleasing surprise and as confirmation of the reader's effective reading of the text. Although the romance script is interwoven with a mystery plot, for enquiry into the past will reveal a triangular love story that still determines the lives of several protagonists and explains the true identity of Lambert, it is finally the coming together of hero and heroine in reciprocal love that will be central to narrative and emotional closure: 'Lambert a pris ma main. C'était une main large, chaude et confiante. Il a murmuré à mon oreille quelque chose d'infiniment doux, et on a rejoint ensemble le monde des hommes.' (539)²⁴

Romance is one of the most consistently popular genres and, in its classic popular form (for the genre's essential elements are also to be found in 'literary' novels, and are not incompatible with an unhappy ending), it certainly observes the conventions of narrative coherence and optimism observed above. The romance element of *Les Déferlantes* heightens the novel's positive charge. Nonetheless, as critical writing on the romance has shown, the narrative core of meeting, development of mutual attraction, negotiation of obstacles and closure in happy union also allows for the staging of less blissful emotions.²⁵ Some elements of popular romance overlap with the recurring themes of more 'literary' or highbrow women's writing, such as the painful contradictions of mother–daughter relations, the difficult assertion of female subjectivity and sexual agency. Two components of the romance plot in *Les Déferlantes* typify both the blurring of division between high and middle or lowbrow, and the modulation of the romance form in twenty-first-century women's best-sellers. Gallay's novel depicts not only the redemptive power of love, but also the heroine's sustained resistance to heterosexual bonding as the form her future will take. And, if romance foregrounds individual happiness, Gallay's novel makes the personal plot inseparable from the social and the collective.

The narrator of *Les Déferlantes*, like almost every romance heroine, resists desire as a threat to the integrity of the self: in women-authored romances, opening up to love generally means at once the promise of self-fulfilment and the threat of self-destruction. In early-to-mid-twentieth-century romances, for example, those of the market-leading Delly, female integrity took the form of virginity, and marriage was resisted until it could be accepted on terms favourable to the heroine's own needs. Gallay's heroine/narrator belongs to an age when virginity has ceased to be a practical and figurative form of self-protection but, as in Delly, or the Harlequin romance, or contemporary 'literary' authors such as Annie Ernaux or Camille Laurens, desire is shot through with anxiety at the self-exposure that accompanies passion. Here the nameless narrator's identity has become, since the pre-diegetic death of her lover, that of a self-in-mourning, and to love another man would mean both to abandon her identity as bereaved lover and to risk opening up again to the vulnerability that love brings: 'Dès que tu aimes, tu portes' (278), as she tersely puts it.[26] It is through the gradual revelation of the lover's own vulnerability, and his capacity for tenderness, that a happy ending becomes possible. Her final affirmation of the desire to be with him ('Vous êtes revenu. Il m'a serrée davantage et j'ai fermé les yeux' (523)) is an assertion of faith in life, and part of the text's typically popular optimism, but it has been won against a powerful sense of the danger of romance for (in particular) female selfhood.[27] The novel's other examples of women-in-love confirm this: half-mad Nan who haunts the village and finally drowns herself, Lili the café's proprietor and her embittered old mother have all invested their happiness in love, and have lost.

The optimism of popular genres then plays out against an undercurrent of apprehension, but nonetheless concludes with the classic denouement of romance. This, however, is only one strand in the comprehensive unknotting of all narrative threads: the mystery of Lambert's past is resolved, and with it the secret history that has poisoned the lives of several of La Hague's inhabitants; each major character achieves a form of resolution, and even happiness; mourning is replaced by love. The personal fate of the lovers is thus closely interwoven with that of the community: romantic union is not only a personal matter but also means 'rejoining the world of men'. The narrator's and Lambert's tenacious search for the truth has led to personal and collective redemption. And, although the remote rural setting means that modernity remains largely offstage, it is clear that La Hague is part of a wider contemporary world that is under threat but potentially redeemable by human intervention: the narrator, a scientist, works towards the protection of sea birds threatened by climate change; asylum seekers gather on the beach ('Je me suis demandé ce qui allait se passer pour eux si le bateau qu'ils espéraient ne venait pas' (73)); a nuclear power station looms along the coast ('le monstre tapi' (84)).[28] If the plot unemphatically shows how human tenacity, imagination and concern for the truth and for others can have real effect on the world, the implication is that this faith in human agency can be generalised.

Les Déferlantes is simply one example of a novel that has caught the popular imagination through its effective deployment of well-tried narrative techniques, and its modulation of these conventions for a contemporary world. That it is a representative example of the twenty-first-century women's best-seller is confirmed by certain elements of resemblance to the work of Anna Gavalda, whose *Ensemble c'est tout* (2004) (*Hunting and Gathering*) and *La Consolante* (2008) (*Consolation*), in particular, have achieved massive sales in France and appeared consistently on the best-seller lists. Gavalda's novels, too, are appealingly substantial books with short chapters and a transparently readable style. The novels' generous size answers the desire often expressed by fiction readers to 'get lost in a book'; as in the case of the *roman-feuilleton*, to be satisfyingly immersive the fictional world needs sufficient dimensions to offer the promise of lengthy and repeated sojourns. Immersion, or imaginary transportation to a universe of heightened meaning, is assured by a strong evocation of place – in Gavalda's fiction both the globalised bustle of contemporary Paris and a rural France characterised as the repository of older French values. Like Gallay's best-seller, Gavalda's novels follow a benevolent, upbeat logic: poverty, loneliness, ageing and dysfunctional family relations are important elements of plot, but they are ameliorated, resolved or transcended through the narrative. And Gavalda's novels also observe, and embroider on, the script of romance, providing similar pleasures through plots that carry the reader from vicarious loneliness to the discovery or achievement of mutual love, from fear of loss of self to recognition of the other's vulnerability and of reciprocity. Like Gallay's, Gavalda's plots also make private happiness inseparable from some form of social resolution: the happy endings of *Ensemble c'est tout* and *La Consolante* take the form not just of the formation of a couple, but of the establishment of new, cross-generational domestic units, based on affinity and choice rather than blood relationships, that replace the traditional family. Despite their absence of any explicitly social or political themes, Gavalda's novels, like Gallay's, propose an inextricable connection between personal well-being and forms of social organisation, between romantic love and altruism, *eros* and *agape*.

Contemporary romantic best-sellers do not forge new feminine languages, nor address explicitly political or social issues. For the pleasure of their readers, they deploy tried and tested techniques of mimetic realism to tell stories that rework the familiar genres of love story, mystery and family melodrama. Their success will most likely be ephemeral. Yet the way that these texts 'work' for their readers, and the reasons for the extreme popularity of certain texts rather than others, is entirely worthy of critical attention. The 'bon roman populaire d'aujourd'hui' succeeds in offering the reader rapid entry into an imaginary world, a portable gateway that can be exited and entered at will and as time allows, lending itself to the enhancement of the unclaimed spaces of the day, such as commuting, lunch breaks, going to bed. The pleasure of briefly inhabiting a more legible, exotically dramatised and, thanks to its optimism, restorative fictional world is by no means enjoyed only by women but, as the pervasive presence of romance and melodrama in contemporary best-sellers suggests, popular narrative fiction has become a predominantly female domain. And what we read matters: temporary transportation to the fictional world does not leave the reader completely unchanged, or as Milorad Pavic puts it: 'the reader who returns from the open sea of his [*sic*] feelings is no longer the same reader who embarked on that sea only a short while ago' (Pavic 1988 [1984]: 294; Ryan 2001: 94). The world-view implied by the recent romantic best-sellers studied here is certainly a comfortingly positive one, and thus radically opposed to the more challenging interrogations of language, postmodern identity and social structures represented in more 'literary' women authors. This does not, however, automatically make for a reactionary or compliant perspective on the contemporary world. These novels model reality in a way that suggests that it is possible to make provisional but workable sense of experience, that we are the agents rather than the victims of our fate, and that the personal is always also the social. The routes to pleasure that they skilfully provide map a journey that is certainly restorative, and is also, overall, empowering.

Notes

1 Though book reading continues to decline in France, as elsewhere in Europe, the most recent edition of the Ministry of Culture's regular survey (Donnat 2008) still shows the French population reading an average of 16 books per year (21 in 1997), of which more than half are novels.
2 Olivier Donnat's regular surveys of French cultural practices register a clear feminisation of reading between 1980 and the present (Donnat 2005: 3). An Institut National de la Statistique et des Études Économiques (INSÉÉ) survey of 2003 already identified 62 per cent of women as fiction readers against 37 per cent of men, and Donnat's work suggests that the trend is still growing.
3 See Morello and Rodgers 2002, for a comprehensive analysis of this phenomenon at the start of the twenty-first century. To take just one example, over the past twenty years there have been just three female winners of the Prix Goncourt.
4 See *http://www.lefigaro.fr/livres/2011/01/12/03005–20110112ARTFIG0 0544-les-dix-romanciers-francais-qui-ont-le-plus-vendu-en-2010.php.* Sales figures do not of course represent completely reliable proof of how many people actually read a book. There are different ways of calculating a book's sales, and publishers may manipulate figures in order to get their books on national best-seller lists and thus further promote sales. However, the figures published by *Le Figaro, L'Express, Livres-hebdo* and the major market research company Ipsos Mori are the best indication available of what readers like best. As Resa Dudovitz (1990: 28) asserts, despite the power of marketing, in the end 'the public decides which book will become a bestseller'.
5 Tatiana de Rosnay is a bilingual French author whose first eight novels were written in French. *Sarah's Key* (2007a) first appeared in English and was rapidly translated into French.
6 Both 2009 and 2010 also contain examples of what might be termed the 'crossover' novel: literary novels propelled to best-selling status by triumph in one of the major national book prizes, and reaching a wide public because, despite departure from conventional modes of storytelling, they strike a chord with a non-elite readership. NDiaye's *Trois femmes puissantes* and Michel Houellebecq's *La Carte et le territoire* (2010a) (*The Map and the Territory*) won the Prix Goncourt in, respectively, 2009 and 2010, propelling their authors onto the best-seller lists as, famously, did Marguerite Duras's *L'Amant* (*The Lover*) in 1984. The extent to which such novels cross the high/low boundary because they also provide 'popular' reading pleasure is an interesting one, too lengthy to be tackled here.
7 'I couldn't stop reading, I was so anxious to know what happened in the end [. . .] It's a fabulous book that really got to me and had me laughing and crying . . . you couldn't stay unmoved by this book.' *http://www.evene.fr/livres/livre/anna-gavalda-ensemble-c-est-tout-32432. php?critiques.* Unless otherwise indicated, translations from the French are my own.

8   Romance is a significant component in the work of each of the top five authors on the 2010 list (Levy, Pancol, Musso, Gavalda, Rosnay).
9   For example, Geneviève Comby's (2008) observation: 'Mais surtout, pour les femmes, lire c'est partager.' ('But above all, for women, reading means sharing.')
10 'the support nowadays for works that "subvert" their own mimetic basis' as opposed to 'the condemnation of those that make good use of imitative techniques'.
11 See Holmes 2010 for an analysis of the radical divide between literary critics and readers of popular fiction in France.
12 The most recent books to survey and analyse contemporary French women's writing (Morello and Rodgers 2002; Rye and Worton 2002; Jordan 2004), and the seminars, conferences and website of the dynamic Contemporary Women's Writing in French group, all encompass a wide range of authors but demonstrate a particular emphasis on the work of, for example, Christine Angot, Marie Darrieussecq, Lorette Nobécourt, authors whose work is characterised by the presence of a 'sujet fracturé, fuyant, recherche identitaire, écriture autobiographique, mélange de genres' ('fragmented, elusive, subject, the search for identity, autobiographical writing, a mingling of genres') and self-reflexive narration (Morello and Rodgers 2002: 44), all of which contrast sharply with the narrative forms employed by the most popular novels.
13 See, for example, Angela McRobbie's early essays, 1976–86, collected in McRobbie 1990; see also Modleski 1982.
14 This prize, awarded by France's most eminent women's magazine to a novel selected by a large jury of readers, is a significant indicator of a novel's popularity with a female readership.
15 'a good popular novel for our times', *http://www.forumdesforums.com/modules/news/article.php?storyid=54815*.
16 'an end-of-the-world sort of place' (Gallay 2011: 3).
17 'it is a matter of skin, La Hague. A matter of the senses.' (98)
18 For example Alexandre Dumas's dramatic land-, sea- and time-scapes in *Le Comte de Monte Cristo* (1844–6) (*The Count of Monte Cristo*) and *Les Trois Mousquétaires* (1844) (*The Three Muskateers*), or Belle Époque *feuilletonniste* (writer of popular serialised novels) Daniel Lesueur's use of Italy in *Calvaire de femme* (1907) (*A Woman's Suffering*).
19 Robbe-Grillet objects to anthropomorphic imagery on the grounds that it attributes to the world a set of pre-existing meanings, thus denying human freedom. The project of a new, authentic form of fiction will demand a complete 'entreprise de nettoyage' ('thorough cleaning out') of all such metaphors (Robbe-Grillet 1963: 48–52).
20 The word 'comfortable' recurs in many negative reviews of popular novels in France, echoing Roland Barthes's characterisation of the mere 'texte de plaisir' ('pleasurable text' as opposed to the 'texte de jouissance' or 'blissful text') as one that offers 'une pratique confortable du texte' (Barthes 1973: 25) ('a comfortable reading practice'). See Holmes 2010. In this volume, Helena Chadderton argues that

reading the work of Marie Darrieussecq involves both Barthesian *plaisir* and *jouissance*.
21 'In the violence, black waves were entwined like bodies [. . .]
    These waves, the breakers.
    I loved them.
    They frightened me.
    It was so dark.' (Gallay 2011: 8)
22 'The first time I saw Lambert was on the day of the big storm' (1).
23 'Lambert was on the handsome side' (2); 'There was something of a brutal tenderness about him, an awkward charm' (84).
24 'Lambert took my hand. He had a big, warm, trusting hand. He murmured something infinitely tender into my ear, and together we went back into the world.' (408) The French reads more literally 'the world of men'.
25 See, for example, Radway 1991; Modleski 1982; Holmes 2006.
26 'The minute you love someone, you carry them' (208).
27 '"You've come back". He held me tighter, and at last I could close my eyes.' (397)
28 'I wondered what would happen to them if the boat they hoped for did not come' (48); 'the lurking monster' (58).

Part Two
Society, Culture, Family

Chapter Four
Vichy, Jews, *Enfants Cachés*: French Women Writers Look Back

LUCILLE CAIRNS

Prior to the 2000s, published testimonies of the *enfant caché* (hidden child) experience from French women were extremely rare.[1] Transhistorically and transculturally, women's focus on children has, with few exceptions, been massively over-determined. Yet when the children concerned are former selves, as is the case here, that focus seems to have been subject to a self-censorship (which may derive from women's acculturation to self-subordination). What changes in the first decade of the 2000s is that such female-authored testimonies begin to multiply, with at least eight appearing between 2002 and 2010.[2] Given the relatively advanced age of the authors concerned, this is an arresting development. In this twenty-first-century trend, Danièle Gervais-Marx's *La Ligne de démarcation* (2004) [1997] (The Demarcation Line) is a signally important – and, as I shall go on to argue, an exemplary – forerunner.

First published in 1997 by the relatively obscure HB Éditions, Gervais Marx's *La Ligne de démarcation* appeared in an entirely new edition in 2004 with the major publisher Hachette Littératures, accompanied by a laudatory preface from the eminent historian Jean-Pierre Azéma. My analysis of this prize-winning book is of most obvious relevance to historiography of the Second World War in France, but it is also pertinent to current global debates about conflict, exclusion, genocide and the uniquely vulnerable position of children therein.[3] Further, I argue for the ethnic, gendered and national significance of *La Ligne de démarcation*, due to its at once singular and, as my conclusion contends, exemplary contribution to post-1945 Jewish women's writing on French experience of the Second World War. *La Ligne de démarcation* re-envisions that war from the perspective of *enfants cachés*, that is, Jewish children who, hidden by non-Jews, survived a genocide in which Vichy France had actively collaborated.[4] Most innovatively, it does so from the perspective of a female *enfant caché*.

The author's stated objective in *La Ligne de démarcation* is to convey the physical dangers and psychological distress of everyday life for Jews living in France during the Second World War: inter alia, dispossession of home, fugitive (sub-)existence and changes of official identity. The text's broadly autobiographical skein integrates experiential strands of other Jews who survived Vichy France, some of whom were family members, others not, others still anonymous figures. As a prelude to this narrative free-ranging, Gervais-Marx situates herself as an eight-year-old child in 1940. Her testimony is a valuable pendant to the more numerous French-language accounts from concentration-camp and death-camp survivors, because it provides documentary evidence about the many Jews who managed to survive in Occupied France, and thus allows a more complete picture of French experience of the Second World War.

The first page of Gervais-Marx's foreword establishes the dual meaning of the eponymous demarcation line (11). The literal obviously denotes the line separating the Occupied Zone from the (so-called) Free Zone in France until 1942. The metaphorical is the line separating life and death for Jews under the Vichy regime. Newly interpellated (like many other *enfants cachés*, as we see in various texts from the 2000s)[5] into conscious, if confused awareness of her Jewishness by Vichy's anti-Jewish statutes, the child is assailed by a sense of the world's murderous absurdity, of estrangement from normality and reality. That sense is generalised from her particular case to that of many other assimilated French Jews. It is further observed that

> [o]n ne se remet pas du constat que le monde peut brusquement perdre tout son sens, qu'une fois franchie la ligne qui sépare habituellement la normalité de l'anormal, la réalité de l'irréel, chaque geste devient lourd de significations particulières dont certaines sont une menace et conduisent à la mort. (11–12)[6]

In the second sentence here, a syntactical distinction is made between normality/the abnormal and reality/the real, through the use of a standard noun for the first part of the binary and, for the second, an adjectival outsider to substantivity which could be aligned with Jewish outsiderhood (11). But Gervais-Marx does not imply any exclusive relationship between outsiderhood and Jews. Instead, she vindicates her testimony as emblematic of an ill that is less obviously atrocious than the Shoah, but more currently resonant: namely, social exclusion in contemporary France (12). Nonetheless, her foreword insists on the right of Jewish non-deportees to reveal their own experience of the Second World War, which has so often been self-censored in awareness of the more obviously horrific experience of deportees (12; again, this phenomenon is documented in other *enfant caché* accounts of the 2000s).[7] Importantly, the final sentence of the foreword suggests an ethical value to ethnically transitive thinking about exclusion: 'Je voudrais que tout lecteur puisse se dire que nul n'est à l'abri d'une aussi étrange expérience, que "l'autre" n'est jamais le seul à qui une telle aventure peut arriver.' (14)[8]

Beyond the author's foreword, her text proper is a generic hybrid whose most obvious constituent is personal history: mainly, although not only, that of a Jewish child forced to assume a new identity in a remote country village far from her Paris home. But she also weaves external history into personal history, indeed manifests a concern meticulously to record such external history, as is evinced by the frequent quotations from or references to professional historians' work, use of footnotes, historico-ethnographical research of her own and interviews with mainly Jewish survivors.[9] After brief consideration of French-Jewish subjectivity as inscribed by Gervais-Marx, this chapter will examine the salient lines of her reflections, first on anti-Semitism and resistance thereto in Occupied France, and secondly on the trauma sustained both during and after the Second World War by Jewish survivors, in particular those child survivors who came to be designated *enfants cachés*.

The reaction of Gervais-Marx's mother to Vichy's anti-Semitic measures shows textbook typicality: an initial myopia paradigmatic of most assimilated French Jews, committed as they were to Republican and patriotic principles, and many of whose male forebears had died during the First World War fighting for France. Given that honourable record, they could not fathom their sudden discursive transformation into enemies of their own country (21). Accordingly, the warning adumbrated by the fate of German Jewish friends exiled from Germany in 1939 was naively rejected by the mother:

> Ma mère, avec beaucoup d'assurance, jugeait ridicule l'idée que les persécutions dont ils étaient l'objet dans leur propre pays puissent être les prémices de ce qui allait survenir en France. En octobre 1940, elle n'avait pas changé d'avis: juive, peut-être; française, sûrement, et à ce titre, elle n'avait rien à craindre du gouvernement de la France. (21)[10]

It is striking that the mother's articulation of her identity (at least as mediated through her daughter) privileges French nationality over Jewishness (through 'sûrement' and 'peut-être' respectively). Significantly, this minimisation of Jewish identity is reflected in her young daughter, who in 1940 still had not understood what anti-Semitism was, for the simple reason that she was not really sure what 'being Jewish' itself meant (25). The pungent irony is that while many Jews made little of their Jewishness, it was to become all in their construction and hounding by the Vichy regime.

La Ligne de démarcation traces a tumescent topography of wartime anti-Semitism in France. One flashpoint singled out for special scrutiny is Alsace, the home region of Gervais-Marx's father, where anti-Jewish feeling is posited as the negative obverse of a long-established, dense Jewish population, and as more virulent than elsewhere in France. Resolved, however, to provide balanced treatment of the French in all their ideological and moral diversity, she also refers to Beulay, on the other side of the Vosges, where residents remained immune to the anti-Semitism of surrounding regions (181). As part of her determined drive to non-partisanship, the anti-clerical Republican tradition of France is valorised as the cause for such resistance to anti-Semitism (181). In this she is not alone – such valorisation occurs in other *enfant caché* narratives of the 2000s[11] – but she is certainly the most categorical. Does this valorisation of France's Republican tradition segue into romanticised idealisation? After all, the Dreyfus Affair had taken place under a Republic, France's Third, as had the rise of home-grown fascistic movements in the 1930s. In the self-circling style that characterises Gervais-Marx's rhetoric, the next chapter concedes that France's logic of universalism and tolerance of difference have definite limits (183). Illustrating this concession is the fact that while her cousin André, a French Jew, was protected in Strasbourg, foreign Jews there were not (183). The point is, again, that toleration of an individual's religious and linguistic differences is contingent on their subordination of such differences to national adhesion.

In keeping with her (arguably quixotic) quest for absolute objectivity, Gervais-Marx charts peaks and troughs in the moral profile of French Gentiles. One anecdote particularly undermines blanket national pride in the Resistance. When, at a post-war reunion, a former Resistance member who was later to become a communist member of parliament discovers that André is Jewish, he quite simply never speaks to him again (192–3). In marked contrast to this stands the experience of Jacques, whose outlook is much more rosy. He professes not to have overheard any anti-Jewish comments in the military camps, either from other French prisoners – mostly peasants – or from the German guards (200). This may seem implausible, but presumably Gervais-Marx would not have falsified Jacques's evidence. Yet, in the absence of knowledge about her processing of raw interview data, we cannot gauge to what extent the direct speech from Jacques represents truly verbatim transcription of his original words. Even the slightest of editorial changes can, after all, have subtly distorting effects, and in this case they may, with respect to the French prisoners recalled by Jacques, both derive from and revive *le mythe résistanciel* that dominated French remembrance of the Second World War until it began to be challenged in the 1970s.[12]

Moreover, desire to pay homage to the courageous actions of at least some French Gentiles leads to a dubious calibration. Of a couple who were deported, it is stated that their three children were saved thanks to the spontaneous intervention of simple people, whose modest courage more than redeemed the thousand acts of cowardice of those who did not want to face the truth or take any risks (168). There are several such tributes to the 'les Justes' of France from other *enfant caché* texts of the 2000s.[13] But faced with Gervais-Marx's extravagant formulation, we might ponder if such redemption should, or even can, be so easily granted. Does one good act genuinely cancel out thousands of *failures* to act to save lives? It is, of course, true that even individual resistance to anti-Semitism could be highly dangerous under Vichy. Moreover, supplementing these apparently isolated cases of individual resistance to anti-Semitism is occasional attribution of it to the entire

French nation, for whom, Gervais-Marx insists, '"être juif" n'avait aucun contenu' (274).[14] The relative weakness of religious faith is adduced as a possible reason why there were fewer Jewish victims in France during the Second World War than in other occupied European countries. So far, so reasonable. But now the reader is confounded by a highly contentious, almost wilfully ingenuous claim: that in France, between 1940 and 1944, Enlightenment philosophy was sovereign, promoting respect for humankind in its universality (275). Gervais-Marx is presumably referring to the proportion of French citizens who actively opposed Vichy ideology, but her failure to denote this specificity and to note its statistical rarity is disarming. This is one of the more flagrant of Gervais-Marx's blind spots, as she vacillates between the wish to condemn Vichy France and the wish nonetheless to believe in an unbroken Republican tradition of French freedom, equality and fraternity. Indeed, Gervais-Marx's whole self-image as configured in *La Ligne de démarcation* is one of national belonging, belonging to a Republican France that is at least partly mythified or sentimentalised. Severance from such belonging is for her clearly inconceivable. And it is within this non-negotiable condition that her discourse develops.

Her general argumentation can be much more nuanced, as when recognising the greater difficulties of individual acts of courage relative to collective acts of courage (276). Her main focus is on the latter, which incidentally are obviously more verifiable from historical documents. So she, like many others, pays tribute to the exceptional bravery of the inhabitants of Chambon-sur-Lignon, a largely Protestant village in the Massif Central that welcomed, hid and thus saved from deportation many Jewish children during the war (276).[15] While this village may have been exceptional, she is at pains to point out that the proportion of children among deported Jews was much lower (about 14 per cent) in France than in neighbouring countries of similar demographic size, such as Belgium or Italy, where the proportion was about 20 per cent (276). But the now familiar mechanism of point-counterpoint again kicks in. So, after acknowledging these relatively heartening statistics, she asserts their incommensurability with individual human beings' experience of death by gassing. She also offsets observation of the greater survival rate of French as opposed to foreign Jews living in France by the trenchant comment that 'cela ne change rien au fait qu'un moment arriva où la machine à tuer commença d'avaler tout le monde. Il n'y eut pas deux façons de mourir, dans les chambres à gaz d'Auschwitz.' (282)[16] In parallel, and on a more personal level, she suggests that generalities like the fact that Strasbourg Jews survived largely due to the resistance of the non-Jewish community in the south-west where they sought refuge meant nothing to her as a bereft twelve-year-old child returning to Paris in 1944 (283–4).

Observation of her bereavement serves as an apt transition to our second axis of enquiry in this chapter, namely the trauma experienced by Jewish survivors of the Second World War, and particularly by *enfants cachés*. One notable device used by Gervais-Marx to render this trauma is a form of sub-looping within her trademark operation of rhetorical looping. Thus she recognises that during the war, she did experience ordinary, pleasant childhood moments set against a backdrop of historical tragedy (76); follows this up shortly afterwards by the implication that, nonetheless, the war years had destroyed her ordinary childhood freedoms (80); yet, later still, downplays her own suffering compared to that of less privileged, usually foreign Jewish children, who were forced into a far more drastic form of clandestinity than mere change of identity. Nonetheless, she states that

> [s]'il me semble néanmoins important de raconter ma propre expérience, c'est justement parce qu'elle est le fait de gens 'ordinaires' qui ne se différenciaient ni par l'accent, ni par l'origine, et qui se retrouvaient néanmoins 'marqués' pour l'abattoir. (82)[17]

The last sentence here may prompt readers to wonder whether they should really be more attentive to the state-planned murder of those who were physically indistinguishable from their murderers than to the state-planned murder of those who were plainly different. While an affirmative reply to that question is affectively understandable, it is surely ethically suspect. To her credit, though, by tapping into the egocentrism lurking in most human beings, Gervais-Marx's stance exposes the cultural bias towards sameness as opposed to alterity. It is this bias that fuels the conflict, exclusion and genocide flagged up in my introduction, and whose trace, though subject to changes of valency and geopolitical location, has been unbroken from Gervais-Marx's childhood to the present of her writing. What is beyond doubt is that Shoah-related suffering did not always issue in death, and that the existential impairment caused by its psychological traumata should not be minimised. Pre-eminent here is the impact of survivor's guilt – a syndrome also discernible in other *enfant caché* testimonies of the 2000s (167).[18] Even fifty years after the war, survivor's guilt can still grip her (300), a vulnerability presented as having enduringly psychopathogenic effects.

In the wide scale of traumatic topoi inscribed in *La Ligne de démarcation*, one in particular is treated curiously elliptically at a personal level, being explored fully only through its location in other victims. This is the enforced assumption of a false identity, stripped of any Jewish vestiges – a potent topos in many *enfant caché* texts from the 2000s (249).[19] When Laure, whose foreign Jewish parents have been deported, signs a school essay with her real name, the teacher balefully intones: 'Le nom que tu as inscrit en tête de la copie n'est pas le tien. Ne fais jamais plus cela, tu m'entends? Ton devoir est bon mais nous allons le déchirer ensemble.' (252)[20] While the teacher is altruistically, and not without danger to herself, protecting a Jewish child, she is also involuntarily reinscribing the symbolic murder of the child's previous identity via the enforced name change. Here, as in another case (253) of a child's imposed identity change, what emerges is the intense psychological strain of dissemblance, in moments when the new identity is questioned by a figure invested directly or indirectly with the powers of life or death.[21] Such strain and the chronic insecurity it induces persist after the war for many Jews (as several of the *enfant caché* texts of the 2000s corroborate).[22] Gervais-Marx brings herself into the equation once more, stating that since the Second World War she has never been able to do anything, however minor, such as parking her car in an unknown spot, without noting it down in writing. She also refers to Denise, who is unable to separate herself from a handbag stuffed full of objects bearing personal memories such as photographs (248). In the case of Denise, what is stressed is the neurotic concern always to keep material signifiers of her identity upon her very person, both literally and figuratively – since in the latter case, the ontological integrity of that person had once been figuratively annulled.

For Gervais-Marx, other effects of trauma persisting after the war are verbal paralysis and impotence (294); inhibition about affirming her Jewish identity in words; and her nervous reaction to hearing the word 'Jew' being spoken by others – an instance of the power of language to crystallise both realities and fearful fantasies.

Such sensitivity to language and its exclusionary power is for her inflamed nowadays by hearing the word 'Arab':

> Aujourd'hui, c'est plutôt, lorsque je l'entends dans une conversation, le qualificatif 'arabe' qui me fait sursauter: j'ai peur de ce qui va suivre. Et le comble de l'imbécillité me parut être cette remarque d'un couple américain, certainement juif, qui visitait en même temps que moi une exposition sur les rafles de 1943 à Marseille: 'Quand je pense, disait la femme, que les Arabes nient l'Holocauste …' Je ressentis l'affirmation comme une blessure. Au Proche-Orient, il y a des Arabes qui le nient, c'est certain; mais 'les' Arabes! Comment cette femme ne comprenait-elle pas qu'elle usait, par une généralisation aussi abrupte et arbitraire, de la même violence que celle qui conduisait à l'Holocauste? (299)[23]

This sensitivity, coupled with her indignation at certain Jews' perception of all Arabs as negationists, implies use of Todorovian (1998) exemplary memory[24] in the most morally exemplary of ways, as well as compliance with Lévinas's (1987: 14) exhortation to 'trouver toujours l'actualité des renseignements de la shoah à partir de nos expériences nouvelles'.[25] Given the vocal hostility expressed in many quarters of contemporary politicised Islam towards not just Israel but Jews generally, who are often excoriated in a synecdochical move *as* Israel, her concern represents a model of ethical integrity. The wider corpus of *enfant caché* texts published in the 2000s also, though not invariably, demonstrates use of such exemplary memory.[26]

Finally, there is the post-war trauma of dealing with betrayal. In Gervais-Marx's experience, although French Jews who survived the camps did not repudiate their country despite its betrayal of them, they faced 'un douloureux travail de deuil' (309)[27] that was usually delayed and preceded by an external silence about their experiences:

> D'autres l'ont dit, quelques-uns l'ont écrit, mais rarement à leur retour. Il a fallu longtemps avant qu'ils puissent se retourner vers le passé proche, contempler à nouveau l'épreuve terrifiante dont ils étaient sortis vivants, et en parler. (309)[28]

Although not a deportee, she herself had had to undertake a work of self-reconstruction, assembling as many photographs, objects and artefacts from her childhood before the war as possible, as evidence of an ontological continuity which would transcend the radical rupture of the war. For all Jewish survivors, whether of the camps or of Vichy, there remains a permanent mental insecurity and loss of any epistemological certainties: '[i]1 n'y a plus de certitudes, la terre devient un univers mouvant aux règles insaississables' (310).[29] While Gervais-Marx had escaped genocide, she had certainly been a victim of conflict and exclusion. The resulting modification to her scale of values – their razing to a bare, vital minimum of attaching importance only to what threatens human life and dignity[30] – could usefully inform global debates about these inveterate ills. Given, evidently, the political will.

This chapter has focused on Gervais-Marx's text as a foundation stone to what was, in the 2000s, to become a sizeable corpus of texts by French Jewish women who had also been *enfants cachés* during the Second World War. I would like to conclude by offering some comparative remarks. Gervais-Marx and her successors all mediate both virulent anti-Semitism generally and the lasting psychological scars of the *enfant caché* experience in particular, the latter often with considerable pathos (and, occasionally, a bathos deriving from excessive use of emphatic stylistic markers such as exclamation marks).[31] Common to all, too, is the erratic quality typifying their representation of Gentile France during the Second World War: a form of narrative zigzagging between exposure of anti-Semitism on the one hand, and homage to 'les Justes' on the other. However, one difference is clear. When Vichy France is arraigned, with Gervais-Marx the censure is explicit, whereas in the later works it tends to be far more implicit. To take just one example, Zaidman's *Mémoire d'une enfance volée (1938–1948)* (2002) (Memoirs of a Stolen Childhood (1938–1948)) makes citations from incriminating official documents, but does not herself directly indict Vichy France. Gervais-Marx's text is exemplary in two senses of the word: as an example of a trend in French women's writing that is being amplified in the 2000s; and as an ethical model of striving for balanced but courageously forthright assessment of Vichy France. That striving is difficult. It sometimes leads to paradox and even historiographical aporia. Gervais-Marx, unlike most of her epigones, takes that writerly risk.

Notes

1 The rare examples I have been able to locate are Kofman 1994 and Krief 1997.
2 Rubinstein 2002; Zaidman 2002; Hannah 2003; Zalberg 2004; August-Franck 2006; Lelaidier-Márton 2006; Burko-Falcman 2007; Zeif 2010.
3 In 2003, it was awarded the Prix Henri-Hertz, created in 1986 by the Chancellerie des Universités de Paris la Sorbonne (Chancellery of the Universities of Paris Sorbonne) to reward the published text most likely to raise awareness of the ethical and civic preoccupations of Henri Hertz, who always sided with the weak and the oppressed against authoritarianism or any form of exclusion at the end of the nineteenth century/first half of the twentieth century.
4 Studies that provide (in varying proportions) consideration of specifically *French* Jewish *enfants cachés* include, listed in order of publication date: Vegh 1975; Delpard 1993; Hazan 2000; Jaron 2002; Bailly 2004; Bailly 2006; Coquio and Kalisky 2007; Feldman 2009; and Samacher 2009.
5 See, for instance, Rubinstein 2002: 59; August-Franck 2006: 28; and Zeif 2010: 34.
6 '[y]ou don't easily get over the realisation that the world is suddenly losing all its meaning, that once the line has been crossed that usually separates normality from the abnormal, reality from the unreal, every gesture becomes laden with particular meanings, some of which are a threat and lead to death.' Unless otherwise indicated, all translations from the French are mine.
7 Zaidman documents a similar phenomenon (Zaidman 2002: 140; see also 187 and 189). And Burko-Falcman (2007: 175) recalls her postwar sensation of '[l]a honte de ne pas avoir souffert comme *les autres*, d'avoir connu des moments délicieux [. . .] La honte de vivre encore' ('the shame of not having suffered like *the others*, of having experienced wonderful moments [. . .] The shame of still being alive').
8 'I'd like every reader to be able to recognise that nobody is protected from such a strange experience, that "the other" is never the only one who might go through such an experience.'
9 I use the term 'survivor' in the inclusive sense of any Jew directly persecuted or indirectly subjected to suffering by Nazi and/or French fascist forces during the Second World War, rather than in the exclusive sense of a Jew who survived a concentration or death camp.
10 'With great confidence, my mother judged ridiculous the idea that the persecutions to which they were subject in their own country could be the warning signs of what was going to happen in France. In October 1940, she hadn't changed her mind: she was Jewish, perhaps; French, certainly, and as such, she had nothing to fear from France's government.'
11 Zalberg 2004: 35, Zaidman 2002: 106–7, and Hannah 2003: 101 and 107, all feature characters who strongly embody the anti-clerical,

anti-fascist, resister ethos of those French citizens who continued to respect Republican ideals even under Vichy. Fittingly, two of these characters are *institutrices* (women primary-school teachers), and so members of a professional class which under the Third Republic had been crucial transmitters of Republican values.

12 Such challenges to *le mythe résistanciel* (the myth that the vast majority of French people had been part of the internal Resistance) came in the wake of the general contestation witnessed in 1968 of French institutions, including the institution of official national memory. Two of the first cultural examples were Marcel Ophüls's film *Le Chagrin et la pitié* (1969) (*The Sorrow and the Pity*), an epic documentary film shown to a restricted public in 1971, but banned from French television until 1981; and Louis Malle's film *Lacombe Lucien* (1974). The best-known historical study to subvert the myth is Rousso 1987; revised and republished 1990.

13 'the Righteous'; see Zaidman 2002: 104; Burko-Falcman 2007: 193; Zalberg 2004: 15; Zeif 2010: 54; Hannah 2003: 169; and August-Franck 2006: 44, 48 and 89.

14 '"being Jewish" had no meaning'.

15 The outstanding courage of Chambon-sur-Lignon's efforts to shelter and protect Jewish children under Vichy has been widely recognised. One other homage among the primary literature of former *enfants cachés* is found in Zalberg 2004, a novel based very closely on the experience of Zalberg's mother, who had been hidden as a Jewish child in Mazet-Saint-Voy, part of the same region.

16 'that doesn't alter in any way the fact that at a certain moment the death machine began to swallow up everyone. There was only one way of dying, in the gas chambers at Auschwitz.'

17 '[i]f it nonetheless seems important to recount my own experience, it's precisely because it's about "ordinary" people who didn't stand out because of their accent or their origins, and nonetheless found themselves to be "marked out" for the slaughter-house.'

18 See, for instance, Burko-Falcman 2007: 59.

19 Representative here are Zaidman 2002: 117; Zalberg 2004: 49; and Zeif 2010: 54 and 69.

20 'The name you've written at the top of your work isn't yours. Never do that again, do you hear me? Your work is good but we're going to tear it up together.'

21 Such a scenario is also powerfully etched in Zalberg 2004: 92–9.

22 Zeif (2010: 205), for one, avers '[i]1 est certain que l'anxiété et l'angoisse me poursuivent. Comme presque tous les enfants cachés.' (I'm certainly hounded by anxiety and anguish. Like nearly all hidden children.')

23 'Nowadays, when I hear it in a conversation, it's more the term "Arab" that makes me jump: I'm scared of what's going to follow. And the height of stupidity seemed to me that remark made by an American couple, obviously Jewish, whose visit to an exhibition on the 1943 round-ups in Marseille coincided with mine: "When I think", said the

woman, "that the Arabs deny the Holocaust . . ." The assertion was like an injury to me. In the Near East, there are some Arabs who deny it, for sure; but "the" Arabs! How could that woman not understand that through such an abrupt and arbitrary generalisation, she was using the same sort of violence that led to the Holocaust?'

24   As I have previously observed, '[f]or Todorov, exemplary memory, unlike literal memory, allows category-links to be made between past and present phenomena of differing contingent forms; through such links, exemplary memory permits the learning of lessons from the past that may improve the present' (Cairns 2011: 27).

25   'always find contemporary relevance in information about the Shoah, on the basis of new experiences'.

26   Thus Burko-Falcman (2007: 101, 95) makes memorial parallels between French police brutality towards Jews in the Second World War and towards Arabs during the Algerian War; and the outbreak of the Iraq War provides a psychological fillip to the text she is writing about her own persecution in the Second World War, namely *Un prénom républicain* (A Republican First Name).

27   'a painful work of mourning'.

28   'Others have said it, some have written it, but rarely just after they returned. It took a long time before they were able to turn back towards the recent past, to contemplate again the terrifying ordeal that they had escaped from alive, to talk about it.'

29   'there are no more certainties, the earth is turning into a moving universe with unfathomable rules'.

30   'une telle expérience m'a obligée à modifier mon échelle de valeurs, à n'attacher de l'importance qu'à ce qui met en cause la vie et la dignité des hommes' (310) ('such an experience forced me to revise my scale of values, to attach importance only to what threatens the life and dignity of human beings').

31   The most egregious case is Zeif 2010.

Chapter Five
Wives and Daughters in Literary Works Representing the *Harkis*

SUSAN IRELAND

A key moment in relations between France and Algeria, the 1954–62 Algerian war of independence is associated with trauma, repression and unhealed wounds on both the individual and national levels. The treatment of the *harkis* in particular has been characterised as 'one of the most ignominious episodes in both Algerian and French history' (Stone 1997: 225), as an estimated 100,000 *harkis* were killed by their compatriots after the signing of the Accords d'Evian, while those who were finally repatriated to France found themselves isolated in temporary housing camps and felt betrayed by the French.[1] While a small number of male-authored novels and personal testimonies first drew attention to the plight of the *harkis* in the 1980s and 1990s, it is only since 2000 that a substantial body of literary works devoted to this taboo topic has finally emerged. Although the term *harki* is generally associated with men, a significant number of the recent texts are written by women, most of them daughters of *harkis*. This chapter examines the gendered nature of their narratives and looks in particular at the ways in which they portray the effects of the father's destiny on the lives of his wife and daughters.

Although allusions to the war of independence appear in texts written by women of Maghrebi immigrant descent before 2000, the conflict has rarely constituted a central focus of their narratives.[2] In contrast, the recent works by Fatima Besnaci-Lancou, Zahia Rahmani and Dalila Kerchouche, which are discussed in this chapter, have the war and its aftermath as their main theme, while at the same time addressing issues characteristic of contemporary women's writing in general, such as the manifestations and effects of trauma and the interrelated topics of women, war and displacement. These texts, which are very different in style and tone, all give voice to the wives and daughters of *harkis* in order to pay tribute to the protagonists' mothers and to create an oppositional discourse that contests official versions of the war story.

The texts in the corpus, which seek to bear witness to an untold story, have several characteristics in common. First, the narratives all possess a strong didactic dimension that uses a 'narrator-as-eyewitness' (Felman and Laub 1992: 101) to document the experiences of the *harkis* and to explore the intersections of family stories and national history. As such, they constitute interesting examples of what Mireille Rosello (2005: 140) calls 'autobio-historical texts'. Secondly, the narrators are explicitly portrayed as belonging to the second or 1.5 generation[3] in relation to the 1962 massacres and the forced uprooting of the survivors. At the same time, recurrent references to wounds and scars evoke a painful inheritance and highlight the ways in which the children have been profoundly marked by their father's past, a situation that leads the authors to emphasise the need for a 'parole cicatrisante' (Besnaci-Lancou 2005: 121). In particular, powerful images of being branded – 'Il fallait à tout prix nous marquer au fer rouge' (Besnaci-Lancou 2005: 28)[4] – suggest how the term *harki* has become a transmittable identity (Charbit 2006: 63), a kind of ethnic marker that is passed down from one generation to the next, along with the stigma associated with it. Finally, the authors' decision to enter the realm of public discourse reflects their desire to put an end to the legacy of shame that makes the daughter of a *harki* the daughter of a traitor (Kerchouche 2006: 50) and signals their intention to provide an alternative account of their lives and identities. Indeed, writing is presented as a potentially reparative process, and frequent allusions to the act of speaking out suggest the idea of narrative recovery,[5] a recovery that, in this case, entails the telling of women's stories in the hope of healing old wounds.

Mothers

In *Nos mères, paroles blessées* (2006) (Our Mothers, Wounded Words), Besnaci-Lancou draws attention to the absence of *harkis*' wives from official narratives of the war in both France and Algeria (20). Likewise, Kerchouche comments on the paucity of media reports and other works devoted to these women who did not 'choose' to be on the side of France during the war, but who nonetheless suffered alongside their husbands (Gladieu and Kerchouche 2003: 85). Recovery of the mothers' stories is evident in two types of text. In the most straightforward form (Gladieu and Kerchouche's *Destins de harkis* (2003) (*Harkis*' Destinies) and Besnaci-Lancou's *Nos mères, paroles blessées*), the mothers' voices are recorded in works that constitute a kind of oral history in that they present a series of first-hand accounts which provide a composite picture of the experiences of the wives of *harkis*, many of whom are illiterate. In *Destins*, the short testimonies are framed by Stéphan Gladieu's black-and-white photos of *harki* families, and the combination of text and visual image gives a strong sense of presence to a community often described as ghosts (Jordi and Hamoumou 1999: 12). Similarly, *Nos mères* is composed of narratives of the lives of twenty women whose names form the table of contents, thus highlighting the importance of each individual voice. Together, the two volumes create a forceful impression of the hardship endured by the women, who evoke similar issues in both books: the violence of the massacres, their fears, their traumatic departure from their homeland, the difficulty of life in the camps in France and the psychosomatic symptoms they still experience, but also the solidarity and support they have encountered, and their desire finally to see an end to the divisions caused by the war. In both works, too, giving the women a voice is clearly portrayed as a form of narrative recovery. Gladieu and Kerchouche's book is described as a 'receptacle' for their hitherto silent suffering (6), while Besnaci-Lancou's subtitle, *Paroles blessées*, points to the 'profonde blessure' she views as the unifying element in the women's lives (20), and she explicitly associates 'la libération de la parole' with 'apaisement' (19, 20).[6]

The homage to the *harkis*' wives also appears in autobiographical works presented from the perspective of their daughters. Here, they are associated in particular with the survival of the family and the notion of heritage in a positive sense. Indeed, all the texts under discussion illustrate sociologist Stéphanie Abrial's (2001: 201) observation that, for the children of *harkis*, the father represents pain, whereas mothers stand for memories of the homeland and of Algerian traditions. In *France, récit d'une enfance* (2006) (France, Story of a Childhood), for example, in which Rahmani addresses her thoughts to her dying mother, the mother is depicted as a strong, generous woman whose skills as a storyteller have enabled her to pass on her culture to her children. Unlike the legacy of shame associated with the father, this 'transmission de la généalogie comme fable' (52) is portrayed as a positive form of inheritance that has enabled the children to remain connected to their roots, and the frequent use of the second-person pronoun 'tu' creates an intimate tone which underscores the depth of the daughter's admiration for her mother: 'Croyant fermement ton héritage, tu as légué à tes enfants un patrimoine inentamé' (43).[7]

The idea of the mother as a bridge to the past is also a central theme in Kerchouche's *Mon père, ce harki* (2003) (My Father, That Harki). As in *France, récit d'une enfance*, the mother is linked to transmission of the family story, and Kerchouche's (2003: 25) depiction of family dynamics strongly recalls Abrial's in that she associates her father with silence and her mother with eagerness to recount life in Algeria and in the French housing camps. Whereas Rahmani focuses on the theme of inheritance, however, Kerchouche's debt to her mother appears primarily in the context of the journey she undertakes in order to learn about her past. When she visits the six camps in which her family lived over a period of twelve years and travels to Algeria for the first time, she follows the same itinerary as her mother, but in reverse, and the framing of her account of the voyage suggests that her mother's oral narratives constitute a model for her own text: 'Je calquerai mes pas sur les siens [. . .] De la même manière qu'elle m'a raconté son voyage, je veux, moi aussi, en écrivant transmettre mon aventure' (32).[8] Likewise, recurrent parallels between the two women's journeys evoke the strong bond between mother and daughter. The expression 'comme ma mère'[9] in particular recurs frequently in the text, and Kerchouche often points to feelings and situations she has in common with her mother. For example, when relating her meeting with the ex-director of the camp at Rivesaltes, who had humiliated her mother by ripping off her headscarf, Kerchouche uses terms related to her mother's experience to convey her own anger and her desire to shame the ex-director in his turn: 'j'arrache moi aussi mon "foulard" et lui balance mon identité au visage.' (117)[10] Furthermore, as Kerchouche reconstructs her parents' trajectory, the stories her mother told her provide her with the insights she needs to recognise the places she visits and to establish an emotional connection with them. In her account of her trip to Algeria, for instance, she explicitly comments on the way in which her experiences are mediated through her mother's narratives, noting especially that she is seeing scenes that her mother had previously described to her (204). By retracing her steps, Kerchouche thus comes to better understand her mother's life and to appreciate fully the important role she has played in providing her children with a sense of rootedness despite her own deracination.

Finally, in Rahmani's *Moze* (2003), which is based on her father's experiences, the repetition of the expression 'la femme de Moze' in the penultimate chapter (145, 159, 160, 162, 163, 165, 166) associates the mother with presence rather than invisibility and highlights the fact that her husband's fate has dramatically changed the course of her life. This emphasis on the effects of war on women is reinforced through the evocation of the mother's 'guerre de femme' (155), her struggle to protect and provide for her children during the five years her husband was in prison in Algeria. As in *France, récit d'une enfance*, the passages depicting the mother in *Moze* portray her as 'experte en histoires et légendes' (165),[11] and storytelling is presented as her means of keeping the family together and of handing down traditions and practical knowledge. Indeed, her voice stands in sharp contrast to the father's silence, and the narrator stresses the idea that, while Moze is associated with rupture, his wife represents continuity and heritage. In a long, lyrical passage evoking her mother's tales of Algeria, for example, her positive legacy is highlighted through references to her native tongue and to '[c]ette parole qui dit cette vie qu'elle n'a pas cédée.' (154)[12] In this sense, Rahmani's mother becomes an emblematic figure who represents the wives of *harkis* in general, and these women's strong influence in their families is encapsulated in the notion of 'la langue des mères', which is portrayed as a life-giving force. This tribute to the *harkis*' wives is further evident in the narrator's recognition of their fortitude and selflessness, and the image of creating songs, which represents the mothers' ability to overcome hardship, serves as a powerful symbol of the gratitude expressed by all the daughters whose works are discussed in this chapter: 'il faut faire du monde un chant. C'est là son secret. Celui de toutes ses femmes. Celles qui il y a quelques années traversaient la Méditerranée, accompagnant, abandonnées et résignées, le destin tragique de leurs hommes déchus' (166).[13]

Daughters

In *Les Harkis, une mémoire enfouie* (1999) (*Harkis*, A Buried Memory), historians Jean-Jacques Jordi and Mohand Hamoumou observe that children of *harkis* are defined by their 'enracinement dans un déracinement' and their 'ancrage dans le silence' (14).[14] The daughters portrayed by Rahmani, Kerchouche and Besnaci-Lancou all grapple with the consequences of their family's uprooting and provide a gendered account of the difficult experience of growing up in France as the child of a *harki*. As might be expected, the daughter's relationship with her father is often problematic and features prominently in the texts. Kerchouche (2003: 24) notes, for example, that history taught her to detest her father, while Rahmani (2007: 250) conveys similar strong emotions in more dramatic terms: 'Meurs ma fille meurs. C'était fait. Tuée je l'étais. Je suis née tuée.'[15] Because their fathers were *harkis*, the daughters also find themselves enmeshed in official war narratives that assign them a predetermined role, which they seek to reject. Indeed, most of the protagonists have internalised the narratives of guilt and shame associated with the *harkis*: Besnaci-Lancou (2005: 18) refers to being crushed by feelings of guilt, and the opening sentence in *Mon père, ce harki* immediately associates being the daughter of a *harki* with dishonour (Kerchouche 2003: 13). At the same time, the daughters' traumatic childhood continues to manifest itself in the psychological problems they exhibit – anorexia in Besnaci-Lancou's *Fille de harki* (2005) (Daughter of a *Harki*), nightmares in Rahmani's *Moze*, suicidal thoughts in Kerchouche's *Leïla* (2006), attempted suicide in Rahmani's *France, récit d'une enfance*, and self-destructive tendencies in Kerchouche's *Mon père, ce harki*. In this sense, Kerchouche's (2003: 100) characterisation of herself as a woman facing her past in order to build a future applies equally well to the protagonists of the other works, who exhume painful memories in an attempt finally to lay the past to rest and reshape the discourses surrounding the *harkis*.

In *Fille de harki*, which documents the collective story of the *harkis* and the personal experiences of the author, Besnaci-Lancou makes an impassioned plea for the existing scripts to be revised. Throughout the text, frequent references to the official French and Algerian accounts of the war draw attention to the ways in which these national narratives have circumscribed the author's identity. On the one hand, her description of life in the camps depicts the *harkis* as a 'héritage encombrant pour la France' (Besnaci-Lancou 2005: 75), an uncomfortable reminder of events the country would rather forget, and the protagonist is conscious of her place in the broader unfolding of French colonial history – 'je fais partie d'une communauté de destin. L'histoire coloniale de la France a fait de moi une fille de harki.' (13)[16] On the other hand, the Algerian script, with its polarised opposition between heroes and traitors, is evoked through Algerian president Abdelaziz Bouteflika's affirmation in June 2000 that the time was still was not right for *harkis* to visit Algeria. In particular, his comparison of the *harkis* to French collaborators during the Second World War is experienced by Besnaci-Lancou as a slap in the face (13), and this 'bannissement présidentiel' (14)[17] is presented as the catalyst that re-opens the original wound and leads the author to revisit her past.

The protagonist's wound, her witnessing of the events of summer 1962 as an eight-year-old child, followed by the fourteen years she spent in camps in France, is clearly described as a form of repressed trauma in which bloody events have been indelibly imprinted in her memory and are described as a monster living in her body (21, 110). Subsequently, recurrent images linking silence to continuing psychological distress suggest the motivation for her writing and introduce the theme of narrative recovery, which is associated with the urgent need to put an end to a curse (20). In her account of her recovery of the past, the combination of information about her family's experiences and her comments on how the text came to be written forcefully brings out the contrast between the personal and official versions of events and thus highlights the idea of a counter-narrative. While Besnaci-Lancou acknowledges that France has gone a good way towards modifying its discourse on the *harkis*, the final words of the text, which are addressed to President Bouteflika, suggest that wounds will not be completely healed, and that the transmission of the curse will not stop, until Algeria in its turn rewrites its national history in order to create a more accurate account of the war to bequeath to future generations (121).

The question of received scripts recurs in Rahmani's *Moze*, where it is related in particular to the themes of branding and filiation.

Like *Fille de harki*, *Moze* stresses the importance of moving from silence to recognition and emphasises the need for both France and Algeria to acknowledge their role in causing the suffering of the *harkis*. As in *Fille de harki*, too, Rahmani relates the word *harki* to the transmission of an unwanted identity, the 'identité honteuse' (46) associated with the father and passed down to his children. Other passages suggest that the term has become a label that imprisons the daughter, and a series of powerful images evokes the pain that results from her being permanently marked by her father's role in the war: 'je porte son matricule' (120); 'la faute de Moze, je veux dire qu'elle est ma chair et mon habit [. . .] Je ne pouvais échapper à sa vie.' (24)[18] The notion of the daughter being a prisoner of her father's past thus suggests a negative form of filiation, and Rahmani's fragmented style serves to underscore the dissolution of the self caused by this unwelcome inheritance.

Throughout the text, the interrelated themes of silence and shame contrast with the image of voice and with the idea that breaking the silence constitutes an integral part of the process of recovery in both senses of the term. As in *Fille de harki*, however, Algeria is depicted as an obstacle to healing and is associated with the stigmatisation, exclusion and continuing demonisation of the *harkis*. The narrator also judges France harshly, accusing the country of abandoning her and of being responsible for her father's death. In particular, in her version of the war story, the verb 'betray', which is often used in relation to the *harkis*, serves to evoke France's dishonour and to portray its treatment of the *harkis* as a crime that should be recognised as such (140).

For the protagonist, then, recovery involves bringing the truth to light, and the first words of the text, which are repeated near the end of the work, explicitly link memory and writing:

> Je me souviens.
> Écris que tu te souviens.
> Que tu t'en souviens. (11, 175)[19]

The importance of narrative articulation for the daughter is also evident in her characterisation of her text as a means of handing Moze back to those responsible for causing his wounds: 'Par l'écriture, je me défais de lui et vous le remets.' (24)[20] In the same passage, the daughter's portrayal of herself as a bequest (*un legs*) and as the continuation of her father suggests a different type of filiation, while at the same time evoking the return of the repressed on the national level. Indeed, this more positive form of transmission is underscored by the idea that the daughter has become her father's voice and will speak for him after his death, an idea reinforced by the fact that she has inherited his handwriting. The final chapter, entitled 'Moze parle, la voix de Moze glisse en sa fille',[21] further suggests that the daughter will continue the father's struggle for recognition and will seek reparation in his name. In the chapter itself, which consists of an imaginary conversation between the daughter and her dead father, the words 'Père je n'ai plus peur' (175)[22] intimate that returning to the past has enabled the daughter to reconcile herself with her father's past. In this sense, her book itself constitutes a memorial to Moze that contrasts strikingly with the description of the official Armistice Day ceremony which took place just before he committed suicide in 1991.

Kerchouche's best-known work, *Mon père, ce harki*, takes up the question of commemoration while raising important questions about how to tell the daughter's story. Early in the text, Kerchouche's (2003: 14) description of her suffering, which she relates to her troubled relationship with her father, evokes many of the classic symptoms of trauma such as shame, rebellion, anger and feelings of aggression. The catalyst that leads her to re-examine this complicated past, her brother's suicide, recalls the slap in the face that precipitated Besnaci-Lancou's coming to writing, and the terms Kerchouche uses to characterise her decision to speak out suggest the force of her repressed emotions – 'je vais [. . .] le dire, l'écrire, le graver, le crier. Hurler ce qu'*ils* m'ont fait.' (31; italics in original)[23] However, references to the difficulty of recovering the past recur frequently in the text as Kerchouche confronts the same challenges as other children of survivors of collective trauma who set out to tell their parents' stories and need to relate events they have not lived through themselves.[24] Indeed, she comments despondently that all that remains of her past are ruined buildings and tattered memories (56). Her solution to this dilemma can perhaps best be described as a form of imaginative re-creation based on archival information, interviews, family memories and places visited. This approach enables her to reconstruct key episodes of her parents' story such as their departure from Algeria and their arrival in Marseille, and her coining of the term 'harkeological' to describe her undertaking (187) underscores the idea that she will need to dig deep in order to recover the past.

Throughout much of the text, references to ghost camps, unmarked tombstones and decaying buildings suggest the erasure of the *harkis* from the French landscape and, by extension, evoke the reluctance to incorporate them into the French war story. Although Kerchouche at first has the impression that she is preparing an 'état des lieux du vide' (85),[25] her narrative attests to an alternative mapping of the events of the war, an idea reinforced by her reference to the star-shaped image the camps form on the map of France. These symbolic places, whose names provide most of the chapter titles, constitute the *harkis*' sites of memory in the sense proposed by Pierre Nora (1984), and Kerchouche's focus on them in her text serves both to commemorate them and to link herself to them. Similarly, the interweaving of past and present highlights the presence of the narrator recording events and thus allows the reader to see her working through the emotions associated with the camps. When she learns about the terrible living conditions at Rivesaltes, for example, her anger is conveyed through a reference to her writing: 'Je suis scandalisée [. . .] J'enfonce les touches du clavier de mon ordinateur avec rage.' (66)[26] This emphasis on the writer-at-work, like the images of voice in *Moze*, draws attention to the narrative process itself and suggests that Kerchouche has become part of the chain of transmission in a positive sense. In this fashion, she emerges as the author and subject of her own story, which now takes its place alongside official narratives, and the end of her voyage into the past is associated with reconciliation and the healing of wounds (195).

While *Mon père, ce harki* relates Kerchouche's own story, *Leïla* is a coming-of-age narrative based on her elder sister's experiences. Although the rehabilitation of the father is one of the main objectives in both texts, *Leïla* focuses primarily on the protagonist's identity crisis and raises the question of gender equality, which is not dealt with in most of the other works.[27] As in *Moze* and *Fille de harki*, the narrator identifies the specific moment (an official dinner) that provided the impetus for her to speak out, a moment that again unlocks painful memories and brings back the ghosts of the past. Likewise, as in the works already discussed, writing is presented as the path to recovery on the personal and collective levels. At the beginning of *Leïla*, the protagonist's dramatic self-description – 'Je suis fatiguée de vivre. J'ai 17 ans et n'ai qu'une envie: m'allonger dans le fossé et mourir' (Kerchouche 2006: 15)[28]

– highlights the psychological distress caused by what she describes as a double curse, the fact of being both a woman and the child of a *harki* (124). On the one hand, recurrent images of imprisonment reveal how Leïla, as the child of a *harki*, feels trapped in the camps, in the daughter-of-a-traitor script (50), and in the 'barbelés dans [s]a tête' (126).[29] Her detailed description of her life during this period thus underscores the idea of being incarcerated in both the physical and psychological senses, and the strong terms she often uses to evoke the debilitating effects of trauma, such as violence, nightmares and mental illness, suggest that the situation in the camps worsened the *harkis*' problems rather than establishing an atmosphere conducive to healing. On the other hand, being a woman requires the negotiation of a further set of restrictions that reflect the *harki* community's expectations regarding gender roles. Although the narrator admires her mother's strength and abnegation, she also describes her as a jailer (41) and associates her with the transmission of inequality and the perpetuation of an unwanted heritage, the 'humiliation ancestrale des femmes de [s]a famille' (124).[30] As in many other works that address gender issues in relation to daughters of Maghbrei immigrants, Leïla is especially worried that she may be married against her will, and it is the threat of an arranged marriage that leads her to run away from home and walk into a pond with intention of drowning herself.

Despite the sombre themes found in much of the text, *Leïla*, like the other works discussed, evokes the possibility of recovery. First, Leïla's fear of transmitting her despair to her younger sister stops her from committing suicide, since she does not wish to pass on the legacy of shame in her turn. Secondly, the awakening of her political and feminist consciousness provides her with a sense of agency. When she participates in the *harkis*' rebellion, for example, the earlier images of imprisonment are replaced by that of self-liberation as Leïla cathartically releases her anger by participating in the destruction of the fencing surrounding the camp. Similarly, pursuing her studies is portrayed as another stage along the road to independence. Finally, the last chapter, which serves as an epilogue, evokes the long process of recovering confidence and self-esteem. Here, Leïla, who is now almost fifty, portrays herself as fulfilled and happily married, while at the same time recognising that many children of *harkis* have not fared so well. In particular, her affirmation 'je suis une rescapée' (145)[31] frames her text as a survivor narrative and thus further underscores the shift from hopelessness to the reappropriation of agency and voice.

At the very end of *Fille de harki*, Besnaci-Lancou (2005: 121) exclaims, 'C'est infernal, comment arrêter cette malédiction!'[32] The texts discussed in this chapter suggest at least a partial answer to her question. Taken together, they illustrate the possibility of writing a new script and of creating a positive inheritance to hand down to future generations – the authors' own version of familial and collective history. Rejecting the role of victim, the authors in the corpus turn to writing as a form of empowerment and demonstrate their intention to enter the realm of public debate in order to bring the situation of the wives and daughters of *harkis* to the fore. In this sense, their texts provide a missing piece of the larger story of the war and take their place alongside the memory work of other groups such as the *pieds-noirs*, French soldiers and the Front de Libération Nationale.

Notes

1 *Harki* is the generic term used to refer to Algerians who worked for the French army during the war; it is often used to describe their families as well.
2 Female authors who give a more prominent role to the war, such as Assia Djebar, are generally not of immigrant descent.
3 See Suleiman 2006: 178, 179, for a definition of these terms.
4 'healing words'; 'We had at all costs to be branded with a red-hot iron.' Unless otherwise indicated, all translations from the French are my own.
5 I am using Suzette Henke's definition of 'narrative recovery' as 'both the recovery of past experience through narrative articulation and the psychological reintegration of a traumatically shattered subject' (Henke 2000: xxii).
6 'deep wound'; 'finding a voice'; 'relief'.
7 'transmission of genealogy in the form of stories'; 'you'; 'Believing strongly in your heritage, you bequeathed to your children a cultural legacy that was still intact'.
8 'I will travel in her footsteps [. . .] Just as she told me about her journey, I too want to pass on my adventure through my writing'.
9 'like my mother'.
10 'I, too, tore off my "headscarf" and thrust my identity in his face.'
11 'Moze's wife'; 'woman's war'; 'skilled in telling stories and legends'.
12 'These words which speak of the life she has not relinquished.'
13 'the language of mothers'; 'the world must be made into a song. That's her secret. The secret of all her women. Those who crossed the

	Mediterranean a few years ago, abandoned and resigned, accompanying the tragic destiny of their fallen men'.
14	'being rooted in an uprooting' and 'anchored in silence'.
15	'Die my daughter die. It had already happened. Killed I was. I was born killed.'
16	'burdensome legacy for France'; 'I belong to a community of destiny. French colonial history has made me a daughter of a *harki*.'
17	'presidential banishment'.
18	'shameful identity'; 'I wear his regimental number'; 'Moze's misdeed, it's my flesh and my clothing [. . .] I couldn't escape his life.'
19	'I remember. Write that you remember. That you remember these things.'
20	'Through my writing, I release myself from him and hand him back to you.'
21	'Moze speaks. Moze's voice slips into his daughter'.
22	'Father, I'm no longer afraid.'
23	'I'm going to [. . .] say it, write it, put it into print, shout it out. Yell out what *they* did to me.'
24	Young 2000: 10, for example, asks 'How is a post-holocaust generation of artists supposed to "remember" events they never experienced directly?'
25	'inventory of nothingness'.
26	'I am outraged [. . .] I pound angrily on the keys of my computer.'
27	See Rice 2009 for a discussion of Rahmani's *France, récit d'une enfance*, which also addresses the issue of gender inequality.
28	'I'm tired of life. I'm seventeen and want only one thing: to lie down in the ditch and die.'
29	'barbed wire fence in her head'.
30	'ancestral humiliation of the women in her family'.
31	'I'm a survivor.'
32	'It's unbearable, how can we put an end to this curse!'

Chapter Six
(Not) Seeing Things: Marie NDiaye, (Negative) Hallucination and 'Blank' *Métissage*

ANDREW ASIBONG

D'un côté, une coupure du doigt sans sang, de l'autre du sang sans coupure de doigt. (Green 1993: 239)[1]

NDiaye's indigestible hybridities

French and francophone women's writing has for some time now been preoccupied with the figure of the 'hybrid' as a heroically postmodern transgressor of the norms, categories and classifications that bind and restrict seemingly more ordinary, monocultural identities. Nuance and complexity notwithstanding, texts as diverse as Leïla Sebbar's *Shérazade: 17 ans, brune, frisée, les yeux verts* (1982) (*Sherazade*), Marguerite Duras's *La Pluie d'été* (1990) (*Summer Rain*) and Marie Darrieussecq's *Truismes* (1996a) (*Pig Tales*) all showcase protagonists whose existence at the crossroads of racialising (or pseudo-racialising) discourses can be seen to contribute, in the final analysis, to an enhanced relationship with pleasure, the body, wisdom, art and, indeed, the secrets of the universe itself. Plunged into moments of inequality, humiliation and sometimes abjection, but equipped with the resources to survive – even revel in – these experiences, Sebbar's adventurous half-Algerian teenager Shérazade, Duras's indescribable, incestuous 'metics' Ernesto and Jeanne, and Darrieussecq's perpetually fluctuating sow-woman are all literary examples of a typically postmodern philosophical *topos* according to which the capacity to move between totalising subject-positions, while painful and quite possibly traumatic, is nevertheless potentially empowering, from both ethical and spiritual perspectives.[2] The literary and theatrical oeuvre of Marie NDiaye (born in 1967, in Pithiviers, north-central France), in conjunction with her frequently disquieting cultural persona, has tended, however, to resist such triumphant representations of 'mixed' subjects.[3] In this chapter, I want to offer an overview of NDiaye's provocative and highly unfashionable presentation of the 'mixed condition', before using her short story 'Les Sœurs' (2008) ('The Sisters') to demonstrate the potential for a radical politicisation by 'race' of the key psychoanalytic concepts of false self, blankness and 'negative hallucination'.

'Les Sœurs', written as the briefest of prefaces for her brother Pap Ndiaye's [*sic*] (2008) sociological study of French blackness, remains Marie NDiaye's most succinct and hard-hitting statement on the near-impossibility of successfully integrating or, indeed, satisfactorily symbolising a split 'mixed-race' subjectivity within a society that obsessively racialises subjects at the same time as prohibiting them from speaking of their racialisation. Long before 'Les Sœurs', though, via the protagonists of her early novels, NDiaye regularly conveyed visions of fundamentally sickening hybridity, a revolting 'mixed-ness' that is always somehow out of joint, either punished for being too foreign, or else never quite foreign enough.[4] The tortured and nameless anomaly (provisionally called 'Fanny') in *En famille* (1990) (*Among Family*) remains NDiaye's most iconic figure of hybrid wretchedness. This protagonist's attempts to gain recognition within her mother's increasingly hostile family are never framed in explicitly racialised terms: the reader will never know for sure exactly why Fanny's maternal family considers her to be so radically beyond the pale. The one indisputable fact we are given to understand, and which is confirmed at some length by Fanny's Aunt Colette, is that Fanny is infected by some kind of ineradicable impurity (derived from her absent father), a quasi-fantastical flaw that has affected not only her physical aspect more and more as the years have gone on, but has even embedded itself into her very soul, to produce a character marked by irremediable arrogance, self-consciousness and paranoia. As for the mediocre half-witch Lucie, the hopelessly passive and compatible narrator of *La Sorcière*

(1996) (The Witch), her magically hybrid status – she is part-sorceress on her mother's side – brings her nothing but alienation and despair: unable to tap into the truly marvellous powers of witchcraft enjoyed by her powerful mother and twin daughters, Lucie is nevertheless tainted by the stigma of being classed as a witch, however weak, and is accordingly despised by both her 'normal' husband and father for this putative, marginalising difference.

From the outset, then, NDiaye's fictions have tended to portray fantastically unnamable 'borderline' subjects who fail to find their place in any social, cultural or political configuration, since they prove undesirable and fundamentally unrecognisable to all of them. Even if one does not wish to 'reduce' such complex and multilayered fictions by claiming that they are simply metaphors deployed by NDiaye to articulate her own feelings about 'race' and/or her experience of being a specifically racialised hybrid subject, it nevertheless seems perverse not to acknowledge the extent to which NDiaye herself has proved – and continues to prove – unrecognisable to the culture that has produced her.[5] A brief analysis of the various silences and distortions surrounding the issue (or non-issue) of NDiaye's brown French skin seems to me to be a useful way into understanding just how awkward, how unstable, how embarrassedly schizoid evocations of 'race', 'origins' and racialised hybridity remain both in NDiaye's writing itself and in her fluctuating self-presentation. NDiaye and her complex fictions have often been wilfully *not seen* by journalists, publishers and academics attempting to impose upon woman and work either a bizarrely hallucinated 'African-ness' that is deeply, stupidly inappropriate, or else, at the other extreme, a blank, pseudo-universalising, post-racial identity that has nothing whatsoever to do with stigmatised minority experience in a white and racialising world.[6] Meanwhile NDiaye's own vaguely self-contradictory statements about her cultural (non-)positioning speak volumes about the paradoxical over- and under-racialising processes that have tended to characterise both her mediatised image and her texts of 'mixed-ness'. In a peculiarly poignant moment of anguished autobiography, NDiaye (1997: 67) bewails her constant sense of displacement on the one hand, while insisting, on the other, that she and her work should be considered in purely (white) French cultural terms: 'Je ne me sens ni cosmopolite ni d'une double culture [. . .] mais principalement l'héritière culturelle de Molière, de Rousseau ou de Proust [. . .] Je suis exclusivement Française.'[7] NDiaye seems torn in two opposing directions, then, drawing the reader's attention to her lifelong sense of 'difference' (a sense deriving, apparently, from the way in which French society has misrecognised her by claiming that she is 'different' when in fact she is entirely the 'same'), while equally vociferously claiming that her writing bears no mark whatsoever of this relentless experience of marginalisation. That the works themselves seem thoroughly haunted by an (unspeakable) question about this (false) thing called blackness – and at times resemble the writings of Toni Morrison at least as much as they do those of Proust – complicates matters still further.

In her writings of the twenty-first century, NDiaye displays a greater confidence in representing *explicitly* how universal mental and emotional dispositions can nevertheless acquire specifically racialised dimensions, particularly in the 'mixed-race' psyche. If the world of *Rosie Carpe* (2001) is populated by all manner of vaguely 'dead' and/or schizoid women, white and black (not to mention red and yellow), it is nevertheless worth noting that the one literal zombie is Lisbeth, little Titi's bewitched, living-dead babysitter, step-grandmother and eventual wife, and brown-skinned *métisse* teenage daughter of Mme Carpe's lover Alex Foret.[8] Similarly, in the play *Papa doit manger* (2003) (Daddy Must Eat), white-blonde Maman and blacker-than-black Papa may both display alarmingly anti-social and non-empathic traits, but it is in the bodies and psyches of the 'mixed-race' daughters Mina and Ami, Maman's 'chères petites mortes' (12),[9] that blank-toned ghostliness is actually named as having set up a permanent home. The diabolically possessed adoptive son in the play *Les Grandes Personnes* (2011) (Grown Ups) is torn apart by conflicting internal forces of (more or less explicitly) racialised culture that will not be reconciled within his splitting hybrid subjectivity until the quasi-redemptive, exorcising denouement.

NDiaye's writing, whether it has specifically named 'race' as the problem or not, then, has always been the writing of an unrepresentable 'hybrid' self, a subject torn in two and blankly (not) watching itself from the outside.[10] Her world and her characters tend to be so deranged (and so deranging) because of the way in which they are forced to carry the burden of a fundamentally macabre duality, a 'split-off', schizoid subjectivity which in turn gives rise to unbearable and unmitigated feelings of misrecognition and, subsequently, disintegration. These feelings become so acute that the only option of texts and characters alike seems to be to double and divide in a constant movement of simultaneous self-exaggeration and self-erasure. Working through the various hallucinatory layers of the exemplary short story 'Les Sœurs', I want to argue that the key feature of NDiaye's silently hyper-racialised and at the same time *almost* post-racial writings is an uncanny hybridity doomed to veer schizophrenically between black and blank.

Justine and Juliette *en métisse*

The plot of 'Les Sœurs' can be summarised quite simply. Bertini, a shy, inarticulate, working-class and rather unattractive schoolboy, forms a friendship with two sisters, Paula and Victoire. Although the sisters have the same mixed parentage (white mother, black father), Paula has turned out with enough European features to 'pass' as white, while Victoire is felt to be simply black. The difference this makes is dramatic: 'Bertini comprit très tôt qu'une telle disparité n'était pas anodine [...] qu'il était impossible d'englober dans un même sentiment, une même représentation, la fille quasi blanche et la fille presque noire.' (10)[11] Bertini's sheepish witnessing of the situation appears at first to do no more than record the fairly predictable differences in the way the two sisters are perceived and treated by the predominantly white world in which they move. Paula is seen by everyone as the more beautiful, more fortunate sister, while Victoire is considered to be fundamentally unlucky, undesirable – hexed, somehow – by her fortuitous overdose of melanin. As Bertini's hungry eyes drink in more and more of the bizarre dynamic, however, it begins to emerge that Paula, the 'light' one, sees herself in exclusively 'black' terms, and behaves in a more and more defensive and self-protecting manner, while Victoire, the one we might expect to develop in such a racialised, even paranoid fashion, seems oblivious to the world's stares and objectifications, appearing to sail through life with confidence and post-racial poise (11–12). It is not until the end of his dealings with the sisters, both of whom eventually vanish from his life, that Bertini comes to realise that victorious Victoire's apparent psychological triumph is swathed in the blank and icy folds of a post-affective psychic shroud, compelling her to disavow – except for one brief, almost divine instant – the racialised discrimination of which she has been a victim, a disavowal which has destroyed her capacity to develop an honest relationship with herself, with Bertini, or, it would seem, with anyone at all:

> Elle avait été contrainte de jouer et de dissimuler bien au-delà de ce qu'on peut raisonnablement admettre. Elle était devenue une femme implacable et sévère, sous ses dehors amènes, et en quelque sorte inaccessible car jamais elle ne se confierait, jamais elle ne laisserait entrevoir de nouveau ce qui lui avait échappé en présence de Bertini. (15)[12]

The two sisters Paula and Victoire operate as a kind of postcolonial equivalent of Justine (Sade 1995 [1791]) and Juliette (Sade 1998 [1799]) insofar as they seem to react to the horrors and injustices with which they are confronted in almost psychotically opposite ways. While Paula-Justine devotes her existence to a self-berating, self-stigmatising revelry in her own (often self-orchestrated) suffering, Victoire-Juliette seems to transcend that oppression in favour of a strangely 'split-off' self-gratification. Unlike Sade's pornographic siblings, however, whose cartoonish travails relate time and again to their respective positions vis-à-vis femininity and sexual oppression, NDiaye's oddly desexualised sisters play out their sadomasochistic dance of self-distortion around the traumatising issue of 'race'. The socially constructed idea of blackness becomes, for both sisters, a psychic object that is seemingly impossible to integrate in a healthy way. Haunting – either in its pathological over-presence or its (equally pathological) pseudo-effacement – blackness is an 'internal object' that simply cannot be used well.[13] Paula's and Victoire's contrasting emotional responses to this awkward and slippery object they carry inside them reveal with terrifying acuity the structuring functions of *false self* and *hallucination* in the self-management of the hybrid subject whose identity has been irremediably spoiled (Goffman 1990 [1963]).[14]

False selves in black and blank

For the British psychoanalyst D. W. Winnicott (1958: 304–5), one of the human subject's most basic, but ultimately self-eroding, responses to early experiences of non-recognition and the concomitant sensation of not being fully alive, is the defensive development of a 'false self', a persona, or set of personas, constructed in infancy, which serve to protect the subject from the psychic annihilation that it imagines will go along with the environment's failure or refusal to recognise it. In the case of the child whose environment fails or refuses to allow it to feel emotionally real, there appears a false self that hides the true self, that complies with demands, that reacts to stimuli, that rids itself of instinctual experiences by having them, but that is only playing for time.

In the universe of Marie NDiaye, one constantly comes across characters whose masks of falseness, often expressed in fantastically blond, black, but most often 'blank' terms, seem to emerge as deranged responses to the way in which nobody around them seems willing or able to hold, contain or truly see them.[15] One way of understanding Paula's and Victoire's respective stances of artifice is to see their flights into insistent and apparently counter-intuitive self-identification as the self-protecting erection of two radically different forms of false self.[16] If Paula increasingly nurtures the delusion that a radical (if largely invisible) blackness inhabits her, affecting and inflecting everything that happens (or does not happen), this must surely be read through the prism of a whole host of information that is simply not placed at the reader's disposal. The information is not at the disposal of the narrator either, or of Bertini, or of Victoire; it may not even be at the disposal of Paula herself. The only thing that we can state with any clarity is that Paula has developed a limited and limiting subjectivity in which 'blackness' becomes the sole receptacle through which she may filter an otherwise unspeakable experience of herself. The artificial category of blackness becomes a discursive catch-all, then, a false (but seemingly solid) container into which Paula can pour all traumatic experience: the unspoken and perhaps unspeakable relationships with her shadowy parents; the inevitable estrangement and guilt felt as a result of being unfairly preferred to Victoire in social terms; the gendered experience of being judged and discussed in terms of beauty and desirability (and about which the narrator has nearly nothing, though not quite nothing, to say); and, of course, the instances of black racialisation which she presumably does, even if only on occasion, experience.

Nobody truly sees Paula: not her schoolmates (whether ignorantly 'pro-white' or hypocritically 'pro-black' (11)); not Bertini (who clearly finds her physically less desirable than Victoire (10)); not Victoire (whose final report on her sad, silly sister towards the end of the story is full of a rancour and contempt that betray her abandonment of any attempt to engage with her sibling's pain (14)); and certainly not the delusional Paula herself. Her false conception and performance of an essentially fantasmatic blackness defensively reacts to the pseudo-magical whiteness with which she was ideologically saddled in her early years, guiltily attempting some kind of reparation, perhaps, for the artificial schism that was imposed between her and her darker sister Victoire.[17] In the final analysis, Paula's racialised internal mirage serves as a supreme and non-negotiable falsifying conduit for a whole host of unspeakable experiences that are for some reason impossible for either character or text to articulate in any other terms.[18]

Paula's *autoportrait en noir* (self-portrait in black) derives, then, from a hallucinated vision of herself: in clinging to the idea of her own omnipresent, insurmountable blackness, she perceives biology and phenomena that are not in fact real. Victoire's own very different 'false self' procedure could also be described as essentially hallucinatory. But, following the conceptual framework of Franco-Egyptian psychoanalyst André Green, I suggest that we consider Victoire's relentlessly blank state of mind as a quintessential machine of 'negative hallucination'. As opposed to the 'positive' hallucinating of Paula – who perceives things that are simply not there – to hallucinate 'negatively', as Victoire does, is to wipe from one's perception the things that *are* there. The subject who hallucinates negatively (like the subject who denies, represses or forecloses) usually does so in order to avoid contact with something s/he finds in some way unbearable. Green (1993: 279) makes the point clearly:

> Il y a toute une série graduée de dénis qui vont de la non-reconnaissance des paroles prononcées à la non compréhension de leur sens et de ce dernier aux associations entretenues avec cet entendement. En outre, l'hallucination négative peut concerner l'affect [. . .] qui servait de marqueur au propos.[19]

In blanking out all 'coloured' perception, Victoire refuses to see (and, apparently, to feel) the ceaseless racialisation that she encounters on a daily basis, a racialisation which may well be a consequence of others' folly and/or stupidity, but which is nevertheless – unfortunately, ineluctably – *real*.

Both sisters' forms of hallucination function, we might argue, as neurotic defences against the anxiety of acknowledging real and complex forms of pain at the heart of all human existence. Paula attempts to give her (presumably) damaged self some form of representation via her 'positively' hallucinated narrative: 'I am black and all these bad things happen to me because of that unalterable fact.' But Victoire's (non-)narrative attempts to do its would-be-reparative work by 'negativising' overly present blackness, removing all solid representations, especially racialised ones, from her story about herself: 'I am nothing but a colourless blank, and nothing bad really happens to me anyway.' Victoire's psychic procedure is seemingly predicated on the erasure of all representation. Not unlike NDiaye herself, in those slightly strange moments when she claims not to be able to see herself or her blackness (Asibong and Jordan 2009: 199), or else, incredibly, complies with white interviewers who inform her that before *Rosie Carpe*'s Guadeloupean hero Lagrand she had never evoked blackness in her writing,[20] Victoire does not so much reverse the black image that other people have of her as *blank that blackness out*, replacing it with. . . well, nothing at all, not even a Fanonian white mask, just an empty space, nothing that could be coherently formulated or shown or described in language. As Green (1993: 244–5) puts it, the subject in this kind of mental (non-) space drifts towards 'les états de non-représentation, de vide, de blanc où la pensée devient exsangue sur fond d'hallucination négative de ses propres productions psychiques'.[21]

If we consider the very few formulations the reticent narrator offers the reader when attempting to convey Victoire's conception of herself, we notice that what binds them all together is their lexical, grammatical or syntactical emphasis on negation. Victoire is, we are told, 'seule à ne pas remarquer sa propre couleur' (12); at another that she 'ne pensait jamais qu'il y avait entre ces figures et la sienne de différence notable' (12).[22] And, as Bertini becomes more and more persuaded of the undeniable acts of racialised discrimination of which Victoire continues to be the object, the narrator insists upon her *ignorance* of the situation, her apparent *inability* to understand it and eventually her possibly contagious *incapacity* for self-perception in terms predicated on blackness (12–13). Rather than saying how Victoire does see herself, we can only be told how she does *not* see herself. Blackness has been eliminated as a viable mode of representation, as have, apparently, its accompanying experiences of racialised pain. Nothing tangible, however, is offered as a replacement representation. In psychoanalytic terms, we might say, then, that Victoire has evolved towards an experience of herself, together with all the unbearable dimensions of a racialised experience she has not chosen, as one big blank: a woman-sized negative hallucination.

In the end, as Bertini notes (14), it is impossible to say who Victoire truly is. She has, apparently, risen above her 'black condition'. She has managed to keep her head, to manipulate the system (15), and, unlike Paula, who is apparently ruined (14), to avoid the frequently racialised conditions of poverty, depression, paranoia and despair. Her capacity for emotional or affective connection has been damaged beyond repair, however. When, for a single instant, the spell of negative hallucination is lifted, and Victoire is induced by her unlikely Prince Charming Bertini to confess to an awareness of her own unwilling racialisation, the unexpected shift is narrated as a sort of miracle, a thunderclap of truth, in which Victoire's negatively sunny persona gives way, for a lightning flash of an instant, to reveal the black clouds of self-recognition lurking beneath the surface of her composure. The moment of careful, resigned acknowledgment morphs almost immediately, however, into a troubling, mad mixture of coldness, resentment, counterfeit smiles and falseness (14). It is as if the humiliation of admitting to Bertini that she has been the victim of something so un-free – so insulting to her true self (Winnicott 1965) – as racialised objectification pushes Victoire into a psychic zone that is both terrifying and fundamentally unmanageable. She cannot integrate this psychic experience into either a continuous emotional reality or a truthful relationship with another person. The intimacy of anything other than blankness threatens to annihilate her.

Beyond hallucination?

In the final analysis, the reader of NDiaye's quite remarkably provocative parable is left with nothing but endlessly thwarted perception. As for Bertini, he lives out the rest of his days bogged down in a morass of his own positive and negative hallucinations. Once Victoire has vanished into the night like some kind of dark-skinned, wounded Cinderella, Bertini is condemned to thinking he sees her everywhere and nowhere at the same time. He hallucinates her forgotten features in every anonymous black face he sees, never glimpsing her or the reality of her unspeakably singular experience ever again (15). Victoire, her mad sister Paula, and the strange, shadowy half-relationship Bertini had (or dreamed he had?) with them both, all disappear into silence, nothingness and blank, ungrievable loss.

Unlike Bertini, we do not have to be plagued by an endless stream of ghostly sighs and romantic regrets. I would like to suggest that we instead try to be haunted by a different kind of interrogation. What might an active, living, 'mixed-race' psyche beyond both Pauline paranoia and Victoirian disavowal look like? Does the writing, the theatre – or even the existence – of a cultural figure like Marie NDiaye provide us with the means of imagining such a healthily integrated psyche? It is important to acknowledge that NDiaye's work – and indeed persona – have been (and continue to be) drawn into precisely the kinds of procedures of identity falsification suffered by the imaginary sisters Paula and Victoire. NDiaye is – and will doubtless carry on being – submitted to all manner of racialised hallucination, both 'positive' and 'negative'. 'Positively' hallucinated dimensions (Africanity, exoticism, foreignness) will doubtless be appended to the texts she creates so long as there exists a market that thrives on precisely such spectacularising appendages.[23] And, at the 'negative' end of the hallucinatory spectrum, the real and painful manifestations of racialised experience that lurk in her texts will be blanked out and disavowed by readers and writers (including, on occasion, NDiaye herself) for whom it is psychically or politically overwhelming to acknowledge the existence of such things. The complex emotional reality of these frightening hybrid texts remains, however. And the soft groans of NDiaye's borderline subjects, leaping in and out of a box of fantasies marked 'race', will continue, in the realms of literature, psychotherapy and perhaps even politics, to do their helpfully schizoid work.

Notes

1 'On the one hand a severed finger without blood; on the other, blood without a severed finger.' (Green 1999: 178)
2 Consider Marie Darrieussecq's unambiguous comments in relation to the shifting narrator of *Truismes*: 'Elle transgresse les races. On peut pas la couper en deux. Donc elle échappe nécessairement à la politique de séparation des races. C'est vraiment un livre contre le racisme, mais de la façon la plus radicale.' (Unpublished interview of the author with Marie Darrieussecq (2003)) ('She transgresses race. She can't be chopped in two. So she necessarily escapes the politics of racial separatism. It's really the most radical kind of anti-racist book.') Unless

otherwise indicated, translations from the French are mine. Darrieussecq's remarks echo the theoretical position of French philosophers of the 'post-' and the 'créole' from Hélène Cixous to Patrick Chamoiseau.

3 In this volume, Helen Vassallo reads Nina Bouraoui's hybridity as fractured.

4 In this sense, NDiaye's hybrids seems to have more in common with the 'tragic mulatto' characters of Duvalier-era Haitian novelist Marie Vieux-Chauvet 2010 [1968] or Danish-Jamaican Harlem Renaissance icon Nella Larsen 2001 [1929] than with contemporary representational trends. Condé 2000 provides an important contemporary theoretical critique of the sometimes simplistic optimism of 'créole' agendas. For further analyses of some of the dilemmas faced by the contemporary 'mixed-race' subject, see Sollors 1997; Brah and Coombes 2000; Parker and Song 2001; Obama 2007; and Ndiaye [sic] 2008.

5 NDiaye (1997: 65) herself frames the narrative of origins thus: 'Mon père est venu du Sénégal [. . .] Il a épousé ma mère, issue, elle, d'une famille d'agriculteurs du centre de la France.' ('My father came from Senegal [. . .] He married my mother, whose own origins were in an agricultural family from the centre of France.') NDiaye's father was not present during her childhood.

6 Consider, on the one hand, the strange, offensive and wholly erroneous claim that 'Marie Ndiaye [sic] is a Senegalese immigrant who writes of African women caught between their traditional cultures, which often include practices like polygamy and female excision, and the fast-paced culture of contemporary France' (Winders 2001: 256), and, on the other, an essay devoted to NDiaye which remains bafflingly silent on the possible significance of 'race' in the texts, while discussing at length the (admittedly important) semiotics of NDiayean suitcases and shoes (Richard 1996).

7 'I feel neither cosmopolitan nor bicultural [. . .] but, in the main, the cultural heir of Molière, Rousseau or Proust [. . .] I am utterly French.'

8 I am grateful to Pauline Eaton for pointing out Lisbeth's textual marking as a clear victim of zombifying *vodun*.

9 'dear little dead things'.

10 The theme of a self apparently unable to contemplate itself (most of all in its racialised difference) runs throughout both NDiaye's writings and her interviews. Consider her enigmatic response to the question 'Est-ce que votre position vis-à-vis de la "race" a changé au cours de votre carrière?': 'Enfin, moi, non . . . je n'arrive pas à me voir, moi, comme une femme noire. Je ne me vois pas, en fait, je crois.' (Asibong and Jordan 2009: 199) ('Has your position with regard to "race" changed at all over the course of your career?' 'Well I, no . . . I just can't quite see myself as a black woman. I don't see myself, in fact, I think.') As for the discreet little Mina in *Papa doit manger*: 'Les peaux, je ne les regarde pas, je ne les vois même pas.' (17) ('Skin, I don't look at it, I don't even see it.')

11 'Bertini quickly realised that such a disparity was far from banal [...] that it was impossible to capture within the same feeling, within the same image, the nearly-white girl and the girl who was practically black.'
12 'She'd been forced to act, to cover up, well beyond the bounds of what anyone could reasonably tolerate. Beneath her pleasant exterior lay a hard, implacable woman who was, in a way, out of reach, for never again would she let anyone catch a glimpse of what had slipped out of her in Bertini's presence.'
13 I find the psychoanalytic concept of 'object relations' particularly helpful when trying to think about different aspects of the psyche which are introjected, projected, repressed or enjoyed in the self's attempt to pursue his or her version of a manageable existence. For a useful introduction to the topic see Fairbairn 1981.
14 It is worth considering both the unnamable dark shape that escapes into the narrator's yard at the climax of *Autoportrait en vert* (2005) (*Self-Portrait in Green*) and the slimy black thing that Nadia gives birth to at the end of *Mon cœur à l'étroit* (2007: 295) (My Heart Hemmed In) in the context of my reading of NDiayean blackness as a spectral or otherwise unmanageable internal object.
15 The eponymous heroine of *Rosie Carpe* is perhaps the ultimate example of this breed of abused, abusive, psychically dead non-character.
16 Sartre 1943, Lacan 1949 and Fanon 1952 all offer accounts of the inauthentic or imaginary self that may usefully complement my own Winnicottian approach; it is Winnicott's 1965 vision of a 'caretaking' falseness, born out of childhood compliance, that I find most rewarding, though, especially when harnessed to NDiaye's texts, preoccupied as they are with subtle gradations of psychic death in the not-good-enough facilitating environment.
17 Paula and Victoire, as two categories of (female) human, one dazzling, the other debased, mirror a whole host of best friend/sister pairs in, respectively, NDiaye 2001, 1989 and 1990: Rose-Marie Carpe I and II; Valérie and the log-narrator; the two shapes of Fanny. The latter example of Fanny, a single (hybrid) character who actually splits into two differently racialised versions of herself, suggests to me, especially read in conjunction with 'Les Sœurs', that we might begin to consider these friend/sister pairs in NDiaye's writing as textual symptoms of an impossibly split 'mixed-race' (or otherwise schizoid) subjectivity, forever dividing into two non-complementary, sadomasochistic, differently psychotic, Jekyll-and-Hyde halves.
18 NDiaye's entire literary project could be said to be the attempt to provide, in opposition to the likes of Paula, and via her writing of an uncategorisable strangeness, sufficiently defamiliarising frameworks for the expression of truly complex and idiosyncratic trauma-experience.
19 'There exists a whole graduated series of denials going from the non-recognition of spoken words to the non-comprehension of their

meaning and from there to the associations related to this understanding. But apart from this, negative hallucination may involve the affect [. . .] which served as a marker for what was said.' (Green 1999: 208)

20   Listen to the CD of interviews with Paula Jacques that accompanies the book *Marie NDiaye* (Rabaté 2008).

21   'states of non-representation, emptiness and blankness in which thought becomes anaemic against the background of the negative hallucination of its own psychical productions' (Green 1999: 182).

22   'the only one not to notice her own colour'; 'never thought there was any difference worthy of note between these faces and her own'.

23   There has been an increased – and clearly lucrative – instrumentalisation of 'positively' hallucinated Africanity in the selling of NDiaye's work in recent years, an instrumentalisation that has, in the case of the Goncourt-winning *Trois femmes puissantes* (2009) (*Three Strong Women*) depended on exoticising and distorting publicity. It all suggests the market-driven forging of a newly black 'false self' with which NDiaye has seemingly complied.

Chapter Seven
Rediscovering the Absent Father, a Question of Recognition: Despentes, Tardieu

LORI SAINT-MARTIN

One of the most significant trends to emerge in French women's writing of recent years is the exploration of the father figure, supplementing and sometimes superseding the writers' interest in the mother–daughter bond. Two novels published in 2002, *Comme un père* (Like a Father) by Laurence Tardieu and *Teen spirit* by Virginie Despentes, illustrate that trend.[1] Though one is dysphoric and the other euphoric in its view of fatherhood, they have much in common. In both, a daughter discovers, after a long separation, that the father she never knew is available to meet her and become a presence in her life. The novel tells the story of their time together. Both fathers are mentally troubled and socially marginalised; both novels are brief and told in a plain, detached style that camouflages strong emotion. Narrative perspective is a major difference: Despentes's father is the narrator; Tardieu focuses on the daughter. In Tardieu's novel, François has been in prison for twenty years and is freed a few months after the mother's accidental death; Louise (his daughter) reluctantly agrees to take him in. Despentes's narrator, Bruno, now thirty, learns from a high-school girlfriend in the early pages of the novel that he is the father of a thirteen-year-old girl, Nancy, who has recently learned of his existence and wants to meet him.

The contemporary focus on the father

Why does recent French women's writing deal increasingly with the father–daughter relationship? Some reasons are circumstantial: for instance, after the father's death, the daughter often returns to his life through fiction or (auto)biography.[2] But we also seem to be experiencing a cultural 'moment' when fathers occupy centre stage in women's writing, perhaps because of a desire to go beyond the still-crucial mother–daughter bond, an interest in male gender identity as problematised by feminist and men's studies scholars and a will to reach out to men after what may have seemed like a feminist rejection of them. More broadly, social changes of the past decades, including rising divorce rates, new family forms such as single-parent or same-sex families and legal changes like the elimination of illegitimacy and of the male's status as head of the household, have led to an intense reflection on fathers and fatherhood in sociology, history, psychology and psychoanalysis, law and literature.[3] The family, paternal power and the father's roles and functions have all been called into question. Women's writing is both a part of a larger trend of reflecting on fathers and fatherhood and one of the strongest forces within that trend, since it is often accompanied by a questioning of male power and authority within the family and in society.

The absent but returning father, the focus of Despentes's and Tardieu's novels, is an important figure.[4] First, because his absence is itself significant: in contemporary literature, while some fathers flee their family responsibilities, many seem to be prevented from involvement because of divorce or ignorance of their paternity; I call them 'les pères empêchés' (Saint-Martin 2010: 239–57).[5] Absence often seems to characterise fathers in literature, even when they still live with the family, in contrast with the often overly present, sometimes invasive mother, a gendered contrast worth exploring. Secondly, the figure of the returning father is interesting because it focuses not only on patriarchal power, a theme of much women's writing, but also on the father's subjectivity, his vulnerabilities and pain, as feminist theorists like Patricia Yaeger (1989) have suggested women writers do. The father in such texts becomes a human being rather than a faceless representative of patriarchal authority as in much feminist theory (see Irigaray 1977, for example). Thirdly, novels about the absent but returning father tend to relate the story from his point of view, a significant change. Marianne Hirsch (1989) has pointed out that women's fiction has been written from the daughter's perspective; the mother's views and voice emerged much later. Most writing about fathers is also told from the child's vantage point; intimations of fathers' subjectivity are a new and important trend. Finally, novels like *Comme un père* and *Teen spirit* are important because they focus not only on the father–daughter relationship, but also on fatherhood itself: what a father is, who determines what it means to be a good father, how questions of recognition and legitimacy are raised and played out.

This chapter will argue that recognition is the critical issue at stake in Despentes's and Tardieu's novels. In both, separation or ignorance of the father's existence have compromised the process of recognition, which implies three stages: physical identification ('I know this person'), acceptance of intimacy and responsibility ('I acknowledge this father/child as my own') and, finally, gratitude ('I recognise what this person means to me and has done for me').[6] Recognition or non-recognition account for positive or negative narrative outcomes in *Comme un père* and *Teen spirit*; narrative perspective – the father's or the daughter's voice – is the other determining factor.

Dimensions of recognition

The ethical as well as personal dimensions of recognition are an essential part of any exploration of father–child relationships. Traditionally, the idea of legitimacy (and its corollary, illegitimacy or bastardy) has upheld traditional family structures and, beyond them, political institutions, including religion and absolute monarchy. In patriarchal societies from ancient Rome – where the paterfamilias could adopt the child or adult of his choice without his wife's consent or even declare illegitimate the children he had fathered during his marriage – to pre-revolutionary France and then, in diminished form, from 1804 to the 1960s, the father was the sole arbiter of legitimacy (Knibielher 1987: 33–6; Mulliez 2000). It is the father's act of naming that *creates* the child, giving birth to it socially and introducing it into the collective order. Becoming a father is thus an act of choice and an act of power. Without that act, the child does not exist socially; the mother's name does not have the weight the father's does.

Many contemporary novels transform the traditional power structure of father-granted legitimacy: the right to 'recognise' and declare legitimate often passes through maternal power, as in Despentes's novel, and then on to the child, who becomes the judge and arbiter of the father's legitimacy. This striking reversal is one of the most significant changes in contemporary fiction on fathers (Saint-Martin 2010: 320–3). In contemporary literature, fathers are constantly on trial by their children for crimes ranging from absence and indifference to violence and incest, all of which are crimes of power. The worst crime fathers can commit is *not* to recognise their children, not to grant them the legitimacy they long for. It is only when the father withholds that legitimacy that fictional sons and daughters retaliate by declaring him illegitimate.[7]

Recognition refers first of all to physical identification: 'I know this person by sight, I know who (s)he is.' This seemingly simple process is often problematic in literary texts. One reason is that fathers may have deserted the family or, in the case of immigrant families, worked overseas for long periods. Recognition may also be impossible because the mother took the child away from the father long before: Bruno, the father in *Teen spirit*, did not even know he had a child until Nancy was 13, and she had been told he was dead. This is a clear-cut case of maternal abuse of power, something often denounced in the contemporary novel, including in works by women (Saint-Martin 2010: 257). Tardieu's narrator, Louise, does physically recognise her father, François, whom she occasionally visited in prison with her mother. Despentes's father and daughter are brought together by a reluctant mother; Bruno's friend Sandra points out immediately how much they look alike, establishing an initial connection for them.

Once visual identification takes place, children long for their father to confirm their identity and his commitment; to 'recognise' in this sense is to accept and love the child, thereby indicating his or her place in the world. In Despentes's novel, this process takes place slowly. Initially, Bruno is like a child himself: he does not work, is supported by his girlfriend Catherine and lives in her apartment, which he has not left for nearly two years; when she finally throws him out, he takes refuge with a friend, Sandra. His agoraphobia reflects his social marginality, experienced partly as a sense of failure, partly as a sign of his rebellious nature (perhaps the 'teen spirit' of the title). Only the news that Alice wants to see him, and the subsequent need to meet Nancy, draw him back into the outside world. Soon, he and Nancy begin to spend time together, going for long walks and exploring the city. Gradually, Bruno learns to become a good father; as he defines it, this means telling her 'no' often (at 13, she needs boundaries) while constantly reassuring her that she is loved and appreciated. Mutual recognition gradually emerges from this process and, although Nancy goes through a phase when she condemns Bruno as a loser, things develop well between them, at the expense of Alice, Nancy's mother, who did all the hard work for thirteen years and is now rejected by Nancy.

In Tardieu's novel, the daughter refuses her father any recognition. Arriving in her apartment after his release from prison, François bares his heart, telling Louise of his affection for her and of his hopes for their future. In response, Louise treats him as a stranger: 'Mais moi, je ne vous ai pas attendu. Je ne vous ai pas préparé de place dans ma vie.' (49–50)[8] To her friend Ana, Louise explains the deep shame she felt when her father was arrested for murder (he killed his wife's lover). At 7, Louise committed a first patricide, telling those who asked that her father was dead. But the ultimate denial comes when her father asks for the opportunity to get to know her. She replies: 'Pour moi vous n'êtes rien! Rien du tout!' (34)[9] In the final pages, the father commits suicide, returning to the 'nothingness' to which his daughter condemned him by her lack of recognition. Ironically, although Louise claims she and her father have nothing in common, she becomes a murderer in her own way, reproducing the very act for which she reviles him; in keeping him at a distance, she shows how close they really are.

In fact, Louise, despite her refusal to make a place for her father in her life, is influenced by the man she barely knew. Looking at him, she sees her own mannerisms, as in this scene where he becomes a mirror image for her, as if she were seeing (her) double: 'Il penche la tête sur le côté, fronce le sourcil gauche (Comme moi!).' (43)[10] The same metaphors recur to describe them: she is 'l'animal pris au piège' (46) and he is 'une bête sauvage' (52) in his prison cage.[11] And even Louise's art, the core of her individuality, was partly inspired by him, as she realises with a shock when he tells her, rightly, that some of her sculptures, displayed throughout the apartment, closely resemble him:

> Sur la cheminée un de mes premiers bronzes: une tête d'homme ... Côte à côte la tête et moi je nous ai contemplées, dans l'immense glace au-dessus de la cheminée.
>
> J'ai éclaté de rire.

Comment peut-on reconnaître une évidence avec dix ans de retard? (69–70)[12]

Again, the father's face is a mirror for the daughter's, although she is incapable of even physical recognition (she did not realise that the head looked like him). The convoluted syntax of this passage ('Side by side I looked at us, the head and myself') reflects confusion in the boundaries between self and other. Louise's laughter here is the reverse of the tears she suppressed earlier, as she realises that her father was an unconscious model for her art, if not a direct influence in her life. Ironically, however, it is only once her father is dead and all contact is impossible that she recognises him with the simple words: 'j'ai perdu mon père' (118).[13]

In contrast, Despentes's novel traces a move from non-recognition (total ignorance of fatherhood) to fully assumed responsibility. At the end of the novel, Nancy runs away, not for the first time, and is caught in Orléans with a boyfriend in a stolen car. It is at that moment that Bruno finally recognises her as his child and himself as an adult: 'C'est cette nuit-là que je suis vraiment devenu son père.' (Despentes 2002: 153)[14] As the Twin Towers crumble on the television screen, Bruno plans to form a family with Sandra, whom he realises he loves, Nancy, and possibly a new baby. Recognising Nancy and his own fatherhood is the key to reaching adulthood and, in a sense, giving (re)birth to a better self, cured of his agoraphobia and of his indifference to others. The passage from recognition in the legal and social sense (his name is not on the birth certificate, so he is not socially the father) to recognition in the personal and emotional sense ('I love this child and we belong to each other') replays, on an individual level, what sociologists such as Christine Castelain-Meunier (2002: 33) have called the shift from authoritarian 'institutional fatherhood' to more intimate 'relational fatherhood'. Despite the years of absence, Bruno is now a modern, rather than a traditional, father. There is also a shift here from maternal possession of the child (symbolised by the mother's name alone on the birth certificate) to mutual child–father recognition.

After physical identification and acknowledgement of a deeper bond, the third and final meaning of *reconnaissance* is gratitude, a meaning absent from the word in many languages, including English. Bruno wins Nancy's gratitude by simply appearing in her life: 'j'ai compris plus tard que tout ce qui comptait pour elle, c'était que je vienne [. . .] Elle m'en était infiniment reconnaissante et ne m'en demandait pas davantage.' (78)[15] In contrast, Tardieu's Louise feels only resentment of her father and explicitly formulates her gratitude to her mother, but not to him. She goes further, relating to her friend Ana what Lacanians would see as a foreclosure of the paternal signifier: 'Ce mot n'a aucune signification pour moi . . . Un père, ça n'a aucune nécessité. C'est la mère qui donne la vie. C'est la mère qui nourrit l'enfant. Le reste, on s'en fout!' (58–9)[16] It is precisely the way the question of recognition plays out that determines how the novel ends. Tardieu's *Comme un père* is dysphoric because the daughter fails to recognise the father and, in essence, sends him to his death. Despentes's *Teen spirit* ends on a positive note, with the father being permanently recognised and integrated into the child's life.

Narrative voice and violence

In both novels, the outcome is closely related to narrative mode. In Despentes's novel, the father is the first-person narrator and is given the chance to defend and exonerate himself. Mother and daughter are seen through his eyes, the first judged severely – she kept him from his daughter, after all – the second with increasing tenderness. Just as Bruno imagines he would have become a different man if Alice had told him at the time that she was expecting his child (65), the novel would be very different if it were told by the mother and/or the daughter. As it stands, it is the story of Bruno's redemption through the acceptance of his fatherhood. This exclusive focus on his point of view highlights his metamorphosis from a man he is ashamed of ('Je serais un gosse, j'aimerais pas apprendre que mon père, c'est moi' (35)),[17] to one who can accept his emotions and take on adult responsibilities. Bruno's situation neatly evolves from being abandoned by his father at 12 to becoming a father unknowingly at 17 and then committing to his own daughter, now 13. This nearly-too-perfect symmetry indicates how Bruno is able to give Nancy what he never received: stability and recognition. While Alice had first told Nancy he was dead and then that he was 'un clodo' (57), Bruno ultimately receives full recognition of his worth from her, but also from Sandra and Alice: 'Pour la première fois de ma vie, j'avais le sentiment . . . d'entrer dans un rôle que j'avais le droit d'assumer et d'aimer' (97).[18] Recognition of his legitimacy as a father gives him full legitimacy as a human being as well. In the end, Alice, who deprived Bruno of his daughter, is left depressed and alone, deprived of her voice and her version of the story, while he takes charge of Nancy and contemplates becoming a father once again with Sandra, knowingly this time and with the intention of being fully involved.

Tardieu's novel is focused exclusively on the daughter's perspective, though the father's point of view comes through in extensive dialogues. Formally, the most striking feature of her narrative is the frequency with which she shifts from the first to the third person, from 'je' to 'elle', to refer to herself. This divided identity began when she was a small child and her mother told her about her father's crime; she repeated the tale to her doll, creating a split between telling and living which persists in her adult life. She imagines herself as being constantly 'sur une scène de théâtre' (30),[19] watched by hostile eyes, or simply without an identity (41). She addresses herself as if she were another person ('Louise, cet homme est ton père' (103))[20] and even discusses herself in the third person:

> Quel âge a Louise?
> Louise a vingt-cinq ans,
> Et Louise est contente?
> Contente de quoi?
> Contente de la vie?
> Non, Louise n'est pas contente ... (83)[21]

The split mirror images we saw earlier (the father as Louise's mirror image, Louise and the bust of him in the mirror) recur here on the narrative level, with 'je', 'tu' and 'elle' both reflecting and opposing one another. These shifts illustrate the split between violence and vulnerability, between Louise's desire for closeness and her rejection of her father, and between her childhood and adult selves.

Despite Louise's denial of his very existence, François, before departing to commit suicide, leaves her a note reading simply: '*Louise, je pense à vous comme un père.*' (82; original italics)[22] He does not confidently claim the role by writing 'I am your father', insisting on his right to her affection; his more tentative words suggest his alienation and her non-recognition as well as his ultimate appeal to her. The novel's title both ironically echoes Louise's verdict (someone who is 'like a father' is not in fact a father) and borrows François's words to crown her narrative. In other words, this novel that so violently rejects the father and denies him voice gives him back that voice in its title, just as Louise belatedly regrets not having reached out to François.

Conclusion

After long years of absence, both fathers studied here try to enter into real fatherhood, but one is recognised by his daughter and the other rejected; as in much contemporary fiction (Saint-Martin 2010: 320–3), it is now the child who grants the father legitimacy, and not the other way around.

In Tardieu's novel, Louise's rejection of her father reflects her own emotional immaturity; Despentes's character finally becomes an adult when he takes on responsibility for his daughter. The agoraphobia both men suffer from is a metaphor for their social and emotional marginalisation: Bruno overcomes his while François, after twenty years of prison, is unable successfully to confront the outside world. In both novels, the father has a troubled relationship with the law: François committed murder, Bruno was a wild teenager and, when he picks up Nancy at the police station, he is bizarrely proud of her non-conformist spirit (152). He revels in the rage she feels, recognising it as his (119). But, as a father, he sees his role as offering Nancy the security of clear-cut boundaries to avoid future brushes with the law.

Another troubling aspect of these novels is that for the father–daughter relationship to be in the foreground, the mother has to be either dead, as in Tardieu's novel, or disqualified, as in Despentes's (Saint-Martin 2010: 240). This silencing of the mother may reflect a vision of parenthood as a war between the sexes: both fathers had been previously murdered symbolically, as Nancy had never known Bruno existed and Louise claimed, from a very early age, that François had died of illness.

Both novels raise important questions about the father and fatherhood today. This anxious questioning speaks to a contemporary doubt about fathers and their roles and functions. It is striking to note how many books on fathers have a question, often a rather apocalyptic one, as their title, usually a question one would never think to ask about mothers: *Y a-t-il encore un père à la maison?*; *Un avenir pour la paternité?*; *Le père, à quoi ça sert?*; 'Le père a-t-il un avenir?' [23] This kind of doubt confirms the transitional period we are living in today, when traditional family roles are disappearing and new forms appearing to take their place both in the real world and in fiction, not without social anxiety, backsliding and persistent doubts. It also reveals that fathers have been absent, either voluntarily or involuntarily, as in the novels studied here, sometimes through the mother's fault, most often through their own. They need to rethink masculinity, fatherhood and their relationships to women, including their daughters. Women's fiction of today is part of that debate and it is important to hear their voices.

Notes

1. The title of the former is referred to several times within the novel; 'comme' is sometimes 'like', sometimes 'as'.
2. See Cixous 1997; Ernaux 1984; and Nimier 2004. See Borgomano 2004 for daughter's texts on the father's death.
3. In sociology, see Castelain-Meunier 1998 and 2002; Dulac 1993; and Neyrand 2000. In history, see Delumeau and Roche 2000; as well as Knibielher 1987. In psychology and psychoanalysis, see Delaisi de Parseval 1981; Hurstel 1996; Le Camus 2004 and 2005; Naouri 1985 and 2004; Prokhoris 2000; Schneider 2005; and Tort 2005. In law, see Legendre 1989. In literature, see Boose and Flowers 1989, as well as Kowaleski-Wallace and Yaeger 1989.
4. In this volume, Barbara Havercroft analyses Christine Angot's confessional treatment of the absent but returning father.
5. 'stifled fathers'. This term refers to men who are prevented from exercising their fatherhood by circumstances or by a hostile or unwilling mother. Unless otherwise indicated, all translations are my own.
6. For a philosophical meditation on the word *reconnaissance* (recognition), see Ricœur 2004.
7. See Saint-Martin 2011 for an overview of contemporary Quebec fiction from the perspective of bastardy, recognition and legitimacy.
8. 'But I didn't wait for you. I didn't make room in my life for you.'
9. 'You're nothing to me! Nothing at all!'
10. 'He tilts his head to one side, lowers his left eyebrow (Like me!).'
11. 'the trapped animal'; a wild beast'.
12. 'On the mantel, one of my first bronzes: a man's head . . . Side by side I looked at us, the head and myself, in the huge mirror over the mantel. I burst out laughing. How can you miss recognising the obvious for ten years?'
13. 'I've lost my father'.
14. 'That was the night I truly became her father.'
15. 'I understood later that the only thing that counted for her was that I was there [. . .] she was infinitely grateful and didn't ask for anything more.'

16 'The word means absolutely nothing to me ... There's no need for a father. It's the mother who gives life. It's the mother who feeds the child. Nobody cares about the rest!'
17 'If I were a kid, I wouldn't be thrilled to discover my father was me.'
18 'a bum'; 'For the first time in my life, I had the feeling ... of taking on a role I was entitled to accept and enjoy.'
19 'on stage'.
20 'Louise, that man is your father'.
21 'How old is Louise? Louise is twenty-five. And is Louise happy? Happy with what? Happy with life? No, Louise is not happy ...'
22 'Louise, I think of you as a father does.'
23 'Is there still a father in the house?'; 'A future for fatherhood?'; 'What good is a father?'; and 'Does the father have a future?' See respectively Arènes 1997; Bruel 1998; Nabati and Nabati 1994; Tombs 1992.

Chapter Eight
Babykillers: Véronique Olmi and Laurence Tardieu on Motherhood

NATALIE EDWARDS

The experience of motherhood has been a primary subject in many texts by women writers, such as Marie Cardinal, Hélène Cixous, Marguerite Duras, Marie NDiaye, Paule Constant and Nancy Huston. More recently, however, a new strand of women's writing that works to resist portraying motherhood as a romanticised, idealised or idyllic experience is discernible. Instead, texts, such as *Le Bébé* (2002) (The Baby) by Marie Darrieussecq, Pascale Kramer's *L'Implacable Brutalité du réveil* (2009) (The Unrelenting Brutality of the Alarm Clock/Awakening), Christine Angot's *Léonore, toujours* (1994) (*Léonore, Always*), Nathalie Azoulai's *Mère agitée* (2003) (Troubled Mother) and Éliette Abécassis's *Un heureux événement* (2005) (*A Happy Event*), represent the difficulties of being a mother in the present day. Similarly, theoretical texts by critics such as Françoise Héritier (2002) and Élisabeth Badinter (2010) question the ways in which discourse about mothering functions in contemporary society. Badinter argues in her controversial *Le Conflit, la femme et la mère* (*The Conflict: Woman and Mother*) that, between 1980 and 2000,

> une révolution s'est opérée dans notre conception de la maternité, presque sans qu'on y prenne garde. Aucun débat, aucun éclat de voix n'a accompagné cette évolution, ou plutôt cette involution. Pourtant son objectif est considérable puisqu'il s'agit ni plus ni moins que de remettre la maternité au cœur du destin féminin. (Badinter 2010: 9)[1]

Badinter's conclusions may be debatable, but her observations of a discourse that operates in a way that places motherhood at the centre of female identity are important for understanding contemporary female experience. After the progress made by second-wave feminism in terms of motherhood (and bearing in mind that this progress is certainly not complete), Badinter's argument that we may have regressed to a place in which motherhood is expected of women should not be overlooked. Her arguments, and those of the literary writers who are engaged in representing the difficulties, the pitfalls and the obstacles inherent in mothering, signal an important trend in French women's writing that merits closer examination.

The 1934 Encyclopædia Britannica defines 'mother' as 'woman who looks after children'. The misunderstanding and the socio-economic class prejudice in this statement are worthy of a separate discussion, but what interests me in recent French women's writing is the woman who does *not* look after children. In this chapter, I examine texts that push the questioning of motherhood to its limits; not simply by representing the difficulties or obstacles involved in mothering, but by focusing on women who have children, who narrate the difficulties of mothering and who commit infanticide. Ever since Medea, examples of infanticide in literature abound, from medieval texts, to colonial and postcolonial literatures, to contemporary writing. It is noteworthy that a significant number of contemporary French and francophone women authors have published texts that include infanticidal mothers. Examples include Paule Constant's *La Bête à chagrin* (2007) (Woeful Beast), Mariama Bâ's *Un chant écarlate* (2005) [1986] (*A Scarlet Song*), Darrieussecq's *White* (2003), Suzanne Jacob's *L'Obéissance* (1991) (Obedience), Ying Chen's *L'Ingratitude* (1999) (*Ingratitude*), Sophie Marinopoulos's *La Vie ordinaire d'une mère meurtrière* (2008) (The Ordinary Life of a Murderous Mother), Mazarine Pingeot's *Le Cimetière des poupées* (2007) (The Doll Cemetery) and Marie NDiaye's *La Femme changée en bûche* (1989) (The Woman Who Turned into a Log). Even a film by a male director, Philippe Claudel, has appeared on the subject, *Il y a si longtemps que je t'aime* (2008) (I've Loved You So Long). What are the reasons for this sustained attention to such a crime? Infanticide is often considered to be one of the most heinous crimes possible. It is a specific threat to the symbolic and social orders in which the mother operates. Not only is it 'unnatural', in the sense that women are supposed to be givers of life and not takers of it, but it also represents female violence, which is profoundly disturbing to the patriarchal norm. It disrupts discourses both of maternity and of patriarchy and presents the maternal body as a contested space.

This is perhaps why infanticidal mothers are so often vilified. Stephanie Chamberlain (2005: 77), who has examined court documents pertaining to infanticide trials throughout history, shows how they have been represented in the legal system as 'monstrous beings who take sadistic delight in butchering babies'. Such is the representation of infanticidal mothers in the contemporary media: sensationalised, often portraying the relatives of the woman as those who are hardest hit, and speculating upon the psychology of the unnatural female mind. Media coverage of recent cases of incidents in France play out this scenario; in July 2010, a woman was arrested for giving birth to eight babies in secret, killing them and hiding them in her garage, and the newspaper articles surrounding her case included comments by neighbours speculating about the woman's marriage, her weight and how her other children could possibly adjust to such a reality (see Maurice 2010). In 1994, French law governing infanticide changed from a definition of 'un bébé de moins de trois jours' with a sentence of fifteen years, to a looser 'homicide volontaire d'un enfant de moins de quinze ans' with life imprisonment.[2] Despite this change in the law, very little discussion of infanticide has taken place. As historian Julie Wheelwright (2002: 275) argues, there is still 'an absence of a philosophical framework beyond the mad/bad framework' in which to understand infanticide.

In this chapter, I discuss two texts that challenge this mad/bad framework in thoughtful and provocative ways. Véronique Olmi, born in 1962, is a playwright who has also published short stories and novels, most of which revolve around intimate relations, notably parent–child and romantic relationships. *Bord de mer* (2001) (*Beside the Sea*) is Olmi's first novel.[3] This won the Prix Alain-Fournier and became a best-seller in France; it has since been translated into several languages and adapted for the stage and for cinema. Told as a first-person narrative from the perspective of the mother, this text recounts the story of a single mother and her two sons who embark on a foreboding journey to the seaside. The unnamed mother is presented as having no family ties and no social connections apart from the (unwanted) social institutions involved in her case. As the difficult relationship she shares with her sons disintegrates, she smothers the two boys in their hotel beds without any clear explanation. As Gill Rye (2009a: 109) writes, 'the reader is impelled to piece together the strands of the narrative in order to speculate on what brings this mother to commit her tragic act'.

Laurence Tardieu, born in 1972, is also a relatively new name in French literature. At the time of writing, Tardieu has published five novels, all of which revolve around intimate relationships between close friends and relatives. *Le Jugement de Léa* (2004) (The Judgement of Léa) is her second. In this text, the main protagonist, Léa, is sitting in an antechamber of a courtroom, awaiting the judgment of a jury that is deliberating its verdict on her alleged infanticide. She is accused of having pushed her four-year-old son down the stairs of her apartment block, and the reader does not know whether she did or not. The trial has taken place, and the text consists of an interior monologue as Léa recounts her thoughts and feelings in the present and jumps back in time to memories of the past that have led up to this moment. First, I analyse how these two texts voice motherhood, using first-person narratives that allow the mothers to express their experience, before examining the inclusion of other voices in the narratives, those of onlookers, of institutions and of society. Finally, I discuss the role of the reader and the ways in which both texts directly manipulate and call into question the reader/onlooker's responsibility.

Voicing motherhood

In *Narratives of Mothering*, Rye demonstrates how mothers are gradually being represented as the speaking subject in recent French literature, as opposed to the object of another's discourse, according to Marianne Hirsh's earlier argument in *The Mother/Daughter Plot* (1989). In both of the novels under discussion here, the mother's voice is the crucial component of the texts. These mothers speak in their own voices about their ambivalence to, discomfort with and even, at times, disdain for motherhood. Tardieu's mother-narrator presents her own childhood as isolated and traumatic. She narrates her story in flashbacks, thinking back over her experience as a mother and interrupting this linear story with memories from her own childhood and adolescence. In her interior monologue, Léa speaks of the distance between her and her mother, and of her father's neglect, and she claims to have rushed into a loveless marriage with her first suitor in order to escape them. Her pregnancy is an accident, and a particularly shameful one. Having avoided all sexual contact with her husband, Léa finds herself the object of a man's attention on a bus, goes to a hotel with him after a brief exchange of words, loses her virginity and conceives. None of this is fully described, since Tardieu's narrative style in this novel consists of staccato phrases that offer very little information and that read like a courtroom account of the facts. Although Léa's monologue recounts her love for her child, she is unable to overcome the shame of this encounter, and it is when her son first enquires about his father that she begins to spiral out of control.

The text includes considerable discussion of the difficulties of motherhood, especially from the perspective of a single mother. Léa describes her pregnancy as uncomfortable due to several weeks of bed rest, yet she is excited about the child's arrival, saying as she thinks back to it, 'je me sens belle. Je suis une femme [...] tout est à sa place' (82).[4] She refuses any romanticised portrayal of the birth, and highlights instead how painful, terrifying and utterly isolating the experience is for her: 'dans les instants où la vie jaillit ou se retire, on est seul: à la naissance, la première fois qu'on fait l'amour, dans la maladie, au moment de la mort' (85–6).[5] Léa's relationship with the child is loving, but Tardieu also emphasises the difficulties of motherhood from within her character's voice. Léa sees nobody, has no contact with her parents, cannot work and is obliged to depend financially upon her ex-husband. In a particularly telling episode, Léa recounts her reaction to her baby's crying: 'Ces pleurs, jusque dans ma chair ... On n'imagine pas jusqu'où peuvent aller les pleurs d'un bébé dans le corps d'une mère. Parce que je suppose ... Les autres mères aussi, n'est-ce pas?' (49)[6] After this much pressure, she seems to hint, surely thoughts of infanticide might arise in a mother's mind. Without completing the thought, Tardieu's narrator goes to the heart of what is, according to Wheelwright (2002: 282), the most emotive part of infanticide, that any mother could be driven to it: 'the infanticidal mother arouses rage because many mothers know how close they may have come to acting out the same desperate fantasy'. By representing these thoughts precisely through the mother's voice, Tardieu confronts this idea head on, lends subjectivity to the infanticidal woman and suggests that she may not be so unnatural, so mad or so bad after all.

Olmi's text is also set in the present of the action and recounts a small segment of the mother's history in first-person narrative. The tale begins as the three characters leave their home and the foreboding atmosphere is clear from the first lines: they take the late bus 'pour que personne nous voie' and the mother regrets that the unfinished pot of jam in the kitchen would 'rester pour rien' (9).[7] In a similar way to Tardieu's novel, Olmi creates a character who divulges very little history. The text reads almost like an official statement, to a court or as a psychiatric evaluation perhaps, in which she recounts the events chronologically, with no attempt at explanation, and she only digresses from the tale to offer brief memories of related incidents or feelings. She never mentions her name, nor does she narrate anything about her family situation. She does not speak of her own mother, or of any social life, friends or relatives, apart from a younger brother, nicknamed Dédé (115). She claims only to be able to remember songs that her father sang to her, which she sings in times of distress, and nothing, the reader infers, about the man himself; she states simply, apparently in a memory of a psychiatric session, 'Est-ce que je me souviens de l'école? Est-ce que je me souviens de mes neuf ans? J'ai tout oublié. À part les chansons de mon père, je me souviens de rien.' (83)[8] These songs function as a phantom of her previous life, spectres that remind her (and the reader) that she had a family but that this is now far away from her. She appears to be in her twenties due to her immature voice, but the reader knows neither where she lives nor the location of the seaside town where she takes her sons. The one thing that she does divulge is that the fathers of her two sons are different and, in a way that is characteristic of the style of this text, only nebulous information is provided about one of them:

> C'est un tout jeune, il avait quitté le lycée et faisait des stages pour devenir plombier, un truc comme ça, ses parents étaient les gardiens de l'immeuble, il était venu une fois à la maison, une histoire de dératisation, je crois, ou d'étrennes de Noël, moi j'avais un problème avec mes radiateurs et il est entré pour voir. (115)[9]

The narrator is so unclear that she cannot remember whether she met the father of her child due to an infestation of rats or during a Christmas visit, giving the impression that she is not deliberately withholding information but that her mind is so confused that she cannot decipher it. In this way, the mother's narration serves to position her as an isolated, abandoned character who struggles to find solace in her lived reality. She clearly suffers from a psychiatric disorder, and explains that she is receiving medical attention and prescription drugs; despite this intervention, it is clear that she suffers alone. Although she quotes the voices of others in her texts, hers is the only voice that speaks directly in this entire novella, and this renders the text almost vertiginous. The reader is so deeply placed within her head, reading only her perspective through her own voice, that the text becomes a powerfully uncomfortable and disturbing testimony of mental illness and maternal desperation.

The way that this character narrates her experience of motherhood is, as is the case for Tardieu's Léa, stark. Her love for her two sons is very evident, as she speaks of her affection for them and of the way in which she attempts to care for them. She worries about their developing a fever and makes sure that she packs clothing to protect them from the rain (ironically, since the hint from the beginning is that they will not survive the excursion). She is very protective of the 5-year-old and feels an affinity with him that she does not share with the older Stan. Even as she recounts how she smothered Kevin, she states: 'Mon Kevin. On a bien ri tous les deux. On a fait des concours de grimaces. Des mimes. Des bisous péteurs. Des blagues. Des tas de choses qui se font pas. Mon Kevin.' (110)[10] This is perhaps the core of her behaviour towards her sons: she cherishes them, but is unaware of how to care for them in conventional terms, leading to these 'choses qui se font pas'. For example, she expresses how difficult it is to explain her behaviour to the social workers who visit her house and see the drawings that she allows Kevin to daub across the wall. She emphasises that she wants Kevin to go to school but is unable to prepare him on time since she sleeps badly, so Stan accompanies him instead. She claims that she is able to dispel their fears by talking about seashells, and adds: 'Je sais bien m'y prendre avec mes gosses, j'ai pensé, suffit qu'on me fiche un peu la paix, est-ce qu'une assistante sociale aurait pensé à ça?' (22)[11]

As she hints here, her experience of mothering is fraught with difficulty. She lives in poverty, claiming never to have left the housing estate in which she lives, and relies upon the welfare state for financial support. Her 'savings' for the trip are so pitiful, just a few coins in a tin, that she can barely afford to feed the children. Unlike Tardieu's narrator, she does not go back in time to recount the birth or first months of her sons' lives, but the reader understands that her life with them has always been harsh. She cannot face getting out of bed to deal with them and is unable to cope with their behaviour, the level of which appears quite normal for their age. Far from conveying an idealised portrait, therefore, this mother narrates an experience of motherhood that would be unliveable to many, even without the added pressures of being a single mother with psychological difficulties.

These two texts thus stack up a list of reasons why motherhood might be experienced in such difficult and disruptive ways, and they do so in the specific voices of the mothers themselves. Rather than being passive earth mothers who feel complete when they become mothers, these narrators express how horrific motherhood can be. Taken together, the force of these texts lies in how these two mothers' voices provide an alternative to media discourses that demand women to be ideal, natural mothers and that proclaim the infanticidal mother as unfeeling, unnatural and wicked.

Voicing social perspectives on motherhood

In addition to the two mothers who narrate their own desperate experience, the voices of social actors, and their perspectives on motherhood, are crucial to the force of these narratives. While both texts are effectively interior monologues, both mothers allude to others, reporting their speech within the first-person narratives. The reader, as recipient of these narratives, is made party to the women's reception of the comments of other people and witnesses their inability to conform to the behaviour of the ideal, 'natural' mother.

In Tardicu's novel, Léa's monologue incorporates the voices of outsiders who reflect society's attitude towards infanticide. Describing the nurse at the prison, for example, she says: 'L'infirmière a eu pitié. Elle m'a regardée longuement, j'ai vu dans ses yeux la tristesse. J'y ai cherché un peu de chaleur [. . .] Au lieu de chaleur j'ai entendu ses paroles: vous deviez être bien mal pour en arriver là.' (10)[12] The contrast between the nurse and the mother is clear; the juxtaposition of the two voices shows the apparent gulf between them as the nurse (who is also a mother) attempts to distance herself and her experience of motherhood from the 'unnatural' mother before her. Fellow female prisoners insult her,

her ex-husband cannot look at her, and the judge, in a comment mediated by Léa's narrative, in reference to her silence, says 'soyez au moins présente à votre propre procès' (25).[13] The condemnation and incomprehension of other characters is clear, but one other voice does move out of the position of distant, judgemental and rejecting onlooker, and this is the prison warden who is guarding Léa. The two strike up a relationship when he begins to tell her of his wife's recent death and his difficulty in being a single parent to his two sons. As they wait together for the verdict, the guard gently encourages Léa to speak. When he tells her that he thinks he understands her, and that she is simply 'égarée' (33),[14] she starts to speak aloud to him about parts of what happened. Although the trial is over and this will not affect the verdict or the sentence, the guard shows that in private, somebody is willing to admit an understanding. The character, even if he serves a metonymical function as a figure of authority and surveillance, offers some comprehension. He does not condone, but he is simply one human being who reacts with understanding to another. This, in my reading, constitutes the crux of this text. Nobody openly admits to understanding infanticide, but we can as human beings have an understanding of desperation, and this desperation should not be silenced. In the position of judge and jury, of those who ordinarily hear the plea of the accused, is the reader, who 'hears' the narrator's story and who is invited not to pass judgment but to view this story, this mother, with empathy.

Olmi's entire text consists of a monologue, since no other voice breaks the stream of the mother's narrative in direct speech. Nevertheless, there are several incidents in which the protagonist quotes the voices of others within her narration. The medical staff with whom she comes into contact during her treatment provide the other main voices in the text. She does not portray them as listening or as offering advice that will help her to overcome her illness; the psychiatrist is merely reported as advising her not to follow 'ces pensées-là' because 'il y a des idées qui emmènent directement au fond du gouffre' (25).[15] She hears the advice of the medical professionals as a long list of items beginning with 'il faut'[16] that she can neither comprehend nor recall (70). The paediatrician to whom she takes the children is distant and presented as oblivious to the family's situation. They have named him 'docteur Flechette',[17] in view of the injections that he gives, and on one visit Kevin addresses him with this nickname. The doctor, unaware, touches his head while looking elsewhere and says 'c'est bien, mon petit', leading the mother to comment wistfully: 'la preuve que le toubib écoute pas ce qu'on lui raconte' (56).[18] Such small incursions into the narrative of the voices of other social actors serve as a reminder that there are people around the mother, specifically professionals who have some responsibility towards her, but who refuse to engage with her in any way other than to objectify her or ignore her. In addition, the voices of outsiders, such as the hotel receptionist and a café proprietor, are hostile and unforgiving; the café owner is reported as pushing over her stack of coins and yelling 'Allez! Allez! Remballez-moi tout ça!' (60)[19] Perhaps the most painful voices are those of the other mothers whom she sees at the children's schools, whom she describes as 'de bonnes mères' in the eyes of society because 'au lieu d'arriver à l'école à dix-huit heures elles se pointent avec leurs pains au chocolat à seize heures vingt-cinq et chopent leur môme en se plaignant Tu es sorti le dernier. Pff!' (23)[20] She knows that she will never speak in such a way to her children and is clearly regretful of her inability to mother in the same way as those whom she sees at the school gates. Perhaps the only voice which is mediated within the mother's monologue and which offers any way out of her predicament belongs to Stan, her 9-year-old son who is presented as becoming increasingly worried and withdrawn. She reports him as offering her small pieces of advice or direction, or reminders of the need to eat, and pleading with her for them to go home. It is he who seems silently to realise the fate that awaits them, and who could potentially take on the role of the prison warden in Tardieu's novel. Unlike the prison warden, though, who appears in the narrative after the infanticide has occurred, Stan may have been able to alert somebody had his mother been able to voice her desperation. As it is, this dizzying monologue includes only the voices of those who condemn, ignore or prescribe, and nobody is willing or able to engage in any sustained way with this mother.

Concluding thoughts

Throughout these two narratives that are based on the mothers' monologues and the mediated voices of others who refuse, for the most part, to understand them, the position of the reader is constantly called into question. Through their first-person testimony and their evidence of irresponsible witnesses, both texts read like court documents that plead the cases of the accused to the reader, who is in the position of judge and jury. The voices of the other actors who enter the narration are all witnesses to the unfolding tragedy of these two mothers, but the final witness is, of course, the person who is reading the testimony itself. Yet the reader is not invited to judge, since these texts do not present explanations or justifications that demand a verdict. Instead, they present characters who are partially guilty and partially innocent and whose plight the reader is simply invited to acknowledge sympathetically. As Anne Mairesse (2006: 491) states in a comment upon Olmi's novel that could easily apply to both texts, 'le lecteur s'y retrouve sans recours, abandonné comme l'enfant, victime et témoin impuissant d'une souffrance provoquée par un acte injustifiable'.[21] The reader is at once in the same position as the children, unable to understand or alter the events, and in the position of the onlookers who are asked to voice their stance. The figure of the prison guard who listens in private to Léa's testimony is a perfect manipulation of the reader, reminding us that we are implicated in such stories, providing examples of those who do and do not listen or voice their understanding, and reminding us that sitting alone in a room hearing or reading a story is not a passive situation that carries no ethical responsibility. Moreover, these courtroom-like narratives similarly invite a critique of the limitations of legal trials; the way in which the reader pieces together the story from little information mirrors the position of a judge and jury, who are obliged to imagine or invent the story from their own (possibly far less sympathetic) perspectives.

Taken together, these two novels represent mothers who make direct appeals to readers as fellow human beings who *can* understand. These texts do not claim that infanticide is not a crime, or that it should not be punishable by the law, but they underscore that the desperation that some mothers may feel is legitimate and should not be ignored or silenced. Ultimately, my reading of these texts argues that they are not really about infanticide, but about the mothers' desperation that is deemed in current media discourse on motherhood to be unsayable, and about the potential destruction of that silencing. Catharine Stimpson (2005: 48) writes that 'The murdering mother [. . .] has travelled beyond the human boundaries within which we normally dwell . . . She signifies the possibility of being us and not-us simultaneously'. In these two texts, the narrating mothers show the possibility of being us. They highlight how it is easier to contemplate sensational representations of infanticide than to confront the reality of this phenomenon. Overall, the current trend of narratives of infanticide in French women's writing points out that such mad/bad mothers do not live in a vacuum, and that there is a society around them that, even if it can only admit to this behind closed doors, has the potential for understanding.

Notes

1 'a revolution has taken place in our conception of maternity, almost without us noticing. No debate, no outcry accompanied this evolution, or rather this involution. Yet its objective is considerable in that it consists no more and no less of putting maternity back at the heart of female destiny.' All translations from the French are my own.
2 'a baby less than three days old'; 'voluntary homicide of a child under fifteen years old'.
3 The French title is a play on the homonym *mer/mère* (sea/mother), so means 'at the edge of the sea' and also 'at the edge of motherhood', hinting at the mother's precarious position, or 'borderline' state (see Morello 2008).
4 'I feel beautiful. I am a woman [. . .] everything is in its place'.
5 'in the moments when life bursts forth or retreats, we're alone: in birth, the first time we make love, in illness, at the time of death'.
6 'Those cries, deep inside of me . . . You can't imagine just how much a baby's crying penetrates a mother's body. Because I suppose . . . other mothers as well, surely?'
7 'so that nobody sees us'; 'be left for no reason'.
8 'Can I remember school? Can I remember being nine years old? I've forgotten everything. Apart from my father's songs, I can't remember anything.'
9 'He's very young, he'd left school and was training to become a plumber, something like that, his parents were the caretakers of the building, he'd come to the house once, something to do with rodents or a Christmas gift, I had a problem with one of my radiators, he came in to see it.'
10 'My Kevin. We had a good time together. We had competitions over who could make the scariest face. Mimes. Raspberry kisses. Jokes. Loads of things you shouldn't do. My Kevin.'
11 'I know how to handle my kids, I thought, just need to be left alone, would a social worker have thought of that?'
12 'the nurse was sympathetic. She looked at me for a while, I saw sadness in her eyes. I looked for some warmth [. . .] Instead of warmth I heard her words: you must have been really bad to get to that.'
13 'at least be present at your own trial'.

14 'lost', as in a lost sheep.
15 'those thoughts'; 'there are ideas that send you straight to the bottom of the abyss'.
16 'you must'.
17 'Doctor Dart'.
18 'that's good, little one'; 'proof that the doc doesn't listen to what people tell him'.
19 'Come on! Come on! Pick all of that up again for me!'
20 'good mothers'; 'rather than arriving at school at 6pm, they turn up with their *pain au chocolat* at 4.25 and take their kid off complaining You were last out. Tsk!'
21 'the reader finds her- or himself without recourse, abandoned like the child, victim of and powerless witness to a suffering brought about by an unjustifiable act'.

Part Three
Body, Life, Text

Chapter Nine
The Becoming of Anorexia and Text in Amélie Nothomb's *Robert des noms propres* and Delphine de Vigan's *Jours sans faim*

AMALEENA DAMLÉ

Introduction

The relationship between femininity and the body that has been a fundamental concern of both French feminist thought and female-authored literature throughout the twentieth century remains a persistent and striking element of women's writing in French in the new millennium. Yet, in contrast to the deliberate attempts of so many late twentieth-century women writers to celebrate the female body in writing, articulations of corporeality in the decades directly preceding and succeeding the turn of the millennium have seen a turn towards visceral extremes of violence and suffering. The female body thus has re-emerged in women's writing in French as a site of both conflict and contestation.

This chapter is concerned with depictions of the female body in twenty-first-century literature that are increasingly (and somewhat paradoxically) marked by their own disappearance. The anorexic, a ghostly figure characterised by a conflict between presence and absence, has in particular haunted the texts of women writing in French in recent years. In its exploration of anorexia in recent writing, this chapter focuses on two particular works: Amélie Nothomb's

114   *Amaleena Damlé*

Robert des noms propres (2002) (*The Book of Proper Names*) and Delphine de Vigan's *Jours sans faim* (2009) [2001] (Days without Hunger).[1] However, the range of authors who have touched upon the subject extends to Nina Bouraoui, Othilie Bailly, Geneviève Brisac, Claudine Galea, Marie Darrieussecq, Ananda Devi, Sabrina Kherbiche and Nathalie Maciel, to name just a few. The prevalence of anorexia as a literary theme is of course a stark reflection of reality, as anorexia has become the (gendered) turn-of-the-millennium epidemic to rival late nineteenth-century hysteria, persisting with tenacity into social contexts in the first decade of the twenty-first century. Underscoring the extent to which individual corporeal practice is embedded in socio-political systems, Susan Bordo (1993: 139–41) has argued that anorexic behaviour illuminates some of the central ills, and appears as a symptom, of the particularities of contemporary Western capitalist society. Yet, moving into the twenty-first century, it is interesting to observe that the range of authors raising the question of anorexia testifies to a wider cultural breadth. The anorexic body, so often theorised as being consigned to affluent Western nations, is becoming an event of significant transnational and transcultural relevance, one that is increasingly reflected in the preoccupations of contemporary female authors writing across cultures and that takes on ever new contexts and meanings.

This proliferation of texts signals the writing of anorexia to represent a significant trend in twenty-first-century women's writing in French. Yet, the problem of representing anorexic experience often rests in the very resistance of this corporeal practice, which exhibits subjectivity through the performance of its own visual code of disappearance, precisely to being held in view. The resistance to scrutiny that is posed by the anorexic logic of invisibility is pertinent on not only a literal but also an interpretative level. In varying attempts to understand anorexia, and particularly as bodily concerns regarding eating disorders have become all the more common in the last twenty years, discourses on the subject have ranged from the medical to the media, the psychoanalytical to the sociological, the feminist to the postmodern, not to mention various intersecting and interdisciplinary combinations of approach (see Heywood 1996: 178). This '*relentless pursuit of excessive thinness*' (Bruch 1978: ix; original italics), propelled through rigorous control and denial, has been interpreted as protest and conformation, rebellion and compliance, an attempt to assert the self and the dissolution of subjectivity, an appropriative decomposition of the body but one that is often complicit with patriarchal ideals of female beauty. An intricate web of conflictual desires and corporeal practices, anorexia is not easily unravelled. As this chapter argues, this very resistance to 'being held in view' – being seen in one's totality, being defined, categorised, interpreted or represented – exposes a heightened tension in the anorexic subject's negotiation between body and signification, one that riddles the endeavour to write about anorexic experience with immense complexity.

This chapter moves away from readings that structure anorexia in either purely sociological terms that view anorexics as victims of their particular (capitalist, (hetero-)patriarchal, postmodern, hyperreal or millennial) social circumstances, purely psychoanalytical terms that focus on subject–object relations, abjection and trauma, or medical/psychiatric terms governed by the straightjacket of pathology. Instead, it looks to the work of Gilles Deleuze, and to Deleuzian feminism, and interprets the anorexic body as a body in becoming, one that recurrently resists systems, systematisations and systematic representations. Wresting anorexia away from the theatre of psychoanalysis in particular, Deleuze figures the anorexic body in terms of the Body without Organs, a concept developed in collaboration with Félix Guattari. Rather than refusing the body in itself, the anorexic creates a Body without Organs that refuses to submit to ideological constraints, and to the concepts of the organism and the organisation of the body (Deleuze and Guattari 1980: 196). Anorexia is not rooted in lack, for Deleuze it is, rather, a means to escape the organic constraints of lack and hunger. Anorexia reforms and redistributes corporeality in an-organic and involuted movements. The involuted body is a body that 'becomes', that inhabits the in-between, within which voids and fullnesses converge, and intensities and flows offer the possibility of floating within one's own body. Anorexia, then, is the attempt to disrupt and destratify the ideology of the unified, hierarchised body, a way of constructing a micro-politics that reveals the multiple layers and codes that signify, construct and constrain corporeality, and of becoming, otherwise and differently (Deleuze and Parnet 1996 [1977]: 132).

Interpreting anorexia as a bodily becoming raises significant questions with regard to its representation. For as Abigail Bray and Claire Colebrook (1998: 35) have argued, Deleuze provides ways of thinking about anorexia and bodily becoming that not only move beyond ideological representation but also beyond the representational antimony that arises in many feminist discourses on anorexia, where the anorexic is viewed as the victim of stereotypical representation, but can only be emancipated through other, less regulative, forms of representation itself. They claim that this antimony only sustains the very mind/body dualism that it supposedly wants to critique, and argue that feminism should instead think through anorexia as a mode of self-formation or creation that jams the Cartesian concept through its very bodily 'deviancy'.[2] As they explain, 'such a body would be precisely where the classical and regulatory "image of thought" as an ordered "theater" would break down' (58). Bray and Colebrook are primarily concerned with reconceiving the relationship between the anorexic body and specular representation. But there are further implications for representation here. For in experimenting with the form of the body, in disrupting idealised corporeality, the anorexic complicates structures of thought through her material communication of difference and performance of body as a visual text that refuses to be tied down to particular, unitary representational meaning. How, then, can one speak, or write about bodily becoming, without necessarily imposing the kinds of ideological and representational constraints that the anorexic body wants to resist?

Various critics have examined the tense relationship between writing literature and starving in recent years (Heywood 1996; Ellman 1993; Meuret 2007). Yet, literary texts that deal with anorexia, whether testimonial or fictional, tend to read (or to be read) as fairly straightforward recovery narratives, insofar as they might not only relate a transition from a pathological body to a 'healthy' one, but also rescue the subject from the maladies of her depleted corporeal existence and reinsert her into language. Writing about anorexia, then, becomes the verbalisation of a trauma that has thus far been corporeally communicated and the body is now reconciled and restituted into words (Havercroft 2007; McIlvanney 2007). Yet, as Deleuze and Guattari (1975: 36) have suggested, the relationship between words and starvation might be more complicated: 'Parler, et surtout écrire, c'est jeûner', they claim.[3] This would counter the Freudian interpretation of language, and specifically the creation of narrative, as providing a sense of resolution to bodily pathology, and instead would posit both writing and anorexia as two sides of the same coin, both endeavours as creative becomings. Indeed, for Deleuze (and Guattari) the work of art exceeds the domain of mimetic representation. Artistic and literary works are forms of becoming that resist resolution and ideological signification, instead creating open-ended and rhizomatic connections to the world (Deleuze 1993: 11, Deleuze and Guattari 1991: 166–7).

This chapter now turns to consider the relationship between the anorexic body and signification in Amélie Nothomb's *Robert* and Delphine de Vigan's *Jours*. Though each author draws on her own real-life experience of anorexia, these works are not autobiographical accounts, but fictionalised third-person narratives. Rather than offering holistic and curative models for the textual restoration of the normative, 'healthy' female body, these authors consciously open out literary spaces that instead evoke anorexic bodily becomings and their complicated relationship with interpretation and signification. Rather than document anorexic experience through testimonial representation, these authors play with language and with representation in creative endeavours that figure the delicate and precarious relationship between materiality and language, and between body and text, that is at stake in anorexic experience. In so doing, they allow for the becoming of both the body and the text through new and different grammars of the flesh.

Resisting representation

Over the past two decades, the prolific and popular writer Amélie Nothomb has exhibited an immensely provocative attitude to the female body in her writing (Amanieux 2005; Bainbrigge and den Toonder 2003). Purity and excess, hunger and denial, beauty and monstrosity, spectacle and disappearance are constantly woven into her depictions of female corporeality, suggesting an anorexic aesthetic that governs her work and, that, as Nothomb has discussed both in interviews (Joignot 2008) and in her writing (Nothomb 2004b), is informed by autobiographical experience.

In *Robert*, the protagonist Plectrude typically develops an ambivalent attitude towards her body as she contemplates her thirteenth birthday, which marks the end of childhood idyll and the threat of messy female metamorphosis (92). But it is not until she goes away to ballet school that this translates into an eating practice of such restraint that she ends up being hospitalised with severe osteoporosis. There are various ways that one might interpret Plectrude's anorexia. The traumatic circumstances of her birth (her mother Lucette murdered Plectrude's father while she was pregnant, and later committed suicide after the child's birth) have haunted Plectrude, so much so that she appears to suffer a psychoanalytical compulsion to repeat experiences of bodily violence and absence (McIlvanney 2007). As an unconscious result of her loss, Plectrude over-identifies with her adoptive mother and exhibits a fervent desire to fix the mother–child bond (93), a resistance to individuation that signals, in psychoanalytical terms, an anorexic fear of adulthood. Clémence is complicit in Plectrude's infantilisation, encouraging her to script her life as a childhood fairytale (36–7), living vicariously through her in a manner that blurs the boundaries between mother and daughter, and later explicitly endorsing (137, 142) and imitating her anorexia (153, 156). Catalysed within the environment of the ballet school, Plectrude's anorexia invites other interpretations in testifying to stringent demands to achieve the dancer's athletic body (119–22) that aspires to a superhuman state attained through control and resilience (130). Finally, the theatrical environment of ballet reveals elements of self-exhibition and performance in Plectrude's anorexia (75), while attitudes of those around her disclose the contemporary socialisation of the aesthetic of thinness and the relationship between food and body in a capitalist logic of consumption (119).

To take a Deleuzian approach to Plectrude's anorexia, one might highlight the opening out of the body and its signifying practices, rather than constrict corporeality in inflexible, interpretative paradigms. Resisting the ideological organisation of the body, Deleuze argues, the anorexic creates a body of lightness and fastness, altering perception and extensive qualities and transforming them into intensities and affects. Plectrude's anorexia enables a redistribution of corporeality and affect, allowing her to experience what Branka Arsic (2008: 36) has referred to as a form of Deleuzian asceticism:

> Ce que Plectrude vivait à l'école des rats s'appelait l'ivresse: cette extase se nourrissait d'une dose énorme d'oubli. Oubli des privations, de la souffrance physique, du danger, de la peur. Moyennant ces amnésies volontaires, elle pouvait se jeter dans la danse et y connaître la folle illusion, la transe de l'envol. (144)[4]

Plectrude's corporeality no longer rests on psychic interiority; rather, it is experienced as a flow of intensities that resists stratification and hierarchisation. In particular, Plectrude's anorexia creates lines of flight ('envol') and allows for intensities of difference in the face of the banality of everyday existence and familiar relationships (133, 141, 147). As such, Nothomb's text is very much in keeping with the Deleuzian idea that anorexia is 'both the process of experimenting with the form of the body [. . .] and the politics of disturbing the socially imposed order of everyday life' (Arsic 2008: 35).

As a text, *Robert* opens out the multifarious possibilities of reading that anorexia itself provokes. Careful not to provide a singular framework to explain Plectrude's anorexia, Nothomb orchestrates various contrapuntal lines that hint at multiple social codes and psychic impulses. Reading Plectrude's anorexia with Deleuze, however, ensures that corporeality is not tied down to a fixed signification and might be understood in terms of ideological resistance as a creative process of becoming-otherwise. But, further allowing Plectrude's anorexia its own bodily becoming, Nothomb's text lacks the resolution of a final perfect cadence: words and representation themselves remain in open-ended becoming alongside the body. The complex relationship between anorexia and words is given a place in the novel, as Plectrude exhibits a contemplative and sparse attitude both to words and to food (29). At school she is indifferent to language acquisition (53), until her mother presents her with a book of fairytales at which point she actively consumes words (57). Plectrude's relationship with words reveals a privileging of creative, artistic language over everyday communication, then. As her anorexia develops, her body itself becomes a keyboard for creative expression, or a 'chart of newly invented signs' (Arsic 2008: 41). Creating different bodily fluxes through dance and lightness allows her a sense of flight from everyday life, and into the inventive becoming of a story: 'Plectrude admirait sa vie· elle sentait comme l'héroïne unique d'une lutte contre la pesanteur. Elle l'affrontait par le jeûne et par la danse' (147–8).[5] Resisting the banality of everyday ideology, Plectrude is instead driven by the creative re-organ-isation of bodies and texts.

By the end of the text, Plectrude appears to have recovered from her anorexia, with a child of her own and a happy ending, having re-encountered her childhood love, Mathieu Saladin. And yet Nothomb's text arguably resists this easy resolution and oppositional passage from disorder to recovery, pathology to language, and difference to normativity, by interweaving words and body together as processes of creative becoming within anorexia. It does so in two further ways, both of which highlight the becoming-otherwise of body and of text. The first involves the opening out of the act of naming. Lucette chose the name Plectrude for her child as she felt it would guarantee her baby's exceptionality, supporting the idea of the power of language in this text to constitute reality (McIlvanney 2007). Yet, by the end of the text, Plectrude has taken the name Robert, 'qui était un nom de dictionnaire et qui convenait ainsi à la dimension encyclopédique des souffrances qu'elle avait connues' (188).[6] Robert thus offers a multiplicity of signification that reflects her anorexic bodily becoming and its resistance to singular meaning. The fact that Robert is a fairly common name in the French language opposes the specificity of Plectrude, and also muddles the signifying act in terms of gender that naming tends to carry. In this creative act of self-signification, then, Plectrude challenges her mother's representational naming, refuses to allow her story to be scripted by another and keeps difference in play at the end of the novel.

The postmodern twist to the tale, in which Nothomb herself appears as a character, Amélie, who befriends and counsels Plectrude before being murdered by her, provides the final element that keeps anorexia's resistance to interpretation and representation alive. It is Amélie who suggests that Plectrude's problems are bound up with her birth and that her only release from the internalisation of violence is to commit murder herself. When Plectrude kills Amélie, this death of the author has clear resonances of matricide. A psychoanalytical reading would maintain that Plectrude is finally able to rid herself of the ambivalent mother–child relationship that has governed her pathology. McIlvanney's argument (2007: 26) that 'Plectrude will no longer passively dance to the tune of another – whether Clémence's or Nothomb's – but will speak her own text' is certainly compelling. But, just as Plectrude's self-re-signification as Robert opens out, rather than fixes, representational naming, there is a sense of openness at the end of this story. Plectrude's actions may in some way reinforce the interpretative paradigm offered up to explain her pathology, insofar as she commits an act of murder that is claimed to be her salvation. However, by killing the very person who offers this interpretation, and who has also thus far narrated her existence, Plectrude ultimately resists the placing of any kind of interpretative or representational frameworks upon her life. Furthermore, as Anna Kemp (2012: 63) has suggested, whether Plectrude can in fact speak her own text remains unclear. It is significant that the novel ends with the unanswerable question 'que faire du corps?',[7] which bears immediate relevance to the corpse lying at her feet, but also recalls the radical interrogation of bodily limits effected through an-organic involution. This suggests a lack of resolution in the relationship between body and text that might signal Plectrude's 'recovery' in normative terms and what is revealed in this resistance is that *neither* Plectrude *nor* Nothomb can conclude the narration of Plectrude's life. Language cannot resolve the question of what to do with the body, precisely because it participates in this inventive text in exactly the same processes of opening out signification as anorexic bodily becoming itself.

In *Robert*, Nothomb's self-conscious treatment of representation exposes the intricacies of the relationship between anorexia and language. Plectrude's anorexia, read alongside Deleuzian philosophy, is bound up creative becoming and self-signifying difference that carries through into the writing of the text. Far from there being any sense of resolution at the end of Plectrude's story, then, Nothomb's creative treatment resists representational structures and allows both bodily and signifying questions to persist.

The parchment of the body

Delphine de Vigan has published an array of texts since the beginning of the twenty-first century and is most well known for *Nô et moi* (2007) (*Nô and me*), recently released as a film of the same name. Originally published under the pseudonym Lou Delvig, *Jours sans faim* is her first literary offering and is concerned with her autobiographical experience of anorexia at a younger age. However, like Nothomb, Vigan deliberately takes an inventive rather than testimonial approach to the past. Indeed, as she has stated in an interview:

> Quinze ans après, on ne raconte pas son passé, on le réinvente [. . .] Si j'avais voulu juste témoigner, je n'aurais pas utilisé la troisième personne. Je l'aurais écrit sur un mode compassionnel, piège que je voulais absolument éviter. (quoted in Cairns 2007: 205)[8]

Where Nothomb's text follows the linear narrative occasioned by the fairytale genre of 'once upon a time', Vigan's third-person narration offers glimpses of 19-year-old protagonist Laure's experience of anorexia and of hospitalisation, avoiding chronological cohesion and thus any semblance of a causal trajectory. And, where Nothomb's text builds up a complex architecture of social and psychical structures that might explain Plectrude's anorexia, while inscribing anorexia's very resistance to these structures, Vigan's text is an altogether more sparse work, with notable gaps and ellipses in Laure's story. Although both texts illuminate the relationship between anorexia and representation, then, Vigan's focus sheds particular light on the Deleuzian notion that to write is to fast in its various evocations of the link between body and text, body as text, and text as body.

It would not be impossible to piece together a psychoanalytical account of Laure's anorexia, but *Jours* certainly does not present an explicit rationale. From the beginning of the text, there is little in the way of contextual detail about Laure's childhood and adolescence. Although fragments do surface, references to family and other relationships are scattered without immediate connections and, although by the end of the text there is a sense of how these relations have influenced Laure, Vigan places greater emphasis on the present corpo-reality of anorexia and Laure's struggle to conform to medical demands. As in *Robert*, starvation is a way of resisting and transforming the organisation of the body through affective becoming, and is described similarly in terms of 'ivresse' and 'envol' (9, 33, 52) that resonate with a Deleuzian ascetics. Anorexia allows Laure to experience corporeality through an evanescent, involuted, in-between existence. Neither firmly rooted in life or death, the body is suspended and lightness creates new intensities of experience: 'Elle se sentait bien. Tellement plus légère. Elle ne voulait pas mourir, juste disparaître. S'effacer. Se dissoudre. Avec un pamplemousse dans le ventre elle volait au-dessus des trottoirs, des journées entières dans la rue, à vider son corps.' (44)[9]

In the fragments that emerge from Laure's past, one aspect seems to persist, and it is that above all language – its weight *and* its possibility – governs Laure's bodily becoming. Both Laure and her sister Louise experience their relationship with their alcoholic father through the violence of the words that he inflicts upon them:

> Toute la nuit, il les abreuve de paroles, des histoires cent fois répétées, des reproches, toute cette haine qu'il vomit, la haine de

leur mère, la haine de toute sa famille à lui, ses frères et sœurs avec lesquels il a rompu, des mots comme des ordures. (46)[10]

The father's words are not only violent in the sense of what they communicate, then, they also appear to take on a visceral, abject materiality, one that is impossible to digest: 'Des mots périmés, avariés, qu'on ne digère pas. Qui restent sur l'estomac.' (46)[11] This over-abundance of words and their materiality lies in stark contrast to the silence of Laure's mother, who is described as not having spoken for some years (27). In a visit home from hospital, Laure observes that words exceed her mother's capabilities (76), and she finds it difficult to put together even a sentence that might communicate unhappiness, either her own or that of her daughter (77). Laure's family relations thus set up a dichotomy between excessive communication of needs that are experienced as a form of force-feeding and suffering that is cloaked in silence.

Deleuze and Guattari argue that language always involves a deterritorialisation of certain body parts. For in articulating sounds, the primitive functionality of the mouth, tongue and teeth – eating – is radically displaced (Deleuze and Guattari 1975: 36). However, it is not Laure's ability to form words that rivals and displaces food; rather, the words of others are ingested and weigh heavily upon her. Resisting the weight of other people's verbal signifiers while imitating her mother's reluctance to enunciate requires Laure to find other forms of communication and self-signification and propels her into creatively becoming-otherwise. Language takes the place of food, then, insofar as words are swallowed, but also because anorexia allows Laure's body itself to become a signifying text. At the beginning of the text, her corpo-reality is expressed in terms of 'ce temps qu'elle n'avait plus à perdre, ce temps ténu, tendu contre la mort comme une dernière virgule, fragile' (11).[12] And this notion of the anorexic body-as-text develops in a story that Laure is told in hospital, of a little girl sitting in a tree, who chews only the pages of books. Little by little, her fleshy existence wanes and she becomes a thin sliver of parchment: 'Bientôt tout son corps devient gris, la pluie laisse des traces d'encre sur sa peau. Bientôt, elle rétrécit, elle devient toute petite, fine comme un parchemin usé, comme une feuille d'or peut-être.' (38)[13] Eventually, after a storm rages at night, the little girl disappears, leaving just a word on a piece of paper, 'un mot qu'on ne peut pas lire' (38).[14] Laure clearly identifies with this story, suggesting that, for her, redistributing the body as a text is an attempt at a self-signifying process. Corporeality is deterritorialised as language rivals food and ink is inscribed onto bodily parchment. And, yet, this bodily text is one that cannot be read, that resists interpretative paradigms. In suggesting that anorexia is bound up with self-signification, then, Vigan highlights its creative bodily becoming, underscoring the extent to which anorexia both exceeds the ideology of the body, as well as systems of representation in and through language, and thus drawing attention to the deterritorialised relationship between body and text.

Interestingly, this story marks the point in the text at which the reader learns Laure's name for the first time. It sparks a desire in her to start writing, about those around her in the hospital, about the visits from her family (39–40). Writing and talking to her doctor, Laure begins to piece together the fragments of her life (46), to script her own life in language rather than to swallow the words of others and exhibit her own text on and through the body. But this is not a simplistic reinsertion into language and Laure struggles with testimonial representation, to the extent that writing a simple sentence to report that her father brought her peanuts provokes the following sentiment: 'sur le papier la phrase est indécente, tellement énorme qu'elle a peine à y croire. C'est pourtant vrai. L'écriture n'y peut rien.' (39)[15] The end of the text evokes a sense of hopefulness for Laure's future and a resolution for her corporeal suffering, one that is bound up with language. Yet, rather than presenting a psychoanalytical account of anorexia in which pathology opposes language and a holistic relationship between body and text is only achieved by means of the recovery of a narrative, Vigan's text reveals the more delicate, deterritorialised relationship between body and words that is involved in anorexic bodily becoming.

If the text explores the notion of body-as-text, the reverse is also true. Vigan's creative endeavour is not to testify to the past, but to invent. Rather than recounting or representing the experience of anorexia, hers is a style of writing that becomes, alongside the body. The resistance of the anorexic body is not merely expressed, then, but produced on the very pages of this skeletal fragmented text. As an inky parchment of the body itself, *Jours* thus figures the deterritorialised relationship between body and text. If to write is to fast, this is because both processes break down the ordered theatre of representation as the image of thought, instead opening out the becoming of both body and text.

Conclusion

This chapter has read depictions of anorexia in twenty-first-century women's writing alongside Deleuzian becoming, in order to highlight the complex interplay between body and signification that is mobilised in anorexic experience. Nothomb's *Robert* and Vigan's *Jours* both underscore the intricate architecture of the anorexic body and the resistance of this body to being held in view. Deleuze provides ways of thinking through anorexia that allow the body to remain suspended in its own creative becoming, rather than being constrained within the specificities of interpretative paradigms, insofar as the very notion of representational thought itself is resisted. In their creative endeavours, Nothomb and Vigan differently figure the complexity of the relationship between body and text: where Nothomb interrogates the very act of representation, Vigan intertwines bodies and words into a new and inventive grammar of the flesh. Refusing conventional narrative forms, their writing captures the becoming of body and text in anorexic experience and resonates with the Deleuzian notion of literature not as a mimetic, representational act that fixes meaning, but as an agentive, aleatory connection to the world. In the words of Deleuze and Guattari: 'La littérature est un agencement, elle n'a rien à voir avec de l'idéologie [. . .] Écrire n'a rien à voir avec signifer' (Deleuze and Guattari 1980: 10–11).[16]

Notes

1. See Anna Kemp's chapter in this volume for a somewhat different reading of Nothomb's *Robert des noms propres*.
2. These thinkers are careful not to valorise anorexia (58), which is a position that resonates with my own in this chapter. To lead an anorexic life is to lead an unliveable life. To think through anorexia as a bodily becoming, or a form of invention, is not to commend it, merely to attempt to open out the complexities of its signifying (designifying, resignifying) practices.
3. 'To speak and above all to write, is to fast' (Deleuze and Guattari 1986: 20).
4. 'What Plectrude was going through at the école des rats was called intoxication: that form of ecstasy that is fed on a massive dose of oblivion. Forgetting privations, physical suffering, danger, fear. Through such voluntary amnesia she was able to throw herself into dancing, and know the mad illusion of it, the trance of flight.' (Nothomb 2004a: 95)
5. 'Plectrude admired her life: she felt as though she was the sole heroine in a battle against gravity. She waged war upon it with the twin weapons of fasting and dance' (97).

6   'which was the name of a French dictionary, and which was thus ideally suited to the encyclopaedic dimensions of the suffering she had known' (125).
7   'what should we do with the body?' (126).
8   'Fifteen years later, one doesn't recount one's past, but rather reinvents it [. . .] If I had merely wanted to bear witness, I wouldn't have used the third person. I would have written it in a compassionate style, a trap that I wanted to avoid above all.' All Vigan translations are my own.
9   'She felt well. So much lighter. She didn't want to die, just to disappear. To erase herself. To dissolve. With just a grapefruit in her stomach, she flew high above the pavements, whole days in the road, emptying her body.'
10 'For the entire night, he drowns them in words, stories repeated a hundred times, reproaches, all that hatred that he regurgitates, hatred for their mother, hatred for all his own family, his brothers and sisters with whom rifts have formed, words that are like pieces of garbage.'
11 'Worn-out words, damaged words, words that cannot be digested. That weigh on your gut.'
12 'time that she no longer had to lose, time suspended, pressed up against death like a final comma, fragile'.
13 'Soon her body becomes grey, the rain leaves traces of ink on her skin. Soon, she shrinks, she becomes tiny, thin like a used parchment, like a gold leaf perhaps.'
14 'a word that cannot be read'.
15 'on the paper the sentence is indecent, so enormous that she can scarcely believe it. It's true though. Writing can't do anything about it.'
16 'Literature is an assemblage. It has nothing to do with ideology [. . .] Writing has nothing to do with signifying' (Deleuze and Guattari 1987: 5).

Chapter Ten
The Human-Animal in Ananda Devi's Texts: Towards an Ethics of Hybridity?

ASHWINY O. KISTNAREDDY

Introduction

Ananda Devi is a prolific Mauritian writer, born in 1957, who has spent the last thirty years in France, on the Swiss border. Holder of a Ph.D. in anthropology from the School of Oriental and African Studies (SOAS) in London, she works in Geneva, Switzerland as a professional translator. Since the 1980s, she has written several short-story collections, a book of poems and ten novels, the first, *Rue la Poudrière* (a street name in Port-Louis, Mauritius), published in 1989, with *Le Sari vert* (The Green Sari) appearing in September 2009. Winner of a number of regional, national and international prizes, Devi is best known in the francophone world as the author of *Ève de ses décombres* (2006) (Eve of her Ruins), which won the Prix des Cinq Continents de la Francophonie. Devi's novels foreground a range of themes and concerns: madness, marginality, transformation, the dialectics of good versus evil, the relationship between appearance and reality, and oppositions and blurred boundaries between humans and animals or monsters. These are more often than not set against a backdrop that details the oppression of women, patriarchal prejudice and interrogates notions of femininity.

This chapter highlights the relationship between humans and animals in Devi's writing, a recurring theme in contemporary women's writing in French. A notable example is the work of Marie

Darrieussecq, who portrays a woman's transformation into a sow in *Truismes* (1996a) (*Pig Tales*). However, Devi's particular treatment of this subject is anchored in the cultural setting of her native Mauritius, where, it will be argued, the implications of hybridity and transformation carry a specific resonance. The chapter focuses on the human-animal hybrid in Devi's work and in particular draws out distinctions between the human-animal monster and the human-animal god. It explores the relationship between these different kinds of hybridity in two novels, *Moi, l'interdite* (2000) (I, The Forbidden) and *Le Sari vert*. Ultimately, the aim is to determine the gendered implications of hybridity, and its relation to the notion of hybrid identity in the Mauritian society depicted by Devi. Mauritius is often hailed as a 'rainbow' nation, as Srilata Ravi points out in the title of her book, *Rainbow Colors* (2007). Indeed, the Mauritian population consists of 70 per cent of people of Indian origin and the rest is divided between those of African descent, mixed and European as well as Chinese. However, just as a rainbow's colours do not mix, the different communities in the society have resisted intermingling for centuries. While, culturally, Mauritius displays hybridity, in the sense that the cuisine is mixed, the music demonstrates the richness of a variety of origins and Mauritian Creole is a hybrid language (broken French, English, African grammar), the various communities have managed to not mix because hybridity is deemed to be a tar. Notions of belonging are, therefore, of paramount importance in this society, since the communities are so divided. A hybrid would essentially not belong to one particular community but two at the same time, and in his or her in-between position s/he would be rejected by both communities.

Lack of belonging and rejection are central to these novels. In *Moi, l'interdite*, Devi depicts a girl born with a harelip, whose facial deformity leads to her marginalisation both from her family and society. Reduced to the state of animality in the limekiln in which she is imprisoned, Mouna transforms into a hybrid, half-dog half-human. Subsequently recognising her apparent inhumanity, she transforms back into a human being and falls in love with a tramp who leaves her pregnant. After giving birth to a deformed child, whom she kills, she is interned in an asylum. It is from this marginal position that she narrates her story to a sympathetic listener, Lisa, her only ally. *Le Sari vert*, on the other hand, is the story of a dying doctor whose daughter and granddaughter are watching over him as he begins a journey into the past, remembering his wife and his mistreatment of her which led to her death. An invalid, he relies heavily on his daughter, while constantly treating her as an animal. Though these two texts both highlight notions of animality, alterity and gender, they raise different questions about the nature of monstrosity: *Moi, l'interdite* focuses on Mouna's physical hybridity, while the idea of moral monstrosity is further evoked in *Le Sari vert*. Both Mouna and Dokter-Dieu, the protagonist of the second novel, are considered to be, alternately, monsters and gods in the novels. This chapter, then, considers the notion of the hybrid as a metaphor in Devi's work and a means of discussing ethics in Mauritian society. It begins by interrogating questions of alterity and hybridity, then proceeds to analyse physical hybridity in Devi's writing. The focus then shifts to the ways in which language is employed to visualise women as animals and confer a new hybrid status upon them. The final section examines the notion of moral hybridity, questioning the boundaries between good and evil, and ultimately interrogating identificatory classifications.

The 'other' body, liminality and hybridity

In *Strangers, Gods and Monsters: Interpreting Otherness*, Richard Kearney suggests that the in-between body is perceived as other, that is, in opposition to the same or self. In Kearney's (2003: 13) words: 'the three figures of our title – strangers, gods and monsters – are three colloquial names for the experience of alterity.' The in-between bodies in Devi's narratives are rarely seen as forming part of the rest of society, insofar as they do not conform to the norm prevalent in that society. In fact, the moment that difference, or alterity, is perceived, the individual is irrevocably marginalised and segregated from the rest of society. Kearney bases his three categories on the fear inspired by those who do not conform, in different ways, to our everyday reality. Instead of understanding what is different, we marginalise them and categorise them in certain groups:

> we often project onto others those unconscious fears from which we recoil in ourselves. Rather than acknowledge that we are deep down answerable to an alterity which unsettles us we devise all kinds of evasion strategies. Primary amongst these is the attempt to simplify our existence by scapegoating others as 'aliens'. (Kearney 2003: 5)

Kearney argues that human beings, whether they be coloniser or colonised, Western or non-Western or, indeed, outside those paradigms, are fundamentally afraid of that which they cannot fathom, and this is a notion that resonates clearly with Devi's work. Thus a body that defies the norms in terms of its incompleteness, or its not belonging to any specific category such as human or animal, will inspire fear in people because such a body is unknowable and reminds them that there is a part of themselves that they do not know.[1]

In Devi's two texts, alterity is closely linked to the hybridity that characters display, and tends to be formulated through the logic of victim and perpetrator. *Moi, l'interdite* is written from the point of view of the victim – albeit narrated in the third person – who transforms into a hybrid entity, and *Le Sari vert* is the narrative of the 'homme bourreau' (Marson 2009).[2] In both novels, women are subjected to oppression and are marginalised in light of their alterity. In the first novel, the human-animal god/monster dialectic occurs with the victim and the perception people have of her or she has of herself as a monster. However, in the second novel, interestingly the perpetrator too develops human-animal god/monster characteristics.

The human-animal hybrid and the blurring of physical boundaries in *Moi, l'interdite*

In *Moi, l'interdite*, Mouna is perceived as a human-animal monster from birth: born with a harelip ('bec-de-lièvre'), animal traits are already assigned to her. The nickname 'Mouna' literally means 'la guenon',[3] thus reinforcing her association with animals rather than humans, especially since at no point she is given a real name. Segregated from the family, she is called 'shehtan, satan ou autre' (9),[4] the multiple language use (Hindi and French/English) illustrating the extent to which she is denied a human identity. Those who label her 'satan' link physical deformity to the forces of evil. Her subsequent transformation into a half-human, half-dog raises questions about the boundaries between humanity, animality and monstrosity. Theriomorphosis, in this case, can be seen as an expression of not only difference, but the will to embrace alterity, in order to question the very basis of humanity.

There are several stages to Mouna's transformation: first, she is 'transformée' (69) when insects accept her; then '[elle] n'étai[t] plus humaine' (72),⁵ and finally she walks on all fours like a dog. Mouna believes love is the reason behind her transformation: 'l'amour seul pouvait opérer cette transformation' (87).⁶ Not having found it within her family, she seeks love and affection where she can find it, mistaking the faithfulness of a dog and her own gratitude for love. Growing hair and claws, Mouna becomes the 'loup-garou' (98),⁷ in-between animal and human, neither one nor the other. However, instead of accepting her transformation, Mouna questions it and ultimately chooses to stay human: 'j'ai vu dans la mare s'échapper le duvet brun, comme si une part de ma vie me quittait en une mue mystérieuse. Ainsi, il fallait que je reprenne mon apparence d'avant' (102).⁸ Reason and humanity appear to prevail as Mouna divests herself of her part-animality. Yet, the process of becoming animal seems to be precisely what enables her to reconnect with her humanity, for it is through fighting with the dogs who are attempting to kill a human family (90–3) that she comes to assume her identity as a human.

According to Marson (2006: 66), 'la "*carnalité*" accroît la pensée et la vie dont le principe anime leur [Devi's characters] corps, leur sens moral, leur sensibilité [. . .] l'esprit humain cède la place au souffle vital. L'"*humanimalité*" se lit alors comme l'apport d'un supplément d'humanité.' (italics in the original)⁹ '*Carnalité*', in Marson's analysis, refers to regression into pure drive, and she argues thus that Devi's characters become more than human through their descent into animality, which recovers or enhances their ability to feel. Marson's own analysis is based on Michel Surya's concept of 'humanimalité'. In an exploration of Franz Kafka's *Die Verwandlung* (1915) (*The Metamorphosis*), Surya (2004: 59) contends that, although Samsa may be a giant insect, this does not compel him to lose his humanity: 'Gregor Samsa ne cessait pas d'être un homme quoiqu'il fût ravalé à l'état de bête.'¹⁰ Even though Samsa will die as an animal, no one, in fact, is as human as him, and Surya thus underscores the supplementary humanity that animality seems to confer to the transformed character. This is supported by Xavier Garnier (2001), who demonstrates that Samsa's sensitive *human* nature becomes apparent through his reaction to the music his sister plays. Similarly, I argue that Mouna's body of becoming – her monstrous, hybrid body – enables her to become increasingly lucid about what is really monstrous, leading her to question the very concept of humanity and ultimately to transform from monster to angel, or the divine. Indeed, the novel ends with the question 'serais-je un ange?' (125).[11]

The semantics of hybridity in *Le Sari vert*

In *Le Sari vert*, language, rather than physical transformation, is the mode through which women are made into animals. The character Dokter-Dieu calls his daughter Kitty 'la chatte' (138) or 'le chat' (14, 71), and of his granddaughter, Malika, he states: 'la fille mâchonne sa langue, plus bovine que jamais' (17).[12] In an extended analysis of the equation of animals and women through language in gender politics, Joan Dunayer (1995: 11) argues that:

> So inveterate and universal is the false dichotomy of animal vs. human – and so powerfully evocative – that symbolically associating women with 'animals' assists in their oppression. Applying images of denigrated nonhuman species to women labels women inferior and available for abuse: attaching images of the aggrandized human species to men designates them superior and entitles them to exploit. Language is a powerful agent in assigning the imagery of animals vs. human. Feminists have long objected to 'animal' pejoratives for women and the pseudogenerics *man* and *mankind*. (italics in the original)

Like the other contributions in the volume in which her article appears (Adams and Donovan 1995), Dunayer's work explores the ways in which animal imagery is used to denigrate women. She focuses in particular on how patriarchal society places women in a domestic position, for example, through common farm animal images. Dunayer's article ultimately emphasises the extent to which humans consider animals as inferior, unintelligent or for the sole benefit of themselves, since 'these linguistic habits are rooted in speciesism, the assumption that other animals are inferior to humans and do not warrant equal consideration and respect' (Dunayer 1995: 11).

Characters who find themselves on the margins of the Mauritian society that Devi creates are often perceived as less than human, and in many cases these characters are female. In Devi's novels, women are secondary to men insofar as they are oppressed and rejected when they do not conform to the accepted standards of normalcy. According to Marilyn French (1985: 314):

Patriarchy is an ideology founded on the assumption that man is distinct from the animals and superior to [them]. The reason for this superiority is man's contact with a higher power/knowledge called god, reason or control. The reason for man's existence is to shed all animal residue and realize his 'divine' nature, the part that *seems* unlike any part owned by animals – mind, spirit or control. (italics in the original)

Man's alleged superiority over all other species is thus extended from the (pseudo)generic to the gendered to imply a superiority of man over woman. In *Volatile Bodies*, Elizabeth Grosz (1994) reminds us that, in Western philosophy, the dichotomy of mind and body separates the two human genders, placing men above women, for the woman is associated with the body, passion, drives and physical needs, while the man is above all considered to be a rational being. And, according to Elizabeth Spelman (1982: 120), this has led to what she terms somatophobia: the equation of women, children, animals and all manner of things 'natural', with one another.

In Devi's *Le Sari vert*, animal name-calling becomes a means of demeaning women. Indeed, the only Creole words that Dokter-Dieu utters in the narrative are '*sorti la alle zanimo*' (156), directed at his wife and bringing out the full force of his anger, since the harshness of the Creole language intensifies the already injurious 'get out you animal'. Dokter-Dieu's use of language is misogynistic throughout in ways that reveal Spelman's somatophobic equation. In his words, his daughter acquires cat-like characteristics: 'Kitty, Kitty, Kitty, viens ma chatte' (14).[13] The disdain and arrogance of the cat transferred to Kitty, who is alternately a cat ('chatte') and like a cat ('comme ces chats' (14)), anger him to the point of violence, so much so that it reveals his own feelings of inferiority. Kitty's true name is Kaveri Bavani, a goddess's name, yet her father's nickname reduces her to the status of an animal. In Dokter-Dieu's language, Kitty becomes an ambivalent human-animal hybrid who changes form on (her father's) whim.

Moreover, Kitty is described 'comme un animal de compagnie' (34), and elsewhere Dokter-Dieu states '[j]'ai besoin de Kitty comme de l'animal familier' (180).[14] The daughter is not only given the name of 'chatte' with its overtly sexual connotations, she is, in line with Kim Alton Robertson's argument (1996), grotesquely transformed through imagery into the feline companion of a man who has lost his wife. However, 'compagnie' takes on other connotations, when he hints on several occasions that he forces her to enter a sexual relationship with him.

As with Mouna in *Moi, l'interdite*, the women in *Le Sari vert* are *animalified* – caught somewhere in-between human and animal – as a way of demeaning them. Devi's female characters suffer at the hands of male protagonists who seek to oppress them by convincing them of their alterity and their animality. Dokter-Dieu calls his wife 'visage de chienne' (30) and claims that following intercourse she has 'une odeur de pelage mouillé' (31).[15] He thus perceives her as an animal because she enjoys copulation, whereas his idea(l) of a woman is passive. In addition, he refers to Kitty and Malika as 'comme des chiennes en manque' (80),[16] thus exacerbating the insult in a manner that plays into heteropatriarchal dictates on femininity, since Kitty has long since lost her husband and Malika is in a lesbian relationship.

Interestingly, however, there are certain instances where Dokter-Dieu places himself in the position of an animal as well: 'je me mis à renifler chaque partie [du sari]' (143).[17] While this may be construed as a slip on his part (if not Devi's) and an unconscious admission of his own part-animality, it is important to note that at no point does he describe himself as a domestic animal but, rather, as one who is superior to the women: 'c'est une espèce de royauté naturelle comme celle du lion ou du tigre' (146).[18] Here, Dokter-Dieu's vision of himself as a lion or a tiger in charge of a pride reveals his perception of his control of the women. In Hindu mythology, half-animal, half-human gods are part of the pantheon and represent the harmony between the two species, and between reason and unreason. Vishnu, the god of preservation, is reincarnated nine times: the first four as animals, the last four as human, while the fifth, Narasimha, is in an in-between state of animal and human, as a lion-man able to defeat a tyrant ruler whose power defies all humans and animals. Narasimha thus represents the blurring of boundaries between human and animal as a necessary condition of the defeat of evil. Dokter-Dieu may not be half-man, half-lion like Narasimha, yet through his own portrayal he nonetheless becomes lion and tiger, symbols of strength and passion in both Hindu and Western mythology. However, the misogynist is also ironically reduced to the status of 'vehicle' for the Hindu goddesses Durga and Kali, who are said to have tamed the passion and impulse represented by these big cats, on which they are portrayed as riding;

an irony, which Dokter-Dieu, with his so-called superior intellectual abilities, fails to perceive (but, again, which Devi surely does not).

God or monster?: blurring moral boundaries

According to Kearney, the other perceived as god is powerful and respected for his feats. Dokter-Dieu is a life-giver by default: as a doctor he is called upon to administer to people's illnesses. As he asserts, God may have given life '[m]ais la guérison et la vie, elles, venaient directement du Dokter' (35).[19] The self-proclaimed Dokter-Dieu is in ascending order, 'un héros' (31), 'un demi-dieu' (38) and 'Dieu' (95), as he likes to remind his audience.[20] However, he is arrogant and despises those who do not conform to his ideals. It is telling, then, that, from his point of view, his patients are also considered to be animals: 'incurables et irrachetables, impossible rédemption des animaux égarés dans un corps humain auquel ils n'auraient pas dû avoir droit' (35).[21] Despite being compared to god and a hero, Dokter-Dieu has no empathy. As such, there is a fundamental difference between appearance and reality in this novel, which complicates the very notion of 'Dieu' and its definition, revealing it to be closely linked to perception.

'Sometimes, in our confusion, we have been known to turn the Other into a monster *and* a God', writes Kearney (2003: 5). Through the figure of the Dokter-Dieu, Devi's text prompts the reader to reconsider accepted definitions and boundaries between animal and human, monster and human, but also between the monster and the god. Dokter-Dieu reflects:

> Celui qu'on appelle monstre est un découvreur de l'âme humaine, celui qu'on appelle monstre est le seul à assumer le courage de son exploration et à le montrer au monde, celui qu'on appelle monstre a la force de sa solitude et l'affranchissement de toute béquille morale, de tout prétexte à ses actes. (181)[22]

However, the question that this raises is whether, by denying the morals associated with society, and therefore civilisation, he is not reverting to primal instincts, *animal* instincts. If the privilege of the human is to think and weigh up the pros and cons of his actions, then the doctor is himself in-between animal and human, and sometimes closer to the animal than to the human. This seems particularly ironic in light of the fact that women are traditionally considered to be inferior to men because of their association with instinct and unreason (Grosz 1994). If the female characters in the text are berated for their impulsiveness and thus equated to animals, it is apparent that Dokter-Dieu, too, is driven by instinct and by unreason. As such, the protagonist's position interrogates the boundaries not only between human and animal but also between male and female, resisting the very gender binary he would want to enforce.

In addition, an elaborate panegyric of monstrosity is given by the doctor, who views the monster as the highest form of human, one who has broken the fetters of decorum and is entirely true to himself. Monsters are cast out of society because society believes that 'un monstre est un monstre, il ne ressent rien, il n'a pas d'émotions, il ne peut pas souffrir, c'est ainsi qu'on le voit' (182).[23] Two things are evident from this: the doctor paints a portrait of himself as a misunderstood individual living in a society where only black and white exist. Yet the actions of someone whose character is so complex will always be misconstrued and, while some may see him as a god, others will perceive only the monster. This is reinforced with the repetition of 'ce dit monstre' (182), emphasising that he might not truly be a monster. And yet the very next sentence, associating himself with the 'dompteur' (182), breaking-in his animals, undermines his own argument: 'le dompteur ne tolère ni négociation avec les chiens ni avec les fauves' (182).[24]

Nevertheless, there are different types of monstrosities: physical monstrosity and moral monstrosity. Dokter-Dieu's monstrosity is grotesque, in the sense of the uncanny grotesque as theorised by Mary Russo (1994: 8), who writes that 'the category of the uncanny grotesque is associated with the life of the psyche, and with the particular "experience" of the "strange" and "criminal" variety'. The doctor may not be physically monstrous, but his mind certainly is, and he crosses the line into evil on a number of occasions with his violent behaviour and thoughts. Christine Rousseau (2009) designates him 'un monstre ordinaire',[25] which might seem a paradox, but her point is that there are monsters all around us and not just those who are physically different.

The human-animal monster/god: towards an ethics of hybridity?

Thus far, the notion of perception has been central to the in-betweenness of both monsters and gods, and, significantly, perception has an important role to play in the moral as well as the physical grotesque. When Mouna's family equates her harelip to animality in *Moi, l'interdite*, it is a form of moral grotesque that leads them to demonise her. Monsters challenge the concept of borders, highlighting the in-between nature of human beings in general. Even more so than traumas from childhood imposed on children or cautions against certain acts, they are both fascinating and forbidding, since

> human existence is always hovering about those frontiers that mark the passage between the same and the other, real and imaginary, known and unknown. Indelibly marked by finitude, the human self has never ceased to ponder its boundaries or to imagine what lies beyond. (Kearney 2003: 230)

Here Kearney underlines the strong links between monstrosity and the human mind, blurring the boundaries between the physical and the mental, while highlighting the different borders that are interrogated and undermined by the very notion of monstrosity, which is again deeply resonant with Devi's work.

In *Moi, l'interdite*, Mouna's own self-awareness and her own reactions to her physical aberrance carry particular significance:

> J'ai contemplé avec horreur mes poils drus, mes griffes, les croûtes qui s'étaient formées sur mes genoux et la paume de mes mains, qui s'étaient endurcies, puis se détachaient périodiquement en libérant une sève blanche, et je ne me suis pas reconnue. Qu'étais-je donc? Quelle créature étais-je devenue? Un bec-de-lièvre m'avait-il excisé de toute humanité? (102)[26]

However, even as a half-animal, half-human, she cannot commit atrocities. Her interrogation of her own transformation is evidence that she is now even more aware of her position, and of her humanity. The question of what precisely the monster consists is highlighted here, for she is kinder to the humans than her family have ever been to her, as the dog reminds her (93). The relationship between physical and moral monstrosity is thus once again foregrounded, as the question is raised: who is more monstrous, Mouna, or her mother who tries to kill her because of her physical deformity? Mouna herself is of the opinion that:

> les gens ont honte de la difformité des autres. Le plus curieux est qu'ils ne voient pas la leur. Pourtant, leur miroir a bien dû leur en parler, à un moment ou à un autre. N'ont-ils jamais vu leurs yeux

torves, leur bouche rancie, leur chair tuméfiée d'envies? [. . .] Tant d'injustice me navre. (56)[27]

The mother, a potential murderer, plotting to kill, is seen as inhumane. On the other hand, Mouna's reason for killing her child is driven by compassion as she does not wish for her child to be rejected by society for being different, just as she was.

Conclusion

In this chapter, I have demonstrated the extent to which name-calling and branding in Devi's *Moi l'interdite* and *Le Sari vert* impact upon the characters who feel both emotionally and physically dislocated. By means of physical difference and by the language used against them, they hover in the space in between animal and human. In her father's mind, Kitty is never a daughter, merely an animal, and his misogynistic treatment of the women in his family leads them, in the end, to treat him as an animal. Mouna was a *mouna* from the outset and her regained humanity is perhaps questionable, since she merely reverts to her previous state, marginal and deformed in society's terms. Devi's novels thus demonstrate an ambivalence towards hybridity: subject to sustained marginalisation, the characters are never at ease in their in-between positions, and yet at the same time hybridity is deemed to be enabling insofar as it undermines identificatory classifications. It is possible that, in showing this ambivalence, the novels themselves display a resistance to classification. They open out enabling perspectives on hybridity without denying its potentially negative impact.

In Devi's work, boundaries between different categories are thus questioned by the characters as well as by the readers. Mouna and Dokter-Dieu in their own ways demonstrate that classifications are futile, that monstrosity is something that changes according to perspective. As a notion, hybridity might be viewed as liberating within the broader context of Mauritian society, insofar as mixing and porosity between communities might pave the way to a more harmonious society, in which the boundaries between different categories of identity on the island are blurred. Interrogating notions of classification, Devi's novels foreground alternative ways of conceiving identity as not necessarily fixed and immutable. This is particularly enabling for women within Mauritian society's patriarchal communities, which have not allowed the trespassing of boundaries for many generations. In these novels, then, hybridity might be read as a way alleviating social pressures on women, and allowing for fluidity of identity, rather than absolute alterity. Ultimately, the undermining of classification through the hybrid positions evoked in these novels calls for acceptance and a new notion of belonging that rests not on otherness, but on an inclusive perception of the multiple differences of identity in Mauritian culture.

Notes

1. In a similar vein, Julia Kristeva, from a psychoanalytical perspective, also speaks of the 'troublante altérité' ('troubling alterity') which we find within us. She further states: 'l'étranger est en nous' ('the stranger is within us') (Kristeva 1989: 284). Unless otherwise indicated, translations from the French are mine.
2. 'the torturer'.
3. 'the female ape'. While we know that it is Mouna's brother who gives her the nickname, we are never given another name for her.
4. 'satan, satan or other'.
5. 'transformed'; 'she wasn't human anymore'.
6. 'only love could have transformed her like this'.
7. 'werewolf'.
8. 'I saw the brownish down wash away in the pond as if a part of my life was leaving in a mysterious moulting. Thus, I had to return to my former appearance'.
9. '"*carnality*" enhances thought processes and lives, whose principles animate their bodies, their sensibilities, their moralities [...] the human mind gives way to the essence of life. "*Humanimality*" is read as affording a supplement of humanity.'
10. 'Gregor Samsa didn't stop being human even though he regressed to the state of beast.'
11. 'might I be an angel?'
12. 'the cat', the former being the feminine form, the latter the masculine; 'the girl chews her tongue, more bovine than ever'.
13. 'Kitty, Kitty, Kitty, come my little cat'.
14. 'like a pet'; 'I need Kitty like you need a pet'.
15. 'bitch-face'; 'smell of wet fur'.
16. 'like bitches in heat'.
17. 'I began to sniff at every part of the sari.'
18. 'it's a sort of natural royalty akin to that of the lion or the tiger'.
19. 'but healing and life would come directly from the Doctor'.
20. 'a hero'; 'a demi-god'; 'God'.
21. 'incurable, unforgivable, the impossible redemption of animals lost in a human body to which they should have had no right'.
22. 'The one we call a monster is the discoverer of the human soul, the one we call a monster is the only one who takes on his exploration with

courage and exhibits it to the world, the one we call a monster is strengthened by his solitude and liberation from any moral crutches, from any justification for his actions'.
23. 'a monster is a monster, he feels nothing, he has no emotions, he cannot suffer, that's how he is perceived'.
24. 'this so-called monster'; 'tamer'; 'the tamer will not tolerate being associated with any dog or beast'.
25. 'an ordinary monster'.
26. 'I contemplated my thick fur with horror, my claws, the crusts formed on my knees and palms, which had hardened and were coming off at intervals accompanied by a white substance, and I didn't recognise myself. What was I? What creature had I become? Had a harelip stripped me of all humanity?'
27. 'people are ashamed of other people's deformities. The curious thing is that they do not see their own. Nevertheless their mirror must have revealed this at some point. Do they not see their skewed eyes, their grim mouths and their envious flesh? [. . .] All this injustice saddens me.'

Chapter Eleven
Embodiment, Environment and the Reinvention of Self in Nina Bouraoui's Life-Writing

HELEN VASSALLO

Introduction: embodiment and environment

Nina Bouraoui was born Yasmina Bouraoui in Rennes on 31 July 1967, to a French mother and an Algerian father. When she was two her family moved to Algiers, where she lived until their return to France due to her mother's ill health when Bouraoui was 14. Her first novel, *La Voyeuse interdite* (1991) (*Forbidden Vision*), won the Prix du Livre Inter, and she was awarded the Prix Renaudot for *Mes mauvaises pensées* (2005) (*My Bad Thoughts*). Bouraoui's work continually engages with the notion of a fractured identity, which can be seen to stem from her own divided heritage, and is frequently concerned with the historical context of Algeria's former colonisation by France. She is commonly considered as a French author rather than a Maghrebi one, and has lived in France all of her adult life. Bouraoui has never returned to Algeria, although it is often alluded to in her oeuvre. Much of her writing is considered as autobiographical or autofictional, due to the preference for a first-person narrator and the similarities between her own life and recurring themes in her work, such as national identity, sexual identity, lesbian desire and the negotiation of subjectivity and identity.

Bouraoui's first autobiographical or semi-autobiographical text *Garçon manqué* (2000) (*Tomboy*) has garnered a solid stream of critical attention (see, for example, Angelo 2010; Fernandes 2005; Jaccomard 2004; Selao 2005; Vassallo 2007). However, her later narratives *Poupée Bella* (2004) (Baby Doll) and *Mes mauvaises pensées*, continuations of the life story first recounted in *Garçon manqué*, and read here as a trilogy, have remained relatively under-examined (see Serrano Mañes 2007; Vassallo 2009 and 2012).[1] The generic categorisation of the narratives is a potentially delicate one: while Bouraoui does not acknowledge the narratives as being autobiographical, the narrators share the name of the author, conforming to Philippe Lejeune's (1975: 32) seminal definition of autobiography as 'un contrat d'identité scellé par le nom propre',[2] and the story of the narrator maps onto that which Bouraoui confirms as being her own. The identity quest of the narrators encompasses both cultural identity (coming from a half-French, half-Algerian background) and sexual identity (negotiating a growing awareness of a lesbian sexuality), and as such exemplifies notions of 'knowing' or 'reclaiming' the self frequently identified in autobiographical writing (see Hewitt 1990: 2).[3] However, the texts offer more than a simple self-story: the engagement with notions of writing as healing and as quest enhances an already valuable contribution to discussions of autobiography and 'scriptotherapy'.[4] It also contributes to discussions of contexts of historical memory (through the evocation of the Algerian War of Independence) and gender and sexuality studies (via the discussion of homosexuality in a society which deems it 'abnormal') (see Bouraoui 2000: 52). The connecting thread between these three *contexts* is the narrative body, from which all three *texts* may be said to stem. Arguing that such texts are not only 'life narratives' (Smith and Watson 2001) but more specifically 'quest narratives' (Frank 1995), this chapter explores Bouraoui's cultural and sexual trajectory via her narrator's literal journeys through France. After a brief consideration of *Garçon manqué* as the first illness or 'quest' narrative, I suggest how *Poupée Bella* might be read beyond a conventional narrative of 'illness' and be considered as one of embodiment (of identity and history). The discussion then moves on to examine *Mes mauvaises pensées* and the more explicit embodiment of memory (historical and personal), before positing this third text as a narrative of reconstruction and reversal rather than 'healing', despite the narrative detailing sessions of psychotherapy (the 'talking cure'). The discussion of the life narrative challenges Lejeune's accepted definition of the autobiographical 'pact', allowing for creativity in the narration of the self, and proposes that the space of the 'quest narrative' allows Bouraoui the possibility to articulate her experience and construct her identity outside the fixed parameters of the autobiographical 'I'. The analysis offers a reading of the texts which suggests that, rather than an explicit 'healing', the narratives represent the possibility of reconciliation and of the reinvention of the self within the space of the text. Finally, the conclusion will turn to Bouraoui's apparently fictional *Appelez-moi par mon prénom* (2008) (Call Me By My First Name) to offer responses to some of the questions raised in the earlier, more recognisably autobiographical works.

My discussion of identity and the relation of self to the environment is framed within a consideration of the theme of illness – both social and emotional – in Bouraoui's life narrative. This is explicit in the last of the three texts, as the narrator recounts sessions with her analyst which conform to an understanding of 'illness', but is also implicit in the preceding two narratives. The narrator-protagonist Nina may not have lived through the Franco-Algerian war herself, but it is an essential part of her family history, since her parents represent a reconciliation between the two sides that was ahead of its time. The stigma attached to this relationship means that it is never overcome by the parents themselves, and is thus passed on to their daughters, taking on the form of guilt, of fault, and of representing a constant reminder of the war. As Nina explains: 'Quelle faute, alors? D'être la fille des amoureux de 1960. De rendre ce temps éternel. Par ma seule présence. Par mon seul regard. Par ma seule voix. Par ma seule identité. De remuer le couteau dans la plaie.' (Bouraoui 2000: 124)[5] Her very existence prolongs (even, as she claims, renders eternal) the time and the suffering of war, and the mixed nationalities of her parents inevitably and perpetually recalls the historical 'wound' and the irreconcilable differences between the two countries, exemplifying Elaine Scarry's (1985: 53) description of the 'dissolution of the boundary between inside and outside' and the 'conflation of private and public'. The 'outside', or the public story and historical context, is thus inseparable from the 'inside', the private experience and the personal story, blurring the boundaries between Nina's body and the historical context. And, thus, the division of the Algerian war of independence is quite literally internalised, with Bouraoui's body carrying both French and Algerian blood. The narrators also incarnate this divide, strengthening the case for a reading of the texts as autobiographical. Nonetheless, hereafter I shall make a distinction between Bouraoui as author and Nina as narrator in all texts, in order to make a similar distinction between the 'life narrative' and autobiography.

Nina's family's troubled past weighs down on her, and is intertwined with wider social and historical issues. She is tortured by her polarised identity, as it leaves her feeling that she belongs nowhere: 'Ici nous ne sommes rien. De mère française. De père algérien. Seuls nos corps rassemblent les terres opposées.' (8)[6] The landscape-related and other-related embodiment, of both the 'terres opposées' and the two family lines uniting in the body, indicate the importance from the outset of social environment in Nina's identity quest. It is, then, precisely Nina's separation between two identities and two countries that approximates this text in particular to the illness narrative. Her claim that 'je suis impuissante. Je reste une étrangère. Je suis *invalide*' (12; added emphasis)[7] evokes the dual meaning of 'invalid' as unwell and not legitimate, her lack of social 'validity' rendering her – at least figuratively speaking – an 'ill' subject, one who is other and 'othered', and who needs to claim subjectivity through the life narrative. Conforming to Arthur Frank's (1995: 115) hypothesis that 'most published illness stories are quest stories', through her writing Bouraoui is searching for a fixed identity, Nina claiming explicitly that 'Je reste entre deux identities [. . .] J'invente un autre monde.' (26)[8] If *Garçon manqué* is a narrative of illness, as I argue elsewhere (Vassallo 2007), then it can also be considered as a 'quest story', in the light of Frank's point above, an attempt to 'invent an other world' through writing. I propose that the same reading can be offered of *Poupée Bella* and *Mes mauvaises pensées*, the literal displacement representing a more nuanced psychological journey towards a sense of self as well as the attempt to carve out a place in the world, and the act of writing being an act of inventing 'an other world'.[9]

Poupée Bella: externalisation and the search for identification

Following on from a quest to establish or assert her cultural and sexual identity in *Garçon manqué*, Bouraoui's second life narrative *Poupée Bella* sees the young adult author/narrator move to a new life in Paris. *Poupée Bella* is written in diary form, as Nina attempts to negotiate a sexual identification, seeking security in an environment in which she is no longer 'other'. The geographical shift that takes place in *Poupée Bella*, and which enables Nina to establish a recognisable sense of self, runs parallel to Frank's (1995: 117) assertion that '[a]s the ill person gradually realizes a sense of purpose, the idea that illness has been a journey emerges'. The sense of purpose is one of a desire for identification, and if Frank writes of the emergence of the idea that illness has been a journey, *Poupée Bella* also offers an example of the reverse: the journey to bring the narrator to Paris has been caused by an 'illness' cast on her in her childhood, which she hopes to reconcile. The quest for the discovery (or *re*covery) of self in *Poupée Bella* thus has its origins in the 'illness' detailed in *Garçon manqué*. The journal form of this narrative distinguishes it from *Garçon manqué*, demonstrating a more evident sense of progression and journey, and representing a self-interrogation that posits *Poupée Bella* firmly within the genre of a quest narrative. As Frank (1995: 117) elaborates,

> [i]f the idea of 'journey' has become a New Age spice sprinkled indiscriminately to season almost any experience, pop psychology could have done worse. The journey may be a fad, but it nevertheless represents a form of reflexive monitoring.

While Frank refers to the phenomenon of the psychological or emotional 'journey', Bouraoui presents in the first instance a literal journey which is both the product and the cause of this 'reflexive monitoring', potentially moving her beyond the 'New Age' or 'pop psychology' accusations levelled at the emotional journey. Indeed, if *Poupée Bella* is read as part of a narrative trilogy, Bouraoui reinvigorates this tired Western phrase through the connection to an Algerian heritage, writing herself instead into the tradition of the novel as a journey to self-understanding.[10]

From the literal displacement stems an emotional journey in *Poupée Bella*: the narrative is not only a quest for identity, but also a quest for love. Now a young woman in Paris, Nina frequents lesbian nightclubs and gay bars in order to find both a community and a special bond. Her search for a sense of self and belonging (Bouraoui 2004: 13) indicates a desire for self-identification, and represents 'un chemin infini vers l'amour' (82).[11] The notion of the 'path' corroborates the idea of a quest, though the fact that it is described as 'infinite' indicates that it will never come to a neat resolution.

Nonetheless, Nina's need to identify herself with a community conforms to Kevin Lynch's (1960: 5) hypothesis that 'a distinctive and legible environment not only offers security, but also heightens the potential depth and intensity of human experience': the security she seeks is a 'legible' environment of identification, and the 'chemin infini vers l'amour' suggests the kind of intensity of human experience alluded to by Lynch. For example, Nina finds a sense of self in the underground lesbian nightclub Le Katmandou, attesting that entering the club is akin finally to inhabiting her own skin, and thus enabling her to find a sense of self through identification with others. Rather than the *environment* being internalised, here it is the narrator herself who decides to enter her own body. Because she has been unable to effect this positive shift between internalisation and externalisation in relation to her nationality or cultural identity, Nina has to find another mode of self-recognition, and this comes through her sexual identity. Asserting her sexuality is only possible in the Western context, evidenced by the juxtaposition of assertions about being in Paris and being lesbian: Paris offers her an identity that relies upon identification, since '[t]rouver sa place dans le cœur d'une fille, c'est enfin trouver sa place dans le monde' (16); 'Je suis à Paris. Je suis en vie. Je suis heureuse [. . .] Je suis une fille qui aime les filles.' (19)[12] The geographical journey is, then, also an emotional journey of the kind described by Frank, an attempt to 'belong' via the ultimate acceptance of unconditional love.

The noise and solidarity of this new Parisian lifestyle eclipses the silence and solitude in which Nina's Algerian childhood was enclosed (Bouraoui 2004: 7 and 2005: 179–80). Thus, in Paris Nina finds a sense of community in the city that allows her a liberation that was unattainable in Algiers, operating *within* the city rather than finding it embodied inside her (Bouraoui 2005: 222). Nina reclaims the cityscape, drawing life from it and reciprocally giving it life through her narrative, describing Western urban living as a lifeline which offers her a place in the world, and inscribing her environment into her text. Nina thus develops a notion of selfhood that is more nuanced than her reclaiming of sexuality via binary gender paradigms in *Garçon manqué*. This comes through a recognition of her own truth, before finally being able to define her identity on her own terms (19), showing that, rather than her body being inscribed with the historical context, she actively inscribes herself into a cultural identity. However, the path towards this sense of belonging is fraught with claims of being 'sick with love' and of going 'mad' with obsession, jealousy or desire – emotions that keep Bouraoui's texts tied to the idea of illness, and that will ensure that her narrator's journey leads her to a psychiatrist's office in her quest to recover herself.

Mes mauvaises pensées: reversing paradigms in pursuit of 'Algeria regained'

The setting for the third in Bouraoui's series of life narratives, *Mes mauvaises pensées*, is a psychiatrist's office. There, Nina navigates memories, experiences and the subconscious in order to understand and redefine herself. This continuation of the emotional journey, corresponding to the kind described by Frank, encompasses a return to her origins. Revisiting in her mind her Algerian homeland, 'un lieu silencieux que je tiens secret' (Bouraoui 2005: 13),[13] Nina gives voice to the silenced cultural identity so paramount in the establishment of her personal one. In so doing, she makes the final steps of her narrative identity quest, negotiating a restricted physical area in order to reach the limitless spaces of her subconscious and her desire. Though the narrative begins with the same desire to ignore the divided cultural identity and to focus instead on relationships and sexuality as in *Poupée Bella*, almost immediately (and against her conscious desire) Nina refers to her fractured cultural identity: 'je vous dis, tout de suite, que je suis de mère française et de père algérien, comme si mes phobies venaient de ce mariage' (18).[14] This indicates the inescapability of her cultural origins and the inevitability of confronting them, and the need to reconcile with both her history and her environment before she can attain any kind of resolution to her 'quest'. From the outset of *Mes mauvaises pensées*, Nina claims to be 'besieged' by memory and history (9), and recognises that, by attempting to come to terms with her heritage, she is engaging with history as well as with her personal story, a history which happens externally, but which is also integrated internally (11).

Mes mauvaises pensées unfolds in real time, in Paris, but constitutes a journey back to Algeria through memory and the subconscious. Unlike the short, staccato or fragmented phrases of *Garçon manqué*, or the diary form (and often similarly brief sentences) of *Poupée*

Bella, Mes mauvaises pensées is not divided into paragraphs, and often the sentences can continue over several pages. This suggests a desire to engage with all that has been silenced, and to find a mode of self-expression via an unrestrained stream-of-consciousness narrative that articulates rather than covers up Nina's cultural complexity. Nina's quest in this narrative is to become 'ma propre fondation, de ma propre pierre' (136),[15] and thus for identity to come from the body rather than being externally imposed or sought via identification. Claiming that she is not 'exiled' but 'uprooted' (18), Nina makes a positive separation with her Algerian homeland, citing Algeria as the locus of her suffering (25) and Paris as the place where she has come to life (222). Algeria is nonetheless an integral part of her, a heritage she can never deny (despite the apparent attempt to do so in *Poupée Bella*): as she explains, 'il y a un lien entre le cœur et la terre' (238).[16] The incorporation of place into selfhood, or the penetration of environment into the body (72), is reflected in the way in which Nina also carries in her body her genealogical history (235) and which is exposed as a wound (50). However, she describes Algeria as the landscape of her childhood, and thus of silence and oppression, and it is in Paris that she is constructing the landscape of her womanhood, or emancipation (220), attempting to liberate herself from an imposed 'fractured identity' and to reconstruct her identity on her own terms. Having previously escaped a judgemental heterosexist and/or misogynist male gaze by living in the shadows, in the lesbian nightclubs of 1990s Paris, and thus attaining a kind of invisibility that Elizabeth Wilson (2001: 93) describes as 'annihilation' and 'a kind of negative freedom', Nina now uses the spaces opened up to her through memory in order to transform this 'annihilation', or denial of alterity, into a 'transparency' (99), or reconciliation thereof.

Continually suggesting that Algeria is incarnated in her, while France is imposed on her, Nina draws a parallel with the colonised land. Her body thus becomes itself a disputed territory, which has to be won or claimed by one side or the other. The war, over in historical terms, is now played out in Nina's body, effectively reversing Scarry's (1985: 81) claim that '[w]ar is relentless in taking for its own interior content the interior content of the wounded and open human body', as the wounded and open human body takes the 'interior content' of the war into itself. Despite Nina's attempts to inscribe herself into a Parisian environment in *Poupée Bella*, Algeria remains embodied in her. However, I propose that the resolution can be found in her claim that 'je suis *dans* Alger, *dans* sa nervure, je suis *dans* le corps d'Alger, je suis *à l'intérieur* de ma tête' (Bouraoui 2005: 216, added emphasis):[17] describing herself as 'inside' the body of Algiers, she dissolves boundaries between inside and outside in a positive way, and collapses fixed ideas of what embodiment represents.

Writing and therapy are the two ways in which Nina attempts to externalise both personal and historical wounds: 'nous sommes une famille éclatée et c'est la raison de ma présence, ici, dans votre cabinet' (81); 'Je ne me suis pas remise de cela, vous savez. L'écriture vient de là [...] l'écriture c'est la terre, c'est l'Algérie retrouvée' (201).[18] Although her claim of not being 'healed' from Algeria, and yet finding some kind of resolution via writing, appears to echo Suzette Henke's (2000: xvi) claim that 'the life-writing project generates a healing narrative', I propose that this analysis would actually, and uncomfortably, place the text in the category of what Frank (1995: 115–19) describes as the 'restitution narrative'. Restitution narratives are a problematic notion for an argument against the pathologising of 'otherness' or identity, as they imply the triumph of medicine, erasing the particularity of the self-story (see Frank 1995: 115). Emphasis shifts from the individual to the medical institution, implying that Bouraoui and her narrators have an 'illness' that can be healed only by a therapist. If the teller of a quest narrative, conversely, 'lives in a world she has traveled beyond' (Frank 1995: 118), then Bouraoui effects, through Nina, a positive reversal of embodiment. Unable to hold Algeria inside her, instead Bouraoui transfers it to the space of her text, travelling beyond the boundaries of cultural stereotype in which she has been imprisoned, and constructing 'Algeria regained' – the object of the quest – through the text.

Conclusion: new horizons in *Appelez-moi par mon prénom*

Claiming that 'ce qui déborde de moi sera, un jour, contenu dans un livre' (Bouraoui 2005: 250),[19] which reiterates both her assertion throughout *Garçon manqué* that writing is a fight for survival, and her claim throughout *Poupée Bella* that love and writing are the same thing, in *Mes mauvaises pensées* Nina externalises in the text what spills out of her body, and this is seen as the possibility for reconciliation. If Nina achieves some kind of exit from her stasis into a new space, it is ultimately the space of her psychiatrist's office, and the 'spilling out' there of what had previously been internalised, which allows her to remember and reconstruct her Algerian past. In all three texts, the author/narrator navigates psychological and/or topographical spaces and places in order to negotiate her personal and historical identity. Nina first attempts to negate her Algerian history via identification, seeking security in a cultural environment in which she is no longer 'other'. However, though Nina seems to *want* to forget (her body is to be a blank canvas, and the only connection that she wants at this point is a sexual one), Algeria returns unfailingly in her narrative: a space which remains un-negotiated, unreconciled, to which it is impossible to return, but which is equally impossible to leave behind.

It is, then, a later work that can perhaps offer the 'new horizons' sought by Bouraoui's narrators, or at least some kind of resolution to the attempts at reterritorialisation evident in the three texts discussed. The subsequent 'fictional' first-person narrative by Bouraoui, *Appelez-moi par mon prénom*, sees a female narrator who is a writer embark on a (heterosexual) relationship with an admirer of her work. Though the less obvious parallels between Bouraoui and her narrator distance this text from those which I have posited as corresponding to certain sub-genres of autobiography, I propose that a reading of *Appelez-moi par mon prénom* can provide a kind of 'epilogue' to this study of *Garçon manqué*, *Poupée Bella* and *Mes mauvaises pensées*, showing how concerns prevalent in these narratives are reconciled to an extent in the later, more fictional work. For example, the narrator's claim that '[j]e montais vers les Champs-Élysées, quartier de mes années d'adolescence lorsque je cherchais quelqu'un qui aurait pu me ressembler' (Bouraoui 2008: 40)[20] can be read as an explicit recognition of *Poupée Bella* (the narrative of the 'années d'adolescence') as a narrative of identification, of searching for someone in whom she could recognise herself. Further reference to the geography of Paris, '[j]e descendais place Saint-Sulpice, désirant traverser la ville qui avait servi de cadre à mes pensées' (62)[21] shows both the importance of the city in the quest for the sense of self and the practice of introspection which is detailed in *Poupée Bella* and *Mes mauvaises pensées*. The subsequent assertion that 'Paris me semblait imprégné de nous deux' (62) has a twofold function.[22] First, it shows the importance of a loving relationship in Bouraoui's narrators' sense of belonging. Secondly, it shows a more definitive reversal of the boundaries between inside and outside indicated by Scarry (1985): the city begins to take on the self, rather than the self taking on the city. Indeed, this notion of reversal is key to my reading of the earlier narratives, and follows on from the development noted in *Mes mauvaises pensées* above. Crucial to this argument is the following reflection: 'Je pensais au silence comme à une défaite. Il fallait baisser nos armes et embrasser *la terre qui nous portait* [. . .] Nous n'étions pas uniquement en vie, *nous étions à l'intérieur de la vie* (Bouraoui 2008 : 112, added emphasis).[23] There is no longer a sense of 'internalising' an environment, the complex embodiment that plagues the earlier narrators. Rather, the land is described as the carrier, with the narrator and her lover embodied in the land, and existing *inside* life, rather than life being battled out inside the narrator.

If the speaking subject of *Appelez-moi par mon prénom* can be read as a continuation of Bouraoui's previous narrators, then a resolution may be found in her claim that '[j]e pensais que l'écriture naissait d'une blessure' (106):[24] the use of the imperfect tense suggests a long period of time in the past – the time, I would suggest, spanned by *Garçon manqué*, *Poupée Bella* and *Mes mauvaises pensées*. Thus, these earlier texts may indeed be narratives of illness and wounding, but they can be read more specifically as 'quest narratives', and Bouraoui's later fictional narrator offers a reversal of the quest, having travelled beyond the earlier restrictive environments by inscribing herself *onto* a landscape rather than embodying it *inside* her. The use of a fictional, heterosexual narrator may appear to offer a problematic 'normative' resolution to an identity quest that stems from a desire to negotiate 'otherness', but I submit that, rather than a reductive return to tropes of sexual 'normativity', this suggests a *lack* of resolution to the illness narrative. If there is any 'definitive' resolution, then it is not a heterosexual one or a fictional one but, rather, a topographical one, offering Bouraoui and her narrators 'new horizons' in both the adopted city and the space of the text. In *Garçon manqué* Nina's identity is 'verrouillée de l'intérieur' (Bouraoui 2000: 63),[25] and it is the perpetual 'unlocking' and externalising of this identity which is so crucial to the ongoing 'never-ending path' of the narrative quest. Thus, from the embodiment of environment comes an externalisation into the text, which leads to an inscription of the self into and onto the environment. This reverses accepted notions of internalisation and externalisation, and the relationship between self and environment, to offer a different perspective as a point along the journey, rather than a destination.

Notes

1. 'Poupée Bella' is a specific brand of French doll popular in the twentieth century. The title thus denotes 'traditional' or conventional notions of artificial femininity.
2. 'An identity contract sealed by the proper name'. Unless otherwise indicated, all translations from the French are mine.
3. The first-person narrative exploration of an alienated self situates Bouraoui within a wider context of francophone women's autobiographical writing: her life-writings can be usefully compared to those of Franco-Algerian author Leïla Sebbar, Algerian writers Malika Mokeddem and Assia Djebar, and *beur* women writers such as Tassadit Imache and Soraya Nini (*beur* is a colloquial term used to signify people of North African origin living in France). In all of these authors' work, issues of gender, history and the imbrication of personal and social contexts are paramount, and all of them engage with questions of alienation, exile and otherness. While Bouraoui cannot be classed as a *beur* writer, or even as an Algerian one (she is, in fact, regularly classed under 'littérature française' (French literature) in French bookstores), her dual heritage locates her firmly within a context of francophone writing, despite not adhering to accepted notions of a politicised 'subaltern' position usually associated with this genre in a postcolonial context. In this volume, see Andrew Asibong's analysis of Marie NDiaye's intervention into racial mixedness.
4. Following Henke 2000: xxii, I understand 'scriptotherapy' as 'the kind of healing made possible through the public inscription of personal testimony'.
5. 'Why am I at fault, then? For being the daughter of the lovers of 1960. For rendering that time eternal. Just by my presence. Just by my voice. Just by my identity. For turning the knife in the wound.'
6. 'Here we are nothing. French mother. Algerian father. Only our bodies unite the opposed lands.'
7. 'I am powerless. I remain an outsider. I am (an) invalid.'
8. 'I remain between two identities [...] I invent an other world.' I make deliberate use of 'an other' rather than 'another', as this is not just about a different world, but also the difference or 'otherness' that the narrator attempts to reconcile.
9. This corresponds to the kind of 'reterritorialisation' associated with francophone women writers of North African origin described in Agar-Mendousse 2006 and Donadey 2001.
10. This exemplifies Mildred Mortimer's (1990: 1) description of 'African reality' as something which reflects 'a history of migrations and

explorations as well as conquest', and thus highlights the North African specificity of Bouraoui's texts despite her frequent categorisation in 'littérature française'.
11 'A never-ending path towards love'.
12 'to find one's place in a girl's heart is to finally find one's place in the world'; 'I am in Paris. I am alive. I am happy [. . .] I am a girl who loves girls.'
13 'A silent place which I keep secret'.
14 'I tell you, straight away, that I have a French mother and an Algerian father, as if all my phobias came from this marriage'.
15 'my own foundation, made of my own stone'.
16 'There is a link between the heart and the land'.
17 I am *in* Algiers, *in* its veins, I am *in* the body of Algiers, I am *inside* my head'.
18 'We are a fragmented family, and that's the reason for my presence, here, in your office'; 'I haven't got over it, you know. That's where writing comes from [. . .] Writing is the land, it's Algeria regained'.
19 'what spills out of me will one day be contained within a book'.
20 'I went up towards the Champs-Elysées, the backdrop to my adolescent years when I was searching for someone who would be like me.'
21 'I got off [the bus] at Place Saint-Sulpice, wanting to cross this city which had been the setting for my thoughts.'
22 'Paris seemed impregnated with the two of us.'
23 'I thought of silence as a defeat. We had to put down our weapons and kiss *the land which carried us* [. . .] We weren't only alive, *we were inside life itself*.
24 'I used to think that writing was born from a wound'.
25 'Locked away from the inside'.

Chapter Twelve
Irreverent Revelations: Women's Confessional Practices of the Extreme Contemporary

BARBARA HAVERCROFT

One of the noteworthy trends in recent French women's writing is the publication of autobiographical and autofictional works which reappropriate, subvert and renew specific features of the confessional genre. In so doing, these writers engage in the practice of textual revelation of intimate, often sexual experiences, developing innovative modes of the confessional in which the subject's endeavour to bare all is no longer an act entirely shrouded in shame or a search for forgiveness or redemption. Authors such as Alina Reyes (*Ma vie douce* (2001) (My Gentle Life)), Catherine Millet (*La Vie sexuelle de Catherine M.* (2001) (*The Sex Life of Catherine M.*)), Annie Ernaux (*Se perdre* (2001) (Losing Oneself)) and Marie Nimier (*La Nouvelle Pornographie* (2002) (The New Pornography)), to name but a few, take a seemingly unmitigated pleasure in revealing sexual acts and fantasies, legitimating the public exposition of female desire and women's sexuality. These irreverent revelations are not exclusively devoted to sexual pleasure, as certain authors choose to narrate more dysphoric or traumatic experiences, such as Christine Angot's ongoing preoccupation with the experience of incest, or Ernaux's narration of abortion (*L'Événement* (2000a) (*Happening*)) and her battle with breast cancer (*L'Usage de la photo* (2005) (The Uses of Photography)). Before going on to examine, as case studies, the reworking of confessional discourse in texts by Angot and Reyes,

I briefly review key concepts and characteristics of the confessional genre, in order, then, to go on to determine how they are adopted and adapted by women authors in the twenty-first century.

Confession: definitions and features

Described by Peter Brooks (1996: 121) as a 'mode' of discourse, 'a crucial kind of self-expression [...] that is supposed to bear a special stamp of sincerity and authenticity and to bear special witness to the truth of the individual personality', confession is characterised by other scholars as a sub-genre of the wider category of autobiography. Hence the inclusion of confession in Sidonie Smith and Julia Watson's *Reading Autobiography* (2001), where they define it as 'an oral or written narrative [...] addressed to an interlocutor who listens, judges, and has the power to absolve' (192). While the double address of the confession was first directed at God and a priest-confessor, since Augustine's *Confessions*, the human reader has replaced the confessor as the recipient of the 'narrative explanation of sinfulness and redemption' (192). Confession traditionally requires what Stephen Spender (1980: 118) terms 'naked truth' and complete sincerity on the part of the narrating subject and typically recounts some sort of error or wrongdoing that has given rise to shame and, until the moment of narrative revelation, the desire to keep this wrongdoing hidden from scrutiny. As Michel Foucault (1976: 83) explains, the confessional speech act is completely bound up with power relations, notably the hierarchy evident in the relationship between the person producing the confession and her interlocutor, who intervenes 'pour juger, punir, pardonner, consoler, réconcilier'.[1] In addition, confessions of sexuality in particular are encouraged in Western cultures since they act as an effective means of surveillance, of policing society and of constructing behavioural norms. According to Biddy Martin (1988: 8–9): '[t]he talk about sex, the obsession with it are part of the operations of power in contemporary society; they make normalization and control possible and invisible'.

For Rita Felski (1989: 87–8), the confession is a subgenre of autobiography that aims at the disclosure of the intimate, personal, and at times traumatic, details of the writer's life. Felski focuses on what she terms the 'feminist confession', which displays two principal features: an emphasis on the relationship between the female author and the female reader, with a concern for communal identity, and, stylistically, a greater use of denotative or referential language than of literary devices or formal experimentation. However, as will be evident in the writings of Angot and Reyes, a lack of literariness need not be a defining feature of confessional discourse penned by women. Felski also delineates two main types of feminist confession: the journal or diary form and the retrospective autobiographical narrative of the author's life, in full or in part. Perhaps the most crucial point Felski makes concerns the possible political import, from a feminist perspective, of the confessional texts she examines, as she wonders if the act of confession 'is a liberating step for women, which uncovers the political dimension of personal experience, confronts the contradictions of existing gender roles, and inspires an important sense of female solidarity', or if it is simply a 'narcissistic soul-searching that uncritically reiterates the "jargon of authenticity" and the ideology of subjectivity-as-truth which feminism should be calling into question' (86). Although these questions certainly merit consideration, they seem to establish a judgment-inducing Manichean binary opposition that does not reflect the nature of certain women's confessional texts that combine elements of both sides of the coin, that is, those exhibiting varying degrees of narcissism, while still packing a political punch. As will become clear, current French women's confessional practices are undoubtedly more complex than Felski's 'either/or' formulation would lead one to believe.

Christine Angot's dysphoric disclosures: incest and paternal phantoms

My focus in this study is on women's confessional discourse that deals with sexual activities, for, as Foucault (1976: 82) has stated, 'depuis la pénitence chrétienne jusqu'à aujourd'hui, le sexe fut matière privilégiée de confession'.[2] One of the most obvious examples of sexual confession in contemporary French women's writing can be found in works by Christine Angot, notably in *L'Inceste* (1999) (Incest), although it is a subject to which she compulsively returns in later works such as *La Peur du lendemain* (2003) [2001] (The Fear of Tomorrow), *Quitter la ville* (2000) (Leaving Town) and *Rendez-vous* (2006). *L'Inceste* could be considered the site of a double confession, in that Angot (or rather her autofictional narrator 'Christine') reveals not merely the episodes of incest with her father, but also the trials and tribulations of a lesbian relationship, to which a good deal of the text is devoted. Citing Kate Millet's *Sita* and Judith Offenbach's *Sonja* as examples, Felski (1989: 118) claims that some feminist confessions feature the detailed narration of a lesbian relationship 'as a political act' in itself, 'a means of breaking the silence which has traditionally denied the existence of relations between women'. However, one might also read the depiction of this relationship as that of a marked desire for fusion, a symbiosis that is often followed by rejection, which Felski has observed in some feminist confessions, and which is demonstrated in Angot's text by Christine's relentless need to speak with her lover Marie-Christine numerous times every day.

Angot's accounts of incest borrow certain elements of confessional discourse, and I show briefly how these are evident in *L'Inceste* before turning to the more recent *Rendez-Vous*. First, *L'Inceste* is a vehicle for the revelation of highly personal thoughts and deeds concerning Christine's life, especially her sex life; one might say that she leaves the private sphere (or the confessional box) to display the most intimate details in the public domain. Secondly, Christine explicitly and repeatedly addresses herself to an interlocutor, be it the reader by the use of the deictic *vous*, or other interlocutors specifically named in the text. According to Irene Gammel (1999: 11), some women authors of confessional texts explicitly 'inscrib[e] their awareness of the role and power of the confessional reader who passes judgment', and Angot is certainly no exception to this practice, as Gill Rye (2010) has shown. Angot even goes so far as to anticipate the reader's reaction – the reader remains ungendered in her text – and is wary of the latter's capacity to judge her in a possibly Manichean manner: '[v]ous, vous public, vous critique [. . .] ne pouvez jamais vous empêcher d'écrire le monde en [. . .] positif-négatif, bon-méchant [. . .] blanc-noir. Moi, je réponds [. . .] Soyez poli' (Angot 1999: 178).[3] Angot's narrating subject evinces an ambivalent attitude toward her reader, as numerous appeals to *vous* indicate. At the beginning of the section of the text in which Christine recounts the story of incest with her father, the sentences are brief and broken, giving voice to a wave of emotion: 'Je déteste à avoir écrire ça. Je vous déteste. Je vous hais [. . .]. Toujours la même chose et tous pareil.' (171)[4] If this passage expresses her hatred of the reader and the wish to establish a conflictual relationship with her or him, other passages indicate the possible desire for a sort of redemption, or at least the reader's acceptance. For example, Christine apologises to the reader for speaking of incest, while pondering the objective of her revelations, or the possible therapeutic effects of her discourse: 'Je suis désolée qu'il faille parler de tout ça. Désolée. Pourquoi j'en parle? [. . .] Ça m'arrache d'en parler.' (169)[5]

This performative gesture of excusing herself, itself a noted feature of confessional discourse, is accompanied by several other discursive traits of the confession, including the revelation of wrongdoing, which is not articulated here in terms of sin as such, but bears the vestiges of it. Although her father clearly initiated the incestuous behaviour, Christine seems to assume partial responsibility for it, as she not only states that she seeks neither to accuse nor excuse her father, but also makes multiple attempts to explain herself and justify her actions, perhaps to assuage her guilt (Angot 1999: 169). There are also frequent instances of self-denigration, where Christine describes herself pejoratively, insulting herself and citing insults she has received from others (for example, 128, 162, 164, 202). It appears that the guilt that should have been borne by the father weighs heavily upon the daughter, who seems to seek a sort of absolution by writing this painful and disjointed narrative, peppered with self-castigating remarks. Further echoes of confessional discourse resound in the construction of a semantic field centred around Christian references, and the onomastic link constructed between 'Christ' and 'Christine', which leads the narrating subject to play with the positions of the confessor, the penitent, the saved and the saviour.[6] Given these multiple confessional indices, it is perhaps not surprising to learn at the end of the text that, upon her father's request, she performs fellatio on him inside a church confessional box (216): it is as if the space of the confessional had in some sense invaded that of her writing, or at least had left its traces within it.

These traces of confessional discourse are but borrowed vestiges, for the generic hybridity of *L'Inceste* prevents it from totally belonging to a particular literary genre or discursive mode: it also bears the marks of autofiction and testimony. Indeed, in *La Peur du lendemain*, Angot denies an affiliation between her writing and the confessional genre. In a rebellious gesture targeting the father of secular confessions, she takes her distance from Rousseau, even if the very evocation of his name might lead one to postulate a possible similarity between their respective scriptural practices: 'Non, pas moi, non, je ne suis pas le nouveau Rousseau. Connais-toi toi-même et je veux faire cette œuvre de parler de moi, qui n'eut jamais d'exemple. Non.' (Angot 2003 [2001]: 13)[7] Despite the disrupted syntax in this passage, one understands that Angot is stating a double refusal: she is simultaneously repudiating the self-knowledge advocated by Socrates and the absolute originality proclaimed by Rousseau in his *Confessions* (1782), he who rejected any previous confessional *exemplum* that could have served him as a model worthy of imitation.

Despite Angot's refusal to acknowledge the confessional features of her writing, they nonetheless resurface in later texts, at times in the context of comments concerning her father. As the narrator avows in *L'Inceste*, 'il m'a marquée' (Angot 1999: 208),[8] and this paternal branding and wounding of the Angotian subject is evident, in *Rendez-vous*, in the account of her relationship with G., a banker. In this autofictional text, a complex series of analepses and prolepses, the narrator Christine recounts her desperate and unrequited love for an actor named Éric Estenoza, while simultaneously revealing intimate details of other past love affairs with different men. While the entire text can be read as an amorous confession, it is the three-month relationship with the banker, instigated by G. and ended by Christine upon meeting Éric, that echoes the incestuous revelations of *L'Inceste*.

Like a malevolent ghost, the father figure is reincarnated in *Rendez-vous* in the guise of the bourgeois banker, who pursues Christine relentlessly, even after she terminates the relationship. The narrator repeatedly underscores the numerous similarities between G. and her father, resorting to the expression 'comme mon père' (Angot 2006: 27, 28)[9] to make the comparison explicit: they were of the same age, social class and milieu; they had similar pretentions to cultural sophistication but were largely materialistic; they were both sadistic, domineering perverts, grimacing at the moment of orgasm (192). So akin are their tastes and temperaments that the narrator employs the third-person plural pronoun *ils* to bind them together in a collective referent, a fitting stylistic reflection of their proximity in her imagination: 'Ils étaient pareils, ils avaient une vulgarité profonde [...] et un rapport tordu à la vérité' (192).[10]

Further resonances of *L'Inceste*'s confessional discourse are evident in the narrator's portrayal of her sexual relationship with the banker, who resorts to the same discourse of seduction as that previously uttered by her father: 'Il me disait qu'il m'admirait, que j'étais extraordinaire, que j'étais une femme inouïe. Le même discours que mon père.' (11)[11] An insidious power struggle begins between G. and the narrator, during which Christine falls increasingly under his controlling, authoritarian influence, becoming incapable of refusing his advances: 'Son regard était un ordre auquel j'allais me plier. Je n'avais éprouvé ça qu'avec mon père, c'était un souvenir qui me ramenait très loin en arrière.' (14)[12] The sexual relationship with G. becomes a repetition of the paternal incestuous scenario of her youth, a return to an unpleasant hierarchical rapport which Christine reluctantly accepts. This return to the status of the suffering victim is expressed in an apt comparison that the narrator uses to describe herself: she is like a fish trapped on the line, the hook in her stomach, just before the fisherman reels in his prey with his fishing rod: '[c'était] comme si j'étais son objet, sa chose, sa victime. Plus le poisson fuyant. Un rapport sado-maso était en train de se nouer.' (15)[13] Elsewhere, the narrator further conflates G. and her father, agreeing to sit on G.'s lap at his request, for refusing to do so, 'ce serait refuser de le mettre en rivalité avec mon père, ce serait protéger la place de mon père' (19).[14] According to this logic of substitution, the narrator fashions a scenario with G. that repeats that experienced with her father, so that G. becomes her father's rival, usurping his place, and thus hopefully banishing his ghost.

If *Rendez-vous* in its entirety can be considered a lengthy confession of amorous adventures, certain sections of the text display overt confessional overtones, such as the letter the narrator writes to G. after his probing question concerning her possible experience of orgasm during the incestuous encounters with her father: 'C'était incroyable d'avoir eu le culot de me demander si je jouissais vite avec mon père.' (19)[15] Shaken and outraged by this question – its effect is likened to a violent blow or slap – the narrator responds in an epistolary confession, cited and embedded in the text, which specifies the reasons for which she committed incest with her father. Once again, the performative gesture of the excuse prevails, as Christine indulges in a discourse of self-justification, repeating the same litany of explanations already uttered in *L'Inceste*: she had never met her father until the age of 14 and had thus been deprived of a father all those childhood years; she shared his predilection for art and intellectual matters; he was the first person in her life with whom she could truly exchange ideas; she repeatedly requested the cessation of the incest, and so on. Faced with the choice between the father's absence or his incestuous presence, she opted, be it for a limited period of time, for the latter: 'Je ne pouvais pas renoncer à tout ce qu'il m'apportait, même si la contrepartie était lourde, mais ça ne me faisait pas jouir' (22).[16] This confessional re-enunciation, in recycling the same discourse of self-justification found elsewhere in Angot's previous texts, accentuates the subject's status as an unhappy victim of male devices and desires.[17]

However, what of more joyous sexual confessions, without the inauspicious shadow of an incestuous father or a domineering banker? French women's confessional discourse of the extreme contemporary is not limited to dysphoric experiences of suffering, as the jubilant, erotic tone of Alina Reyes's diary demonstrates.

Exuberant revelations: the joys of sex in Alina Reyes's *Ma vie douce*

Alina Reyes's voluminous, 400-page journal *Ma vie douce* contains excerpts of her diaries dating from 1979–2000. Divided into nine sections, each of which bears its own title, the text generally corresponds to Felski's first type of confession, as the first six sections follow the familiar diary format of dated entries detailing the author's everyday activities, thoughts and emotions. The final three chapters, however, present a poetic departure from the diary entries, as they contain memories, fantasies and prose poems with little emphasis on recounting the quotidian, thereby experimenting with the habitual generic characteristics of the diary. Given Reyes's celebrity and success as an acclaimed writer of erotic fiction, it is not surprising that she includes details of her sex life and sexual desires, or that she stresses the physical and sensual aspects of life-writing in this autobiographical tome, and for that reason, parts of this text can be considered as a sexual confession.

The nine chapters are preceded by a brief metatextual preface explaining the author's objectives in gathering together these excerpts from her journals, dream diaries and notes (Reyes 2001: 10). This preface also features two canonical traits of the confessional speech act: the invocation of the interlocutor (here, the reader) and a declaration of honesty. The reader is addressed directly, on the very first page of the book, as Reyes recounts a discussion with her editor, who questioned the choice of the adjective 'douce' in the title, given that Reyes's eventful life was rather turbulent and difficult at times. The narrator subsequently speaks directly to the reader, asking her and him: "Lectrice, lecteur, votre vie n'est-elle pas dure aussi? Dure et douce à la fois?" (7)[18] In contrast to Felski's uniquely female reader of feminist confessions, Reyes inscribes both female and male readers – note that the former is named first – but not in a way which would put the female reader under erasure with the masculine plural form *lecteurs*. Reyes then describes the aims of her text and the author–reader relationship:

> Le but de tous ces efforts est moins d'obéir au *connais-toi toi-même* [. . .] que de communiquer avec les autres par un langage supérieur à celui du quotidien. L'écriture établit entre deux personnes, l'auteur et le lecteur, un lien et un échange d'une profondeur qu'on ne peut atteindre dans la 'vraie vie' que par la promiscuité physique. (11; original italics)[19]

What is striking here is not simply the refusal – as in Angot's text – of Socrates' famous dictum and thus a repudiation of self-knowledge as the text's main objective, but also the importance accorded to the egalitarian exchange with the reader, who is not offered the hierarchically superior position of judge in the author–reader relationship. Also noteworthy is the reference to 'promiscuité physique', which is just one of the many components of a lexical field relating to the body, physicality and sexual activities that is developed throughout the text.

A second confessional element that surfaces in the preface is the narrator's stated desire for honesty and authenticity, which harks back to Spender's claim that confession demands 'naked truth'. Reyes seems to respond to this challenge quite literally, as the following remarks indicate: 'Avec *Ma vie douce*, j'ai voulu me montrer nue. La nudité physique est un bonheur très important pour moi. Nue, je me sens mieux, autrement belle, sans souci des canons esthétiques en vigueur' (Reyes 2001: 10).[20] This nudity can be understood in two ways, as referring at once to the sincerity and honesty with which Reyes will recount all matters in her text, be they explicitly related to carnal matters or not, and to the candid revelations of her sensual and sexual life (which may be written in an unclothed state). Further comments in the preface link the concern for authenticity to the possibility of novelistic (*romanesque*) effects of her writing, thus departing from Felski's insistence on the use of purely denotative language in feminist confessions. The journal oscillates in style, at times employing ordinary, denotative language in the description of daily affairs, while elsewhere becoming poetic and literary and, in certain passages, producing a hybrid combination of the two.

The sexual revelations of *Ma vie douce* are largely, but not exclusively, limited to the third and fourth chapters, respectively entitled 'Hommes' ('Men') and 'Cahiers d'une amoureuse' ('Notebooks of a woman in love'). Although not as explicit or as detailed as her erotic fiction – and here, the sizzling encounters with the butcher of *Le Boucher* (1988) (*The Butcher*) and the firemen of *Derrière la porte* (1994) (*Behind Closed Doors*) may spring to mind – the accounts of Reyes's sexual activities are frank and at times humorous. One unnamed lover, for example, is obsessed with the volume and consistency of his semen, leading the diarist to criticise his preoccupation with his production: 'Comme si toute la frénésie sexuelle n'avait eu d'autre but que de voir jaillir de son pénis ces geysers plus ou moins hauts, plus ou moins abondants, plus ou moins spéctaculaires, plus ou moins réussis' (Reyes 2001: 202).[21] The diarist's candour and sensuality are also evident in her poetic description of Jean-Paul, where she uses certain discursive devices to create a veritable ode to her lover's body: 'Sa chair . . . blanche et ferme près des os . . . Ses épaules larges, coque de voilier sous sa nuque bouclée. Sa tête sombre comme ses yeux, son visage taillé ferme et fin, son menton qui pique et son rire qui transperce . . . Sa façon de faire l'amour [. . .] Élan, joie, excès' (211).[22] In this excerpt, the diarist expresses her desire and excitement in incomplete sentences separated by ellipses, creating a panting rhythm that evokes the lovers' breathing. The series of body parts, each of which begins with the possessive adjective 'his', culminates in a ternary group of three nouns that aptly describe the diarist's own unbridled state.[23]

The main thread weaving its way throughout the narration of Reyes's amorous adventures is that of multiple lovers, not in the sense of the group sex so clinically captured in Millet's *La Vie sexuelle de Catherine M.*, but in that of pursuing sexual relations with two or more men at once (not in the same bed). The diarist candidly confesses this overwhelming desire and need for new lovers: 'Je pense aussi beaucoup à Daniel, et un peu à Roland. Je sais bien que, si je vivais avec Florent ou même avec Daniel, je chercherais encore ailleurs d'autres amours, d'autres émois' (226).[24] To describe her urgent need to change lovers frequently, the diarist uses the metaphor of the serpent who sheds its skin: 'Je suis le serpent, et les hommes sont les arbres contre lesquels je me frotte, pour me débarrasser de mon ancienne peau' (226).[25] Although the serpent figure evokes biblical connotations of sin and evil, Reyes considers it as the expression of her need to 'renaître constamment' (226), a process which allows her to become 'plus forte, plus moi-même' (226).[26]

Despite being married with two sons (she would later give birth to two more), the diarist's infidelity, seemingly insatiable sexual appetite and love of sensuality and the flesh do not result in the sense of guilt often expressed in confessional writing: 'Pas trop de sentiment de culpabilité: après tout, je suis tellement sincère avec chacun' (222).[27] Indeed, the guilt she does feel arises not from any moral dilemma relating to satisfying her physical desires as such, but from the hurt she is possibly causing certain people involved in this scenario of multiplicity, such as Henry (her main partner at one point) or Sylvie, Florent's girlfriend. In other words, it is not a question of abandoning the multiple-partner script, but of attempting to mitigate the emotional havoc it is wreaking on others. Eventually, the diarist finds the ideal solution, even if it is but temporary: in a nod to Virginia Woolf, she resolves to obtain a room of her own, 'le moyen d'apaiser [s]a soif énorme d'indépendance et de solitude' (222),[28] a studio in which she can write and entertain the various men at will. Instead of the arduous quest for forgiveness of typical confession, then, *Ma vie douce* is an unabashed performance and expression of female sexuality; the diarist takes 'ownership of [her] erotic body pleasures and self-representations, actively constructing [her] sexual identit[y] in life writing' (Gammel 1999: 11).[29]

Confessional subjectivities

This brief study of Angot's and Reyes's texts illustrates the engagement of certain contemporary French women writers with confessional discourse. Indeed, there is a deliberate play with particular features of the genre in order to manipulate the traditional frames of hierarchy, subjection, guilt and shame, which are inherent in it. While the texts examined here do not necessarily conform to Felski's model of feminist confession, particularly in the sense that they do not deliberately seek to establish a feminist community or to emphasise non-literary language, they do exhibit an interrogation of the construction and identity of the female subject which claims the authority to affirm itself and speak publicly about private, sexual matters while rejecting shame, especially in Reyes's case, a defining trait of traditional confession.[30] Secondly, there is a different representation here of the relationship between women and their bodies. As Sidonie Smith (1993: 11, 16) has shown,

> female identity [traditionally] inheres in women's embodiment as procreator and nurturer [...] [t]o the extent that woman represses the body, erasing her sexual desire and individual identity while embracing encumbering identities in service to family, community, and country, she positions herself as a proper lady who surmounts her negative identification with the body through selflessness.

In Angot's and Reyes's writings, the authors, far from being demure and selfless, audaciously articulate intimate sexual experiences in a public voicing of their sexuality, be it a difficult coming-to-terms with the status of the incest victim in Angot's case, or the unrestrained affirmation of erotic pleasure as a central component of subjectivity in Reyes's journal. In these confessional narratives, the narrators adopt a provocative stance as they redefine the stakes and boundaries of women's sexual self-representations.

Notes

1 'To judge, punish, pardon, console, reconcile'. All translations from French texts are mine.
2 'Since Christian penance until today, sex has been a privileged subject of confession'.
3 'You, you the public, you the critic [...] can never prevent yourself from writing the world in terms of [...] positive-negative, good-bad [...] white-black. Me, I respond [...] Be polite'.
4 'I hate having to write that. I detest you. I hate you [...] Always the same thing and all of you the same.'
5 'I'm sorry that I must speak of all that. Sorry. Why do I speak of this? [...] It pains me to talk about it.'
6 For a more detailed discussion of these and other features of confessional discourse in *L'Inceste*, see Havercroft 2013a, forthcoming. Faerber 2002: 61 also explores Angot's identification with Christ in *L'Inceste*.
7 'No, not me, no, I am not the new Rousseau. Know thyself and I want to make this work speak of me, who has never had any example. No.'
8 'he marked me'.

9   'like my father'.
10 'They were the same, they were profoundly vulgar [. . .] and they had a twisted rapport with the truth'. This same use of *ils* to denote both G. and Christine's father occurs elsewhere in the text (25, 75, 237).
11 'He told me that he admired me, that I was extraordinary, that I was an incredible woman. The same discourse as my father.'
12 'His glance was an order to which I was going to submit. I had only ever experienced this with my father; it was a memory that took me very far back.'
13 '[It was] as if I were his object, his thing, his victim. More, the fleeing fish. A sado-masochistic rapport was beginning.' The narrator employs a similar image of herself as an older man's prey later in the text, comparing herself to a bird caught in a net, when thinking of both G. and her father (192).
14 'it would be to refuse to make him [G.] my father's rival, it would be to protect my father's place'.
15 'It was unbelievable to have had the nerve to ask me if I climaxed quickly with my father.'
16 'I couldn't relinquish everything he gave me, even if it was a big price to pay, but it didn't make me come'.
17 This epistolary confession addressed to *tu* (you), the referent of which is the banker, forms part of the larger confessional narrative (*Rendez-vous* in its entirety) offered to *vous* (you), the readers: in this way, the confessor/receiver of the discourse is doubled.
18 'Reader, isn't your life hard as well? Hard and gentle at the same time?'
19 'The objective of all of these efforts is not so much to obey the [saying] *know thyself* [. . .] as to communicate with others in a language superior to the quotidian. Writing establishes between two people, the author and the reader, a link and an exchange of a depth that one can only attain in "real life" by physical closeness.'
20 'With *Ma vie douce*, I wanted to show myself naked. Physical nudity is an important source of happiness for me. Nude, I feel better, beautiful in another way, without a care for prevailing aesthetic norms'.
21 'As if all of the sexual frenzy had no other goal but to witness, gushing forth from his penis, those geysers that were more or less high, more or less abundant, more or less spectacular, more or less successful'.
22 'His flesh . . . white and firm on his bones . . . His wide shoulders, sailboat's hull under the curly nape of his neck. His head dark like his eyes, his face carved and fine, his chin that prickles and his laugh that pierces . . . His way of making love [. . .] *Élan*, joy, excess'.
23 The same candour and joyful attitude towards sexuality are found in *La Vérité nue* (2002) (The Naked Truth), which contains three long conversations between Reyes and Stéphane Zagdanski. The interlocutors, each playing the role of the other's confessor, speak of their intimate, sexual experiences in explicit detail.

24 'I also think a lot about Daniel and a bit about Roland. I know that if I lived with Florent or even with Daniel, I would still search elsewhere for other loves, other emotions'.
25 'I am the serpent, and men are the trees against which I rub myself to remove my former skin'.
26 'to be constantly reborn'; 'stronger, more myself'.
27 'Not too great a feeling of guilt: after all, I am so sincere with each one [of them]'.
28 'the means of appeasing [her] enormous thirst for independence and solitude'.
29 Reyes has published several mystical, religious texts, inspired by her recent conversion to Christianity (see Reyes 2008a; 2008b; 2009; 2010a; 2010b). The confessional character of certain of these writings is most obvious in *Lumière dans le temps* (Light in Time), the story of her conversion that bears some affinities to Augustine's *Confessions*, but the multiple lovers of the past have been replaced by one partner, God, the unique object of the narrator's passion. See Havercroft 2013b, forthcoming.
30 On shame in confession, see Tambling 1990: 70 and Taylor 2009: 8.

Chapter Thirteen
Contamination Anxiety in Annie Ernaux's Twenty-First-Century Texts

SIMON KEMP

Is Annie Ernaux an anxious narrator? The term has been linked to her writing before, notably by Jennifer Willging in her 2007 monograph, *Telling Anxiety*. Willging's exploration of 'anxious narration' in Ernaux focuses on the twenty-year gap between Ernaux's first fictionalised account of her childhood and parents and the inclusion into this picture of the incident of domestic violence between them, of which the first account is given in *La Honte* (1997a) (*Shame*). The anxiety that is my subject here, though, has less in common with the post-traumatic shame evoked by Willging, than it has with the concern to exercise control over the reader's interpretation. Ernaux's insistence that her depiction of the self be understood by the reader in the manner intended by the writer suggests an anxiety on the author's part about readers' freedom to interpret as they see fit. It is my contention here that Ernaux's twenty-first-century texts show a heightening and concentration of this concern around a single aspect of Ernaux's autobiography: her status as an author.[1]

Ernaux's desire to guide, or perhaps to police, her readers' interpretation of the text is the main theme of Siobhán McIlvanney's 2001 study, *Annie Ernaux: The Return to Origins*. McIlvanney (2001: 94) comments on a pair of Ernaux's earlier texts, *La Place* (1984) (*A Man's Place*) and *Une femme* (1988) (*A Woman's Story*):

> The narrators in both *La Place* and *Une femme*, by their repeated narrative interventions, clearly do view it as essential to justify the particular generic framework they adopt in the works and to

instruct the reader of their writerly intentions in order to aid – or, more bluntly, to manipulate – them in their interpretation of the texts. As I have argued elsewhere, Ernaux's narrator attempts to influence the reader by a variety of means, not least by the existence of such comments in the first place, which flatter the reader by their confessional nature, inducing a sense of intimate dialogic exchange. The narrator may 'share' her literary objectives with the reader, yet the narrative hierarchy remains firmly in place, with the narrator striving to control readerly interpretation of the works.

For McIlvanney, Ernaux's oeuvre as a whole is marked by its metanarrative interventions, as the narrator breaks into her narration to comment explicitly on the objectives behind her writing. Such procedures serve primarily to align reader's interpretations with Ernaux's intentions – in McIlvanney's (2001: 91) view, 'to move beyond the subjective and the personal to the typical' – and discourage any reading 'against the grain', which might, say, focus on what is individual and unique in Ernaux's experience as if reading a confessional memoir.

McIlvanney highlights an important characteristic in Ernaux's style, although it must be conceded that not all of Ernaux's admonitions steer the reader away from the personal. Perhaps her most unequivocal instructions to the reader, from the preface to the published extracts of her private diary, *'Je ne suis pas sortie de ma nuit'* (1997) ('I'm Still In My Night'), declare the very opposite:

> En aucun cas, on ne lira ces pages comme un témoignage objectif sur le 'long séjour' en maison de retraite, encore moins comme une dénonciation (les soignantes étaient, dans leur majorité, d'un dévouement attentif), seulement comme le résidu d'une douleur. (12)[2]

But these lines are guiding readers about the interpretation of texts that were not written with the intention of being read by anyone other than Ernaux herself (as she claims in the preface). Where writing for publication is concerned, it is the general that is emphasised, even more so in the twenty-first-century texts than in those analysed by McIlvanney. In *L'Occupation* (2002) (*The Possession*), for instance, the account of Ernaux's obsessive jealousy over her ex-partner's new lover is given a strikingly impersonal gloss: 'ce n'est plus *mon* désir, *ma* jalousie, qui sont dans ces pages, c'est *du* désir, *de la* jalousie.' (48; italics in the original)[3]

Such interventions divide Ernaux's texts between a narrated self in the autobiographical past and a narrating self in the writing present who exhibits explicit concern about how the reader should interpret the autobiographical content. While the main characteristic of the present narrator is her status as writer, the past protagonist is, if not exactly an everywoman, then a figure designed to emphasise what is typical in Ernaux's experience and may be generalised to a broader group – those who share with Ernaux a class, a sex or a generation, say, or those who have shared with her an experience of intense passion or obsessive jealousy. Lynn Thomas's (1999: 107–39) study of Ernaux's fan mail demonstrates that these groups are well represented among her readers, who often come to identify strongly with the protagonist as a result.

Since the year 2000, Ernaux has published two short *récits*, *L'Événement* (*Happening*) in 2000 and *L'Occupation* in 2002, a second volume of sociological *journal extime* (unprivate diary), *La Vie extérieure* (Life Outside) in 2000, a substantial extract from her private diary, *Se perdre* (Losing Oneself) in 2001, a co-written photography project and memoir of her cancer treatment, *L'Usage de la photo* (The Uses of Photography) in 2005, with Marc Marie, and most recently, the entwined personal and social history of *Les Années* (2008) (The Years). During this period, too, Ernaux has become ever more established as a major voice in French literature, consolidating best-seller status with overdue recognition in French academic criticism (Thumerel 2004, following a 2002 conference on the writer, is one example). Although her subject matter is as firmly autobiographical as ever, her literary life is strictly compartmentalised in her work. Indeed, one of the most striking aspects of narrative form in her texts is the way she makes use of her narratorial persona as the locus of all self-conscious, writerly considerations in the text. In her twenty-first-century texts, this division becomes increasingly explicit. She writes in *Se perdre*: 'Je ne *suis* pas écrivain, j'écris, puis je vis' (299; italics in the original); and in *L'Écriture comme un couteau* (2003) (Writing Like a Knife), the year-long email 'interview' with Frédéric-Yves Jeannet, she tells him: 'Je ne me pense jamais écrivain, juste comme quelqu'un qui écrit.' (19)[4] Writing seems almost to occur in a parallel existence from her lived experience: 'Je vois le temps filer comme, à une échelle plus grande, la vie. L'écriture est juste l'inverse, l'absence de temps.' (Ernaux 2001: 124)[5]

The unified writer-protagonist is missing from Ernaux's writing for publication, but can be seen in her private diaries – written 'sans visée littéraire particulière, simple confident et aide-à-vivre' (Ernaux and Jeannet 2003: 22)[6] – extracts from which have been retrospectively published as companion-pieces to her *récits*. *Se perdre* is filled with the day-to-day activities of the author: Ernaux has dinner with Pascal Quignard, lectures on Alain Robbe-Grillet, watches a monologue performance of *La Place*, goes on book tours, deals with publishers and struggles with *La Honte* (55, 70, 71, 219, 300). None of this material is to be found in the corresponding accounts of this time in *Passion simple* (1991) (*Simple Passion*). The literary life has been expunged from the *récit*, perhaps in part simply because Ernaux did not consider it relevant. But perhaps also because Ernaux wished *Passion simple* to be the account of a *woman* in a passionate love affair, and was uncomfortable with any elements that might turn the text into the account of a *writer* in a passionate love affair. In *Se perdre*, a comment suggests that the idea of such an interpretation displeases her: 'Je ne fais pas l'amour comme un écrivain, c'est-à-dire en me disant que "ça servira" ou avec distance. Je fais l'amour comme si c'était toujours – et pourquoi ne le serait-ce pas – la dernière fois, en simple vivante.' (32)[7]

L'Écriture comme un couteau draws attention to a more dramatic expurgation of writerly aspects from the protagonist's persona. Ernaux published four texts in her mother's lifetime, depicting the mother with often brutal honesty, while exposing intimate details of her own life and sexual history. Ernaux's own writing never mentions how the mother was affected by her daughter's decision to reveal private details of their lives to the general public. While Ernaux's relationship to her mother is one of the most important themes in her work as a whole, it is presented as if entirely unaffected by its public exposure. Only when she is directly questioned on the matter by Jeannet does Ernaux admit otherwise:

> [*Les Armoires vides*] sera lu par la critique comme un roman, par les lecteurs comme un roman autobiographique. Pas comme un roman par mes proches, évidemment. En premier lieu ma mère, qui vivait alors chez moi. Avec beaucoup d'intelligence mais aussi de soumission devant la violence que je lui infligeais – elle a dû souffrir énormément à cause de ce livre – elle a joué le jeu, fait comme si tout était inventé [...] Elle avait souhaité que j'écrive, elle n'avait pas imaginé que ce serait ça, un livre qui n'avait rien à voir avec ce

qu'elle aimait, l'amour – 'la romance' comme elle disait –, et tout avec le réel, avec notre vie, le commerce, avec elle. (27)[8]

Even in the most recent *récits*, Ernaux's status as the most famous autobiographical author in France is often presented as immaterial in her dealings with those who will later appear in her texts. The affair with W. recounted in *L'Occupation* occurs nine years after the publication of *Passion simple*, of which W. must surely have been aware, but the book's effect on her subsequent relationships is unexplored. When W. refuses to describe or give the name of his new lover, Ernaux (2002: 29) interprets this as 'une crainte que je ne m'en prenne à elle de façon violente ou retorse, que je fasse un esclandre', rather than a concern for her privacy.[9] Ernaux (2002: 34) recounts her fantasy of telephoning the woman to abuse her verbally, but records no scruples about infringing the woman's privacy through her writing. Aside from a brief footnote to inform us that certain names and places have been changed, there is no discussion in the text of how the book itself, potential and actual, might have had a bearing on the actions of those involved.[10]

Ernaux is not an absolute or systematic writer, and will freely admit when a finished text departs from her more rigorous original intentions, as when, in the preface to the collection of sociological fragments, *Journal du dehors* (1993) (*Exteriors*), she tells the reader: 'j'ai mis de moi-même beaucoup plus que prévu dans ces textes' (9).[11] Thus, it comes as no surprise to find that the division of personas into writing narrator and experiencing protagonist is not hermetic, and there are moments of slippage, which are often telling in themselves. There is, for instance, the moment when the protagonist of *L'Usage de la photo* is accused by Marc Marie, 'tu n'as eu un cancer que pour l'écrire' (76), and a similar incident in *Passion simple* where S. tells her: 'tu n'écriras pas un livre sur moi' (76).[12] In these instances, the protagonist is clearly presented as a writer. They are notable for their rarity, however, and it is interesting that each provides the opportunity for the narrating persona, in reflecting upon them, to reinforce the writing/experiencing division. The narrator of *Passion simple* claims she has done as her lover asked: *Passion simple* is not a book about him, as it is a book about passion itself. The narrator of *L'Usage de la photo* uses Marie's comment to argue that she does not wait for life to provide her with subjects for writing. The element of defensiveness in both these claims points to the anxiety that motivates them.

Perhaps most interesting, though, is an instance of *L'Usage de la photo* where the experience is unavoidably contaminated by the writing project that will result from it. Marie and Ernaux began taking the photos that chronicled their love affair before *L'Usage de la photo* was conceived. Once they begin writing, the situation changes:

> Nous continuons les prises de vue [. . .] Mais il me semble que nous ne regardons plus de la même façon le spectacle que nous découvrons, qu'il n'y a plus cette douleur qui nous poussait à fixer la scène. Photographier n'est plus le *dernier* geste. Il appartient à notre entreprise d'écriture. Une forme d'innocence est perdue. (171; italics in the original)[13]

It is unclear whether the final published version contains any of these contaminated photos, but it seems likely that it did not.

Ernaux's work in the twenty-first century is dominated by one text, the magisterial *Les Années* of 2008. The book has developed over the course of the decade – its writing interrupted by Ernaux's cancer treatment early in the new century – and stands apart from everything else she has published in this period through its length and complexity, and through the critical acclaim and best-seller status it has received. At first glance, it appears to stand as an exception to this tendency to separate writer from protagonist. Uniquely among Ernaux's autobiographical texts, it lacks a present-tense authorial commentary; just as uniquely, it recounts the processes of its own inspiration, development and production as they occur within the chronology of Ernaux's life story. And, yet, despite this narrative, *Les Années* represents the most dramatic and wide-ranging suppression of the author's writerly self to be found anywhere in her work.

Ernaux inserts at intervals into her socio-historical narrative the creative decisions which will lead to the writing of *Les Années*, marking, for instance, the moment at which the premise of the book becomes fixed:

> Ce que ce monde a imprimé en elle et ses contemporains, elle s'en servira pour reconstituer un temps commun, celui qui a glissé d'il y a si longtemps à aujourd'hui – pour, en retrouvant la mémoire de la mémoire collective dans une mémoire individuelle, rendre la dimension vécue de l'Histoire. (239)[14]

In the same way, each aspect of the book's development, from choice of tense and pronouns to the selection of subject matter, is recounted within the narrative itself, not as the thoughts of the narrator as she writes, but as the ideas of the protagonist, Ernaux's former self from around the 1980s (when the idea first arises) to the present. Like the quotation above, the descriptions of the aims and choices of the project are very much of a kind with the authorial commentaries of her other texts: only the use of tense and the choice of the third person distinguishes them. They would seem to fit McIlvanney's view of Ernaux's writing as attempting to guide or manipulate the reader's interpretation of the text. Yet what prevents *Les Années* from being a long-delayed reintegration of the writing persona into the experiencing persona is the expurgation of Ernaux's entire career as a published writer from the text.

The story of Ernaux's life recounted in *Les Années* contains several of the episodes that form the heart of other texts, such as the domestic violence of *La Honte*, the obsessive jealousy of *L'Occupation*, or the breast cancer of *L'Usage de la photo* (58, 234, 235). At no point does she signal that these events became published *récits*, or acknowledge that she has discussed them previously. She writes of Bernard Pivot as one of the faces familiar to her from her TV viewing, without mentioning that he was also familiar to her in person, due to her various appearances on his *Apostrophes* show (132). Her early, unpublished writings *are* accorded a mention: 'Elle a commencé un roman où les images du passé, du présent, les rêves nocturnes et l'imaginaire de l'avenir alternent à l'intérieur d'un "je" qui est le double décollé d'elle-même.' (89)[15] Her diary writing is also referred to, and quoted from (88). Once it is a matter of writing for publication, however, absolute silence descends. Throughout her adult life she presents herself as an educator, focusing on her teaching career in detail, and allowing it to appear her sole occupation. She writes of herself in 1974, the year when her first novel was published: 'Le soir venu, on avait l'impression de n'avoir rien fait, sinon de vagues cours à des classes énervées.' (127)[16] School scenes enable her to include the younger generation in the text, and comment on its changing mores. One classroom scene, an account of a video recording of Ernaux speaking to lycée students, has the protagonist answering personal questions about her life in a manner that would seem more plausible if she were there in the capacity of a visiting author than a teacher (155–7); the situation is not explained. In the early 1990s, when she reaches the height of her fame with the popular and controversial *Passion simple*, she sums up her day-to-day life thus: 'En dehors de ses obligations de travail, cours et copies, son temps est consacré à la gestion de ses goûts personnels et de ses désirs, lecture, films, téléphone, correspondance et aventures amoureuses.' (175)[17] Only when the premise of *Les Années* comes to her does the protagonist finally allow herself to be seen as a writer. It is striking that the project's gestation appears as if it has only personal, rather than literary antecedents: Ernaux recounts how in the 1990s she remembers moments of her past 'dans ses insomnies', and feels the desire to 'réunir ces multiples images d'elle, séparées, désordonnées, par le fil d'un récit, celui de son existence.' (178–9)[18] When the time comes to write, the preparations are recounted as follows:

> L'an prochain, elle sera à la retraite. Elle jette déjà des cours, des notes sur des livres et des ouvrages qui lui ont servi à les préparer, se dépouillant de ce qui a été l'emballage de sa vie, comme pour faire place nette à son projet d'écrire, n'ayant plus aucun motif à invoquer pour le repousser. (205)[19]

Ernaux presents herself as leaving behind her life as a teacher to become a writer, as if *Les Années* were her first writing project, rather than her fifteenth.

Why should Ernaux's narrator display this anxiety about contaminating the persona of the experiencing protagonist with the traits of the narrating author? The answer lies in her desire to generalise the protagonist's experience to that of her readers and the social groups to which she belongs. Ernaux describes her writing on several occasions as an objective study, calling it sociology, history or ethnology. In the outward-looking texts she attempts to suppress the personal, labelling *Les Années* an 'autobiographie impersonelle' (240), for instance, and in texts which look inward to her emotional experiences, the collective is still emphasised over the individual: 'Je me demande si je n'écris pas pour savoir si les autres n'ont pas fait ou ressenti des choses identiques, sinon, pour qu'ils trouvent normal de les ressentir.' (Ernaux 1991: 65)[20] The persona of Ernaux's past life is presented as 'l'objet du récit et de l'analyse' conducted by the narrator (Ernaux and Jeannet 2003: 151).[21] This critical distance is essential to her work, as she explains to Jeannet:

> Il y a la même *objectivation*, la même mise à distance, qu'il s'agisse de faits psychiques dont je suis, j'ai été, le siège, ou de faits socio-historiques. Et, dès *Les Armoires vides*, mon premier livre, je ne

dissocie pas intime et social [...] Quand j'écris, tout est chose, matière devant moi, extériorité, que ce soit mes sentiments, mon corps, mes pensées ou le comportement des gens dans le RER. Dans *L'Événement*, le sexe traversé par le sonde, les eaux et le sang, tout ce qu'on range dans l'intime, est là, de façon nue, mais qui renvoie à la loi d'alors, aux discours, au monde social en général.

Existe-t-il un intime à partir du moment où le lecteur, la lectrice, ont le sentiment qu'ils se lisent eux-mêmes dans un texte? (152–3; italics in the original)[22]

This attitude is clearly shown in *Les Années*, which goes as far as to remove the first person singular from the text, in order to merge the protagonist with the others of her generation whose changing habits and attitudes she shared. In place of the *je* comes a constantly shifting *on* or *nous*, which stands in turn for each of the groups in which she has a stake: she offers herself as an example of an intellectual, a socialist, a consumer, a French citizen, a working-class child and a middle-class adult; she presents herself as a daughter, a parent, a lover, a wife and a divorcee, and as a woman. In the commentaries on personal photographs that appear at intervals as markers of passing time, the third person and an external perspective maintain the impression of objectivity, even as the photographs come up to date with the writer's present self in the final pages. In an interview on the book's publication, she detailed her aim of making use of the private and personal as a means to attain broader truths shared by wider parts of society:

> Avec ce livre, en particulier, j'ai voulu créer une fusion. J'ai utilisé le 'on', le 'nous', le 'elle' comme une forme collective, impersonnelle. Sans pour autant me passer de l'intime. Habituellement, le 'je' de la première personne est le signe de l'autobiographie. Mais il est également un moyen de dire le monde qui est autour. À condition qu'il ne s'agisse pas d'autobiographies bêtement centrées sur soi, bien sûr! Moi, j'ai fait l'inverse. Grâce aux photos qui ont permis ces arrêts sur mémoire. Grâce à l'utilisation de mon journal, de mes notes et de souvenirs personnels. Toutes ces écritures différentes m'ont permis de dire à la fois l'intime, l'historique, le changement des choses de la vie, de la mémoire. C'est un livre sur le temps et la mémoire. (Ferniot and Delaroche 2008)[23]

Ernaux's writing stance at times appears less that of the autobiographer than the biographer: a carefully researched, objective and critical study of a stranger's life. The distance she puts between herself as a writer and the protagonist of the text allows the gap to narrow between protagonist and reader, who is likely to share some of the protagonist's life experiences and group identities. An integrated author-protagonist would be a less universal figure, less open to readers' recognition and identification. Worse still, the sociological, historical and psychological evidence that the text lays before its readers would become suspect. Ernaux's divided persona suggests an anxiety on her part that readers might interpret her life experience cynically, that they might be tempted to accuse her of living out these experiences in the second degree, with an eye to later publication. It is not that Ernaux rejects her status as a writer: rather, writing for her is the *medium* for the transmission of authentic life experience, and it cannot be allowed to become the message.

Ernaux's twenty-first-century texts show a clear increase in contamination anxiety from the narrating persona, and a more radical purging of writerly attributes from the experiencing persona. This purging is at its most dramatic in *Les Années*, where the presentation of the self is so selective as occasionally to be disingenuous – a difficult stance for a writer who seems to place so high a price on sincerity. It is possible that, at this point in her career, Ernaux's prominent status in French society as a celebrated feminist, writer and autobiographer has become such an important aspect of her own identity, and of others' interactions with her, that it threatens to derail her project. What this anxiety suggests is that her very success in connecting with her readership, through the social groups and life experiences she holds in common with them, ironically risks damaging this connection, as literature begins to dominate life.

Notes

1 In this volume, Shirley Jordan discusses Ernaux's anxiety about losing autobiographical autonomy through her use of the visual. In contrast, see also Anna Kemp's chapter on the all-powerful author in the work of Amélie Nothomb.
2 'Under no circumstances are these pages to be read as objective testimony on the "long stay" in a retirement home, less still as a denunciation (the carers were, on the whole, dedicated and attentive), only as the remnants of sorrow.' Unless otherwise indicated, all translations from the French are mine.
3 'it is no longer *my* desire, *my* jealousy, which is to be found in these pages, it is simply *desire*, simply *jealousy*.'
4 'A writer is not what I *am*; I write, then I live'; 'I never think of myself as a writer, just as someone who writes.'

5   'I see time flying by, as, on a larger scale, does life. Writing is the exact opposite, the absence of time.'
6   'with no particular literary aim, simply as something to confide in and to help in life'.
7   'I don't make love as a writer, telling myself, "I'll be able to use that", or distancing myself. I make love every time as if it were the last – and why wouldn't it be? – simply as a living being.'
8   '[*Cleaned Out*] was read by the critics as a novel, as an autobiographical novel by the readers. Not as a novel by my family, obviously. Particularly my mother, who lived with me at the time. With great intelligence, but also submission to the violence I was inflicting on her – she must have suffered terribly because of that book – she played the game, pretended it was all made up [. . .] She had wanted me to write, she had never imagined it would be that, a book that had nothing to do with what she liked, love – "romance" as she would say – and everything to do with reality, with our life, the shop, with her.'
9   'a fear that I will get at her in a violent or underhand way, that I might make a scene'.
10 Privacy issues in French autofiction have led to several major literary scandals in recent years. Serge Doubrovsky was accused of contributing to his wife's suicide through his representation of her in Doubrovsky 1989; Michel Houellebecq's mother, published Ceccaldi 2008 as a refutation of what she saw as an unflattering portrait of her in Houllebecq 1998; more recently, Christine Angot was twice accused by Élise Bidoit of invasion of privacy, after the latter claimed to recognise herself and her children in Angot 2008 and 2011.
11 'I put much more of myself into these texts than I had intended'.
12 'You only got cancer so you could write about it'; 'you won't write a book about me'.
13 'We carry on taking pictures [. . .] But it seems to me that we are no longer looking at the spectacle we discover in the same way, that there is no longer this pain that pushes us to fix the scene. Taking the photo is no longer the *final* act. It is a part of our writing project. A kind of innocence has been lost.'
14 'She will make use of what this world has imprinted on her and on her contemporaries to reconstruct a common time, the time which slipped from so long ago until today, in order to recreate, in rediscovering the memory of collective memory in an individual memory, the lived dimension of history.'
15 'She began a novel in which images from the past and present, her dreams and her imagined future take their turn within a first person that is the detached double of herself.'
16 'By evening, you had the impression of having done nothing, apart from giving vague lessons to classes of irritated students.'
17 'Outside of her work obligations, lessons and marking, her time is devoted to managing her personal tastes and desires, reading, films, letters and love affairs.'

18 'while lying awake at night'; 'to reunite these multiple, separate, disordered images of herself with the thread of a story, the story of her existence.'
19 'The following year she will be retired. She is already throwing away her lessons, the notes about books and the texts she's used to plan them, getting rid of what has been the wrapping of her life, as if to make room for her writing project, no longer having any excuse to draw on to postpone it further.'
20 'impersonal autobiography'; 'I wonder whether I'm writing to see if others have done or felt the same things, or if not, so that they might consider it normal to feel such things.'
21 'the object of the narrative and of the analysis'.
22 'There is the same *objectivising* process, the same distancing, whether it's a matter of the mental facts for which I am, or I was, the locus, or of socio-historical facts. And right from *Cleaned Out*, my first book, I have not distinguished between the private and the social. When I write, everything is substance, matter in front of me, exteriority, whether it be my feelings, my body, my thoughts, or the behaviour of people on the commuter train. In *Happening*, the probe in the vagina, the waters and the blood, everything that is considered private is there, exposed, but reflecting the laws of the time, the way people talked, society in general. Is anything private from the moment that the readers, male or female, feel they are reading about themselves in a text?'
23 'With this book in particular, I wanted to create a fusion. I used "one", "we" and "she" as a collective, impersonal form. Without for all that dispensing with the private. Usually the first-person "I" is the sign of autobiography. But it can also be a way to recount the world around you. As long as we're not talking about autobiographies stupidly focused on oneself, of course! I did the opposite. Thanks to the photos which allowed me these pauses on a memory. Thanks to the use of my diary, my notes and personal memories. All these different writings allowed me to recount the private, the historical, the changes in matters of life, or memory, all at the same time. It's a book about time and memory.'

Part Four
Experiments, Interfaces, Aesthetics

Chapter Fourteen
Experience and Experiment in the Work of Marie Darrieussecq

HELENA CHADDERTON

Marie Darrieussecq has firmly established herself as one of France's leading young writers, producing fifteen full-length works between 1996 and 2012, and demonstrating an erudite interest in time, memory and the subconscious, love, death, familial relationships and female identity. Born in Bayonne in 1969, Darrieussecq found fame and best-seller status in 1996 while aged only 27, with the publication of her first novel, *Truismes* (*Pig Tales*), which sold over a million copies worldwide and was translated into forty languages, a feat which had not been achieved by a French author since Marguerite Duras and *L'Amant* (*The Lover*) in 1984 (Valéry 1999: 67). Since then Darrieussecq has produced an eclectic mix of novels, autobiography, autofiction, short stories, a translation of Ovid's *Tristrium* and *Ex Ponto* letters, a play, a treatise on literary plagiarism, a children's book and a number of texts to accompany artists' work. She has expressed a desire to reinvigorate the French novel, declaring in an interview for *L'Humanité*: 'En tant qu'écrivain, je donne un grand coup de pied dans le château de cubes et j'essaie de le reconstruire différemment' (Nicolas 2001: 22).[1] Certainly Darrieussecq's ambivalent literary reputation suggests she may have achieved this. Critics have commented on her ability simultaneously to embrace and subvert traditional elements of storytelling such as character, plot and setting.[2] Catherine Rodgers (2009a: 105) describes her as a writer of 'l'entre-deux'.[3] Despite commercial and media success, the author has stated her desire to avoid populism

(Sauvage 1999: 65) and to write novels that demand a brave and participating reader (Terrasse 2003: 262).

It is Darrieussecq's dual appeal as an author concerned with capturing the essence of lived experience, and her metatextual exploration of the textual processes required to do this, which is of interest here. Darrieussecq treats human events and relationships, preoccupied with a textual expression of individual emotion and sensation. Fulfilling a trend apparent in French women's writing since the 1970s, to seek to write the unnarratable, her interest is in experiences which are not codified by language, or in which everyday expressions become redundant. In *Naissance des fantômes* (1999) [1998] (*My Phantom Husband*), the protagonist's husband's disappearance is: 'entièrement nouveau, sans syntaxe et sans contenu, informe' (Darrieussecq 1999: 49).[4] Darrieussecq proclaimed with regard to *Bref séjour chez les vivants* (2001) (*Brief Stay with the Living*): 'Cette famille n'est capable d'aborder ce deuil que par bribes, par souvenirs refoulés, en deçà du langage. Donc, la narration est impossible' (Nicolas 2001: 22).[5] In *Tom est mort* (*Tom is Dead*), the protagonist asks 'Quelle est la langue de la mort de Tom?' (Darrieussecq 2007: 42-3)[6] As such, Darrieussecq's protagonists make innovative use of language, and sometimes writing, to express their singular experience (Lambeth 2006: 807-9). As Shirley Jordan (2002: 153) has noted: 'The ultimate interest for the reader of her works [. . .] [lies] in the moments of intense identification provoked by the astonishingly original outcomes of her resolve to say the unsayable.' Darrieussecq often disassociates language from the pre-established, referential meanings that distance it from lived emotion and sensation. Instead, she concentrates on the poetic function, highlighting patterns of rhythm and sound, exploiting the graphic surface of the text, and making use of narrative strategies that allow her to embody her subjects and their experiences. Yet Darrieussecq's texts can also be read as metatextual commentaries on the process of reading and the complex relationship between text and 'reality'. Her techniques call into question the representative relationship between language and the external world. She uses strategies that both highlight and subvert the artificiality of established conventions in the construction of words, sentences and text in order to suggest the active role of linguistic and textual features in the process of meaning creation. In this way, the representative possibilities of language are challenged and the location of meaning is questioned. This duality – the desire to find an expression for experience, and the simultaneous problematisation of that expression – recalls and rejuvenates the separation and interaction between Roland Barthes's (1973) *texte de plaisir* and his *texte de jouissance*,[7] which in turn suggests the multiple reading pleasures of Darrieussecq's novels.

Barthes's concentration on the ambiguities of language in literature leads him to distinguish between the *texte de plaisir*: sayable, expressable, satisfying and comfortable for the reader; and the *texte de jouissance*: concerned with the impossibility of expressing reality and the unfinished, problematic, plural nature of language:

> Texte de plaisir: celui qui contente, emplit, donne de l'euphorie; celui qui vient de la culture, ne rompt pas avec elle, est lié à une pratique *confortable* de la lecture. Texte de jouissance: celui qui met en état de perte, celui qui déconforte (peut-être jusqu'à un certain ennui), fait vaciller les assises historiques, culturelles, psychologiques, du lecteur, la consistance de ses goûts, de ses valeurs et de ses souvenirs, met en crise son rapport au langage. (Barthes 1973: 25–6; italics in the original)[8]

The *texte de jouissance* 'discomforts' because it reveals the inadequacy of socially agreed language; it refuses to adhere to the indirect and collective nature of discourse. Yet Barthes also demonstrates the crossover of *plaisir* and *jouissance*, the text which attains readability while nonetheless making holes in discourse, simultaneously using and undermining language: 'la narrativité est déconstruite et l'histoire reste cependant lisible' (18).[9] Barthes focuses on the presence of this gap, or tension, between satisfying and problematic processes of reading, and suggests that this is the real *texte de jouissance*: a text that reveals both processes of reading at once (18–19). As Jonathan Culler (1983: 99) puts it: 'Avant-garde techniques, or disruptions of traditional expectations are more pleasurably startling as gaps in a readable discourse'.

Taking Darrieussecq's novels *White* (2003) and *Le Pays* (2005b) (The Country) as case studies, this chapter draws attention to the plural nature of Darrieussecq's texts. It will simultaneously show how her work has the capacity to satisfy the desire of both narrator and reader to find expression for seemingly 'unnarratable' experience, recalling Barthes's *texte de plaisir*, and how her linguistic and textual experiments constantly evoke the unfinished difficulty of expression, creating a problematic text, destabilising the reader's certainties, and recalling Barthes's *texte de jouissance*. In this enactment of both expression of experience and practice of experiment, both processes of reading are heightened, leading to the conclusion that Darrieussecq's work demonstrates the co-existence of *plaisir* and *jouissance*. Furthermore, the 'plaisir' engendered in the reading of Darrieussecq's novels persists, despite, and perhaps due to, her evasion of the use of socially agreed representative codes of language. The chapter focuses on four of Darrieussecq's textual strategies: her concentration on sound, her use of elliptical syntax, aspects of the layout of the texts, and, finally, her choice of narrative voice. In relation to each, I show how Darrieussecq captures the paradox inherent in the language of literature: the inadequacy of language as an instrument of expression and the continued desire to record intensity of experience. First, however, I introduce the novels and define the unnarratable aspects they attempt to express.

Both *White* and *Le Pays* are poetic novels pledging to express identity. Michael Worton (2005) describes *White* as an 'unfinished meditation on space, time, physicality and love', which is in fact an apt description of them both. In both novels, a young female protagonist attempts to understand and, in the case of *Le Pays*, to write, a specific place, and to comprehend her relationship with this place and her position in the world around her. In *White*, Edmée Blanco joins an isolated expedition team in Antarctica for six months in an attempt to escape the disturbing events of her past. The alien emptiness and monotony of Antarctica provide her with the space to ponder her self and her future. In *Le Pays*, the protagonist, Marie Rivière, relocates from Paris to a fictional post-independent Basque country, from where Darrieussecq hails. The text explores the notion of belonging, and sets out to redefine identity, its principal preoccupation being, as Nathalie Crom (2005) declares: 'la question de l'appartenance (à une langue, à une terre, à une nation), sans entretenir la moindre nostalgie pour la vision classique ou traditionnelle de l'enracinement'.[10] Indeed, in *Le Pays*, Darrieussecq directly and continuously addresses issues of local, national and international identity, desire for individuality and rejection of group identity.

Significantly, both the novels' subjects lend themselves to an examination of the nature and function of language, emphasising Darrieussecq's own expressed interest in this (Gaudet 2002: 115; Terrasse 2003: 266). The international environment in which *White* is set, involving characters from all over the world working together and using what Edmée Blanco calls 'leur anglais de contrebande' (Darrieussecq 2003: 171),[11] encourages situations in which use of language is constantly highlighted and questioned. Furthermore, the unfamiliar and extreme surroundings of Antarctica demand a new vocabulary which none of the participants speak: 'Ceux qui . . . y séjourneront . . . parlent entre eux le pidgin anglais international et se contentent de *snow, ice, white*, osent *desert* et *flat*, et dans les moments d'épanchement, *solitude*' (84; italics in the original; see also 17, 29, 33, 35, 71, 161).[12] The protagonist, Edmée, mentions several times the irrelevance and unsuitability of established words to such an inhuman place as Antarctica – 'C'est un endroit auquel les humains ont, de visu, peu attribué de mots' (84) – and Peter Tomson, the technician and Edmée's future lover, lamely declares, 'Il fait si . . . beau dehors' (89), as he struggles for a description which captures the specificity of what he is experiencing.[13] In *Le Pays*, Marie Rivière has returned to the country in which she was born and brought up, whose official language has changed in her absence, and which she does not speak, inevitably raising questions about the politics of language. Similarly to *White*, Marie struggles for words, this time to capture *le pays* and her relationship with it in a way which satisfies her, baldly repeating, 'Elle ne parvenait pas à englober le pays' (Darrieussecq 2005b: 85, 88),[14] recalling Michel Butor's *Mobile* (1962) in its listing of facts and use of poetic images. Thus the subject of difficulty of expression, of representation, is both explicit, as an aspect of the fictional worlds Darrieussecq creates, and implicit, in the writing challenge she sets herself, as we will now see.

Darrieussecq uses innovative strategies in both *White* and *Le Pays* to embody experience: to manifest authentically the otherworldliness and extreme sensations of the Antarctic in the former, and the slippery notion of identity in the latter. J. M. G. Le Clézio, who declared *White* to be 'sans doute le roman le plus inventif de l'année 2003', emphasises the innovative nature of Darrieussecq's choices of language in the novel, and, in particular, notes her emphasis on sound: 'De *White*, je dis voyage, mais non dans un pays, ou dans un temps. Un voyage dans le sens, dans les mots, dans les sons' (Amette 2003).[15] Darrieussecq is renowned for her concentration on sound and, in particular, is infamous for her use of onomatopoeia. Indeed, it seems to be this element of her work, seen to be somehow unnecessary or indulgent, which has infuriated some of her readers.[16] Of all Darrieussecq's texts, onomatopoeia is most liberally employed in *White* and *Le Pays*. The choice of language in *White* is reflective of the intensely physical and unfamiliar surroundings the protagonist finds herself in: 'BLÂM' goes the ship against the waves (Darrieussecq 2003: 16), '*bada-bang!*' and '*crac!*' goes the ice-breaker (38), 'RrRrRrRrRrRrRrRrRrRrRrRrRrRrRrRr' goes the motor of the heating system as Peter Tomson forces it into life, the striking typography expressing his panic (48). *Le Pays*, focusing on the elements which make us what we are, and thus mindful of the seven senses, also makes use of a profusion of onomatopoeia. In relation to the hologram of Marie Rivière's dead grandmother, the direct attempt to convey sound suggests the poignancy of the attempt to bring Amona back to life: '*Cling clong*, les assiettes, les verres.' (Darrieussecq 2005b: 205)[17] The experience of memory here is evoked by sound, not vision. In the same way, the physicality of Marie's mother's work as a sculptor, compared to the incessantly intellectual craft of Marie Rivière the writer, is captured in the following example: 'Le bronze bougeait, instable, en faisant *dong dong.*' (287)[18] Yet use of onomatopoeia serves two distinct roles in the texts. First, as shown, it allows Darrieussecq to capture perception and sensation as authentically as possible in situations where ordinary language is inadequate. However, in exploring the possibility of a 'natural' link between signified and signifier, the technique also problematises non-onomatopoeic language. In giving sounds the value of semantically established and organised words, Darrieussecq is challenging the limits of linguistic convention and what one is able to express within the limits of the representative linguistic sign.

Secondly, moving from individual words to sentences, in both texts Darrieussecq often refuses classical syntax and employs elliptical and repetitive structures. Yet this syntactic breakdown nonetheless creates meaning, allowing a more visceral, mimetic connection with reality to be made, and embodying both the experience of selfhood in the texts and the incompleteness of discourse. In *Le Pays*, use of anaphora, for example, embodies the relationship between self and place. The word 'Quand', with which paragraphs very frequently open, serves to position the self squarely in a concrete time and place:

> Quand je sors de l'hôpital (31)
> Quand Pablo est devenu fou (104)

Quand la télé locale avait émis ses premiers programmes (132)
Quand ils quittèrent le pays (140)
Quand elle partit à Londres puis à New York (158)[19]

This plethora of concrete indicators of time and place detail the many different experiences captured in *Le Pays*, embodying the self as it moves through space and time, and the multiple situations which combine to construct a sense of self. Similarly, repetition within sentences serves to emphasise the sheer quantity of aspects that make up a country: 'Un pays, ça dispose d'un État. Ça a des traditions frontalières. Ça mène des guerres officielles. Ça contient souvent une nation, parfois plusieurs. Ça forme un paysage. Ça supporte les conflits' (153).[20]

In *White*, the various sensations Edmée experiences on her trip are equally expressed using elliptical and repetitive syntax. For example, the constant disturbing movement of the ice-breaker as she approaches her destination is captured using the repetition of simple terms of location as the vessel rolls, 'poupe . . . proue . . . proue . . . poupe' (Darrieussecq 2003: 15), and of parts of the body as she lies in her moving bunk, 'Tête . . . pieds. Pieds . . . tête' (18).[21] Again, within sentences, key terms are repeated, as in poetry: 'C'est vide d'un vide parfait, vide jusqu'à eux, un vide primal.' (169)[22] The repetition here of 'vide' alerts the reader to its significance and its double meaning in the novel: both of the physical emptiness of the landscape and the state of being without encumbrance, free of the ghosts of the past, which Peter and Edmée, by the end of the novel, have finally reached. In addition to repetition, both texts also manifest a tendency to list. In the context of *Le Pays* and the protagonist's desire to encapsulate the essence of a place, this listing suggests a cramming of information, an overload:

> Lumière soudaine. Air, pesanteur, rupture. (Darrieussecq 2005b: 234)
> C'est le sol de Paris. Calcaire et silice; humus de marronnier, fiente, carburants: ce qui s'use et ce qui pousse, ce qui fait la poussière ici comme ailleurs, graines et pollen, météores, squames, cendre . . . (45)[23]

Yet, again, this search for the appropriate term can equally be seen as a commentary on the language itself and its inability to capture reality. In a sense, each new signifier in fact distances the reader further from the desired signified in its evocation of multiple meanings. Nominal construction is also a recurring feature of Darrieussecq's style, described by Marcel Cressot (1974: 193) as disassociating a phrase from either a cause (in its lack of subject), or a goal (in its lack of object). In both novels, this technique, involving a series of disjointed impressions, captures the immediacy and fragmentation of memory, increasing the poignancy of the protagonists' recollections: 'Dans le bruit d'élytres des arroseuses, le ronron de la climatisation . . . les baies vitrées immenses . . . les ondulations de la chaleur à ras de bitume, à ras de gazon' (Darrieussecq 2003: 134);[24] 'La déréliction douce de la Porte d'Orléans. Le sentiment de la périphérie.' (Darrieussecq 2005b: 50)[25] The lack of analysis in each case allows the phrase its own weight, implying complexity and emotion. These arhytmic, elliptical techniques subvert normal syntactic relations and undermine the norms of grammar in order to enhance the reader's understanding of the experiences. Meaning is viscerally produced: as a result of associative relations between signs rather than socially agreed ones, ensuring a productive rather than representative role for each sentence, and, ultimately, the text.

The third aspect of Darrieussecq's innovative textual strategy to be addressed here is her use of layout. Her employment of unconventional punctuation and pictorial image both add to the embodiment of experience in *White* and *Le Pays*, and bring into question the possibility of textual representation. In terms of punctuation, both novels make use of the slash: 'elles s'étaient déjà rencontrées, à un congrès art et médécine / à un dîner d'anciens lycéens / sur un plateau télévisé' (Darrieussecq 2005b: 163–4).[26] Here, in *Le Pays*, the seemingly rather frivolous expression of multiple-choice options highlights Marie Rivière's mother's socialite existence and the narrator's own nonchalance towards it. In the following instance in *White*, the choppy punctuation captures Edmée's inexpert use of binoculars and the slashes embody the physical action of the sudden flashes of focus on different things in her field of vision: 'Noir mer / tache rouge (géranium) / noir mer / gris zigzagant du ciel / – ah: le paroi blanche.' (Darrieussecq 2003: 28)[27] Much like use of shifters, the reader's dependence on textual context, in order to understand the different effects of the slash in the novels, emphasises the importance of textual relations to the creation of meaning, dismissing language's role as representative tool. In the same way, dashes are employed in order to express the monotony of the American suburbia Edmée has left behind in *White*: 'une–maison–une–pelouse–une–maison–une–pelouse.' (120)[28] Similarly, Edmée's physical state is described using mathematical symbols, recalling a scientific formula:

> Depuis toutes ces semaines le corps d'Edmée c'était: gorge sèche + transpiration + extrémités froides + muscles toniques (grattage quotidien de la parabole) + conjonctivite (opthalmie légère) + amenorrhea conjoncturelle (perte des repères jour/nuit). (137)[29]

The punctuation here suggests the physicality of the protagonists' existence in Antarctica and their dependence on an understanding of science for survival. At the same time, the unusual punctuation – the slashes and the dashes – suggest that conventional linguistic code is insufficient and questions the utility of its representative qualities to expression.

Furthermore, in *Le Pays* Darrieussecq bypasses the linguistic sign by making use of pictorial images to present the protagonists' pre-linguistic thoughts. Marie Rivière graphically depicts the chart with which she learned to write at school (Darrieussecq 2005b: 25; see Figure 14.1). Not only her non-linguistic thought process, but also her childhood lack of writing skills, are highlighted by lack of phonetic text. Similarly, she draws the split of the Transfrontalière road linking the main towns of the Basque coast (98; see Figure 14.2). These reflections and memories are more easily represented pictorially than linguistically, thus allowing the reader better to experience the protagonist's life. The use of diagrams allows Darrieussecq to present, to manifest experience, instead of describing it via language. Yet they also directly replace language and thus emphasise that language has failed. While the relationship between the socially approved linguistic sign and referent does not allow for either free association or direct presentation, an image avoids this formulaic link and thus images which replace text not only suggest the insufficiency of text, but also open it up to multiple meanings and interpretations.

Finally, the choice of narrative voice in the novels, while bringing the reader ever closer to the protagonists' experiences, equally draws attention to the difficulty of their expression. In *Le Pays*, fragmentation of identity is expressed through the creation of referential instability. Darrieussecq makes use of both standard and bold type to express Marie Rivière's thought process, each representing a distinct voice and contributing to a sense of the difficulty of

munauté brute, la nuée du sans-moi... Les hirondelles sur les fils, à l'automne. Et les portées d'hirondelles à la maternelle, pour apprendre à écrire

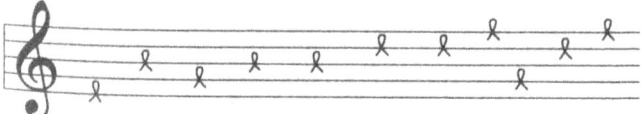

pour apprendre qu'on a un pouce opposable et tenir un crayon... Assez. Molécules lâchées dans la nuit, où tout renvoie toujours à tout. Dormir. Quand sa grand-mère

Figure 14.1 'Learning to write', Marie Darrieussecq, *Le Pays* (2005). By kind permission of P.O.L.

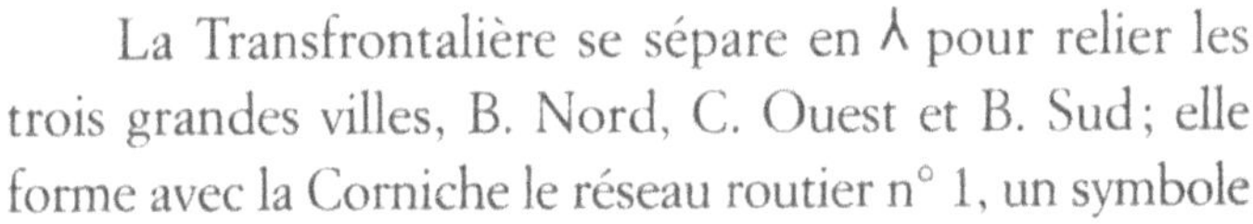

La Transfrontalière se sépare en Λ pour relier les trois grandes villes, B. Nord, C. Ouest et B. Sud; elle forme avec la Corniche le réseau routier n° 1, un symbole

Figure 14.2 'La Transfrontalière', Marie Darrieussecq, *Le Pays* (2005). By kind permission of P.O.L.

presenting a unified self. First- and third-person pronouns are also measuredly and alternately employed, sometimes commenting on or resuming the previous section, sometimes changing the subject entirely.[30] In addition, the narrator at times includes a *Je scindé* (split 'I'), 'J/e', an effect the protagonist compares to disappearance of, or escape from, her 'official' identity: 'Le psychologique et l'étatique, le privé et le familial avaient disparu.' (13; see also 11 and 42)[31] In *White*, referential instability is also created, this time by the constantly changing multiple viewpoints, as the novel is narrated alternately by Edmée, Peter and the chorus of ghosts which surround them, representing their previous lives and painful memories. The ghosts also embody social cliché, filling Peter's head with doubt about his relationship with Edmée: '"*Cette femme est trop bien pour toi*" [. . .] "*ça ne marchera jamais!*"' (Darrieussecq 2003: 164; italics in the original).[32] It is the protagonists' challenge to get rid of the ghosts, to overcome their difficult memories and find their own voices, a recurring concept in Darrieussecq's work, and linked to the struggle for authentic means of expression. In both texts, then, identity struggle is manifested in the dialogic multivocality and lack of a coordinated narrative voice. Additionally, on a metatextual level, this strategy again suggests the need for experimentation in the expression of complex experience. Furthermore, this refusal of an authoritative, unified narrator calls into question the existence of an independent and detached source of meaning, again emphasising the production of meaning through multiple elements of the text itself.

In each of the narrative techniques discussed, the representative and socially agreed role of language is replaced by the visceral connection of 'embodiment', in which the signifier does not function as a referent to a pre-established signified; rather, the signifier itself embodies lived experience. Darrieussecq allows us to see the layers of the text; she reveals the materiality of language, and carries out a 'critique du signifiant' (Barthes 1973: 27).[33] This refusal of social code recalls the inadequacy and discomfort of Barthes's *jouissance*. Yet Darrieussecq concurrently succeeds in manifesting physical otherness, memory and sensation in *White* and fragmented and shifting identity in *Le Pays*, recalling Barthes's 'dicible' (36)[34] and the satisfaction of the *texte de plaisir*. Barthes's distinction was not about texts, but about processes of reading. In the pages of Darrieussecq's novels the reader finds both satisfaction and frustration; an attempt mimetically to record emotion and experience and an attempt to dispute metatextually the possibility of doing this; Darrieussecq performs both the insufficiency of social discourse and the necessity of some form of language to the expression of the totality of individual experience. Thus Darrieussecq's work demonstrates the crossover of *plaisir* and *jouissance*. Furthermore, her work highlights Barthes's insistence that the real *texte de jouissance* is one that reveals both processes of reading at once. Indeed, the gap or the tension, and, by extension, the coexistence, described in Barthes's work, between satisfying and problematic processes of reading, is apparent in *White* and *Le Pays*. Furthermore, although Darrieussecq sidesteps social code in the expression of authentic emotion and sensation, the pleasures of her texts are still multiple. In this way, Darrieussecq's novels rejuvenate Barthes's concepts, with language always in crisis but still producing *plaisir*. The experimental self-awareness of Darrieussecq's novels does not prevent their more accessible experiential pleasures. Indeed, her capacity to unite experience and experiment, and *plaisir* and *jouissance* in the reader, contributes to the breaking down of barriers between 'accessible' and 'challenging' reading.

Notes

1. 'As a writer, I'm kicking over the tower of bricks and trying to reconstruct it differently'. All translations are my own unless otherwise specified.
2. See Jordan 2005: 65; Fiemeyer 2002; Burnside 2001; Kemp 2008: 434; Rodgers 2009b: 30; Rye 2009b: 31.
3. 'the in-between'.
4. 'entirely new, without syntax or content, unformed'.
5. 'This family is only capable of talking about this tragedy in bits, in repressed memories, beyond language. Therefore narration is impossible'.
6. 'What is the language of Tom's death?'
7. Translated as 'text of pleasure' and 'text of bliss' by Richard Miller (Barthes 1975).
8. 'Text of pleasure: the text that contents, fills, grants euphoria; the text that comes from culture and does not break with it, is linked to a *comfortable* practice of reading. Text of bliss: the text that imposes a state of loss, the text that discomforts (perhaps to the point of a certain boredom), unsettles the reader's historical, cultural, psychological assumptions, the consistency of his tastes, values, memories, brings to a crisis his relation with language' (Barthes 1975: 14; italics in the original).
9. 'narrativity is dismantled yet the story is still readable' (9).
10. 'the question of belonging (to a language, a land, nation), without showing the slightest nostalgia for the classical or traditional vision of roots'.
11. 'their international pidgin' (Darrieussecq 2005a: 132).
12. '. . . those who will stay here . . . will speak international pidgin English and will content themselves with *snow, ice* and *white*, or hazard a *desert* or *flat*, or when effusive *solitude*.' (61; italics in the original)
13. 'This is a place to which visiting humans have given very few names.' (61); 'It is so . . . so beautiful outside' (65).
14. 'She couldn't encompass the whole country.'
15. 'without a doubt the most inventive novel of 2003'; 'Of *White*, I say journey, but not in a country, or in time. A journey in meaning, in words, in sounds'.
16. An example of some of the vociferous attacks on her by members of the reading public: 'Marie Darrieussecq, l'inénarrable auteur du Bébé! La pasionaria des Pampers! La spécialiste mondiale des onomatopées ridicules! La reine du Brr, du Pshit, du Blblblblo et du Flouip!

Normale Sup rencontre la crèche municipale du sixième! Hervé Guibert meets Playskool!' (*http://vipere-litteraire.over-blog.com/article-27230160.html*) ('Marie Darrieussecq, the priceless author of *Le Bébé*! The ardent champion of Pampers! The world specialist in ridiculous onomatopoeia! The queen of Brr, Pshit, Blblblblo and Flouip! Oxbridge/Normale Sup meets the state nursery school of the sixth arrondissement! Hervé Guibert meets Playschool!'). See also Liger 2005, who talks of '[les] onomatopées superflues' ('[the] superfluous onomatopoeia').

17   '*Cling clong*, the plates and glasses.'
18   'The bronze moved around, unstable, going *dong dong*.'
19   'When'; 'When I come out of hospital'; 'When Pablo went mad'; 'When local TV had broadcast its first programmes'; 'When they left the country'; 'When she went to London then to New York'.
20   'A country, it has a State. It has border traditions. It wages official wars. It often contains a nation, sometimes several. It forms countryside. It endures conflict'.
21   'poop... prow... prow... poop' (Darrieussecq 2005a: 6); 'Head... feet. Feet... head' (8).
22   'It is a perfect nothingness of nothing.' [*sic*] (131)
23   'Sudden light. Air, gravity, rupture.' 'It's the earth of Paris. Chalk and silica; chestnut mulch, droppings, fuel: what is worn down and what grows, what makes up the dust here as elsewhere, seeds and pollen, meteors, squama, ash...'
24   'Through the noise of the sprinklers, the purr of the air conditioning ... the huge bay windows ... the waves of heat across the tarmac and the grass...' (Darrieussecq 2005a: 103).
25   'The gentle dereliction of the Porte d'Orléans. The sense of periphery.'
26   'they had already met, at an art and medicine conference / at a former students' dinner / on a TV set'.
27   'Black sea / red blotch (geranium) / black sea / grey zigzags in the sky / and there: the white wall.' (Darrieussecq 2005a: 17)
28   'house–lawn–house–lawn.' (91)
29   'For weeks now, Edmée's body has been: dry throat + perspiration + cold extremities + hardened muscles (the daily scraping of the satellite dish) + conjunctivitis (slight ophthalmia) + contextual amenorrhoea (loss of day/night references).' (105)
30   See Rye 2009b: 33, for a fuller exploration of the dual narrative voice in *Le Pays*.
31   'The psychological and the non-governmental, the private and the familial had disappeared.'
32   '"That woman is too good for you!" ... "It will never work out!"' (Darrieussecq 2005a: 127)
33   'criticism of the signifier' (Barthes 1975: 15).
34   '[what] can be expressed in words' (Barthes 1975: 21).

Chapter Fifteen
Interfaces: Verbal/Visual Experiment in New Women's Writing in French

SHIRLEY JORDAN

The period of creativity explored in this book is characterised by pronounced fascination with the visual image in all its categories and manifestations and by enthusiasm for refashioning writing practices around, or alongside, visual material. A special issue of *Yale French Studies* entitled *Writing and the Image Today* contends that we are witnessing the emergence of 'a new kind of hybrid textuality' which privileges intermediality and implies 'the waning autonomy of any one medium' (Baetens and Blatt 2008: 3). While this phenomenon is, of course, not confined to women's cultural production, it is to female-authored verbal/visual narratives and their various strategies that this chapter turns its attention. The range of experiment is excitingly wide in terms of subject matter, category of text, type of image and word/image distribution and writers as diverse as Annie Ernaux, Catherine Cusset, Leïla Sebbar, Catherine Millet, Marie NDiaye, Chloé Delaume, Marie Desplechin and Pierette Fleutiaux have recently opened their writing to the visual.[1] The area calls out for more extensive analysis than it has yet received.[2] This modest contribution to debate explores visual/verbal interfacing in two autobiographical projects, concentrating on the unsettling ways in which, as openings are made for the visual, the production and reception of narrative are restructured. First, a broad outline of my area of study is needed.

The visual swell

Factors which have fostered the recent visual swell, or 'swerve' (Harrow 2010: 256), in literature include contemporary culture's generalised shift towards visual media; a deepening of interest in popular cultural forms such as the comic strip and the graphic novel; and intensifying fascination with photography, associated with the medium's dual transition from 'art moyen' (Bourdieu 1965) (middlebrow art) to recognised high-art form, and from analogue to digital technology. Other stimuli include the technologies that generate experimental installation or web-based visual/verbal mixes such as those explored by Sophie Calle or Chloé Delaume.[3] Critical too is the readiness of mainstream as well as newer, specialist publishers to commission hybrid works. Verbal/visual-friendly publishers now include not only established operations such as Actes Sud, but new ventures such as Les Éditions du Chemin de Fer, begun in 2004, which is dedicated to experimental collaborations between writers and illustrators.[4] There have emerged new verbal/visual adventures such as Mercure de France's 'Traits et portraits' ('Traits and Portraits') series launched by Colette Fellous in 2004, which focuses on self-portraits and includes Marie NDiaye's *Autoportrait en vert* (2005) (Self-Portrait in Green) and Catherine Cusset's *New York: journal d'un cycle* (2010) (New York: Cycle Diary). Finally, a readiness to engage with visual material is also newly in evidence in mainstream literary publishers, as exemplified by the works on which this chapter will settle, Annie Ernaux's and Marc Marie's *L'Usage de la photo* (2005) (The Uses of Photography) and Sigolène Prébois's *Version live* (2010) (Live Version). The first, a cancer narrative constructed around a cluster of domestic photographs, was published by Gallimard; the second, a graphic response to bereavement, was published by P.O.L.

The communicative potential of the visual/verbal interface lends itself to a wide spectrum of subject matter. Essays collected in *Writing and the Image Today* show how writers have 'mobilized the visual as a conduit for sustained consideration of [...] national identity, ethics, aesthetics, globalization, race, terrorism, the family, class, politics [and] the reshaping of new individual and collective subjectivities' (Baetens and Blatt 2008: 2). Essays in Harrow's *New Ekphrastic Poetics* argue that visual/verbal hybrids are fruitfully engaged in interrogating postcolonial identities and relationships, especially as they explore hierarchies between word and image. My own contention regarding verbal/visual experimentation among women writers is that these writers are producing hybrids in order to communicate with fresh impact, often within ongoing autobiographical projects, on a range of critical issues: intimate relationships; the drama of reproduction; displacement and transcultural longing; illness and ageing; bereavement; gender differences and so forth. I am especially interested here in those hybrids which deal with dark matter: those which harness the visual as a partial solution to the challenge of expressing trauma, loss, grief, pain, rejection, or identity disturbance. I am curious to explore how visual images can tap into interstitial and affectively slippery matter, thickening the significance of a work by providing openings for such matter to coalesce and become operative. What is important in my own take on the visual is not the question of hierarchy between word and image but what Catherine Poisson (2007) has productively called the 'friction' between them; not the problem of illustration, but of inflammation. Further, as the visual becomes overwhelmingly pervasive and as innovations in the technologies of image reproduction and transmission romp ahead, it seems increasingly important that works organised around the verbal/visual interface bring us to question what it means to look and position us so that we are brought to consider the ways in which our perceptions are increasingly entangled with visual images. In different ways, both the works I now move on to analyse fulfil this function.

The instances of verbal/visual interface chosen for analysis here involve photography (Ernaux and Marie) and graphic art (Prébois). Both provide highly original ways of dealing with the dark material that is a key part of contemporary women's writing; both concern illness and loss. Other reasons for drawing them together include the density and dominance of their visual material; the ways in which they confront us with the *shock* of seeing; and their harnessing of visual images for a function which we might theorise as reparative, or more specifically as palliative. Both are works of mourning in progress and both resort conspicuously to visual images as a strategy for dealing with the pain of actual or anticipated loss. In temporal terms, both are confined by the onset of a life-threatening illness and its resolution – in *L'Usage de la photo*, through cure; in *Version live*, through death. Both raise acutely the issue of how verbal/visual mixes resituate us as readers. What kinds of questions do these new interfaces bring us to ask? What kinds of distinctive new contact spaces do they inject into the reading process? What kinds of productive complication do they give rise to as they knot us differently into their textual fabric? How do they position us as they ask us to reflect on their author's private fear, suffering and grief?

Reading Ernaux's photographs

Articles on Ernaux's and Marie's phototext have sought to provide readings of the peculiar photographs which structure it and of its thematic interest in photography. It is generally acknowledged that the images of garments hastily abandoned on the floor in Ernaux's home as she and Marie began to make love create a new, especially difficult textual space. Critics have focused on Ernaux's resort to photography as a solution to a particular life-writing problem, on the work's central tension between Eros and Thanatos, and on the ontology of photography (specifically analogue photography, frequently linked theoretically to loss, disappearance and death) as an appropriate framework given Ernaux's cancer.[5] *L'Usage de la photo* is indeed a specific kind of autothanatography, one that intensifies Nancy K. Miller's (1994: 12) contention that all life-writing contends with non-existence and is, for that reason, autothanatographical. These distinctively 'belated' photographs anticipate the moment when the subject's death will make of her, to quote Susanna Egan (1999: 212) who has written on terminal illness and autothanatography, 'an object entirely exposed to being read, entirely dependent on its reader for constructions of meaning'. In her subsequent work, *Les Années* (2008) (The Years), Ernaux indeed seems increasingly haunted by the fear of losing autobiographical autonomy, a fear that she begins intensively to address in the visual/verbal interface of *L'Usage de la photo*. In some respects these works are companions, in tight dialogue with each other despite their differences: both experiment with new ways not only of seizing experience but of relinquishing control over it; both dramatically intensify Ernaux's habit of worrying at photographic images and processes (from pre-digital photography in *L'Usage de la photo* to digital photography in the latter stages of *Les Années*); and between them they pursue a broad, troubled meditation on what it means to live within and understand ourselves through a culture of visual saturation.[6]

The fascination exercised by *L'Usage de la photo* stems from its hybridity (it is at once life-writing and photographic exhibition);

from the eroticised and excessively intimate nature of its photographs; from its overwhelming emphasis on the seductiveness of visual images; and from its sustained interrogation of how we make use and sense of them. Casting psychoanalytic light upon visual encounters in her exploration of sexuality in the field of vision, Jacqueline Rose (1986: 224) remarks upon moments wherein 'the pleasure of looking tips over into the register of excess', as when a child first sees or imagines sex. Such jolting acts of viewing turn the spectator back upon her self to revisit the fundamental relationships that she sustains with others. Borrowing Rose's idea, one might argue that visual scenes in *L'Usage de la photo* confront us with just such tipping points. Not that they lay bare the passion of lovemaking; instead, the remnants they display are cold and forlorn. Unexpected images of a quite *differently* overwhelming intimacy, they constitute disturbing puzzles drawing us to ask what it is that we are seeing and provoking fresh interrogations about photographs and looking. The scopophilic (and haptic) pleasures generated as we visually sift through Ernaux's effects are troubled by the sheer excess of questions posed by the text's visual component. These photographs set us intellectual exercises, which give them a generic value beyond their very particular value within Ernaux's narrative of illness and erotic drive.

Abruptly confronted with Ernaux's kitchen, study or hallway (see Figure 15.1), what questions are we brought to ask? Here are just some: what is at stake for Ernaux in these interfaces? How are *we* at stake? What is *our* role in the verbal/visual contract? Why this whiff of violence/violation? Are we investigating a crime (following Susan Sontag (1978), Ernaux and Marie link photographic enigma to the puzzles set by crime scenes)? Are there victims? Are we *committing* a crime in terms of propriety? Are the images then a comment on *us*? And if these abandoned clothes belong to us all, what do they tell us about who we are, what fascinates us and what we have prompted? Perhaps they offer compact enactments of the *extime* (unprivate), of its combination of the intimate and the alien and of all the unresolved problems that its extreme instances entail.

Ernaux herself, like us and like Marie, worries over the images. She occupies *with* us the verbal/visual interface and asks us to witness her own attempts to make sense of what she sees – through meticulous ekphrastic reworking of each image, through scrutiny of the photographic impulse and through persistent searches for

Figure 15.1 *L'Usage de la photo*, 'a register of excess' (2005), © Annie Ernaux and Marc Marie, reproduced by kind permission.

meaning in what are by any standards recalcitrant scenes. The problems of interpreting visual images and the unavailability of the self within them are thus both foregrounded and there is a multiple puzzling-over. Ernaux peers at her photographs and we witness her peering. We can usefully link the tracery of questions involved here to that prompted by Hal Foster's (2004: 302) consideration of an intimate and uncanny diorama wherein artist Robert Gober is seen peering at a leg – perhaps his own leg – extruding from a gallery wall. To compare this surreal image with Ernaux's photographs is not as long a shot as it might at first seem. As Foster encounters

Gober's encounter with an absent part of himself, he muses as follows:

> Does [Gober] investigate a crime or revisit a deed of his own [...]? Is he the witness of the event? Its perpetrator? Its victim? Or is he somehow all three? Clearly the man is a voyeur; but if the leg is somehow his, is he not an exhibitionist as well? To gaze so seems a little sadistic; yet, if this humiliated leg is somehow his, is he not a little masochistic too? [...] This ambivalence of active and passive roles is performed in visual terms; both an active seeing and a passive being-seen are in play here, and they meet in a reflexive seeing oneself. (Foster 2004: 303)

For the spectator too, Gober's work probes 'the strange sense of [...] revisiting the crime that is oneself' (Foster 2004: 303). Given the enduring presence of shame and of shame's contagion in Ernaux's life-writing (see, for example, Miller 1999), this idea of the crime of the self resonates especially interestingly.

Staying with analogies from installation art to conclude this brief discussion of *L'Usage de la photo*, I want to suggest that we might usefully consider Ernaux's photographs in relation to what Jennifer A. Gonzáles (1995) calls 'autotopography'. Gonzáles's term is generated by the increasing importance attributed in recent years to autobiographical 'evidence' in installations, by creators such as Sophie Calle or Christian Boltanski. Crucially, it refers to spatial sites rather than narratives; sites which display arrangements of personal effects. Like many installation pieces, Ernaux's photographs constitute material landscapes imbued with the self. The connection with the ways in which we are called to make sense of installation art is a useful one which has not yet been remarked upon. What is especially useful in Gonzáles's (1995: 147) concept is that autotopography is frequently conceived of as a 'countersite to all that is readily legible'. As such, it manifests resistance to mass-media images: in spite of its apparent intimacy, its impenetrability provides a strong statement about what is *not* yielded in the visual image. It makes us question what images can tell us about an author and redoubles the emphasis, already foregrounded in certain strands of autofiction, on authorial unavailability. I have argued elsewhere that *L'Usage de la photo* is one of a significant cluster of autobiographical/autofictional phototexts by women (including Camille Laurens, Marie NDiaye and Anne Brochet) which coincidentally harness photography in the middle of our decade, and which use it to deny or to question access to the autobiographical self (Jordan 2011). Significantly, images of the author do not figure in these works. Further, in looking backwards to the kinds of self-knowledge associated with pre-digital photographic technology, and in sitting self-consciously on the cusp of that technology's disappearance, these phototexts mark what is clearly a major turning point in photographic self-narrative practice.

Graphic pain

Sigolène Prébois's *Version live* uses visual material to probe something that can be especially hard to get at: the interfacing within us, at different life stages, of childhood and adult subject positions. As such it is consistent with the pronounced interest among contemporary women's writing in French in child/adult interferences (consider for instance the ways in which writers such as Marie NDiaye or Agnès Desarthe weave into tales for adults traces of story patterns that we associate with children's narratives, or deal with similarly dark matter in works for children as they do in works for grown ups).[7] It is also richly comparable with the verbal/visual venture that recently put artist Gaël Davrinche in collaboration with Béatrix Beck to produce *L'Épouvante l'émerveillement* (2010) (Terror and Wonder), the first-person narrative of a little girl's discovery of the world from the age of two months to 13 years. Beck's 1977 narrative, revitalised in a new publication by Les Éditions du Chemin de Fer, is now newly layered with marks and drawings which interrupt and thicken it and which we might readily analyse as inflammatory (see Figure 15.2)

Prébois's autobiographical narrative concerns the ordinary, yet extraordinarily difficult subject of a mother's illness, the final days of her life and her death, as experienced by a daughter who is responsible for organising her care. The narrative thus belongs within a substantial tradition of works wherein daughters explore illness, death and mourning, through the loss of their mothers (we think of Marguerite Yourcenar, Simone de Beauvoir, Ernaux and more controversially of Sophie Calle's 2007 video installation of her mother's last moments).[8] Prébois's text is a sparse, staccato record of an all too rapid sequence of events, from a telephone call at the onset of her mother's illness to the latter's hospitalisation, the problems surrounding her treatment, her death, the planning of her

10 mois

Dans le noir, comment être sûre que Palmyre est toujours là ? Glisser de mon lit. Ramper. Escalader son lit. S'asseoir sur le visage de mon amour. Mon derrière sur sa bouche, son nez, ses yeux, la voici immobilisée. Elle ne peut plus disparaître. Joie. Sécurité. Modulons des sons pour nous-même et pour plaire à Palmyre, pour resserrer encore les liens entre elle et moi.

1 an

On m'a mis des bottines qui font un bruit agréable. Mes bottines marchent quand mes pieds sont dedans. En me pliant en deux, je vois mes bottines de tout près, je les touche avec mon nez. Elles sont lisses. Je marche partout, je peux aller partout, je peux tout.

15 mois

Pourquoi Palmyre met-elle des aliments dans sa bouche, pas dans la mienne ? Souffrons en silence. Essayons de ne pas crier. J'ouvre grand ma bouche mais Palmyre se trompe

12

Figure 15.2 *L'Épouvante l'émerveillement*, 'inflammatory marking', Béatrix Beck (illustrations by Gaël Davrinche), © Les Éditions du Chemin de fer, 2010.

funeral, the visit to the crematorium and the final distribution of her effects among friends and family.

Like *L'Usage de la photo*, *Version live* seeks a solution through the visual that will permit both distance and proximity. It is remarkably restrained. Each double-page spread consists of a simple line drawing to the right, sometimes incorporating handwritten snatches of speech or thought attributed to protagonists, and to the left a brief ekphrastic text that confirms what the image shows and that maintains the overall informality of register. The most remarkable aspect of this work is the way in which Prébois allows us access to the intimate nub of events through an unusual and difficult device: that of depicting the members of her close family as animals. The author is drawn as a squirrel; her mother, Claire, as a green woodpecker; her brother as a duck-billed platypus. Prébois's drawings present a combination of animals and human beings: for instance, officials involved with the funeral are penguins, while hospital staff, neighbours and more distant relatives are sketched, in Thurberesque idiom, as human forms.

At first glance, Prébois's visual material gives *Version live* the appearance of a slight, perhaps unserious work. What kind of autobiographical record is this when set beside the documentary gravitas of Ernaux's and Marie's black-and-white photographic evidence? Yet this return to tactics of childhood image-making and image-reception subtly raises important questions about experiencing and expressing loss, affording a productive vehicle for conveying complex layers of affect and putting the visual in the persistent service of a fundamental truth: that the death of a parent returns us, in more ways than one, to the child that we remain. The representation of Prébois and her siblings as cuddly animals is, among other things, a projection of the mother's protective attitude towards them, while it accounts at the same time for the surreal strangeness of the distressing activities into which they are abruptly plunged. There are comparisons to be drawn between Prébois's testimonial work and that of Art Spiegelman whose project of mourning and postmemory *Maus* explores the question of how his family experience of the Holocaust might be represented. As Spiegelman narrates his father's story of surviving Auschwitz, he too uses cartoon drawings of mice, cats, pigs, frogs and ladybirds, with similar disjunctive effects (see Hirsch 1997 for an analysis of Spiegelman's *Maus*).

A rapid look at some of the tough material illustrated by Prébois will allow us to see the powerful dichotomy in her drawings between closeness and distancing; a dichotomy which, as in the case of Spiegelman's *Maus*, combines 'an almost obsessive desire for accuracy and, at the same time, clearly abandon[s] (or refigure[s]) that desire by setting the story in an animal fable' (Hirsch 1997: 26). Prébois draws Claire sick, dying and dead. She sketches the moment when she finds Claire confused on her hospital bed, her mouth caked in dried apple compote. She draws the classic mother/daughter mirroring scene which she experiences, in which she not only recognises herself in Claire, but sees, proleptically, her own death (see Figure 15.3) The image brings to mind Ernaux's (1997b: 23, 74) succinct remarks a propos of her own declining mother: 'Impression terrible de dédoublement: je suis moi et elle' and 'elle est le *temps* pour moi. Elle me pousse aussi vers la mort' (italics in the original).[9] Prébois juggles with intractable ethical questions:

Figure 15.3 *Version live*, 'daughter/mother identification', Sigolène Prébois, © P.O.L., 2010.

should Claire be taken to the hospital or cared for at home? Should she be kept alive whatever the costs? At what point is it right to let her die? The wrench of having to take adult decisions when one feels like a child, of seeing a confused parent infantilised, or of being oneself infantilised within the often impersonally authoritative care system, is powerfully conveyed not only via the inherent vulnerability of all Prébois's animal forms, but in particular scenes such as her meeting with the *médecin-chef* (senior consultant) wherein she relives school-day encounters with the headmistress. The complex interplay between child and adult subject positions also includes the dreadful feeling of reversal for which no child is ever prepared: the one that leads Ernaux (1997b: 29) to protest a propos of her own mother: 'Je ne PEUX pas être sa mère.'[10] Many of Prébois's images depict the intensive round of tending – of touching, washing, feeding and dressing – which invert maternal and filial gestures (see Figure 15.4) Significantly, these gestures of tending are supplemented by the gesture of drawing itself: Prébois's rapidly sketched images, attentive, loving and redolent with affect,

Figure 15.4 *Version live*, 'drawing as tending', Sigolène Prébois, © P.O.L., 2010.

also pursue a relationship with the mother, and this too accounts for their emotional charge: drawing is one more way of attending to the dying. It is in this sense that the image-making in *Version live*, just like the image-making in *L'Usage de la photo*, is integral to a process of managing loss and approaching mortality; indeed, both texts are very deliberate in their *mise-en-scène* of image-creation and the vigour with which images are pursued and multiplied certainly suggests that they are instrumental in a vital function. One might wonder too if there is something here concerning a necessary swiftness of gesture in recording painful subject matter: the rapidly taken photograph and the quick sketch both bring to mind Ernaux's (1997b: 88, 38) assertion that on her return from visits to her mother in the care home she writes 'le plus vite possible' and 'en évitant de me laisser aller à l'émotion'.[11]

One of my guiding questions for this chapter is how word/image combinations resituate us as readers. How do we read a work such as *Version live* whose graphic properties contrast so problematically with its disturbing adult narrative? Prébois creates within us a productive unease, a sense of embarrassment at her device and of uncertainty as to its value. She activates, within an adult narrative of mourning, the childhood pleasure of seeing toads career in cars or rabbits run along with pocket watches; she presses a range of interpretative buttons, none of which is allowed to hold sway, and gains her disturbing effect through their disjunctive combination. We are caught between an unwelcome sense that animals are out of place in such a narrative, and a raw reminder of the child who always reads within us. Part of the power of *Version live* is that it opens up pockets of affect related not just to loss, but to childhood spaces of reading, of being read to and of the proximity with a loved adult that reading often entailed when we were learning about life through picture books. Prébois's word/image interface thus provides us with a peculiar contact space: while our adult intellect is busy assessing the author's devices and their troubling effects, the potent affect of the images is nevertheless undiminished: they speak to the layering and complexity of our relationship to a parent without that complexity being teased out in words.

Let us return for one moment to the importance not simply of the image but of image-making; more especially of image-making as palliative. *Version live* is, as its title suggests, performative. As with Ernaux's phototext, illness, loss and grief are worked out *through* images and image-making, which become compelling and compulsive during these painful cycles. In both *Version live* and *L'Usage de la photo* there is a sense of simultaneity: the visual material constitutes a diary; it is not created post-mortem (in Prébois's case) or post-cure (in Ernaux's). Each author seeks to grasp and concretise scenes that have only just been lived through, to provide a 'looking on' for both author and reader. Each uses the visual image to help make sense of painful experiences; in each case it is the visual element that makes articulation possible, and that provides such subtle expression of what is at stake.

Conclusion

To conclude, I should like to raise the idea that women's recent work at the verbal/visual interface has ushered in not only a rich crop of experiments with an extraordinary range of communicative potential, but more fundamentally a new questioning of the visual image's provision of knowledge and of the act of viewing; a questioning which is consistent with and necessary in our increasingly ocular-centric culture. As feminist theory has long told us, acts of viewing have been especially important for women and working with visual images remains a very powerful way of both questioning and reappropriating the gaze. Many verbal/visual adventures, and certainly the two which I have analysed in this chapter, offer powerfully self-referential statements about the contemporary insistence on the visual of which they are a part. As autobiographical explorations, they push *against* the availability of the self in the visual image, radically confounding any notion of the self as accessible and penetrable. Rather than offer the self up to the gaze, they draw the reader into a sophisticated assessment of how we attain knowledge of self and other via visual media. Both eschew the current culture of direct visibility by showing extraordinarily intimate material indirectly and with discretion. In these as in a number of other recent visual/verbal autobiographical works by women, the autobiographical subject evades the gaze, refuses to become its object, and brings us instead to question both the nature of visual evidence and our increasingly imperious demands for something to see.

Notes

1 See Ernaux and Marie 2005; Cusset 2010; NDiaye 2005; and Fleutiaux and Cartier 2006 for autobiographical or autofictional texts which operate at the interface between writing and photography. Works by and about Millet (Millet 2001 and Henric 2001) derive part of their meaning from the interface between the written texts and the numerous erotic photographs taken of the author by her partner and are in this sense companion works. Sebbar 2004 gathers and displays a highly eclectic range of visual material related to the ways in which visible traces of French/Algerian interfaces punctuate the environment of metropolitan France. Certain of Desplechin's fictional narratives (see Desplechin and Lambé 2004 and 2005) are illustrated by line drawings which intriguingly imitate a photographic aesthetic. Delaume's fertile autofictional writing 'laboratory' (see Delaume 2010a) opens out to explore a wide range of image-producing technologies and the interactive narrative opportunities that these provide. Such projects represent just a small sample of the diverse experiments with the verbal/visual interface by women writing in French over the last decade.
2 While a range of articles has appeared on various female-authored verbal/visual projects, there are few more sustained examinations of the field. A good selection of essays on verbal/visual mixes in contemporary women's autobiographical and autofictional work is available in Edwards, Hubbell and Miller 2011 and in Jordan 2013b, forthcoming.
3 See for example Calle's extravagantly multi-layered installation *Prenez soin de vous* (Take Care of Yourself) (the book of the same name (2007) contains a combination of written texts, photographs and DVDs), the interactive version of her book *Vingt ans après* (Twenty Years After) (2001) and Delaume's online game-book, *La Nuit je suis Buffy Summers* (2007) (At Night I am Buffy Summers).
4 See *www.chemindefer.org*.
5 See Cotille-Foley 2008; Delvaux 2006; Fayet 2006; Havercroft 2009; Jordan 2007; and Kawakami 2010.
6 See Arribert-Narce 2011, for an excellent interview with Ernaux which focuses on the shifting emphases in her work on photographs and photography and is the richest source of information to date on this subject. Simon Kemp's chapter in this volume also discusses Ernaux's anxieties as an author.
7 See Connan-Pintado 2009 and Jordan 2004: 185–218.
8 For a study of filial bereavement in Yourcenar, Beauvoir and Ernaux, see Fort 2007. Calle's uncomfortable project, which records her failure to connect with her mother at the precise moment of the latter's death, is entitled *Pas pu saisir la mort* (Not Able to Capture Death) and was shown at the 2007 Venice Biennale; see also Calle 2012.

9 'A terrible impression of doubling: I am me and her.' 'she is *time* for me. She pushes me towards death too.' Translations from the French are mine.
10 'I CANNOT be her mother.'
11 'as quickly as possible'; 'preventing myself from giving in to emotion'.

Chapter Sixteen
'Autofiction + x = ?': Chloé Delaume's Experimental Self-Representations

DEBORAH B. GAENSBAUER

Invited to participate in a 2008 colloquium on the subject of autofiction, Chloé Delaume proposed a title with an Oulipian ring: 'S'écrire mode d'emploi' ('Self-writing a user's manuel').[1] In her address, the then 35-year-old writer, performance artist and musician elaborated:

> J'ai pour seul objectif la variation d'un genre via mode combinatoire [. . .] Faire un objet hybride, qui écrirait le Je en lui faisant incarner le plus de strates possible. Auteur, narrateur directif, personnage, lecteur. Une forme d'autofiction interactive, qui se jouerait sur et à plusieurs niveaux. (Delaume 2010b: 120)[2]

This explanation conveys Delaume's drive to keep contemporary autofiction innovative and inclusive by means of multisensory and multimedia experiments in a broad range of print, musical and electronic media. Product of an interactive media generation disposed, as Serge Tisseron (2005: 274) observes, to co-construction and exteriorisation of elements of personal experiences in order to re-interiorise them in a new form, Delaume is drawn to the unruly but fertile 'clinamen' generated by ungovernable reader or audience response. She often refers to her autofictions as laboratory experiments and has described herself as a researcher who is almost more interested in exploring autofictional methodologies, structures and languages than in the fictions themselves (Guichard 2009b: 23). This chapter examines the progression of Delaume's experiments with constraints and formulas in multimedia formats as she moves her autofictions away from a confrontational practice of literary self-exposure in the style of Christine Angot, who is just one of Delaume's influences, towards a more reader/audience-inclusive approach to reconstructions of identity, and where, among the many 'strata' of the autofictional 'I', the political tier is primary. Tracing the evolution of Delaume's Oulipo-inspired experimentation with forms of autofictional narration from her debut novel, *Les Mouflettes d'Atropos* (2000) (Atropos's Kids), to her recent *Une femme avec personne dedans* (2012) (A Woman with No-One Inside), with particular emphasis on her two most explicitly autobiographical works, *Le Cri du sablier* (2001) (The Cry of the Hourglass) and *Dans ma maison sous terre* (2009a) (In My Underground House), the chapter argues that her work represents a significant contemporary revitalisation of autofictional practice.

'Personnage de fiction'[3]

Delaume's nineteen published works to date (2012) and numerous sound and performance pieces have been considerably influenced by the Oulipo. This would seem to be a natural fit with her work given the central importance to both of memory and autobiography, humour, language play, mathematical formulas and the collaboratively oriented practice of writing under arbitrary constraints, in order to provoke clinamen that stimulate the imagination of writers and their readers by liberating the creative process from habit and the literary canon. Motivating Delaume's self-invention as an autofictional persona is a processing of trauma by means of the invention and full assumption of a liberating fictional identity conceived and experienced in a manner very similar to an Oulipian constraint: 'je réinvente ma personnalité et mon existence par la littérature, en reconstruisant mon identité réelle à partir d'un changement de nom.' (Delaume 2010a: 61)[4] In an early entry on her website, she sketches an autobiographical portrait with characteristic black humour:

> Je m'appelle Chloé Delaume. Je suis un personnage de fiction. J'ai pour principal habitacle un corps féminin daté du 10 mars 1973. Conception franco-libanaise, le néant pour signe particulier. Les locaux étaient insalubres lorsque j'en ai pris possession.[5]

Behind the darkly droll portrait lies a disturbing history of imposed alterations of identity. '[N]ée d'une fiction qui s'est très mal finie' (Delaume 2009a: 69),[6] with nearly each permutation of her experimental identity she confronts anew consequences of a grisly family drama that left her an orphan at the age of 10. Chloé Delaume began life as Nathalie Abdallah. Born in 1973 to a French mother and a Lebanese father, she lived until the age of 5 in civil-war-torn Beirut. Following relocation with her parents to the Paris suburb of Bourg-la-Reine, a racially motivated maternal subterfuge transformed the young Nathalie Abdallah into Nathalie Dalain, daughter no longer of Selim but of Sylvain. For her severely abusive father, she remained an essentially nameless *elle* (she/her) or *l'enfant* (the child). In 1983, in her close presence, the man she was led to believe until adulthood to be her biological father murdered her mother and then shot himself in the head.[7] In *Les Juins ont tous la même peau* (2005) (Junes All Have the Same Skin), an hommage to Boris Vian, she credits her adolescent discovery of his *L'Écume des jours* (1997) [1947] (*Foam of the Daze*) for her realisation that to survive 'sans avoir à palper ces carcasses confites de sang noir dès le réveil [. . .] je devais trouver la formule qui change les jeunes filles dépressives en personnages de fiction propre' (34).[8] In 1999, with the launch of her literary career in *EvidenZ*, a radical literary and philosophical review founded by Mehdi Belhaj Kacem, her first husband, she recreated her identity as an author-narrator-protagonist, taking Chloé from the young heroine who dies of cancer in *L'Écume des jours* and creating Delaume from *L'Arve et l'aume* (1989) [1947], Antonin Artaud's title for his translation of the Humpty Dumpty chapter of Lewis Carroll's *Through the Looking Glass* (1871).[9]

'S'écrire, non pas à nu, mais parfaitement à vif'[10]

Creating a new identity by means of a genre in which the match of author, narrator and protagonist was posited as a key element by a number of autofiction's principal early theorists allows Delaume to seize some control of externally manipulated identities.[11] However, coming to autofiction as her exclusive mode of self-expression at the turn of the century, she adopts the genre, in vogue by then for some two decades, at a time when commercial exploitation and growing critical denigrations of autofiction as an exhibitionist fixation on sexual feats and defeats were taking a toll on its capacity to remain a revolutionary voice for women writers.[12] Delaume's (2010b: 110) response is to declare as her objective: '(s)'écrire, non pas à nu, mais parfaitement à vif'. The statement pays tribute to Vian who, according to the author, had taught her that literature is 'tout le contraire d'une vérité toute nue' (Delaume 2005: 30).[13] It also distinguishes Delaume's focus on formal experimentation with the genre from the legacy of self-writing as a more personally confrontational *mise à nu* (exposure) that has been a primary feature of autobiographical fictions by contemporary French women writers since the publication of Duras's *L'Amant* (1984) (*The Lover*). Variously represented in the writing of Angot, Catherine Cusset, Annie Ernaux and Catherine Millet, among others, for Delaume this legacy is most compellingly portrayed by Angot, whose work is complexly omnipresent in Delaume's fictions, essays, interviews and blogs, both as an authorising model and point of resistance.

In 'S'écrire mode d'emploi', Delaume (2010b: 120) posits a quasi-mathematical formula for her work: 'Autofiction + x = ?'. The unsolvable equation aligns her experiments with the Oulipo. It also makes a caricatural nod to often oedipally charged attempts by some male theorists to mount a definitive critical 'takeover' of a hybrid genre that came into being with Serge Doubrovsky's (2001:10) seminal description of the neologism he created to describe his 1977 novel, *Fils*, as follows: 'Fiction, d'événements et de faits strictement réels; si l'on veut, *autofiction*, d'avoir confié le langage d'une aventure à l'aventure du langage.'[14] It is this definition that Delaume mobilises as the overarching constraint that governs her experiments with self-writing. The 'x' also refers to the menacing genetic heritage that motivates her self-re-creation as a fictional character. She recounts in *Le Cri du sablier* that, from the time she learned about Arabic numbers, she associated mathematics with the language of her abusive father (Delaume 2001: 32). Just as crucially, the unsolvable equation challenges her audiences to participate in the practice of autofiction by bringing their own variables to the equation as a means of resisting being otherwise written by social conventions.

Oulipian constraints in *Les Mouflettes d'Atropos* and *Le Cri du sablier*

Delaume's debut novel, *Les Mouflettes d'Atropos*, much of it drawn from her personal journal, depicts her experience working as a call girl and responds with considerable, if blackly droll, fury to her husband's infidelity.[15] It also makes an initial foray into confronting 'un roman familial putride et affligeant auquel je me refuse' (Delaume 2005: 32).[16] Initial critical response, attentive to the misandry, gritty language and perverted eroticism in this angry autofictional social critique has already assigned the new writer a place in the lineage of Angot, Virginie Despentes and Marie Nimier. In post-publication interviews, however, Delaume (2010a) has distinguished herself from such authors by highlighting instead the Oulipian features of this novel. Noting, as an example, that a passage in *Mouflettes* incorporates all the footnote matter from a page in a volume of Rimbaud's poems that was lying on her writing table, she emphasises that the foundation for her work was laid by the pataphysicians, the Oulipo, Queneau and the work of linguistic constraints (Tran Huy 2001). *Mouflettes*'s layers of palimpsestic referentiality, syntactical distortions and punning language blown up to gargantuan proportions mirror the explosive nature of the traumatic events and relationships that have distorted or buried the author's identity in the ruins of personal catastrophes. The reader also gets a sense of the author's talent for mobilising language as a battering ram, both to bludgeon the objects of her wrath in the novel and to ward off readers primarily drawn to a spicy scandal. In this first novel, however, Delaume's Oulipian play with language and vocabulary is too obviously an attempt at a virtuosic performance to be fully integrated into the autofictional substance of the work. By the time of her second novel, however, *Le Cri du sablier*, she has refined the influence of the Oulipo and the pataphysician and jazz musician, Vian, into a unique autofictional language and voice.[17]

As in *Mouflettes*, punning homophonies of sound and meaning, extensive citations and ludic substitutions weave abundantly through *Le Cri du sablier*. However, cadenced by the alexandrine rhythms, blank verse, idiosyncratic punctuation and fractured syntax, 'meurtrie, à l'image de l'enfant' (Delaume 2010a: 84)[18] that have become Delaume's literary signature, they are more tightly integrated into the traumatic pulse of the autofiction. The constraint of the blank verse that dominates the narrative, for example, takes on an integral autofictional significance as an unobtrusive means of relating the play of language and form to the traumatic effects of the parental murder and suicide, the event that dominates the novel. Playing on the double meaning of *vers blancs* (meaning both blank verse and white worms), allows, according to the author, the language to be 'contaminée par les vers blancs, comme les vers blancs contaminaient les corps des parents. Le vers blanc est attaché à la mort' (Guichard 2009a: 25).[19]

Structured as a dialogue with a fictive psychiatrist who treats her post-traumatic mutism, *Cri*, like *Mouflettes*, is a settling of scores. It documents paternal and spousal abuse, the murder-suicide, the damaging incomprehension of her caretakers and doctors and the first of several attempts to take her own life. Developing a fertile constraint provided by the artist, Michèle Khan, who, while creating a frontispiece for the still developing work, suggested its title, Delaume configures her traumatic experiences as the contents of an hourglass. Assigning negative qualities to time, sand and silex (associated in the novel with her father and ex-husband and with her fear that 'le mica serait génetique' (Delaume 2001: 89)), she seeks to shatter the metaphorical hourglass that imprisons and distorts her identity with a strident cry:

> le sable peut [. . .] se kafkayer en verre [. . .] Le verre au cri aigu ne peut lui résister. Ils diront sournoisement elle nous joue la diva oui mais seules les altos maîtrisent l'aigu pointu qui peut en vocalises faire voler en éclats le père cristallisé. (Delaume 2001 : 124)[20]

What draws her to music, according to the author, is not the melody but the sounds, 'les séquences, les cahots' (Noudelmann 2010).[21] Joltingly rendered musical metaphors in *Cri* enable the author to veer away from the directly cathartic and anecdotal in her representation of trauma, allowing her to find her own voice both as a fictional character and an author. In this work she describes as 'le cri primal qui brise le temps, qui vient amorcer la musique, la langue personnelle' (Noudelmann 2010),[22] Delaume begins to personalise her writing as an autofictional experiment in which music will play an increasingly key role, both metaphorical and concrete:

> L'instrument hurle bleu. Il est bien sec le bruit que fait le verre nocturne dépeçant ses debris aux lattes du plancher [. . .] Nulle

urne c'est acquis. Une fois le sablier braillant déflagration les vestiges familiaux fondront comme l'on s'en doute. (Delaume 2001: 127)[23]

The passage recalls the 'pianocktail' in Vian's *L'Écume des jours*, but the message is far more urgent. Delaume's instrument is intended not to distil from literature and music synaesthetic jazz cocktails as Vian's fantastical piano does but, rather, to liberate a strong and distinctive personal voice. Her literary voice is both particularised and fortified by the success of *Cri*, awarded the Prix Décembre in 2001, and as a young writer she becomes well positioned to explore through experimental autofiction 'où est son Je, comment il se positionne et comment il défend l'intégrité de son individualité' (Delaume 2010b: 125).[24] This quest becomes increasingly oriented to interactive media.

Ludic experiments

Following the publication of *Cri*, Delaume began to explore the range of her autofictional voice across multiple genres and media, conceiving her work as laboratory research where explorations of media other than writing, particularly electronic music, the Internet and video games, as well as experiments with form and language take precedence over the development of autobiographical material (Guichard 2009b: 23). Several of these experiments format the reinvention of her identity as games that permit construction of her fictional character as a joint venture with the reader. The sexualised body that has been a principal locus and focus of women's autofiction since the 1970s, although quite differently expressed over the decades, largely disappears from these works. Bodies do not disappear though; they are omnipresent. However, variously uninhabitable (Delaume 2003b), virtual (Delaume 2003a), figured as game pieces (Delaume 2004), swallowed by media (Delaume 2006), they are ludic constructions that invite the reader into the construction of autofiction as a multimedia process not a portrait. The most elaborate of these works is *Corpus Simsi* (2003a) (Sim's Body) in which Delaume takes up residency in the life-strategy computer game, *The Sims*. Published in 2003, the project began in 2002 with a series of live performances integrating Delaume playing her video avatar, projections of the *Sims* and electronic music. Directed at breaking down barriers between the virtual and the real, print, performance and cyberfiction, and author and reader, *Corpus Simsi* also developed as an interactive autofiction during a period when the author's avatar could be downloaded and manipulated by her fans from her website.[25] *Certainement pas* (2004) (Certainly Not) is a partially autofictional version of the society game, Cluedo, based on the author's experiences in the Sainte Anne psychiatric hospital. *La Nuit je suis Buffy Summers* (2007) (At Night I am Buffy Summers), a create-your-own-adventure story inspired by an episode of the television series in which Buffy the Vampire Slayer is revealed to be a hospitalised schizophrenic, replicates the interactive format of fan fiction. The author's website advises readers to name the heroine Chloé Delaume at the beginning of the game: '[s]achant que ce livre est autant inspiré par ses propres nuits [. . .] vous obtiendrez une forme d'autofiction jouable'.[26] *Certainement pas*, where the well-elaborated characters and creatively personalised twist on a familiar society game simultaneously draw the reader into solving a murder mystery and exploration of the writing process, is the most engaging of these ludic experiments. Each of these novels holds considerable interest, however, as an autofictional work that integrates the perspective of the reader into the creative process.

The Doubrovskian constraint called into question: *Dans ma maison sous terre*

In *Dans ma maison sous terre*, Delaume returns specifically to the family drama portrayed in *Cri* from the space of a breach in the shield of her autofictional identity: 'Dans mes mains plus de sable, juste de la poussière' (105).[27] This highly poetic novel was generated by a 'clinamen' more radical than anything previously conceived in her 'laboratory'. In 2004, her maternal grandmother charged a cousin with informing her that Sylvain Delain was not her biological father. *La bonne nouvelle* (the good news), as the cousin phrased it, called into question the legitimacy of Delaume's self-reconstruction: 'les fondations du *Cri du sablier* ne tenaient plus debout, avec l'impression d'avoir menti' (Guichard 2009a: 27).[28] Like *Cri*, *Dans ma maison* was conceived as a performative autofiction. The author's expressed initial intent for writing the novel was literally to kill with public shame her maternal grandmother who had not only concealed the circumstances of her birth but explicitly contributed to her fear that she had inherited her father's schizophrenia (Delaume 2009a: 9). The principal catalytic figure in this novel, which opens with Chloé seated on her mother's grave, is not the grandmother in the end but her dead mother who, as the cousin's message makes cruelly clear, was more than just a victim in the saga that led to her murder. Chloé's obsession with witnessing an embalming as an aid to reconfiguring her portrait of her own mother and also to anchor her autofictional project and her references to her mother in the 'real' connects the various threads of the novel: the family drama, a trenchant critique of contemporary literature and, in the last part of the novel, a reassertion of autofiction's power when it moves beyond the therapeutic and the cathartic to contest dehumanising 'groupthink' (Janis 1972: 188).[29]

Chloé is accompanied throughout the novel, set entirely in a cemetery, by a fantastical necrophile, a failed writer named Théophile who attempts to wean her from her macabre project to more acceptable subjects by guiding her to other tombs where she can hear the voices of 'fantômes présents passés futurs' (23).[30] Théophile plays a double role: functioning similarly to the psychoanalyst in *Cri* and epitomising a conventional reading public. Using Théophile as a foil permits Chloé to mount a sustained critique of a literature that has become the domain of commerce and entertainment and to argue, even as she grapples with the validity of her own *personnage* (fictional character), that literature is 'avant tout, une arme' (118).[31] The tone is set during their first excursion that takes them to the tomb of Clotilde Mélisse (1973–2069), an alter ego for the author in several of her works. Allowed to look into the future by means of a futuristic wireless reader at the grave marker, she learns that, by the time of Clotilde's peaceful suicide in 2069, all of her work will be available electronically. The revelation leads to a condemnation of the mediocrity of the current market-driven publishing industry and a spirited defence of systems that can circumvent it, most particularly digital formats with their capacity to engage readers in a non-passive role.

At Clotilde's graveside, Chloé also hears the first of the sound pieces that are integrated into the fabric of *Dans ma maison*, musical elaborations of the affective tone of the experiences described by the voices she hears in the cemetery. Joca Seria's *Extraction* series, which Delaume currently directs, announces as its *raison d'être* to give a voice to writer-researchers who produce unique textual forms and devices working with language, sound and images: 'Une littérature aux frontières d'autres arts, intégrant d'autres pratiques que l'écriture'.[32] Very much in this vein, a 'musique intérieure' (interior music) was created simultaneously with their prose narratives for each of the tombs' inhabitants. Twenty sound tracks, two composed by the author, the others by Aurélie Sfez, who also performed the music, constitute an integral part of the work.[33] By summoning the reader from the printed page to her website to hear the music, the author draws the reader into a challenging interpretive process.[34] The musical rendition of these inner experiences highlights, moreover, the critical importance of non-verbal autofictional modes at a time when *la bonne nouvelle* has sapped Chloé's confidence in the power of words to construct her identity: 'Les mots ne suffisaient plus [...] il me fallait m'entendre, et surtout m'écouter. Pour tenter de savoir si j'existais vraiment' (Delaume 2009a: 105).[35]

As the novel draws to a close, she experiences her decision to forego witnessing an embalming as a further deterioration of her autofictional voice. The decision, spurred by her physician's insistence that the consequence would be a re-descent into psychosis, constitutes a break with the constraint of Doubrovsky's definition of autofiction that has been a foundational tenet of Delaume's laboratory: 'c'est annuler le pacte. Vécu mis en fiction mais jamais inventé' (186).[36] Ultimately, as she opts for life and the apparent undoing of her autofictional practice, she realises that she is not retiring Chloé Delaume but, rather, finally writing a requiem for the invasive phantoms of her discarded civil status as Nathalie Dalain, deceased in 1999 (202). The *bonne nouvelle* has called into question the Doubrovskian constraints but not the liberating processing of identity made possible by her experiments: 'Personnage de fiction = suicider le Je. Pour le redéfinir, pour le réinvestir, par la littérature' (Delaume 2010a: 13).[37]

Revising the equation

In *La Règle du je*, an essay on autofiction published a year after *Dans ma maison*, Delaume substitutes 'L'autofiction = un pas de côté = réappropriation de sa vie par la langue = mon Je est politique' for 'Autofiction + x = ?' (81).[38] The modification aligns with her statement that what she wants readers to take from *Dans ma maison* is the importance of mastering their own fictions (Guichard 2009b: 23).

Her concept of autofiction makes extremely high demands on readers' creativity, a central theme in *Une femme avec personne dedans*. This novel opens with the announcement of the suicide of an avid reader of her work. The victim, a self-styled double for the author, commits suicide after Chloé Delaume refuses to recommend publication of a book in which the reader had uncannily mimicked her own autofictional performances of identity. Delaume's (2005: 30) position that '[a]rpenter les romans pour y quêter émois sensations et transferts c'[est] leur faire outrage' has been clearly stated and multiply illustrated.[39] Consistent with the thrust of her highly varied experiments, she continues to insist that if autofiction is to retain a revolutionary status, its fundamental dynamic must not promote reader/writer transference, positive or negative, but rather stimulate collective creativity: 'Au commencement était, ne l'oubliez jamais, vous qui êtes le lecteur [. . .] je vous lègue la formule, quelle vie en ferez-vous?' (Delaume 2012: 139–40).[40]

Notes

1 The Ouvroir de Littérature Potentielle (Workshop of Potential Literature), or Oulipo, was founded in 1969 by Raymond Queneau and the mathematician, François de Lionnais. Motte 1998 is a useful reference as is Mathews and Brotchie 2005. A *mode d'emploi* (user's manual) frequently prefaces Oulipian works. Delaume's title also references the Oulipo's best known novel, Georges Perec's *La Vie mode d'emploi* (1978) (*Life A User's Manual*).
2 'My only objective is to vary genre via a combinatory mode [. . .] To make a hybrid object that would write the I making it embody as many strata as possible. Author, narrative director, character, reader. A form of interactive autofiction that would play on and at several levels.' All translations from French are my own.
3 'Fictional character'.
4 'I reinvent my personality and my existence through literature, reconstructing my real identity starting from a change of name.'
5 'My name is Chloé Delaume. I am a fictional character. My principal abode is a female body dating from 10 March 1973. Franco-Lebanese conception, nothingness as my distinguishing mark. The premises were insalubrious when I took possession.' (*http://www.choledelaume. net/bio.remarquesetcie/bio*)
6 'Born from a fiction that ended very badly'.
7 'J'ai attrapé la maladie de la mort le 30 juin 1983', she notes in one of many plays on Marguerite Duras's titles in her work (Delaume, 2009a: 127) ('I caught the malady of death on 30 June 1983'). Her autofictional accounts have triggered multiple psychotic episodes. She

reports her diagnosis in several works and interviews as bipolar disorder with psychotic tendencies.
8   This title is a play on *Les Morts ont tous la même peau* (1947) (*The Dead All Have the Same Skin*), published by Boris Vian under the pseudonym Vernon Sullivan; 'not to be fingering carcasses preserved in blackened blood from the moment of waking [. . .] I had to find the formula that changes depressive young girls into characters in their own fiction'.
9   The Arve is a river in France; 'aume' is not a French word, but is used to mimic Carroll's nonsense poetry. Vian's Chloé's cancer manifests itself on an x-ray as a waterlily, and this flower figures prominently in Delaume's fictions as a symbol of her precarious identity. Throughout her work she also portrays herself as a botched, auto-destructive version of Lewis Carroll's Alice: 'Je finis toujours face au miroir en train de me décomposer.' (Delaume 2009b: 7) ('I always end up in front of the mirror in a process of disintegration.')
10 'Writing the self, not bared but like an open wound'.
11 See Darrieussecq 1996b: 369–70 and Gasparini 2008: 272.
12 She recites a litany of these denigrations in Delaume 2010a: 28.
13 'The exact opposite of a naked truth'.
14 'Fiction, from strictly real events and facts; if you like, *autofiction*, from giving over the language of an adventure to the adventure of language.' Philippe Vilain (2009: 49), for example, attributes the 'legitimacy' of autofiction to the work of Philippe Lejeune, Jacques Lecarme, Vincent Colonna, Jean-Louis Jeannelle and Philippe Gasparini.
15 After completing a degree in modern languages, Delaume worked for two years as call girl to support herself while she was writing.
16 'A putrid and distressing family romance that I refuse'.
17 Claude Burgelin (2001:16) notes of Oulipian autobiographical texts: '[p]ar la simple exigence d'un refus de certaines stéréotypes verbales, par la façon toute pratique de faire que des structures de syntaxe ou de genre se fendillent, le je est sollicité d'avoir recours à de nouvelles configurations de mots, d'images, peut-être de mythologies secrètes.' ('By the simple requirement of rejection of certain verbal stereotypes, by the entirely practical way of crazing syntactical and generic structures, the I is called upon to turn to new configurations of words, images and perhaps secret mythologies.')
18 'wounded, in conformity with the image of the child'.
19 'contaminated by blank verse, just as white worms contaminated the parent's bodies. Blank verse is attached to death'.
20 'the mica would be genetic'; 'Sand can [. . .] Kafka itself into glass [. . .] Glass to a high-pitched cry has no resistance. They will say deceitfully she is playing the diva yes but only altos master the shrill note in a singing exercise that can shatter the crystallised father.'
21 'the sequences, the jolts'.
22 'the primal cry that breaks time, that primes music, personal language'.
23 'The instrument howls blue. It is very dry the noise made by the nocturnal glass breaking up its pieces on the floorboards [. . .] No container is a given. When the hourglass is a bawling explosion the familial vestiges will dissolve as one might suspect.'

24 'where the I is, how it positions itself and how it defends its individual integrity'.
25 For extensive analyses of *Corpus Simsi*, see Goggin 2009 and Ducas 2010.
26 'knowing that the book is equally inspired by her own nights [. . .] you will arrive at a form of playable autofiction'. (*http://www.chloedelaime.net/publications*)
27 'In my hands no more sand, just dust'.
28 'The foundations of *Le Cri du sablier* no longer held up, with an impression of having lied'.
29 The term created by social psychologist Irving Janis matches well Delaume's notion of 'la fiction collective' ('group fictions').
30 'present, past, future phantoms'.
31 'above all a weapon'.
32 'A literature at the frontier of other arts, integrating practices other than writing', *http://www.0extraction0.net/collection-extraction/demarche/*.
33 Much of Delaume's recent work involves collaborative ventures incorporating text and sound. Several of her sound pieces can be downloaded from her website. A 2010 performance of *Waterlilith* is available from the sound archives of the Bibliothèque Centre Pompidou, *http://archives-sonores.bpi.fr/index.php.urlaction*.
34 Delaume had previously experimented with this interactive model in Delaume 2006.
35 'Words no longer sufficed [. . .] I needed to hear myself, and above all to listen to myself. To try to find out if I truly existed'.
36 'It breaks the pact. Lived experience fictionalised but never invented'.
37 'Fictional character = suicide of the I. In order to redefine it, reinvest it, through literature'.
38 'Autofiction = a step aside = re-appropriation of one's life through language = my I is political'.
39 'To survey novels in search of emotions sensations and transferences is an outrageous violation'.
40 'In the beginning was, never forget it, you, the reader [. . .] I bequeath you the formula, what life will you make of it?'

Chapter Seventeen
Beyond Antoinette Fouque (*Il y a deux sexes*) and Beyond Virginie Despentes (*King Kong théorie*)? Anne Garréta's Sphinxes

OWEN HEATHCOTE

Anne Garréta came to public attention in 1986 with the publication of her first novel, *Sphinx* (1986). What particularly intrigued readers of *Sphinx* was the sexual ambiguity of Garréta's narrator and his/her lover. As Lucille Cairns (2002a: 399) writes in *Lesbian Desire in Post-1968 French Literature*, 'Garréta displays immense technical virtuosity in her manipulation of the French language's gendered grammar to prevent [...] sexed identification of either narrator or his/her partner A***.' More recently, Delphine Naudier (2008: 61) confirms Garréta as an example of authors who 'mettent au cœur de leur œuvre la question des identités sexuées, en jouant précisément sur l'absence de marque de genre dans la définition des personnages'.[1] The figure of the sphinx can, moreover, be said to recur in different guises in later Garréta works such as *Ciels liquides* (1990) (Liquid Skies), where, again, the sex of a would-be lover seen in a cemetery is never specified and in *La Décomposition* (1999) (The Decomposition), where otherwise unnamed 'characters' are identified with those in Marcel Proust's *À la recherche du temps perdu* (1913–27) (*In Search of Lost Time*) before being summarily executed and erased by an even more anonymous narrator. Indeterminacy and enigma also feature in Garréta's more recent writings such as

Pas un jour (2002) (Not a Day), where a similarly unnamed narrator describes a series of 'tricks' with lovers or potential lovers known only by a letter of the alphabet, and such as *Éros mélancolique* (2009) (Melancholy Eros), jointly authored with Jacques Roubaud, a prominent member of the Oulipo group, and thus, in its way, another, differently ambiguous, hybrid production (see Oulipo 1973, 1981, 1988). Along the way, Garréta has published a number of short stories such as 'La Pyramide' (1991) ('The Pyramid') and 'Nuits' (1994) ('Nights'), together with a provocatively entitled essay, *Pour en finir avec le genre humain* (1987) (Putting an End to Human- and Gendered-Kind). As this brief overview shows, the sexually unmarked in Garréta has spread like a virus throughout her writings, taking in character, identity, personhood and even *life*. It is, therefore, an appropriate moment to take stock of the nature and implications of the phenomenon of the 'sphinx'. Does the 'sphinx' incorporate or supersede sex and gender – and, thus, perhaps, also incorporate or supersede women? And what, then, are the implications of such sphinx-imbued texts for the category and practice of women's writing in the twenty-first century?

Before embarking on a closer analysis of Garréta's sexually ambivalent sphinxes, it will be useful briefly to situate her work in the context of two contrasting contemporary approaches to sex and gender, as represented by Antoinette Fouque and Virginie Despentes. These two writers have been chosen partly because of their prominence and partly because of their very different positions and writing careers. Antoinette Fouque is known particularly for her role in co-founding the Mouvement de la Libération des Femmes (MLF), arguably in 1968 (other feminists date it to 1970), the research group Psychanalyse et Politique (Psychoanalysis and politics) and the publishing house, les Éditions des femmes–Antoinette Fouque, which, at the time of writing, is about to publish *Le Dictionnaire des créatrices* (The Dictionary of Creative Women).[2] Virginie Despentes, on the other hand, is known for her provocatively violent, highly sexualised novels such as *Baise-moi* (1993) (Fuck Me), which she and Coralie Trinh-Thi adapted as a film under the same title in 2000. Similarly audacious is Despentes's recent novel, *Apocalypse bébé* (2010) (Apocalypse Baby), which, according to its back cover, is 'entre satire sociale, polar contemporain et romance lesbienne'.[3]

In successive works, such as *Il y a deux sexes* (1995) (There are Two Sexes) and *Qui êtes-vous, Antoinette Fouque? Entretiens avec Christophe*

Bourseiller (2009) (Who Are You, Antoinette Fouque? Conversations with Christophe Bourseiller), Fouque emphasises what is for her the unavoidability of binary sexual difference, as exemplified in the essentially different female body or in what she calls 'la *géni(t)alité des femmes*' (Fouque 1995: iii; italics in the original).[4] As a result of her belief in 'l'œuvre de corps ou de chair qui échoit spécifiquement aux femmes', she identifies a particular 'écriture génitale' or 'écriture utérine',[5] which she sees as 'femelle', or, in English, female, thereby distancing herself from the less essentialist, more sexually ambivalent, 'écriture féminine' (Fouque 1995: 61; 2009: 114, 70).[6] Since her awareness of 'la *géni(t)alité* des femmes' was prompted in particular by the birth of her daughter, Vincente, a key feature of women's difference lies for Fouque in procreation and maternity and thus in 'un défi permanent à la guerre et à la pulsion de mort' (Fouque 1995: xviii, xix).[7] Unlike what we have seen of Garréta, then, Fouque seeks to downplay ambiguities of sex, gender and sexuality, with the homosexual being primarily associated with mother–daughter relationships: 'L'alliance des femmes entre elles inclut l'homosexualité primaire, l'*homosexuation, une pensée de ce qui se transmet entre mère et fille*' (Fouque 2009: 92; italics in the original).[8] Unlike Garréta, where the viral sphinx embodies and transmits death, Fouque's female body is a constantly reiterated affirmation of (new) life: 'penser c'est procréer' (101).[9]

Equally different from both Garréta and Fouque is the work of Virginie Despentes, as exemplified in her short but predictably feisty 'theoretical' essay, *King Kong théorie* (2006) (*King Kong Theory*). In true Beauvoirian tradition, Despentes (2006: 27) vehemently argues that women are made not born, not least through a claustrophobic identification of women and maternity: 'la mère investie de toutes les vertus, c'est le corps collectif qu'on prépare à la régression fasciste.'[10] Rather than rehabilitate her femaleness or her femininity, Despentes sees herself gendered as male: 'Tout ce que j'aime de ma vie, tout ce qui m'a sauvée, je le dois à ma virilité' (11).[11] And, rather than seeing men as embodiments of essential heterosexual maleness, they, too, for Despentes, are constantly constructed and reconstructed as masculine. Despite the fact that 'les hommes aiment les hommes',[12] men are consistently socialised as virulently homophobic and 'straight' (141). Whilst this gendered approach to sex and sexuality is clearly different from that of Fouque, it would also seem to be different from that of Garréta. For whilst, for Despentes, artificially constructed sexual difference is exploited to impose unequal relations of gendered power, Garréta would seem to be abolishing sexual difference altogether in a new, sex-free and gender-free culture and society. Through her sphinxes and her characterless characters, Garréta seems, in every sense, to be foreseeing and hastening the end of 'le genre humain'.[13] Having situated what may be Garréta's unique contribution to sex and gender, at least as made possible through its written representations, we can now turn more specifically to the role and import of the sphinx in her works.

Although the main emphasis in this chapter will be on Garréta's two latest works – *Pas un jour* and *Éros mélancolique* – it will be helpful to begin by looking briefly at the role of the sphinx in the earlier texts – in *Sphinx* itself, *Ciels liquides* and *La Décomposition*. As indicated above, *Sphinx* is noted for its erasure of sex or gender distinctions in respect of its two protagonists so that, as Garréta (2000: 8) herself has remarked in interview, it might be 'une histoire entre un homme et une femme ou entre deux hommes ou deux femmes'.[14] Later in the interview, and thereby adopting a stance akin to Despentes rather than Fouque, Garréta confirms her desire to use *Sphinx* to subvert sexual difference: 'Faire la preuve empirique, expérimentale, non seulement de la contingence du genre, mais de son inanité ou de son insignifiance comme catégorie' (8).[15] This exposure of sexual difference as both arbitrary and yet programmed is, moreover, replicated in literature itself since, as the narrator of *Sphinx* points out: 'mon désir voyait sa réalisation dans une feinte, s'éprouvait dans la fiction.' (Garréta 1986: 66)[16] Gender difference has the same programmed arbitrariness as the literature of the above-mentioned Oulipo group and as in Paul Valéry's famous reference to 'La marquise sortit à cinq heures' (Genette 1969: 92–3).[17] Fiction and gender are both arbitrary and programmed and, in an additional tightening of the link, gender itself can also be described as a convenient but constraining *fiction*.

What is, however, less noted in respect of *Sphinx* is that the sexual indeterminacy of the two protagonists is framed by a text where the sexual identity of other characters is not in the least ambiguous. The narrator is introduced to the night club, L'Apocryphe, by an academic *padre*, whose sex seems in no doubt; the narrator replaces a male disc jockey when he dies of an overdose in the club lavatories; after the death of A*** on the dance floor, the narrator revisits

A***'s dying mother in New York; at the end of the narrative, the narrator is stabbed to death by two black males in Amsterdam. Any sexual ambiguity is, therefore, confined to the two main protagonists whilst other characters are clearly sexed, even to the point of being defined in terms of spiritual paternity (the *padre*) or, as in Fouque, in terms of biological maternity (A***'s mother). All the main characters are also defined in terms of death: the DJ dies of drugs; A*** dies in an accident; A***'s mother dies of old age; the narrator is stabbed and thrown in a canal. By saying that Garréta 'efface toute référence, toute trace d'appartenance à un genre masculin ou féminin, mâle ou femelle dans la totalité de son roman',[18] Anne Mairesse (2008: 93) does, therefore, give an incomplete, even distorted, version of a text which combines gender neutrality with gender certainty and where all the main characters share similar fates whatever their sexual status. Even the death of gender dies when all the characters disappear, as characters do, at the end of their 'play'. Not only gender, but the death of gender, is, in the end, a *fiction*.

Given the self-consciousness of Garréta's fiction, it is perhaps not surprising that her next texts, *Ciels liquides* and *La Décomposition* are, like *Sphinx*, labelled *romans* (novels) on the title page, even though they depart further and further from conventional stories in terms of plot, character and setting. Although the main character of *Ciels liquides* can be identified as male, he is of no fixed abode, unless living rough in a cemetery can be seen as 'fixed', and all his encounters seem to be both fortuitous and with 'characters' of uncertain sex and even identity – an anonymous sunbather in the cemetery and a real or hallucinated angel, who/which drowns, like the narrator of *Sphinx*, in a canal and ends up in the morgue where the narrator works as a dissector of corpses: 'Sur le billard d'acier froid, dans la lumière étale, gisait l'ange, son cadavre de chair, son modèle, sa statue.' (Garréta 1990: 143).[19] It can be seen, then, that the questioning of sexual difference in *Sphinx* is now extending to a questioning of human difference: in what sense are the silent, recumbent sunbather, the angel and the corpses actually real or human?[20] Do they really 'exist' or are they the hallucinated others of a deranged mind? In *La Décomposition*, too, reality seems to be displaced by the potentially disturbed if seemingly logical mind of the (male) narrator who identifies unknown others with characters in Proust so that he can explain to himself why he needs to eliminate both them and electronic versions of 'their' text. The narrator of *La Décomposition* thus emphasises not only the contingency of gender, but, again, the contingency of the human via a writing that becomes a 'littératuerie' or a 'thanatographie' (Garréta 1999: 226).[21] As in *Sphinx*, moreover, where the narrator is also murdered, in *La Décomposition* the virus of deconstruction infects the narrator himself, whose 'system' for killing his real or fictional others finally disintegrates when targeted victims themselves escape or mutate before he has time to execute them. Once again, then, the text itself is condemned to self-destruct – 'c'est la mort, cette main invisible du Temps, qui le décompose' (Garréta 1999: 224)[22] – and sex or gender are the inevitable casualties of conceptual systems that are either perfect but impossible to implement or imperfect but impossible to improve. Moreover, systemic and conceptual 'decomposition' not only affects the narrator – 'Oui, j'irais jusqu'à attenter au narrateur' (133) – but the identity and status of the reader: 'L'espace du langage est un piège que je vous tends.' (159)[23] Gender, text, narrator and reader all seem to destroy and self-destroy in 'un petit programme tueur, sorte de virus kamikaze dont je suis l'auteur' (236) and where even 'Sa Majesté le Je' (228) is but fantasy or fiction.[24]

Now that the sphinx has invaded not just gender but the whole of Garréta's writing, it may be something of a relief to turn to her next novel, *Pas un jour*, published in 2002 and winner of the Prix Médicis in that year. For, since the title *Pas un jour* is short for 'pas un jour sans une femme',[25] and since the female narrator is recounting a series of twelve encounters with twelve other women (or, in one case, a transgender partner) over a sequence of twelve nights, neither gender nor the novel's structure seems open to quite the same 'decomposition' as in the previous texts. Since, in addition, all the characters seem to outlive their textual representation, recounting *Pas un jour* should not produce 'un grand mausolée' like *À la recherche du temps perdu* or *La Décomposition* (Garréta 1999: 25).[26] More reminiscent of Renaud Camus's *Tricks* (1988) than of Hervé Guibert's *Le Mausolée des amants* (2001) (The Lovers' Mausoleum), *Pas un jour* would seem to be a refreshingly straightforward text, even, just possibly, a straight or at least sexually unmarked one: Garréta eschews the category of lesbian in her writing not just because she 'distrust[s] categories and the attendant compulsory identification with them' (Garréta 1996: 223) but because she sees the lesbian as 'a male fictional construct' (208) and explicitly lesbian characters as functioning 'as a screen [...] for an ambiguous male identity' (209). Thus, unlike, Didier Éribon (2001: 86), for example, who starts from a position of 'enfant de l'injure', and Guillaume Dustan (1997: 18) who speaks of '[s]es frères du ghetto', Garréta's narrator in *Pas un jour* writes of and to herself: 'tu n'as jamais eu pour le ghetto la moindre affinité. Le langage t'y paraît pauvre, aussi pauvre que celui de la norme.' (Garréta 2002: 51)[27]

At the same time, the very distance that Garréta puts between herself and both lesbian writing and autofictional writing means that *Pas un jour* is likely to be less straightforward than it might at first appear.[28] *Pas un jour* may not be readily co-optable as lesbian, but that does not necessarily mean that it has to be *straight*. The first way in which *Pas un jour* is far from straight is shown by the narrator's detached, cavalier or playful attitude towards her own material. For example, by using both the first person and, as seen above, the second person in relation to herself, the narrator is both self-absorbed and yet detached. As she opines of one of her encounters: 'Distante et absorbée tout ensemble...' (143)[29] Secondly, the narrator reveals, in the latter stages of the narrative, that all the encounters are authentic, with one exception, but that the identity of the one fictional episode she will not disclose but leave to the reader to decide: 'Cherchez la fiction.' (169)[30] Thirdly, although a developmental sequence of encounters is implied by identifying the different women with progressive letters of the alphabet, the order of these encounters is, arbitrarily, numerical not 'alphabetical'. In *Pas un jour*, both letters and numbers are, differently, deceptive, contradictory and arbitrary. Since, moreover, the encounters are taken out of any chronological, logical, emotional or even alphabetical order, what she refers to as 'l'alphabet bégayant du désir' (12) cannot build into what she also claims they represent – '[une] mémoire du corps' (19).[31] Although Garréta (2000: 2) claims she is no realist but, nonetheless, 'un écrivain exact',[32] her precision seems to be undermined by her wilful and seemingly wayward jettisoning of *both* order *and* disorder. Even more radically than the narrator of *La Décomposition*, whose system is eventually disrupted by the understandable unpredictability of his victims, the narrator's 'system' in *Pas un jour* is disrupted from the outset by a Scheherazade who turns a contract for the story of thirty nights into a mere twelve and who repeatedly backs away from what one might expect is her other narrative contract – 'dénouer le fil du désir' (Garréta 2002: 157).[33] *Pas un jour*, therefore, builds up into neither a 'grammaire du genre' nor a Queneau-like 'exercice du style', nor, even a narrative as wilfully wayward as *Jacques le fataliste*.[34] Still less does Garréta endorse or rebut Wittig's (1992: 32) claim that 'lesbians are not women' since the encounters of *Pas un jour* are not identified or self-identified as either. In contrast, for example, to Despentes's *Apocalypse bébé*, which features an out, proud and provocative lesbian, nicknamed La Hyène (The Hyena), the encounters in *Pas un jour* have no such memorable identity, even for the narrator. The encounters in *Pas un jour*, revealingly dedicated 'À nulle',[35] overlap and merge in seamless succession – just like the endless series of records played nightly by the narrator of *Sphinx* in the appropriately named L'Apocryphe.

Although Garréta's most recent text, *Éros mélancolique*, is co-authored with Jacques Roubaud and thus only partially attributable to Garréta herself, this very hybridity fits perfectly with a text which is itself not just hybrid but multiple, even viral. The title *Éros mélancolique*, deriving from the title of a parasite computer file passed on to Garréta by Roubaud and from a film found in the box of a second-hand camera, describes a student's obsession with a mysterious woman met at a party and seen undressing in a nearby, supposedly uninhabited apartment in Paris. The woman, known as Raymonde, disappears and reappears at various rendez-vous before 'fading into gray' (Roubaud and Garréta 2009: 295)[36] as her photograph and memory evaporate from the file, film and text – and thereby from the so-called reality she barely seems to inhabit. It can be seen that, like the previous texts discussed, *Éros mélancolique* is populated by sphinxes, not just the mysterious Raymonde, but file-owners, file-users, photographers and narrators whose eminent reproducibility is only matched by the evanescence and the corruptibility of the material they access. If gender remains identifiable throughout, the media conveying or reproducing the supposed reality of that gender are not. Gender is, therefore, undermined here not just by the sexual ambiguity of the sphinx, nor just by the disruptive power of 'queer',[37] nor even by a mixture of Haraway-style cyborgs and what Teresa de Lauretis (1987) has called the 'technologies of gender', but by a combination of textual/ontological erasures and self-erasures, fades and dissolves. Gender, like any other imposed category, is subject to programmed or unprogrammed dissolution, and thus, like Prospero's 'insubstantial pageant', is finally 'melted into air, into thin air'.[38]

In conclusion, then, it can be said that, whilst explicitly feminist in her positions (Garréta 2000: 10), Garréta does indeed seem to go beyond what some would see as the biological essentialism of Fouque[39] and the gender essentialism of Despentes by offering one of the most radical and disturbing assaults on both sex and gender among current feminist writers. This assault is all the more radical since the characters in Garréta manage to combine sexual and gender indeterminacy with a certain critical detachment and, indeed, a certain strength of personality and personhood. For, however impossible they are to categorise, Garréta's characters do not dissolve into (mere) energy flows or libidinal urges but retain, despite their uncertain identities, a sense of self, a sense of humour and a certain nostalgia for a seemingly lost community. Even the hero/heroine of *Pas un jour* seems to be on a quest for new forms of relations and relationships and, indeed, however jadedly, for more contact and more *fun*. For what is unusual here is that by circumventing both the isolation of Despentes's rampaging women *and* the would-be homosexual motherhoods and daughterhoods of Fouque, Garréta paves the way for new forms of post-human humanity – and, therefore, for new forms of what may still be called 'women's writing'.

Notes

1 'put the question of sexual identities at the heart of their works, by taking full advantage of the absence of gender markers which might define a given character'. Unless otherwise indicated, translations from the French are my own. Although, like many modern writers, Garréta does not figure in Martine Reid's (2010) survey of 'des femmes en littérature' ('women in literature'), she is singled out in an interestingly entitled article, 'Les laborantines du verbe' ('Laboratory assistants in language'), in a special issue of *Le Magazine Littéraire* on 'les romancières françaises' ('French women novelists'), for 'le rythme distinctif, sophistiqué et captivant de l'écriture' ('the distinctive, sophisticated and captivating rhythm of the writing') which gives her fictions 'une dimension impétueuse, presque violente, comme avec *Pas un jour*' ('an impetuous, even violent dimension, as in *Pas un jour*') (Hoctan 2010: 92). I am grateful to Michèle A. Schaal for drawing this special, 500th issue of *Le Magazine Littéraire* to my attention.
2 Fouque is Commandeur de la Légion d'honneur and Grand officier de l'Ordre du Mérite.

3   'between social satire, modern thriller and lesbian romance'.
4   'the geni(t)ality of women'. Fouque is clearly playing here with at least three words: gender, genius and genitalia.
5   'the work of body and flesh that belongs specifically to women'; 'genital writing'; 'uterine writing'.
6   It should be said, however, that Fouque does not see herself as having an essentialist approach to sex and sexuality. As an example of this, her notion of 'écriture utérine' combines not only characteristics associated with both sexes but also the potentiality for the presence of a third party – the child. For Fouque, then, 'écriture utérine' is, or at least can be, tripartite, representing both creation and procreation (personal conversation of the author with Fouque in Paris, 27 November 2010). I would like to thank Antoinette Fouque most sincerely for her comments on these issues. My gratitude goes too to Michèle Idels and Sylvina Boissonas for our helpful discussion of this chapter at the Espace des femmes, 25 November 2010.
7   'an unremitting challenge to war and the death drive'.
8   'The alliance between women among themselves encompasses a primary homosexuality, or *homosexuation*, an idea of what is passed on from mother to daughter'. This aspect of the mother–daughter bond can be seen as the cornerstone of Fouque's more general foregrounding of the homosexualisation of women's relationships. In an interesting article, Marie-Hélène Devoisin (2010) shows to what extent Fouque 'refusait la séparation homo/hétéro' (21) ('refused the separation homo/hetero') and, for feminist reasons, advocates female-to-female bondings and groupings in order to counter 'la domestication [de la femme] dans le couplage hétéro' (8) ('the domestication [of the woman] in the heterosexual couple'). It should be noted that the 'homosexual' here does not have for Fouque any erotic connotations (personal conversation with Antoinette Fouque, 27 November 2010).
9   'thinking is procreating'.
10 'the mother, endowed with every imaginable virtue, is the collective body being prepared for fascist regression.'
11 'everything I love about my life, everything that has saved me, I owe to my virility'.
12 'men love men'.
13 'gendered-/humankind'.
14 'a story between a man and a woman or between two men or two women'. It should be pointed out that, in her post-1990 work, Anne Garréta became Anne F. Garréta.
15 'Offer the empirical, experimental proof not only of the contingency of gender, but of its stupidity or of its meaninglessness as a category'.
16 'my desire became fulfilled through a sham, was felt via fiction.' See also Garréta 1986: 77: 'Cela s'offrait à moi, chuchoté, sous les espèces extraordinaires d'une fiction.' ('It offered itself to me in a whisper, under the extraordinary guise of a fiction.')
17 'The marchioness left at five o'clock'. As Gérard Genette (1969: 92) writes: 'Il faut partir comme d'une donnée fondamentale, de cet

arbitraire du récit [. . .], qui fascinait et repoussait Valéry, de cette liberté vertigineuse qu'a le récit [. . .] d'adopter à chaque pas telle ou telle orientation (soit la liberté, ayant énoncé *La marquise*. . ., de poursuivre par *sortit*, ou aussi *rentra*, ou *chantait*, ou *s'endort*, etc).' (italics in the original) ('What has to be a basic given here is *this arbitrariness of narrative* [. . .], that Valéry found both fascinating and repellent, this vertiginous freedom of narrative [. . .] to go in one direction or another at any moment (in other words, the freedom, having mentioned *The Marchioness* . . ., to continue with *left*, or *came back*, or *sang*, or *goes to sleep*, etc).') Long before Valéry, a work such as Denis Diderot's *Jacques le fataliste* (1962) [1796] (*Jacques the Fatalist*) took full of advantage of this freedom to tease and taunt the reader. Garréta's exploitation of the problematics of fiction – and of the self – can, moreover, be seen as an aspect of her indebtedness not just to Oulipo but, more generally, to the French *moraliste* tradition.

18 'erases any reference, or any sign of belonging, to gender, be it masculine or feminine, male or female, throughout the whole of her novel'.
19 'On the cold steel bench, in the still light, lay the angel, its corpse of flesh, its model, its statue.'
20 Interestingly, the angels in Monique Wittig (1985: 137–8) are alternately or cumulatively male and female.
21 'L'accord en genre est une mise jetée sur le tapis à la case pair ou impair, rouge ou noir.' (Garréta 1999: 132) ('A gender agreement is a wager placed on either odds or evens, red or black.'); 'literaslaughter'; 'thanatography'.
22 'it is death, that invisible hand of Time that decomposes it'.
23 'Yes, I would even go so far as to waylay the narrator'; 'The space of language is a trap I am setting for you.'
24 'a deadly little programme, a sort of kamikaze virus which I create'. It is worth pointing out that Wittig adopts a different way of dethroning 'Sa Majesté le Je' ('His/Her Majesty the I') – by splitting that 'Je' into 'J/e', notably in Wittig 1973.
25 'not a day without a woman'.
26 'a great mausoleum'.
27 'child of insult'; 'his brothers in the ghetto'; 'you never had the least affinity for the ghetto. You find the language of the ghetto impoverished, as impoverished as that of the norm.' This offers another glimpse of Garréta positioning herself within, if also against, French literary and philosophical (rather than popular) tradition. Hence perhaps the recurrent references in her work to Albert Camus, notably *La Chute* (*The Fall*) (Garréta 1986: 109) and, in *La Décomposition*, to Proust.
28 On Garréta's rejection of her writing as autofictional, see Garréta 1996: 223.
29 'Distant and absorbed, at one and the same time. . .'
30 'You find the fiction.'
31 'the stammering alphabet of desire'; '[a] memory of the body'. Any repudiation of the body as a site of memory can be seen as departing

from approaches to 'women's writing' linking the female body and trauma, as represented, for example, by Cardinal 1975; Chawaf 2010; and Hyvrard 1975.
32 'an exact writer'.
33 'to unravel the skein of desire'.
34 'gender grammar'; 'stylistic composition'.
35 'To nowoman'.
36 In English in the text ('Fade to gray'). For Ward Jouve 1977, the colour grey conveys the flexibility and the strength of a certain gender indeterminacy, most readily available perhaps to women.
37 See Garréta 2000: 11: 'Je n'ai pas de religion queer ou gay and lesbian, ni Women Studies [sic] ou gender studies.' ('I have no religion, queer, gay and lesbian, nor Women Studies or gender studies.')
38 Shakespeare, *The Tempest*, Act 4, Scene 1.
39 However, see note 6 above.

Chapter Eighteen
Amélie the Aesthete: Art and Politics in the World of Amélie Nothomb

ANNA KEMP

Amélie Nothomb's writing has both intrigued and perplexed feminist critics. On the one hand, her foregrounding of body issues and female psychology, along with her frequent nods to feminist thought, seem positively to invite interpretations of her work as feminist. Yet, at the same time, her seeming disdain for adult female sexuality and valorisation of feminine narcissism have been cause for concern. While some critics have been troubled by the apparent misogyny of Nothomb's world-view,[1] others have sought to recuperate her writing to a feminist narrative.[2] However, Nothomb's texts continue to resist definitive categorisation as either pro- or anti-feminist. My aim in this chapter is to explore Nothomb's awkward fit with feminism in terms of what I shall call her 'decadent aesthetic'. In my view, Nothomb's work might be seen to resist (without fully obstructing) recuperation to a feminist perspective primarily because it aspires towards an ideal of art that is indifferent to moral or political concerns. In other words, what seems to matter most in Nothomb's work is not what is good or what is true but what is beautiful and, in line with decadent aesthetics, beauty appears as an ideal with no social or moral purpose. This is not to say, however, that it is impossible to claim Nothomb's work (or aspects of it) as feminist. Instead, my argument is that the perceived politics of Nothomb's work needs to be seen to be in tension with an aesthetic that is indifferent to political matters. As I shall demonstrate, Nothomb's writing is often less concerned with political power than it is with creative power, and less invested in social freedoms than it is in the freedom of the imagination. Indeed, rather than privileging women's collective voices or lives, Nothomb's work foregrounds the singular power of the artist by transforming life into literature.

This chapter will look backwards as a means of looking forwards. It will look back to the *fin de siècle* of the decadents, before considering Nothomb as a writer at the turn of the millennium. I will consider a selection of texts from across her oeuvre, with a view to showing how her early work lays the foundations for her twenty-first-century aesthetic. Just as the decadents posed a challenge to contemporary morality, Nothomb's work, I shall argue, resists recuperation to the ethical concerns of political literary criticism and invites a re-evaluation of the critical habits that we bring to work by women writers.

A decadent aesthetic

Nothomb's writing reveals a number of continuities with an aestheticism that is not confined to but perhaps finds its purest expression in *fin-de-siècle* Decadence. So, before I continue, I will briefly sketch out some of the key characteristics of this movement. In some ways, Decadence can be understood as a reaction against the perceived concerns of Realism and its legatee, Naturalism. While writers like Émile Zola sought to document gritty social realities in a bid to mobilise political reform,[3] the decadents professed a profound lack of interest in reflecting reality or engaging in politics. For decadent writers like Joris-Karl Huysmans, art was first and foremost a means of transforming or escaping 'real life' in order to accede to a superior plane of being characterised by an intensity of aesthetic experience.[4] Indeed, decadent artists and writers are defined, above all, by their dedication to beauty. For decadents, beauty is the ultimate value, surpassing all social or moral concerns and, importantly, this beauty arises from artifice and artistry. Unlike Zola's desire to show nature unadorned, the decadent sensibility abhors the blunt facticity of the world and seeks instead to escape it or redeem it via the artist's imagination. Decadent heroes like Huysmans's des Esseintes retreat into highly wrought, artificial environments that expel the natural and social world and construct, in its place, an artificial paradise over which the artist reigns supreme. This withdrawal from the world brings us to another defining characteristic of decadent art and literature: its anti-social individualism. Rather than associating themselves with any community or collective, decadent artists and protagonists place a high value on the uniqueness and originality of the individual. Indeed, the decadent hero is intensely narcissistic, his artificial paradises leaving no room for others. In short, then, decadent writing tends towards an evacuation of the natural world, society and other people in favour of an ideal aesthetic vision that is the product of a singular artistic imagination.[5]

Unsurprisingly, decadent aesthetics does not mix easily with feminist imperatives. In fact, decadent art and writing is notoriously misogynistic. As Sandra Gilbert and Susan Gubar (1979) have demonstrated, the decadent exaltation of art over nature, the individual over the collective, frequently maps onto the 'masculine' domination of the 'feminine'. In the decadent imagination women are typically made to embody everything Decadence rebels against: nature, bourgeois morality and sexual and artistic reproduction. The female body is frequently figured as unstable, impure and with a capacity to proliferate that undermines the uniqueness and integrity of the individual. It is the 'feminine', therefore, that must be transcended and redeemed by a 'masculine' artistic sensibility and, following the Pygmalion myth, women frequently appear as privileged art objects. One classic example of this is Baudelaire's *Éloge du maquillage* (1961) [1863] (*In Praise of Cosmetics*) that celebrates the triumph of man-made artifice over women's base bodily nature. The decadent aesthetic then is far removed from the 'feminine' aesthetic sensibility favoured by much feminist literary criticism. Not only do decadents distance themselves from any notion of a political collective or moral agenda, but their emphasis on the monadic individual and hostility to the female reproductive body are a far cry from the tropes of relationality, fluidity and an ethical openness to the other that permeate feminist readings. As this chapter argues, Nothomb's writing unapologetically (though not uncritically) aligns itself with many of these decadent prerogatives.

Prétéxtat Tach, c'est moi'[6]

With a Flaubertian flourish, Nothomb once declared that the protagonist of her first novel *Hygiène de l'assassin* (1992) (*Hygiene and the Assassin*), Prétéxtat Tach, was her literary alter ego. As a 'grotesque parody of the great, dead, white, male author' (Gorrara 2003: 106), and a raging misogynist to boot, the fictional writer seems an unlikely avatar for a young female novelist, and critics have, therefore, tended to dismiss Nothomb's words as mischievous provocation. However, it is my view that Tach's aesthetic ideals are consistent with those espoused in Nothomb's work as a whole.

Tach's aesthetic is resolutely decadent in character. Despite his own hideous vulgarity, he claims to be a dedicated worshipper at the temple of beauty and, like his decadent predecessors, he flees life to seek refuge in art. He writes not to produce a copy of reality, 'comme s'il pouvait y avoir quelque jouissance à créer une chose aussi triste et moche que la vie', nor to communicate with others, 'écrire n'est pas chercher à communiquer', but simply 'pour jouir' (87).[7] This *jouissance* arises from what he sees as the clarity and purity of his literary ideals. In keeping with decadent traditions, Tach's literary ideal does not represent the world so much as create an alternative world: a separate, private space that sustains its own reality and gives rise to intense aesthetic pleasure. This is apparent in his solipsistic attachment to a private language that is accessible to him alone. Tach claims that his writing constitutes an ideal language that is perfectly literal and univocal, saying exactly what it means and obeying no law other than its own. However, only he is able to perceive the utterly transparent truth of his writing while his readers, he claims with a sneer of derision, insist on hunting for metaphors and allegories or (in a sideswipe at political criticism) impose 'grille[s] de lecture' derived from 'manuel[s] de sociologie' (157).[8] Tach is his own ideal writer and reader, and although he is aware that his fantasy of a private language is an impossible ideal – 'cette lecture-là n'existe pas' (156)[9] – he clings to it to the very end.

Furthermore, following the decadents, Tach's aesthetic vision is highly gendered. The author's disdain for his readers corresponds to his fearful loathing of others more generally and of women in particular as the embodiment of a threatening otherness. Indeed, Tach's writing and corresponding *jouissance* is the antithesis of the 'feminine' *jouissance* favoured by the critical legacy of *écriture féminine*. Whereas Cixousian *jouissance* envisages an ethical openness to the Other,[10] 'Tachian' *jouissance* is a highly narcissistic affair that fantasises the integrity of the individual self. And, while *écriture féminine* is associated with a polysemous, poetic writing that finds its organising metaphor in the fluidity of the female body, Tach expresses a virulent loathing of proliferating metaphors with their 'effroyable polysémie' (22),[11] describing his style in hypermasculine terms that figure *la bite* (cock) and *les couilles* (balls) as proof of the writer's mastery and virtuosity. Indeed, in line with Baudelairean misogyny, the reproductive female body is associated with 'toutes les saloperies de la vie' (159)[12] that must be disciplined in order for the ideal art form to emerge.

In *Hygiène de l'assassin*, this sacrifice of the female body to art is made explicit in the story of Tach's beloved childhood companion Léopoldine. In Tach's telling of the story, he and the beautiful Léopoldine enjoyed an edenic and isolated childhood during which they remained exclusively devoted to one another. As I have argued elsewhere (Kemp 2012), the Nothombian child can be seen to represent a narcissistic aesthetic ideal characterised by purity and integrity of form. The young Prétextat and Léopoldine may be seen as the first examples of this. In Tach's story, he and his companion do everything in their power to preserve their perfect bubble, artificially extending their childhood by fasting. However, knowing their artificial paradise cannot last, Léopoldine consents to be strangled the moment she begins menstruating in order to preserve the perfection of her child's body. As a child, Léopoldine is not, according to Tach, 'un personnage féminin' and, therefore, 'pas un autre' (172).[13] But, as soon as she becomes a woman, she must die in order to maintain the integrity of Tach's aesthetic. In an echo of Edgar Allen Poe's (1846: 4) assertion that 'the death of a beautiful woman is unquestionably the most poetical topic in the world', Léopoldine's murder is represented as the transfiguration of life into the perfection of art. At the moment of her death, the young woman is transmuted into pure artifice, 'un cadavre abstrait' (192),[14] and this transmutation is imagined by Tach as a moment of sublime beauty. Indeed, her death is not cause for real grief, only the exquisite pain one feels at the perfectly executed death of a literary character.[15] This pygmalionesque story is the quintessence of Tach's decadent aesthetic: the substitution of life for art.

Tach's exaggerated horror of women turns him into a grotesque caricature of 'masculinist' artistic imperatives, but it would be wrong to reduce this to a straightforward feminist critique. As is often the case in Nothomb's work, monsters are sympathetically drawn and represented as strangely admirable. Prétextat Tach may, in many respects, be a preposterous character but his decadent aesthetic and desire to transform life into literature is treated with a certain veneration and resonates in Nothomb's work as a whole.

The self as work of art

Like Tach, many of Nothomb's protagonists are (or become) committed aesthetes for whom art offers the promise of a perfection that was lost with childhood. However, while Tach seeks to transform female others into artworks, Nothomb's heroines (as they already inhabit female bodies) seek to transform themselves into their own ideal creations or works of art. In order to explain this notion of the self as work of art a little further, I shall enlist the help of Nothomb's favourite philosopher, Nietzsche.

Nothomb is a self-professed Nietzsche fan and critics have remarked on various affinities between Nothomb's aesthetic and that of her hero, for example her Dionysian taste for extremes (see, for example, Amanieux 2005: 243). But, in my view, there is another reason why Nietzsche is her philosophical soul mate. Nothomb, like Nietzsche, thinks of the ideal self as a perfected literary character – a singular, self-constructed being who has succeeded in fashioning himself or herself into a fascinating, admirable but not necessarily moral individual. For this view of Nietzsche I am indebted to Alexander Nehamas's *Nietzsche: Life as Literature* (1987), and it is his reading that I am following here. Nehamas argues that Nietzsche's ideal self turns the substance of life into a work of art by integrating life's conflicts and tensions into a unique and harmonious whole. This ideal is achieved by subjecting oneself to one's own laws, becoming both artist and artwork as the brute matter of one's existence is sculpted towards the perfect life story. This story is not necessarily morally improving nor even strictly true; rather, it is an admirable interpretation that produces a unique and inimitable literary character that testifies to the superior creative powers of the artist-self.

This tendency to see and value oneself as a self-fashioned work of art or literary character can be detected in a number of Nothomb's novels,[16] but it is perhaps most clearly crystallised in the figure of the tiny ballerina, Plectrude, heroine of *Robert des noms propres* (2002) (*The Book of Proper Names*). Like Léopoldine, Plectrude fears the development of her adolescent body and does everything she can to maintain the aesthetic ideal of childhood. In Plectrude's case this means submitting herself to the rigorous artistry of ballet, seeking, through dance, to transcend her body and become a weightless ideal of form. When Plectrude dances she feels transported, sublimated; it is as if she leaves her body behind to become pure art. As I have argued elsewhere (Kemp 2012), for Plectrude dance is 'l'art total' (Nothomb 2002: 130)[17] in which the dancer is both artist and artwork, ridding herself of the weight of the world and aspiring towards empty abstraction. As for Léopoldine, this substitution of art for life tends dangerously towards self-destruction. Under the school's iron rule, Plectrude endures a crippling anorexic phase during which she replaces her intake of food with the reading of words from the dictionary – 'le dictionnaire Robert lui fournit l'alimentation qu'elle n'avait plus' (130).[18] Again, female flesh is substituted by form as the development of her body is exchanged for the categorical orderliness of words.

At certain moments the narrator strongly criticises the school's treatment of young girls, but at others the intense *jouissance* to which Plectrude's self-discipline gives rise appears to justify her suffering. Ballet is 'l'ivresse absolue' (125), 'la seule transcendance' (133).[19] This kind of ambivalence means that, while some see Nothomb's work as a feminist critique of the disciplining of women's bodies (for example, Le Garrec 2003: 69), others criticise it for its romanticisation of anorexia (for example, Rodgers 2003). Both readings may be justified, but it is my view that such readings exist in tension with an overarching value system that (although it hesitates between ethics and aesthetics) ultimately privileges art over life. In other words, as a feminist reader, one is inhibited by an evaluation within the text that discourages moral or political readings and encourages an appreciation of the characters first and foremost *as characters*; that is, as artistic creations whose aesthetic value trumps moral concerns. This does not immunise Nothomb from feminist criticism but it does complicate the picture.

Ethics versus aesthetics

This tension between ethics and aesthetics is perhaps most clearly played out in Nothomb's novel, *Mercure* (1998) (Mercury) in which feminist prerogatives are explicitly staged and brought into conflict with a resolute aestheticism. *Mercure* tells the story of Hazel, a beautiful young woman kept prisoner on a remote island by her elderly captor Omer. Years before, Omer rescued Hazel from a bombing in which her entire family was killed, tricked her into thinking that she had been horribly disfigured and transported her to his isolated mansion from which all reflective surfaces had been banished. Françoise, a no-nonsense nurse, is Hazel's only visitor and she is allowed to tend to her patient on the condition that she does not reveal the truth about the young woman's sublime appearance. Over time, the two women develop an intense friendship, and this friendship is mediated by literature. Hazel is an avid reader and the friends' conversations revolve around the books they borrow from Omer's immense library. But this is not any old book club. Hazel fantasises herself and Françoise as characters in their own fiction and takes particular delight in comparing their fates to those of the imprisoned heroes of Dumas and Stendhal. Through these literary games of 'let's pretend', Hazel confirms an idealised image of herself and, like Plectrude, values herself as a singular work of art – in this case a marvellous literary character.

Despite some potential for feminist interpretation, *Mercure* puts up considerable resistance. The struggle between moral and aesthetic values is most fully played out in the endings of the story (there are two). Françoise is in many ways a pragmatic, feminist character concerned to liberate Hazel from Omer's tyranny and in the first ending she creates an opportunity for Hazel to escape. However, Hazel does not at first collaborate. 'Si vous avez de l'amitié pour moi', Hazel pleads, 'laissez-moi tranquille' (141).[20] Françoise's mistake is to believe that Hazel values her person more than her *personnage* (character). Hazel may well complain about her treatment at Omer's hands, but he has offered her something that she is very reluctant to sacrifice: a marvellous image of herself as a tragic princess. In Omer's majestic manor that she believes to have been built especially for her, Hazel is an adored devotional object, a broken beauty to Omer's Beast. As Omer puts it, 'Grâce à moi [. . .] Hazel a une vie de princesse romantique. Elle était faite pour ça, non pour devenir une reproductrice bourgeoise.' (127)[21]

When Françoise does eventually persuade Hazel to leave Omer, it is not for the reasons she had foreseen. Hazel is less appalled by the fact of her treatment, than she is to hear that another woman, Adèle, had been treated this way before her. Although she is ready to forgive Omer's cruelty, she is unable to forgive this terrible 'faute de goût'. She tells him: 'Vos méfaits en sont comme banalisés: ils tiraient leur grandeur de leur caractère *exceptionel*, de leur *unicité*. Si je ne suis qu'une répétition, alors oui, je vous en veux et je vous déteste.' (159; italics in the original)[22] Knowing that her story is merely a replay of somebody else's vulgarises and devalues Hazel as a work of art. She is not a precious masterpiece so much as a cheap copy and it is on these grounds that she breaks with Omer – not because of his cruelty but because he has undermined her integrity as a literary character.

Even Nothomb's most resilient feminist characters are liable to be seduced by the dominant aesthetic regime. In the second ending of *Mercure*, Françoise is transformed from sensible nurse to delicate aesthete on glimpsing the full force of Hazel's beauty as she watches her step into the sunlight: 'En un instant d'éblouissement, les plans de Mlle Chavaigne changèrent de tout au tout' (180).[23] In one sublime moment, Françoise's values radically alter and she aligns herself with Omer who, pages earlier had pleaded 'Cessez donc de me juger selon les ukases de la morale et mesurez mon mérite à l'aune de Prométhée' (175).[24] Slipping slyly into (the now dead) Omer's shoes, Françoise decides to maintain his lie so that she alone may enjoy the spectacle of Hazel's beauty. This second ending sees Hazel and Françoise live out their days in devoted seclusion. Decades later, once Hazel's beauty has faded, Françoise reveals the lie upon which their friendship has been founded. 'Vous étiez si sublime', she tells Hazel, 'que pas un instant je n'ai eu honte de mon crime. Sachez au moins ceci : jamais beauté ne fut aussi gaspillé que la vôtre. Grâce à notre bonheur insulaire, je n'ai pas perdu une miette de votre visage.' (188)[25] Far from being outraged, Hazel believes that Françoise did the right thing: 'Si vous me l'aviez révélé il y a cinquante ans, je n'aurais pas résisté à la tentation d'aller me montrer au monde entier [. . .] Jamais je n'aurais connu l'existence idyllique que vous m'avez offerte.' (188)[26] Hazel remains true to her values, and these are purely aesthetic. As with other of Nothomb's works, *Mercure* ends with an open indifference to moral, political or worldly matters, the Second World War meriting only the following remarks:

> Une vingtaine d'années plus tard, il y eut une guerre. Les habitantes de Mortes-Frontières s'en aperçurent à peine et s'en soucièrent encore moins.
> Quand les Alliés débarquèrent, non loin de là, elles se plaignirent un peu :
> 'Pourvu que ce soit vite fini. Ces gens sont bruyants.' (186–7)[27]

In a similar fashion, Tach's interlocutor Nina ends up repeating the gestures of her adversary. In *Hygiène*, Nina variously represents the common sense point of view and the perspective of contemporary literary and feminist approaches to Tach's misogynist conception of literature. A duel ensues between ethical concerns (voiced by Nina) and an impossibly pure aesthetics (defended by Tach). But, despite Tach's death at the end of the novel, there is no clear sense in which Nina has won. In fact, quite the opposite appears to be true. Tach persuades Nina to strangle him in an act that doubles his own strangling of Léopoldine, putting a suitably aestheticised end to his life. Nina, by this point, has assumed the role of Tach's 'avatar' and her precise execution of his commands signals the triumph of Tach's aesthetic regime: 'Ce fut rapide et propre. Le classicisme ne commet jamais de faute de goût.' (223)[28] Indeed, by murdering the writer, Nina enacts the fundamental principle of Tach's literary universe: in order to establish one's own singular vision of the world, in order to 'rétablir le singulier' (220),[29] all others must be eliminated. For the One to survive, the Other must die. As we have seen, this singularising world-view is not only that of Tach, it is also present in the deadly single-mindedness of Plectrude, and in Hazel's (and eventually Françoise's) perception of life as literature. Although this self-aestheticisation may often be destructive, the protagonists' creative power nonetheless allows them a strong sense of control, individuality and integrity. I will conclude this chapter with a brief consideration of this creative power – the power of the artist – via a reflection on the figure of Amélie Nothomb herself.

Amélie the artist

Like her protagonists, Nothomb may be seen to style herself as her own literary character and this self-aestheticisation serves to draw attention to her as an artist. Not only does she appear as a character in her ostensibly autobiographical texts,[30] but she frequently appears as a character in her own fictions[31] or draws attention to herself as an author-character directing the story. Indeed, these self-representations and authorial interventions are often bound up with fantasies of absolute creative power that resemble those of Tach. The pseudo-autobiography *Métaphysique des tubes* (2000) (*The Character of Rain*) stages the ludicrously grandiose solipsism of its child protagonist who, with self-deprecating irony, imagines herself as the origin and end of all creation and nurtures a fantasy of a perfected, private language similar to Tach's.³² The God complex of the young Amélie is reflected in the characterisation of Nothomb the author-character. Even when Amélie Nothomb does not step into the action of the story, Nothomb frequently draws attention to herself as an author-character interrupting the narrative, commenting on it and asserting control over the story as if to remind us that these fictional universes are presided over by the all-powerful figure of the author who can alter her characters' destinies at will.³³ These fantasies may be treated with a certain self-ironising humour but Nothomb's work demonstrates an enduring attachment to them.³⁴

So is there any sense in which Nothomb's self-creative/destructive aesthetic might (despite its misogynist heritage) be reconciled with feminism? There are two senses in which this is arguably the case. First, Nothomb's conception of life as artwork may be seen to offer an analysis of a culture that holds out to women the promise of total self-control and self-creation. At the end of the decade, technology, surgery, fashion and consumption all feed the fantasy that we may create and control our own bodies, personas and substitute selves. Nothomb's preference for the possibilities of art over the limitations of life might be seen to shed light on these fantasies of self-perfection and the anxieties they foster. But there is another way in which Nothomb's aestheticism might be reconciled with feminism, if not exactly seen as feminist. The desire of Nothomb's protagonists to transform life into literature foregrounds a fantasy of creative power that women are frequently denied (and nowhere more so than in the decadent tradition). Decadent aestheticism may be narcissistic, solipsistic and amoral, but it aspires towards an absolute creative and imaginative freedom that is (at least artistically) empowering. Nothomb's creative fantasies, though they repeat some of the misogynist tropes of Decadence, stake a claim to these freedoms and the traditionally 'masculine' capacity to create ideal beauty.

On this point, one may detect similarities with the only woman writer to be associated with Decadence, Rachilde. Elitist, uninterested in politics and unwilling to associate herself with any collectivity, Rachilde was notoriously hostile to the feminism of her day but, as Liz Constable and Melanie Hawthorne (2004) have argued, Rachilde's public persona and her powerful female artist-protagonists subvert nineteenth-century gendered hierarchies in their insistence on a kind of creative power from which women artists have been excluded. In Rachilde's day, this power was denied by patriarchal discourses, but a century later the woman-writer-as-aesthete may be seen to clash with a different set of assumptions about women-authored work, namely the tendency of some feminist criticism to construct work by women writers as representative and political. Unlike Rachilde, Nothomb is not openly hostile to feminism but her decadent attachment to singularity and amorality nonetheless strains against political readings that rely on notions of collectivity and ethical commitment. However, as for Rachilde, the resolute amorality and unworldliness of the decadent aesthetic offers women artists another kind of freedom: the freedom to fantasise literature as a flight from the world and a space of infinite possibility.

Notes

1. See, for example, Rodgers 2003.
2. Caine 2003, for example, argues that Nothomb's cartoon-like narratives in fact subvert misogynist stereotyping.
3. One might take as an example Zola 1885, a novel that seeks to represent the grim realities of a miner's strike in northern France.
4. See, for example, the decadent classic, Huysmans 2010 [1884], in which the decadent hero des Esseintes retreats into an ideal, highly aestheticised world of his own creation.
5. For an analysis of Decadence (in particular with reference to feminism), see Holmes 2001; Paglia 2001; and Hawthorne 2002.
6. 'I am Prétéxtat Tach'. Unless otherwise indicated, all translations from the French are mine.
7. 'as if there could be any pleasure in creating something as depressing and ugly as life'; 'to write is not to seek to communicate'; 'to take pleasure'. It should be noted that the French verb *jouir* and its corresponding noun *jouissance* refer to an intense pleasure analogous to that experienced at orgasm.
8. 'interpretative grids'; 'sociology textbooks'.
9. 'no such reading exists'.
10. See Cixous 1975, for an elaboration of her notions of textual *jouissance* and *écriture féminine*.
11. 'dreadful polysemy'.
12. 'all the filth of life'.
13. 'a female character'; 'not an other'.
14. 'an abstract corpse'.
15. Even her parents, we are told, do not mourn their daughter; rather, they mourn the drowned maiden 'Ophélie' (192).

16 Nothomb 2010 is a particularly recent and explicit example of this, in which the character Melvin Mapple, a fictitious American soldier with a rapidly expanding waistline, transforms his body into a work of art by meticulously documenting his consumption and physical appearance.
17 'the total art form'.
18 'the Robert dictionary gave her the sustenance that she was lacking'. In this volume, see Amaleena Damlé's different reading of anorexia in Nothomb's *Robert des noms propres*.
19 'absolute intoxication'; 'the only transcendence'.
20 'If you are truly my friend, then let me be'.
21 'Thanks to me, Hazel has the life of a romantic princess. She was made for this, not for becoming a bourgeois baby-maker.'
22 'lapse of taste'; 'Your crimes now seem banal: it was their *exceptional*, their *unique* character that endowed them with grandeur. If I am nothing but a repetition, then yes, I hate you for it.'
23 'In one dazzling moment, Mlle Chavaigne's plans were radically altered'.
24 'Stop judging me on moral grounds and measure my worth against that of Prometheus'.
25 'You were so sublime that I was never ashamed of my crime, not for an instant. Know this at least: never has beauty been so well spent. Thanks to our isolated happiness, I have not lost a single fragment of your beautiful face.'
26 'If you had revealed it to me fifty years ago I would not have been able to resist the temptation to show myself to the whole world [. . .] I never would have known the idyllic existence that you have offered me.'
27 'Twenty years later, there was a war. The inhabitants of Mortes-Frontières hardly noticed it and it bothered them even less.
When the Allies landed, not far off, they complained a little.
"Let's hope it ends quickly. Those people make such a noise."'
28 'It was quick and clean. Classicism never commits an error of taste.'
29 're-establish the singular'.
30 These texts seem less concerned with self-expression than self-mythologisation, the narrator of *Métaphysique des tubes* candidly admitting that she does not see the point in being truthful given that nobody can check the facts (35).
31 See, for example, Nothomb 2010, or the ending of Nothomb 2002.
32 In this fantasy, the child appears as the divine creator of her own universe, bringing things into being by means of her perfected language. For the little Amélie, there is only one true language and it is her own. 'Pour moi', she explains, 'il n'y avait pas des langues, mais une seule et grande langue dont on pouvait choisir les variantes japonaises ou françaises, au gré de sa fantaisie.' (49) ('For me, there were not languages plural, but rather one single, great language from which one could choose Japanese or French variations.')
33 To give an example from *Mercure*, no sooner has the story drawn to a seeming close when the text is interrupted by a *note de l'auteur* (author's

note) in which the writer explains that the internal logic of her characters compelled her to write a second, equally possible, ending. She even directs us to the necessary page from which we are to paste on this alternative denouement. This rupture in the narrative draws attention to the characters precisely *as characters* dancing to the author's tune (171).
34 In this volume, see also Simon Kemp's chapter on authorial anxiety in the work of Annie Ernaux.

Conclusion

AMALEENA DAMLÉ AND GILL RYE

Anna Kemp's reading of Amélie Nothomb's work confronts us with the political (and emotional) investment that feminist readers and critics may have in women-authored texts. It also explicitly explores the creative endeavour and the relationship between life and literature. As we have seen, women writers in twenty-first-century France are engaging with real-life issues – the fallout from historical tragedies, family relations, violence, illness, death, racial, sexual and gendered identities, and the practice and role of writing itself. In analysing how women's writing interacts with sociocultural and political issues in France (and beyond) today and exploring the insights it offers, our contributors have drawn on a wide range of theoretical perspectives, they have situated their analyses of individual texts and authors in the broader literary context, and they have all paid close attention to the textual, the literary, the aesthetics of the texts they discuss. At a time when literary scholars – indeed, the whole of the humanities – are under pressure to justify their existence and to identify the social impact of what they do (and what the texts they work on do), it is important to communicate, to our funding bodies, to the general public, to each other, just how creative production engages the reader, whether it be through offering pleasurable experiences, confronting prejudices, challenging norms, shocking sensibilities, or stretching minds and imaginations. Reading is thus an important ingredient in the relationship between life and literature, life as literature. As this volume attests, in twenty-first-century women's writing in France the experiential and the experimental work together to create the reading experience as a dynamic process of exchange and information, engaging readers with difficult social issues, inviting them to bear witness to past traumas, revealing inner and intimate worlds, exploring new forms of expression, generating moral and ethical reflection, changing the way we look at the world we live in.

The chapters in this volume offer a glimpse of where women's writing is in twenty-first-century France. The collection does not aim to be comprehensive but, rather, it profiles trends and issues that the editors and contributors see as key. The limitations of space, personal choice and editorial decisions mean there will always be omissions. Endeavours such as this may risk becoming a snapshot and fixing perceptions of what the period has to offer. Women's writing in contemporary France is not, however, frozen in the first decade of the twenty-first century. It is an ongoing work in progress, and that is what makes it such an exciting field of research, of teaching and of reading. We hope that this volume will serve not only to take stock of authors, texts, trends and issues, but also to open up the literary production of the decade. The intention is certainly not to corral writers and texts into any form of literary movement or *tendance* or to force coherence where there is diversity and dynamism. Rather, we hope the volume not only points to what *we* think is interesting and important, but also that it will encourage other scholars and readers to explore further and more widely the rich offerings of contemporary women's writing in French.

Works Cited

Abécassis, Éliette (2005) *Un heureux événement* (Paris: Albin Michel).
Abrial, Stéphanie (2001) *Les Enfants de harkis: de la révolte à l'intégration* (Paris: L'Harmattan).
Adams, Carol and Josephine Donovan (eds) (1995) *Animals and Women: Feminist Theoretical Explorations* (Durham, NC: Duke University Press).
Agar-Mendousse, Trudy (2006) *Violence et créativité: de l'écriture algérienne au féminin* (Paris: L'Harmattan).
Amanieux, Laureline (2005) *Amélie Nothomb: l'éternelle affamée* (Paris: Albin Michel).
Amette, Jacques-Pierre (2003) 'Interview avec Jean-Marie Le Clézio', *Le Point*, 21 November, http://www.arabesques-editions.com/fr/articles/061702.html.
Angelo, Adrienne (2010) 'Vision, voice, and the female body: Nina Bouraoui's sites/sights of resistance', in *Francophone Women Between Visibility and Invisibility*, ed. Cybelle H. McFadden and Sandrine F. Teixidor (New York: Peter Lang), pp. 77–98.
Angot, Christine (1994) *Léonore, toujours* (Paris: Gallimard).
Angot, Christine (1999) *L'Inceste* (Paris: Stock).
Angot, Christine (2000) *Quitter la ville* (Paris: Stock).
Angot, Christine (2003) [2001] *La Peur du lendemain* suivi de *Normalement* (Paris: Stock/Le Livre de Poche).
Angot, Christine (2006) *Rendez-vous* (Paris: Flammarion).
Angot, Christine (2008) *Le Marché des amants* (Paris: Seuil).
Angot, Christine (2011) *Les Petits* (Paris: Flammarion).
Arènes, Jacques (1997) *Y a-t-il encore un père à la maison?* (Paris: Fleurus).
Arribert-Narce, Fabien (2011) 'Vers une écriture "photo-sociobiographique" du réel: entretien avec Annie Ernaux', *Roman 20–50*, 51, 151–66.
Arsic, Branka (2008) 'The experimental ordinary: Deleuze on eating and anorexic elegance', in *Deleuze and Gender*, ed. Claire Colebrook (Edinburgh: Edinburgh University Press), pp. 34–59.
Artaud, Antonin (1989) [1947] *L'Arve et l'aume, suivi de 24 lettres à Marc Barbezat* (Paris: L'Arbalète).
Asibong, Andrew and Shirley Jordan (eds) (2009) *Marie NDiaye: l'étrangeté à l'œuvre*, a special issue of *Revue des Sciences Humaines*, 293, 1.
August-Franck, Francine (2006) *Les Feux Follets de Bourg d'Iré: espoir et survie d'une âme d'enfant* (Paris: L'Harmattan).
Azoulai, Nathalie (2003) *Mère agitée* (Paris: Seuil).
Bâ, Mariama (2005) [1986] *Un chant écarlate* (Dakar: Les Nouvelles Éditions Africaines du Sénégal).

Badinter, Élisabeth (2010) *Le Conflit, la femme et la mère* (Paris: Flammarion).
Baetens, Jan (1999) 'La crise des romans ou le crise du roman', in *Écritures contemporaines 2: États du roman contemporain, Revue des Lettres Modernes*, ed. Jan Baetens and Dominique Viart (Paris: Minard), pp. 9–16.
Baetens, Jan and Ari J. Blatt (eds) (2008) *Writing and the Image Today*, a special issue of *Yale French Studies*, 114.
Bailly, Danielle (ed.) (2004) *Traqués, cachés, vivants* (Paris: L'Harmattan).
Bailly, Danielle (ed.) (2006) *Enfants cachés: analyses et débats* (Paris: L'Harmattan).
Bainbrigge, Susan and Jeanette den Toonder (eds) (2003) *Amélie Nothomb: Authorship, Identity and Narrative Practice* (New York: Peter Lang).
Barbery, Muriel (2006) *L'Élégance du hérisson* (Paris: Gallimard).
Barbery, Muriel (2008) *The Elegance of the Hedgehog*, trans. Alison Anderson (London: Gallic Books).
Barnet, Marie Claire (2007) 'Introduction', in *Affaires de famille: The Family in Contemporary French Culture and Theory*, ed. Marie-Claire Barnet and Edward Welch (Amsterdam and New York: Rodopi), pp. 11–20.
Barnet, Marie-Claire and Edward Welch (eds) (2007) *Affaires de famille: The Family in Contemporary French Culture and Theory* (Amsterdam and New York: Rodopi).
Barnet, Marie-Claire and Shirley Jordan (eds) (2010) *Space, Place and Landscape in Contemporary Francophone Women's Writing*, a special issue of *Dalhousie French Studies*, 93 (winter).
Barthes, Roland (1973) *Le Plaisir du texte* (Paris: Seuil).
Barthes, Roland (1975) *The Pleasure of the Text*, trans. Richard Miller (Oxford: Blackwell).
Barthes, Roland (1984) 'La mort de l'auteur', *Essais critiques IV: le bruissement de la langue* (Paris: Seuil), pp. 61–7.
Baudelaire, Charles (1961) [1863] 'Éloge du maquillage', in *Œuvres complètes* (Paris: Gallimard), pp. 1182–5.
Beauvoir, Simone de (1967) *La Femme rompue* (Paris: Gallimard).
Beauvoir, Simone de (1969) *The Woman Destroyed*, trans. Patrick O'Brian (New York: Pantheon Books).
Beck, Béatrix, illustrated by Gaël Davrinche (2010) *L'Épouvante l'émerveillement* (Paris: Chemin de Fer).
Besnaci-Lancou, Fatima (2005) *Fille de harki* (Paris: Atelier).
Besnaci-Lancou, Fatima (2006) *Nos mères, paroles blessées: une autre histoire de harkis* (Léchelle: Zellige).
Best, Victoria and Martin Crowley (2007) *The New Pornographies: Explicit Sex in Recent French Fiction and Film* (Manchester: Manchester University Press).
Boose, Lynda E. and Betty S. Flowers (eds) (1989) *Daughters and Fathers* (Baltimore and London: The John Hopkins University Press).
Bordo, Susan (1993) *Unbearable Weight: Feminism, Western Culture and the Body* (Berkeley: University of California Press).
Borgomano, Madeleine (2004) 'L'ombre du père', in *Le Roman français au tournant du XXIe siècle*, ed. Bruno Blanckeman, Aline Mura-Brunel and Marc Dambre (Paris: Presses Sorbonne Nouvelle), pp. 249–61.

Bouraoui, Nina (1991) *La Voyeuse interdite* (Paris: Gallimard).
Bouraoui, Nina (2000) *Garçon manqué* (Paris: Stock).
Bouraoui, Nina (2004) *Poupée Bella* (Paris: Stock).
Bouraoui, Nina (2005) *Mes mauvaises pensées* (Paris: Stock).
Bouraoui, Nina (2008) *Appelez-moi par mon prénom* (Paris: Stock).
Bourdieu, Pierre (ed.) (1965) *Un art moyen: essai sur les usages sociaux de la photographie* (Paris: Minuit).
Bragard, Véronique and Srilata Ravi (eds) (2011) *Écritures mauriciennes au féminin: penser l'altérité* (Paris: L'Harmattan).
Brah, Avtar and Annie E. Coombes (2000) *Hybridity and its Discontents: Politics, Science, Culture* (London: Routledge).
Braidotti, Rosi (1994) *Nomadic Subjects: Embodiment and Sexual Difference in Contemporary Feminist Theory* (New York: Columbia University Press).
Braidotti, Rosi (2002) *Metamorphosis: Towards a Materialist Theory of Becoming* (Cambridge: Polity Press).
Bray, Abigail and Claire Colebrook (1998) 'The haunted flesh: corporeal feminism and the politics of (dis)embodiment', *Signs* 24, 1, 37–67.
Brooks, Peter (1996) 'Storytelling without fear? Confession in law and literature', in *Law's Stories: Narrative and Rhetoric in the Law*, ed. Peter Brooks and Paul Gewirtz (New Haven, CT: Yale University Press), pp. 114–34.
Bruch, Hilde (1978) *The Golden Cage: The Enigma of Anorexia Nervosa* (London: Open Books).
Bruel, Alain (1998) *Un avenir pour la paternité?* (Paris: Syros).
Burgelin, Claude (2001) 'Quelques remarques sur le sujet oulipien en guise de préface', in *Un art simple et tout d'exécution: cinq leçons sur l'Oulipo*, ed. Marcel Bénabou, Jacques Jouet, Harry Mathews and Jacques Roubaud (Paris: Circé), pp. 9–20.
Burgelin, Claude, Isabelle Grell and Roger-Yves Roche (eds) (2010) *Autofiction(s): colloque de Cérisy* (Lyon: Presses Universitaires de Lyon).
Burko-Falcman, Berthe (2007) *Un prénom républicain* (Paris: Seuil).
Burnside, Anna (2001) 'Flesh and fantasy', *Sunday Herald*, 27 May, 19.
Butler, Judith (1990) *Gender Trouble: Feminism and the Subversion of Identity* (New York: Routledge).
Butor, Michel (1962) *Mobile: étude pour une représentation des États-Unis* (Paris: Gallimard).
Caine, Philippa (2003) '"Entre-deux": inscription of female corporeality in the writing of Amélie Nothomb', in *Amélie Nothomb: Authorship, Identity and Narrative Practice*, ed. Susan Bainbrigge and Jeanette den Toonder (New York: Peter Lang), pp. 72–84.
Cairns, Lucille (2002a) *Lesbian Desire in Post-1968 French Literature* (Lewiston: Edwin Mellen Press).
Cairns, Lucille (2007) '*Dissidences charnelles*: the female body in revolt', in *The Flesh in the Text*, ed. Thomas Baldwin, James Fowler and Shane Welter (Bern: Peter Lang), pp. 205–25.
Cairns, Lucille (2011) *Post-War Jewish Women's Writing in French* (Oxford: Legenda).
Cairns, Lucille (ed.) (2002b) *Gay and Lesbian Cultures in France* (Oxford: Peter Lang).

Calle, Sophie (2001) *Vingt ans après*, http://www.panoplie.org/ecart/calle/calle. html.
Calle, Sophie (2007) *Prenez soin de vous* (Arles: Actes Sud).
Calle, Sophie (2012) *Rachel Monique...* (Paris: Éditions Xavier Barral).
Camus, Renaud (1988) *Tricks*, preface by Roland Barthes (Paris: P.O.L.).
Cardinal, Marie (1975) *Les Mots pour le dire* (Paris: Grasset & Fasquelle).
Cardinal, Marie (1984) *The Words to Say It*, trans. Pat Goodheart (Cambridge, MA: Van Vactor and Goodheart).
Cardinal, Marie (1987) *Les Grands Désordres* (Paris: Grasset).
Cardinal, Marie (1991) *Devotion and Disorder*, trans. Karin Montin (London: Women's Press).
Carroll, Lewis (1871) *Through the Looking Glass, and What Alice Found There* (London: Macmillan).
Castelain-Meunier, Christine (1997) *Cramponnez-vous, les pères: les hommes face à leur femme et à leurs enfants* (Paris: Albin Michel).
Castelain-Meunier, Christine (1998) *La Paternité* (Paris: Presses Universitaires de France).
Castelain-Meunier, Christine (2002) *La Place des hommes et les métamorphoses de la famille* (Paris: Presses Universitaires de France).
Ceccaldi, Lucie (2008) *L'Innocente* (Paris: Scali).
Célestin, Roger, Eliane DalMolin and Isabelle de Courtivron (eds) (2003) *Beyond French Feminisms* (London: Palgrave Macmillan).
Chamberlain, Stephanie (2005) 'Fantasizing infanticide: Lady Macbeth and the murdering mother in early modern England', *College Literature*, 32, 3, 72–91.
Charbit, Tom (2006) *Les Harkis* (Paris: La Découverte).
Chawaf, Chantal (2010) *Je suis née* (Paris: des femmes).
Chen, Ying (1999) *L'Ingratitude* (Arles: Actes Sud).
Cixous, Hélène (1975) 'Le rire de la Méduse', *L'Arc*, 61, 39–54.
Cixous, Hélène (1976) 'The laugh of the Medusa', trans. Keith and Paula Cohen, *Signs*, 1, 4 (summer), 875–93.
Cixous, Hélène (1997) *Or, les lettres de mon père* (Paris: des femmes).
Cixous, Hélène and Catherine Clément (1975) *La Jeune Née* (Paris: 10/18).
Cixous, Hélène and Catherine Clément (1986) *The Newly-Born Woman*, trans. Betsy Wing (Minneapolis: University of Minnesota Press).
Colonna, Vincent (2004) *Autofictions et autres mythomanies littéraires* (Auch: Tristram).
Comby, Geneviève (2008) 'Les femmes lisent plus que les hommes', *Le Matin*, 4 May, http://archives.lematin.ch/LM/LMD/-/article-2008-05-07.
Condé, Maryse (2000) 'Order, disorder, freedom and the West Indian writer', *Yale French Studies*, 97, 151–65.
Connan-Pintado, Christiane (2009) 'L'univers étrange et familier de Marie NDiaye: trois paraboles à l'usage des enfants', *Marie NDiaye: l'étrangeté à l'œuvre*, ed. Andrew Asibong and Shirley Jordan, a special issue of *Revue des Sciences Humaines*, 293,1, 39–52.
Connon, Daisy (2010) *Subjects Not-at-home: Forms of the Uncanny in the Contemporary French Novel, Emmanuel Carrère, Marie NDiaye, Eugène Savitzkaya* (Amsterdam and New York: Rodopi).

Constable, Liz and Melanie Hawthorne (2004) 'Rachilde: a decadent woman rewriting women in decadence', in Rachilde, *Monsieur Vénus: roman matérialiste*, ed. Liz Constable and Melanie Hawthorne (New York: The Modern Language Association of America), pp. ix–xxxiv.
Constant, Paule (2007) *La Bête à chagrin* (Paris: Gallimard).
Coquio, Catherine and Aurélie Kalisky (eds) (2007) *L'Enfant et le génocide: témoignages sur l'enfance pendant la Shoah* (Paris: Laffont).
Cotille-Foley, Nora (2008) 'L'usage de la photographie chez Annie Ernaux', *French Studies*, 62, 442–54.
Cressot, Marcel (1974) *Le Style et ses techniques: précis d'analyse stylistique* (Paris: P.U.F.).
Crom, Nathalie (2005) 'Marie Darrieussecq, née quelque part . . . Sur les questions de l'identité, de l'appartenance, l'écrivain livre un roman très simplement beau, fluide et entêtant', *La Croix*, 8 September, 12.
Cruickshank, Ruth (2009) *Fin de millénaire French Fiction: The Aesthetics of Crisis* (Oxford: Oxford University Press).
Culler, Jonathan (1983) *Roland Barthes* (New York and Oxford: Oxford University Press).
Cusset, Catherine (2010) *New York: journal d'un cycle* (Paris: Mercure de France).
Damlé, Amaleena (2011) 'Nomadic trajectories: postfeminism and contemporary women's writing in French', *Parcours de femmes: Twenty Years of Women in French*, ed. Maggie Allison and Angela Kershaw (Bern: Peter Lang), pp. 133–50.
Damlé, Amaleena (2014, forthcoming) *The Becoming of the Body: Contemporary Women's Writing in French* (Edinburgh: Edinburgh University Press).
Dandrieu, Laurent (2006) [2001] 'Le grand marasme de la littérature contemporaine', *http://www.ichtus.fr/article.php3?id_article=118*.
Darrieussecq, Marie (1996a) *Truismes* (Paris: P.O.L.).
Darrieussecq, Marie (1996b) 'L'Autofiction un genre pas sérieux', *Poétique*, 107 (September), 369–80.
Darrieussecq, Marie (1998) *Pig Tales: A Novel of Lust and Transformation*, trans. Linda Coverdale (London: Faber and Faber).
Darrieussecq, Marie (1999) [1998] *Naissance des fantômes* (Paris: P.O.L.).
Darrieussecq, Marie (2001) *Bref séjour chez les vivants* (Paris: P.O.L.).
Darrieussecq, Marie (2002) *Le Bébé* (Paris: P.O.L.).
Darrieussecq, Marie (2003) *White* (Paris: P.O.L.; Folio).
Darrieussecq, Marie (2005a) *White*, trans. Ian Monk (London: Faber and Faber).
Darrieussecq, Marie (2005b) *Le Pays* (Paris: P.O.L.).
Darrieussecq, Marie (2007) *Tom est mort* (Paris: P.O.L.).
Davis, Colin and Elizabeth Fallaize (2000) *French Fiction in the Mitterand Years: Memory, Narrative, Desire* (Oxford: Oxford University Press).
Delaisi de Parseval, Geneviève (1981) *La Part du père* (Paris: Seuil).
Delaume, Chloé (2000) *Les Mouflettes d'Atropos* (Paris: Farrago).
Delaume, Chloé (2001) *Le Cri du sablier* (Paris: Farrago/Léo Scheer).
Delaume, Chloé (2003a) *Corpus Simsi* (Paris: Léo Scheer).
Delaume, Chloé (2003b) *La Vanité des somnambules* (Paris: Farrago/Léo Scheer).

Delaume, Chloé (2004) *Certainement pas* (Paris: Verticales).
Delaume, Chloé (2005) *Les Juins ont tous la même peau* (Paris: La Chasse au Snark).
Delaume, Chloé (2006) *J'habite dans la télévision* (Paris: Verticales).
Delaume, Chloé (2007) *La Nuit je suis Buffy Summers* (Paris: Ère).
Delaume, Chloé (2009a) *Dans ma maison sous terre* (Paris: Seuil).
Delaume, Chloé (2009b) *Éden matin midi et soir* (Paris: Joca Seria).
Delaume, Chloé (2010a) *La Règle du je* (Paris: Presses Universitaires de France).
Delaume, Chloé (2010b) 'S'écrire mode d'emploi', in *Autofiction(s): colloque de Cérisy 2008*, ed. Claude Burgelin, Isabelle Grell and Roger-Yves Roche (Lyon: Presses Universitaires de Lyon), pp. 109–26, *www.publie.net*.
Delaume, Chloé (2012) *Une femme avec personne dedans* (Paris: Seuil).
Deleuze, Gilles (1993) *Critique et clinique* (Paris: Minuit).
Deleuze, Gilles and Félix Guattari (1975) *Kafka: pour une littérature mineure* (Paris: Minuit).
Deleuze, Gilles and Félix Guattari (1980) *Capitalisme et schizophrénie 2: mille plateaux* (Paris: Minuit).
Deleuze, Gilles and Félix Guattari (1986) *Kafka: Toward a Minor Literature*, trans. Dana Polan (Minneapolis: University of Minnesota Press).
Deleuze, Gilles and Félix Guattari (1987) *A Thousand Plateaus: Capitalism and Schizophrenia*, trans. Brian Massumi (London: Continuum).
Deleuze, Gilles and Félix Guattari (1991) *Qu'est-ce que la philosophie?* (Paris: Minuit).
Deleuze, Gilles and Claire Parnet (1996) [1977] *Dialogues* (Paris: Flammarion).
Delpard, Raphaël (1993) *Les Enfants cachés* (Paris: J.-C. Lattès).
Delumeau, Jean and Daniel Roche (eds) (2000) *Histoire des pères et de la paternité* (Paris: Larousse).
Delvaux, Martine (2006) 'Des images malgré tout: Annie Ernaux/Marc Marie: *L'Usage de la photo*', *French Forum*, 31, 3, 137–55.
Despentes, Virginie (1993) *Baise-moi* (Paris: Florent Massot).
Despentes, Virginie (2002) *Teen spirit* (Paris: J'ai lu).
Despentes, Virginie (2006) *King Kong théorie* (Paris: Grasset & Fasquelle; Livre de Poche).
Despentes, Virginie (2010) *Apocalypse bébé* (Paris: Grasset).
Desplechin, Marie and Éric Lambé (2004) *Le Sac à main* (Tournai: Estuaire).
Desplechin, Marie and Éric Lambé (2005) *La Photo* (Tournai: Estuaire).
Devi, Ananda (1989) *Rue la Poudrière* (Abidjan: Nouvelles Éditions Africaines).
Devi, Ananda (2000) *Moi, l'interdite* (Paris: Dapper).
Devi, Ananda (2006) *Ève de ses décombres* (Paris: Gallimard).
Devi, Ananda (2009) *Le Sari vert* (Paris: Gallimard).
Devoisin, Marie-Hélène (2010) '*MLF*: l'invention au XXe siècle d'une *homologia parrêsia* côté femmes', *Quid pro quo*, 5 (June), 3–30.
Diderot, Denis (1962) [1796] *Jacques le fataliste et son maître* (Paris: Livre de poche; first published in a German version in 1792).
Donadey, Anne (2001) *Recasting Postcolonialism: Women Writing Between Worlds* (Portsmouth, NH: Heinemann Studies in African Literature).

Donnat, Olivier (2005) 'La féminisation des pratiques culturelles', *Développement culturel*, 147 (June), http://www2.culture.gouv.fr/culture/deps/2008/pdf/dc147.pdf.
Donnat, Olivier (2008) *Les Pratiques culturelles des Français à l'ère numérique*, ch.6., http://www.pratiquesculturelles.culture.gouv.fr/08resultat_chap6.php.
Doubrovsky, Serge (1989) *Le Livre brisé* (Paris: Grasset).
Doubrovsky, Serge (2001) [1977] *Fils* (Paris: Gallimard).
Doubrovsky, Serge (2007) 'Les points sur les "i"', in *Genèse et autofiction*, ed. Jean-Louis Jeanelle and Catherine Viollet with Isabelle Grell (Louvain-La-Neuve: Academia-Bruylant), pp. 53–65.
Ducas, Sylvie (2010) 'Fiction auctorial, postures et impostures médiatiques: le cas de Chloé Delaume, "personnage de fiction"', *Le Temps des Médias*, 14 (January), 176–92.
Dudovitz, Resa (1990) *The Myth of Superwoman: Women's Bestsellers in France and the United States* (London and New York: Routledge).
Dulac, Germain (1993) *La Paternité: les transformations sociales récentes* (Quebec: Conseil de la famille).
Dumas, Alexandre (1981) [1844–6] *Le Comte de Monte-Cristo*, ed. Gilbert Sigaux (Paris: Gallimard).
Dumas, Alexandre (1984) [1844] *Les Trois Mousquétaires* (Paris: Flammarion).
Dunayer, Joan (1995) 'Sexist words, speciest roots', in *Animals and Women: Feminist Theoretical Explorations*, ed. Carol Adams and Josephine Donovan (Durham, NC: Duke University Press), pp. 11–32.
Duras, Marguerite (1958) *Moderato cantabile* (Paris: Minuit).
Duras, Marguerite (1960) *Moderato cantabile*, trans. Richard Seaver (New York: Grove Press).
Duras, Marguerite (1984) *L'Amant* (Paris: Minuit).
Duras, Marguerite (1990) *La Pluie d'été* (Paris: P.O.L.).
Duras, Marguerite (1993) *The Lover*, trans. Barbara Bray (London: Bloomsbury).
Dustan, Guillaume (1997) *Je sors ce soir* (Paris: P.O.L.).
Edwards, Natalie (2011) *Shifting Subjects: Plural Subjectivity in Francophone Women's Autobiography* (Newark: University of Delaware Press).
Edwards, Natalie and Chris Hogarth (eds) (2008) *Gender and Displacement: 'Home' in Contemporary Francophone Women's Autobiography* (Newcastle: Cambridge Scholars Publishing).
Edwards, Natalie and Chris Hogarth (eds) (2010) *This 'Self' Which is Not One: Women's Life-Writing in French* (Newcastle: Cambridge Scholars Publishing).
Edwards, Natalie, Amy Hubbell and Ann Miller (eds) (2011) *Textual and Visual Selves: Photography, Film and Comic Art in French Autobiography* (Lincoln, NE: University of Nebraska Press).
Egan, Susanna (1999) *Mirror Talk: Genres of Crisis in Contemporary Autobiography* (Chapel Hill: University of North Carolina Press).
Ellmann, Maud (1993) *The Hunger Artists: Starving, Writing and Imprisonment* (Cambridge: Virago).
Éribon, Didier (2001) *Une morale du minoritaire: variations sur un thème de Jean Genet* (Paris: Fayard).

Ernaux, Annie (1984) *La Place* (Paris: Gallimard).
Ernaux, Annie (1988) *Une femme* (Paris: Gallimard).
Ernaux, Annie (1991) *Passion simple* (Paris: Gallimard).
Ernaux, Annie (1993) *Journal du dehors* (Paris: Gallimard).
Ernaux, Annie (1997a) *La Honte* (Paris: Gallimard).
Ernaux, Annie (1997b) *'Je ne suis pas sortie de ma nuit'* (Paris: Gallimard).
Ernaux, Annie (2000a) *L'Événement* (Paris: Gallimard).
Ernaux, Annie (2000b) *La Vie extérieure, 1993–1999* (Paris: Gallimard).
Ernaux, Annie (2001) *Se perdre* (Paris: Gallimard).
Ernaux, Annie (2002) *L'Occupation* (Paris: Gallimard).
Ernaux, Annie (2008) *Les Années* (Paris: Gallimard).
Ernaux, Annie and Frédéric-Yves Jeannet (2003) *L'Écriture comme un couteau: entretien avec Frédéric-Yves Jeannet* (Paris: Stock).
Ernaux, Annie and Marc Marie (2005) *L'Usage de la photo* (Paris: Gallimard).
Etcherelli, Claire (1967) *Élise ou la vraie vie* (Paris: Denoël).
Etcherelli, Claire (1969) *Elise, or the Real Life*, trans. June P. Wilson and Walter Benn Michaels (New York: William Morrow).
Even-Zohar, Itamar (1990) *Polysystem Studies* (Durham, NC: Duke University Press).
Faerber, Johan (2002) 'Le bruissement d'elles ou le questionnement identitaire dans l'œuvre de Christine Angot', in *Nouvelles écrivaines, nouvelles voix?*, ed. Nathalie Morello and Catherine Rodgers (Amsterdam and New York: Rodopi), pp. 47–62.
Fairbairn, W. R. D. (1981) *An Object-Relations Theory of the Personality* (London: Routledge).
Fallaize, Elizabeth (1993) *French Women's Writing: Recent Fiction* (London: Macmillan).
Fanon, Frantz (1952) *Peau noire, masques blancs* (Paris: Seuil).
Fayet, Agnès (2006) 'Les images fantômes du texte: usage romanesque de la photographie dans trois textes contemporains (Guibert, Ernaux, Toussaint)', *Études romanesques*, 10, 305–14.
Feldman, Marion (2009) *Entre trauma et protection: quel devenir pour les enfants juifs cachés en France (1940–1945)?* (Toulouse: Érès).
Felman, Shoshana and Dori Laub (1992) *Testimony: Crises of Witnessing in Literature, Psychoanalysis, and History* (New York and London: Routledge).
Felski, Rita (1989) *Beyond Feminist Aesthetics: Feminist Literature and Social Change* (Cambridge, MA: Harvard University Press).
Fernandes, Martine (2005) 'Confessions d'une enfant du siècle: Nina Bouraoui ou la batârde dans *Garçon manqué* et *La Vie heureuse*', *L'Esprit Créateur*, 45, 1 (spring), 67–78.
Ferniot, Christine and Philippe Delaroche (2008) 'Entretien: Annie Ernaux', *L'Express*, 1 February, http://www.lexpress.fr/culture/livre/annie-ernaux_813603.html.
Fiemeyer, Isabelle (2002) 'L'univers ouaté de bébé', *Lire*, 3 April, http://www.lire.fr/critique.asp?idC=39800/idTC=3/idR=218/idG=3April 2002.
Fleutiaux, Pierrette and J. S. Cartier (2006) *Les Étoiles à l'envers: New York* (Arles: Actes Sud).
Fontanel, Sophie (2011) *L'Envie* (Paris: Robert Laffont).

Fort, Pierre-Louis (2007) *Ma mère la morte: l'écriture du deuil au féminin chez Yourcenar, Beauvoir et Ernaux* (Paris: Imago).
Foster, Hal (2004) *Prosthetic Gods* (Cambridge, MA and London: MIT Press).
Foucault, Michel (1976) *Histoire de la sexualité 1: la volonté de savoir* (Paris: Gallimard).
Fouque, Antoinette (1995) *Il y a deux sexes: essais de féminologie*, new and expanded edn (Paris: Gallimard).
Fouque, Antoinette (2009) *Qui êtes-vous, Antoinette Fouque? Entretiens avec Christophe Bourseiller* (Paris: Bourin Éditeur).
Frank, Arthur (1995) *The Wounded Storyteller: Body, Illness, and Ethics* (Chicago: University of Chicago Press).
French, Marilyn (1985) *Beyond Power: On Women, Men and Morals* (New York: Summit Books).
Frith, Simon (1998) *Performing Rites: On the Value of Popular Music* (Cambridge, MA: Harvard University Press).
Gallay, Claudie (2008) *Les Déferlantes* (Paris: Rouergue).
Gallay, Claudie (2011) *The Breakers*, trans. Alison Anderson (London: Maclehose Press).
Gammel, Irene (1999) 'Body politics and confessional interventions', in *Confessional Politics: Women's Sexual Self-Representations in Life Writing and Popular Media*, ed. Irene Gammel (Carbondale: Southern Illinois University Press), p. 11.
Garnier, Xavier (2001) *L'Éclat de la figure: étude sur l'antipersonnage de roman* (Brussels: Peter Lang).
Garréta, Anne (1986) *Sphinx* (Paris: Grasset & Fasquelle; Livre de Poche).
Garréta, Anne (1987) *Pour en finir avec le genre humain* (Paris: François Bourin).
Garréta, Anne (1990) *Ciels liquides* (Paris: Grasset).
Garréta, Anne F. (1991) 'La Pyramide', *La Règle du jeu*, 5, http://cosmogonie.free.fr/pyramide.html.
Garréta, Anne F. (1994) 'Nuits', *Le Serpent à plumes*, 24, http://cosmogonie.free.fr/nuits.html.
Garréta, Anne F. (1996) 'In light of invisibility', in *Same Sex, Different Text: Gay and Lesbian Writing in French*, ed. Brigitte Mahuzier et al., a special issue of *Yale French Studies*, 90, 205–13.
Garréta, Anne F. (1999) *La Décomposition* (Paris: Grasset).
Garréta, Anne F. (2000) 'Entretien avec Anne F. Garréta', by Eva Domeneghini (13 October), http://cosmogonie.free.fr/interview.html.
Garréta, Anne F. (2002) *Pas un jour* (Paris: Grasset & Fasquelle; Livre de Poche).
Gasparini, Philippe (2008) *Autofiction: une aventure du langage* (Paris: Seuil).
Gaudet, Jeannette (2002) 'Des livres sur la liberté: conversation avec Marie Darrieussecq', *Dalhousie French Studies*, 59, 108–18.
Gavalda, Anna (2004) *Ensemble, c'est tout* (Paris: Le Dilettante).
Gavalda, Anna (2006) *Hunting and Gathering*, trans. Alison Anderson (London: Chatto and Windus).
Gavalda, Anna (2008) *La Consolante* (Paris: Le Dilettante).

Gavalda, Anna (2010) *Consolation*, trans. Alison Anderson (London: Chatto and Windus).
Genette, Gérard (1969) 'Vraisemblance et motivation', in *Figures II* (Paris: Seuil), pp. 71–99.
Gervais-Marx, Danièle (2004) [1997] *La Ligne de démarcation* (Paris: Hachette Littératures).
Gilbert, Sandra and Susan Gubar (1979) *The Madwoman in the Attic: The Woman Writer and the Nineteenth-Century Literary Imagination* (New Haven, CT and London: Yale University Press).
Gladieu, Stéphan and Dalila Kerchouche (2003) *Destins de harkis* (Paris: Autrement).
Goffman, Erving (1990) [1963] *Stigma: Notes on the Management of Spoiled Identity* (London: Penguin).
Goggin, Joyce (2009) 'A body hermeneutic? *Corpus Simsi* or reading like a Sim', in *The Hand of the Interpreter: Essays on Meaning after Theory*, ed. G. F. Mitrano and Eric Jarosinski (Oxford and Bern: Peter Lang), pp. 205–21.
Gonzáles, Jennifer A. (1995) 'Autotopographies', in *Prosthetic Territories: Politics and Hypertechnologies*, ed. Gabriel Brahm Jr. and Mark Driscoll (Boulder: Westview Press), pp. 133–50.
Gorrara, Claire (2003) 'L'assassinat de l'écriture: Amélie Nothomb's *Les Combustibles*', in *Amélie Nothomb: Authorship, Identity and Narrative Practice*, ed. Susan Bainbrigge and Jeanette den Toonder (New York: Peter Lang), pp. 105–13.
Green, André (1993) *Le Travail du négatif* (Paris: Minuit).
Green, André (1999) *The Work of the Negative*, trans. Andrew Weller (London: Free Association).
Grosz, Elizabeth (1994) *Volatile Bodies: Toward a Corporeal Feminism* (Bloomington: Indiana University Press).
Guibert, Hervé (2001) *Le Mausolée des amants: journal 1976–1991* (Paris: Gallimard).
Guichard, Thierry (2009a) 'L'Adieu à Nathalie D', *Le Matricule des Anges*, 100 (February), 24–7.
Guichard, Thierry (2009b) 'Laboratoire de génétique textuelle', *Le Matricule des Anges*, 100 (February), 22–4.
Hannah, Ettel (2003) *Le Caillou de lune* (Paris: Michalon).
Haraway, Donna J. (1991) *Simians, Cyborgs, and Women: The Reinvention of Women* (London: Free Association Books).
Haraway, Donna J. (1992) *Primate Visions: Gender, Race, and Nature in the World of Modern Science* (London: Verso).
Haraway, Donna J. (1996) *Modest_Witness@Second_Millennium.FemaleMan©_ Meets_Oncomouse*™ (New York: Routledge).
Hargreaves, Alec G., Charles Forsdick and David Murphy (eds) (2010) *Transnational French Studies: Postcolonialism and Littérature-monde* (Liverpool: Liverpool University Press).
Harrow, Susan (2010) 'New ekphrastic poetics', *New Ekphrastic Poetics*, ed. Susan Harrow, a special issue of *French Studies*, 64, 3, 255–64.
Havercroft, Barbara (2007) 'Paper thin: agency and anorexia in Geneviève Brisac's *Petite*', in *Unfitting Stories: Narrative Approaches to Disease, Disability*

and Trauma, ed. Valerie Raoul, Connie Canam, Angela D. Henderson and Carla Paterson (Waterloo: Wilfrid Laurier University Press), pp. 61–9.

Havercroft, Barbara (2009) 'L'autre "scène": l'écriture du cancer dans *L'Usage de la photo* d'Annie Ernaux et Marc Marie', in *Annie Ernaux: approches critiques et interdisciplinaires*, ed. Sergio Villani (Ottawa: Legas), pp. 127–37.

Havercroft, Barbara (2013a, forthcoming) 'Le refus du romanesque? Hybridité générique et écriture de l'inceste chez Christine Angot', in *Le Romanesque dans la littérature française contemporaine*, a special issue of *Revue des Sciences Humaines*.

Havercroft, Barbara (2013b, forthcoming) 'Splendeurs et misères de la confession au féminin au XXIe siècle', in *Narrations d'un nouveau siècle: romans et récits français (2001–2010)*, ed. Bruno Blanckeman and Barbara Havercroft (Paris: Presses Sorbonne Nouvelle).

Havercroft, Barbara, Pascal Michelucci and Pascal Riendeau (eds) (2010) *Le Roman français de l'extrême contemporain: écritures, engagements, énonciations* (Quebec: Nota Bene).

Havercroft, Barbara and Michael Sheringham (eds) (2012) 'Fictions de soi/Self-Fictions', a special issue of *Revue critique de fixxion française contemporaine/Critical Review of Contemporary French Fixxion*, 4 (June).

Hawthorne, Melanie (2002) *Rachilde and French Women's Authorship: From Decadence to Modernism* (Lincoln, NE: University of Nebraska Press).

Hazan, Katy (2000) *Les Orphelins de la Shoah: les maisons de l'espoir (1944–1960)* (Paris: Les Belles Lettres).

Henke, Suzette (2000) *Shattered Subjects: Trauma and Testimony in Women's Life-Writing* (Basingstoke: Macmillan).

Henric, Jacques (2001) *Légendes de Catherine M* (Paris: Denoël).

Héritier, Françoise (2002) *Masculin-féminin*, tome 2: *Dissoudre la hiérarchie* (Paris: Odile Jacob).

Hewitt, Leah (1990) *Autobiographical Tightropes: Simone de Beauvoir, Nathalie Sarraute, Marguerite Duras, Monique Wittig and Maryse Condé* (Lincoln, NE and London: University of Nebraska Press).

Heywood, Leslie (1996) *Dedication to Hunger: The Anorexic Aesthetic in Modern Culture* (Berkeley: University of California Press).

Hirsch, Marianne (1989) *The Mother/Daughter Plot: Narrative, Psychoanalysis, Feminism* (Bloomington: Indiana University Press).

Hirsch, Marianne (1997) *Family Frames: Photography, Narrative and Postmemory* (Cambridge, MA: Harvard University Press).

Hirsch, Marianne (2012) *The Generation of Postmemory: Writing and Visual Culture after the Holocaust* (New York: Columbia University Press).

Hoctan, Caroline (2010) 'Les laborantines du verbe', in *Les Romancières françaises*, a special issue of *Le Magazine Littéraire* (September), 90–2.

Holmes, Diana (2001) *Rachilde: Decadence, Gender and the Woman Writer* (London: Berg).

Holmes, Diana (2006) *Romance and Readership in Twentieth-Century France: Love Stories* (Oxford: Oxford University Press).

Holmes, Diana (2010) 'The comfortable reader: romantic bestsellers and critical disdain', in *Story-Telling in Contemporary French Fiction: le*

'*prêt-à-penser*' and *Reading Pleasure*, ed. Diana Holmes and David Platten, a special issue of *French Cultural Studies*, 21, 4 (November), 287–96.
Houellebecq, Michel (1998) *Les Particules élémentaires* (Paris: Flammarion).
Houellebecq, Michel (2010a) *La Carte et le territoire* (Paris: Flammarion).
Houellebecq, Michel (2010b) *The Map and the Territory*, trans. Gavin Bowd (London: Heinemann).
Hurstel, Françoise (1996) *La Déchirure paternelle* (Paris: Presses Universitaires de France).
Hutton, Margaret-Anne (ed.) (2009) *Redefining the Real: The Fantastic in Contemporary French and Francophone Women's Writing* (Oxford: Peter Lang).
Huysmans, Joris-Karl (2010) [1884] *À rebours* (Paris: Gallimard).
Hyvrard, Jeanne (1975) *Les Prunes de Cythère* (Paris: Minuit).
Hyvrard, Jeanne (1976) *Mère la mort* (Paris: Minuit).
Hyvrard, Jeanne (1977) *La Meurtritude* (Paris: Minuit).
Hyvrard, Jeanne (1988) *Mother Death*, trans. Laurie Edson (Lincoln, NE: University of Nebraska Press).
Hyvrard, Jeanne (1990) *La Jeune Morte en robe de dentelle* (Paris: des femmes).
Hyvrard, Jeanne (1996a) *The Dead Girl in a Lace Dress*, trans. Jean-Pierre Mentha and Jennifer Waelti-Walters (Edinburgh: Edinburgh University Press).
Hyvrard, Jeanne (1996b) *Waterweed in the Wash-Houses*, trans. Elsa Copeland (Edinburgh: Edinburgh University Press).
Irigaray, Luce (1977) *Ce sexe qui n'en est pas un* (Paris: Minuit).
Jaccomard, Hélène (2004) '"Cours, cours Nina!": *Garçon manqué* de Nina Bouraoui', *Essays in French Literature*, 41 (November), 43–61.
Jacob, Suzanne (1991) *L'Obéissance* (Paris: Seuil).
Janis, Irving L. (1972) *Victims of Groupthink* (New York: Houghton Mifflin).
Jaron, Steven (2002) 'Autobiography and the Holocaust: an examination of the liminal generation in France', *French Studies*, 56, 2, 207–19.
Jeanelle, Jean-Louis (2007) 'Où en est la réflexion sur l'autofiction', in *Genèse et autofiction*, ed. Jean-Louis Jeannelle and Catherine Viollet with Isabelle Grell (Louvain-La-Neuve: Academia-Bruylant), pp. 17–37.
Jeannelle, Jean-Louis (2009) *Autofiction en théorie* (Paris: Transparence).
Jeannelle, Jean-Louis and Catherine Viollet, with Isabelle Grell (eds) (2007) *Genèse et autofiction* (Louvain-La-Neuve: Academia-Bruylant).
Joignot, Frédéric (2008) 'Amélie Nothomb: l'enfance à en mourir', *Le Monde*, 29 September, *http://fredericjoignot.blog.lemonde.fr/2008/09/29/73/*.
Jordan, Shirley (2002) 'Saying the unsayable: identities in crisis in the early novels of Marie Darrieussecq', in *Women's Writing in Contemporary France: New Writers, New Literatures in the 1990s*, ed. Gill Rye and Michael Worton (Manchester: Manchester University Press), pp. 142–56.
Jordan, Shirley (2004) *Contemporary French Women's Writing: Women's Visions, Women's Voices, Women's Lives* (Bern: Peter Lang).
Jordan, Shirley (2005) '"Un grand coup de pied dans le château de cubes": formal experimentation in Marie Darrieussecq's *Bref séjour chez les vivants*', *Modern Language Review*, 100, 1, 51–67.

Jordan, Shirley (2007) 'Improper exposure: *L'Usage de la photo* by Annie Ernaux and Marc Marie', *Journal of Romance Studies*, 7, 2, 123–41.
Jordan, Shirley (2011) 'Chronicles of intimacy: photography in autobiographical projects', in *Textual and Visual Selves: Photography, Film and Comic Art in French Autobiography*, ed. Natalie Edwards, Amy Hubbell and Ann Miller (Lincoln, NE: University of Nebraska Press), pp. 51–77.
Jordan, Shirley (2013a) '*État présent*: Autofiction in the feminine', *French Studies*, 67, 1, 76–84; online version available at http://fs.oxfordjournals.org/content/67/1/76.full.html?etoc.
Jordan, Shirley (2013b, forthcoming) *Private Lives, Public Display: Intimacy and Excess in French Women's Self-Narrative Experiment* (Liverpool: Liverpool University Press).
Jordi, Jean-Jacques and Mohand Hamoumou (1999) *Les Harkis, une mémoire enfouie* (Paris: Autrement).
Kafka, Franz (1915) *Die Verwandlung* (Leipzig: Kurt Wolff Verlag).
Kawakami, Akane (2010) 'Annie Ernaux's "proof of life": *L'Usage de la photo*', *French Studies*, 64, 4, 451–62.
Kearney, Richard (2003) *Strangers, Gods and Monsters: Interpreting Otherness* (London and New York: Routledge).
Kemp, Anna (2010) *Voices and Veils: Feminism and Islam in French Women's Writing and Activism* (Oxford: Legenda).
Kemp, Anna (2012) 'The child as artist in Amélie Nothomb's *Robert des noms propres*', *French Studies*, 66, 1 (January), 54–67.
Kemp, Simon (2008) 'Darrieussecq's mind', *French Studies*, 62, 4, 429–41.
Kemp, Simon (2010) *French Fiction into the Twenty-First Century: The Return to the Story* (Cardiff: University of Wales Press).
Kerchouche, Dalila (2003) *Mon père, ce harki* (Paris: Seuil).
Kerchouche, Dalila (2006) *Leïla: avoir dix-sept ans dans un camp de harkis* (Paris: Seuil).
Kermode, Frank (1967) *The Sense of an Ending: Studies in the Theory of Fiction* (Oxford: Oxford University Press).
Knibiehler, Yvonne (1987) *Les Pères aussi ont une histoire* (Paris: Hachette).
Kofman, Sarah (1994) *Rue Ordener, rue Labat* (Paris: Galilée).
Kowaleksi-Wallace, Beth and Patricia Yaeger (eds) (1989) *Refiguring the Father: New Feminist Readings of Patriarchy* (Carbondale and Edwardsville: Southern Illinois University Press).
Kramer, Pascale (2009) *L'Implacable Brutalité du réveil* (Paris: Mercure de France).
Krief, Evelyne (1997) *Une enfance interdite ou la petite marrane* (Paris: L'Harmattan).
Kristeva, Julia (1989) *Étrangers à nous-mêmes* (Paris: Fayard).
Lacan, Jacques (1949) 'Le stade du miroir comme formateur de la fonction du Je telle qu'elle nous est révélée dans l'expérience psychanalytique', *Revue Française de Psychanalyse*, 4, 449–55.
Lambeth, John (2006) 'Entretien avec Marie Darrieussecq', *French Review*, 79, 4, 806–18.
Larsen, Nella (2001) [1929] *Quicksand and Passing* (London: Serpent's Tail).

Lasserre, Audrey and Anne Simon (eds) (2008) *Nomadismes des romancières contemporaines de langue française* (Paris: Presses Sorbonne Nouvelle).
Lauretis, Teresa de (1987) *Technologies of Gender: Essays on Theory, Film, and Fiction* (Basingstoke: Macmillan).
Le Bris, Michel and Jean Rouaud (eds) (2007) *Pour une littérature-monde* (Paris: Gallimard).
Le Camus, Jean (2004) *Le Vrai Rôle du père* (Paris: Odile Jacob).
Le Camus, Jean (2005) *Comment être père aujourd'hui* (Paris: Odile Jacob).
Le Garrec, Lénaïk (2003) 'Beastly beauties and beautiful beasts', in *Amélie Nothomb: Authorship, Identity and Narrative Practice*, ed. Susan Bainbrigge and Jeanette den Toonder (New York: Peter Lang), pp. 64–70.
Legendre, Pierre (1989) *Le Crime du caporal Lortie: traité sur le père* (Paris: Flammarion).
Lejeune, Philippe (1975) *Le Pacte autobiographique* (Paris: Seuil).
Lelaidier-Márton, Liliane (2006) *Une ombre entre deux étoiles* (Paris: Velours).
Lesueur, Daniel (1907) *Calvaire de femme* (Paris: Alphonse Lemerre).
Lévinas, Emmanuel (1987) 'La mémoire d'un passé non révolu: entretien avec Foulek Ringelheim', *Les Juifs entre la mémoire et l'oubli*, a special issue of *Revue de l'Université de Bruxelles*, 1–2, 11–20.
Liger, Baptiste (2005) 'Le match Marie Darrieussecq – Éliette Abécassis', *Lire*, September, *www.lire.fr/critique.../idC=49022&idTC=3&idR=218&idG=3*.
Lynch, Kevin (1960) *The Image of the City* (Cambridge, MA: The M.I.T. Press and Harvard University Press).
Mairesse, Anne (2006) 'Le roman spectaculaire à l'épreuve du quotidien: l'œuvre de Véronique Olmi', *Contemporary French and Francophone Studies*, 10, 491–8.
Mairesse, Anne (2008) 'La traversée du genre: le héros-narrateur chez les romancières contemporaines', in *Nomadismes des romancières contemporaines de langue française*, ed. Audrey Lasserre and Anne Simon (Paris: Presses Sorbonne Nouvelle), pp. 93–102.
Marinopoulos, Sophie (2008) *La Vie ordinaire d'une mère meurtrière* (Paris: Fayard).
Marson, Magali (2006) 'Carnalité et métamorphoses chez Ananda Devi', *Notre Librairie*, 143, 64–9.
Marson, Magali (2009) 'Notes de lecture: *Le Sari vert*', *Cultures Sud*, http://www.culturessud.com/contenu.php?id=42.
Martin, Biddy (1988) 'Feminism, criticism, and Foucault', in *Feminism and Foucault: Reflections on Resistance*, ed. Irene Diamond and Lee Quinby (Boston, MA: Northeastern University Press), pp. 3–19.
Mathews, Harry and Alastair Brotchie (eds) (2005) *Oulipo Compendium* (London: Atlas Press).
Maurice, Stéphanie (2010) 'Dominique C., une mère qui ne voulait plus d'enfants', *Libération*, 30 July, http://www.liberation.fr/societe/0101649670-dominique-c-une-mere-qui-ne-voulait-plus-d-enfants.
McCracken, Scott (1998) *Pulp: Reading Popular Fiction* (Manchester: Manchester University Press).
McIlvanney, Siobhán (2001) *Annie Ernaux: The Return to Origins* (Liverpool: Liverpool University Press).

McIlvanney, Siobhán (2007) '"Il était une fois...": trauma and the fairytale in Amélie Nothomb's *Robert des noms propres*', *Dalhousie French Studies*, 81 (winter), 19–28.
McRobbie, Angela (1990) *Feminism and Youth Culture* (Basingstoke: Macmillan).
Meuret, Isabelle (2007) *Writing Size Zero: Figuring Anorexia in Contemporary World Literatures* (Brussels: Peter Lang).
Miller, Ann (2007) *Reading the Bande dessinée* (Bristol: Intellect).
Miller, Nancy K. (1994) 'Representing others: gender and the subjects of autobiography', *differences*, 6, 1, 1–27.
Miller, Nancy K. (1999) 'Memory stains: Annie Ernaux's *Shame*', *a/b: Auto/Biography Studies*, 14, 1, 38–50.
Millet, Catherine (2001) *La Vie sexuelle de Catherine M.* (Paris: Seuil).
Modleski, Tania (1982) *Loving with a Vengeance: Mass Produced Fantasies for Women* (Hamden: Archon Books).
Morello, Nathalie (2008) 'Débordements d'une mère *borderline*: écriture de l'état limite dans *Bord de mer* de Véronique Olmi', in *Les Mères et la mort: réalités et représentations*, ed. É. LaMothe, P. Sardin and J. Sauvage (Bordeaux: Presses Universitaires de Bordeaux), pp. 211–27.
Morello, Nathalie and Catherine Rodgers (eds) (2002) *Nouvelles écrivaines: nouvelles voix?* (Amsterdam: Rodopi).
Mortimer, Mildred (1990) *Journeys Through the French African Novel* (Portsmouth, NH: Heinemann).
Motte, Warren F. Jr (ed.) (1998) *Oulipo: A Primer of Potential Literature* (Champaign: Dalkey Press).
Motte, Warren (2003) *Fables of the Novel: French Fiction since 1990* (Normal: Dalkey Archive Press).
Motte, Warren (2008) *French Fiction Now: The French Novel in the Twenty-First Century* (Champaign and London: Dalkey Archive Press).
Mulliez, Jacques (2000) 'La désignation du père', in *Histoire des pères et de la paternité*, ed. Jean Delumeau and Daniel Roche (Paris: Larousse), pp. 43–72.
Nabati, Simone and Moussa Nabati (1994) *Le Père, à quoi ça sert? La valeur du triangle père-mère-enfant* (Geneva: Jouvence).
Naouri, Aldo (1985) *Une place pour le père* (Paris: Seuil).
Naouri, Aldo (2004) *Les Pères et les mères* (Paris: Odile Jacob).
Naudier, Delphine (2008) 'Assignation à "résidence sexuée" et nomadisme chez les écrivaines', in *Nomadismes des romancières contemporaines de langue française*, ed. Audrey Lasserre and Anne Simon (Paris: Presses Sorbonne Nouvelle), pp. 51–62.
NDiaye, Marie (1989) *La Femme changée en bûche* (Paris: Minuit).
NDiaye, Marie (1990) *En famille* (Paris: Minuit).
NDiaye, Marie (1996) *La Sorcière* (Paris: Minuit).
NDiaye, Marie (1997) 'Mon quatrième roman', in Thierry Fourneau, Marie-Thérèse Humbert and Marie NDiaye, *Tombeau du cœur de Francois II, Adeline et un voyage* (Tours: CRL), pp. 65–8.
NDiaye, Marie (2001) *Rosie Carpe* (Paris: Minuit).
NDiaye, Marie (2003) *Papa doit manger* (Paris: Minuit).

NDiaye, Marie (2005) *Autoportrait en vert* (Paris: Mercure de France).
NDiaye, Marie (2007) *Mon cœur à l'étroit* (Paris: Gallimard).
NDiaye, Marie (2008) 'Les Sœurs', in Pap Ndiaye, *La Condition noire: essai sur une minorité française* (Paris: Calmann-Lévy), pp. 9–15.
NDiaye, Marie (2009) *Trois femmes puissantes* (Paris: Gallimard).
NDiaye, Marie (2011) *Les Grandes Personnes* (Paris: Gallimard).
NDiaye, Marie (2012) *Three Strong Women*, trans. John Fletcher (London: Maclehose Press).
Ndiaye, Pap (2008) *La Condition noire: essai sur une minorité française* (Paris: Calmann-Lévy).
Nehamas, Alexander (1987) *Nietzsche: Life as Literature* (Cambridge, MA: Harvard University Press).
Neyrand, Gérard (2000) *L'Enfant, la mère et la question du père: un bilan critique des savoirs sur la petite enfance* (Paris: Presses Universitaires de France).
Nicolas, Alain (2001) 'Marie et les cerveaux', *L'Humanité*, 13 September, 22.
Nimier, Marie (2002) *La Nouvelle Pornographie* (Paris: Gallimard).
Nimier, Marie (2004) *La Reine du silence* (Paris: Gallimard).
Nora, Pierre (1984) *Les Lieux de mémoire* (Paris: Gallimard).
Nothomb, Amélie (1992) *Hygiène de l'assassin* (Paris: Albin Michel).
Nothomb, Amélie (1998) *Mercure* (Paris: Albin Michel).
Nothomb, Amélie (2000) *Métaphysique des tubes* (Paris: Albin Michel).
Nothomb, Amélie (2002) *Robert des noms propres* (Paris: Albin Michel).
Nothomb, Amélie (2004a) *The Book of Proper Names*, trans. Shaun Whiteside (London: Faber and Faber).
Nothomb, Amélie (2004b) *Biographie de la faim* (Paris: Albin Michel).
Nothomb, Amélie (2010) *Une forme de vie* (Paris: Albin Michel).
Noudelmann, François (2010) 'Je l'entends comme je l'aime', *France Culture*, 10 October, http://www.franceculture.fr/emission-je-1-entends-comme-je-1-aime-chloe-delaume-2010–10–10.html.
Obama, Barack (2007) *Dreams from my Father: A Story of Race and Inheritance* (New York: Random House).
Olmi, Véronique (2001) *Bord de mer* (Paris: Actes Sud).
Olmi, Véronique (2010) *Beside the Sea*, trans. Adriana Hunter (London: Peirene Press).
Ouellette-Michalska, Madeleine (2007) *Autofiction et dévoilement de soi* (Montreal: XYZ Éditeur).
Oulipo (or OuliPo) (Ouvroir de littérature potentielle) (1973) *La Littérature potentielle* (Paris: Gallimard; Folio essais).
Oulipo (1981, 1988) *Atlas de littérature potentielle* (Paris: Gallimard; Folio essais).
Paglia, Camille (2001) *Sexual Personae: Art and Decadence from Nefertiti to Emily Dickinson* (London and New Haven, CT: Yale University Press).
Parker, David and Miri Song (2001) *Re-Thinking 'Mixed Race'* (London: Pluto Press).
Pavic, Milorad (1988) [1984] *Dictionary of the Khazars: A Lexicon Novel*, trans. Christina Pribicevic-Zoric (New York: Knopf).
Pearce, Lynne (1994) *Reading Dialogics* (London: Edward Arnold).
Pearce, Lynne (1997) *Feminism and the Politics of Reading* (London: Arnold).

Perec, Georges (1978) *La Vie mode d'emploi* (Paris: Hachette).
Pingeot, Mazarine (2007) *Le Cimetière des poupées* (Paris: Julliard).
Poe, Edgar Allen (1846) *The Philosophy of Composition* (Philadelphia: G. R. Graham).
Poisson, Catherine (2007) 'Frictions: mot et image chez Marie NDiaye et Camille Laurens', *Contemporary French and Francophone Studies*, 11, 4, 489–96.
Prébois, Sigolène (2010) *Version live* (Paris: P.O.L.).
Prokhoris, Sabine (2000) *Le Sexe prescrit: la différence sexuelle en question* (Paris: Flammarion).
Rabaté, Dominique (2008) *Marie NDiaye* (Paris: Textuel).
Radway, Janice (1991) [1984] *Reading the Romance: Women, Patriarchy and Popular Literature* (London: Routledge).
Rahmani, Zahia (2003) *Moze* (Paris: Sabine Wespiesier).
Rahmani, Zahia (2006) *France, récit d'une enfance* (Paris: Sabine Wespiesier).
Rahmani, Zahia (2007) 'Figure d'un homme', in *Mon père*, ed. Leïla Sebbar (Montpellier: Chèvre-Feuille Étoilée), pp. 245–56.
Rakocevic, Robert (2007) 'Quelle politique de (la) crise d'après la critique littéraire française à partir de 1980? Une enquête bibliographique', *Trans: Revue de littérature générale et comparée*, 12 ('La Trace'), http://trans.univ-paris3.fr/spip.php?article182.
Ravi, Srilata (2007) *Rainbow Colors: Literary Ethnographies of Mauritius* (Lanham: Lexington Books).
Redonnet, Marie (1986a) *Splendid Hotel* (Paris: Minuit).
Redonnet, Marie (1986b) *Doublures* (Paris: P.O.L.).
Redonnet, Marie (1987a) *Forever Valley* (Paris: Minuit).
Redonnet, Marie (1987b) *Rose Mélie Rose* (Paris: Minuit).
Redonnet, Marie (1992) *Candy Story* (Paris: P.O.L.).
Redonnet, Marie (1994a) *Forever Valley*, trans. Jordan Stump (Lincoln, NE: University of Nebraska Press).
Redonnet, Marie (1994b) *Nevermore* (Paris: P.O.L.).
Redonnet, Marie (1994c) *Rose Mellie Rose*, trans. Jordan Stump (Lincoln, NE: University of Nebraska Press).
Redonnet, Marie (1994d) *Splendid Hotel*, trans. Jordan Stump (Lincoln, NE: University of Nebraska Press).
Redonnet, Marie (1995) *Candy Story*, trans. Alexandra Quinn (Lincoln, NE: University of Nebraska Press).
Redonnet, Marie (1996) *Nevermore*, trans. Jordan Stump (Lincoln, NE: University of Nebraska Press).
Redonnet, Marie (2005) *Understudies*, trans. Jordan Stump (Raleigh: Leaping Dog Press).
Reid, Martine (2010) *Des femmes en littérature* (Paris: Belin).
Resnick, Margery and Isabelle de Courtivron (eds) (1984) *Women Writers in Translation: An Annotated Bibliography 1945–1982* (New York and London: Garland Publishing).
Reyes, Alina (1988) *Le Boucher* (Paris: Seuil).
Reyes, Alina (1994) *Derrière la porte: une aventure dont vous êtes le héros/une aventure dont vous êtes l'héroïne* (Paris: Robert Laffont).
Reyes, Alina (2001) *Ma vie douce: journal 1979–2000* (Cadeilhan: Zulma).

Reyes, Alina (2008a) *La Jeune Fille et la Vierge* (Montrouge: Bayard).
Reyes, Alina (2008b) *Lumière dans le temps* (Montrouge: Bayard).
Reyes, Alina (2009) *Psaumes du temps présent: 70 prières pour Son retour* (Paris: Presses de la Renaissance).
Reyes, Alina (2010a) *Souviens-toi de vivre* (Paris: Presses de la Renaissance).
Reyes, Alina (2010b) *Charité de la chair: le sexe et le sacré* (Paris: Presses de la Renaissance).
Reyes, Alina and Stéphane Zagdanski (2002) *La Vérité nue* (Paris: Pauvert).
Rice, Alison (2009) 'Answering to "Muslim" language, country, and religion in Zahia Rahmani's *"Musulman" roman*', *Women's Studies International Forum*, 32, 347–53.
Richard, Jean-Pierre (1996) 'Le trouble et le partage', in *Terrains de lecture* (Paris: Gallimard), pp. 161–86.
Ricœur, Paul (2004) *Parcours de la reconnaissance* (Paris: Gallimard).
Robbe-Grillet, Alain (1963) *Pour un nouveau roman* (Paris: Minuit).
Robertson, Kim Alton (1996) *The Grotesque Interface* (Frankfurt: Vervuert).
Robson, Kathryn (2004) *Writing Wounds: The Inscription of Trauma in post-1968 French Women's Life-Writing* (Amsterdam: Rodopi).
Rochefort, Christiane (1958) *Le Repos du guerrier* (Paris: Grasset).
Rochefort, Christiane (1959) *Warrior's Rest*, trans. Lowell Bair (New York: David McKay Co.).
Rodgers, Catherine (2003) 'Nothomb's anorexic beauties', in *Amélie Nothomb: Authorship, Identity and Narrative Practice*, ed. Susan Bainbrigge and Jeanette den Toonder (New York: Peter Lang), pp. 50–63.
Rodgers, Catherine (2009a) 'Marie Darrieussecq: écrivaine de l'entre-deux', in *Women in the Middle*, a special issue of *Women in French Studies*, 105–17.
Rodgers, Catherine (2009b) 'Between "white" and "blanc": the margin of the fantastic in Marie Darrieussecq's *White*', in *Re-Defining the Real: The Fantastic in Contemporary French and Francophone Women's Writing*, ed. Margaret-Anne Hutton (Oxford: Peter Lang), pp. 13–30.
Rose, Jacqueline (1986) *Sexuality in the Field of Vision* (London: Verso).
Rosello, Mireille (2005) *France and the Maghreb: Performative Encounters* (Gainesville: University Press of Florida).
Rosnay, Tatiana de (2007a) *Sarah's Key* (New York: St Martin's Press).
Rosnay, Tatiana de (2007b) *Elle s'appelait Sarah*, trans. Agnès Michaux (Paris: Héloïse d'Ormesson).
Roubaud, Jacques and Anne F. Garréta (2009) *Éros mélancolique* (Paris: Grasset).
Roudinesco, Élisabeth (2002) *La Famille en désordre* (Paris: Fayard).
Rousseau, Christine (2009) 'Écrire avec cette voix m'a effrayée', *Le Monde des Livres*, 13 November, *http://www.lemonde.fr/livres/article/2009/11/12/ananda-devi-ecrire-avec-cette-voix-m-a-effrayee_1266067_3260.html#ens_id=1232414*.
Rousso, Henry (1987) *Le Syndrome de Vichy: 1944–1987* (Paris: Seuil).
Rousso, Henry (1990) *Le Syndrome de Vichy: de 1944 à nos jours* (Paris: Seuil).
Rubinstein, Marianne (2002) *Tout le monde n'a pas la chance d'être orphelin* (Paris: Verticales/Le Seuil).

Russo, Mary (1994) *The Female Grotesque: Risk, Excess and Modernity* (London: Routledge).
Ryan, Marie-Laure (2001) *Narrative as Virtual Reality: Immersion and Interactivity in Literature and Electronic Media* (Baltimore and London: The John Hopkins University Press).
Rye, Gill (2001) *Reading for Change: Interactions Between Text and Identity in Contemporary French Women's Writing (Baroche, Cixous, Constant)* (Oxford and Bern: Peter Lang).
Rye, Gill (2009a) *Narratives of Mothering: Women's Writing in Contemporary France* (Newark: University of Delaware Press).
Rye, Gill (2009b) 'Marie Darrieussecq's *Le Pays*: threshold worlds', in *Re-Defining the Real: The Fantastic in Contemporary French and Francophone Women's Writing*, ed. Margaret-Anne Hutton (Oxford: Peter Lang), pp. 31–44.
Rye, Gill (2010) 'Christine Angot et l'écriture de soi', in *Le Roman français de l'extrême contemporain: écritures, engagements, énonciations*, ed. Barbara Havercroft, Pascal Michelucci and Pascal Riendeau (Quebec: Nota Bene), pp. 423–39.
Rye, Gill (ed.) (2002) *Contemporary Women's Writing in French*, a special issue of *Journal of Romance Studies*, 2, 1 (spring).
Rye, Gill (ed.) (2004) *Hybrid Voices, Hybrid Texts: Women's Writing at the Turn of the Millennium*, a special issue of *Dalhousie French Studies*, 68 (fall).
Rye, Gill (ed.) (2005) *A New Generation: Sex, Gender and Creativity in Contemporary Women's Writing in French*, a special issue of *L'Esprit Créateur*, 45, 1 (spring).
Rye, Gill and Michael Worton (eds) (2002) *Women's Writing in Contemporary France: New Writers, New Literatures in the 1990s* (Manchester: Manchester University Press).
Sade, D. A. F. de (1995) *Œuvres II* (Paris: Gallimard).
Sade, D. A. F. de (1998) *Œuvres III* (Paris: Gallimard).
Saint-Martin, Lori (2010) *Au-delà du nom: la question du père dans la littérature québécoise actuelle* (Montreal: Presses de l'Université de Montréal).
Saint-Martin, Lori (2011) 'Bastards, legitimacy and new families in contemporary Québec fiction', *American Review of Canadian Studies*, 41, 2 (June), 126–37.
Samacher, Robert (2009) *Sur la pulsion de mort: création et destruction au cœur de l'humain* (Paris: Hermann).
Sarrey-Strack, Colette (2002) *Fictions contemporaines au féminin: Marie Darrieussecq, Marie NDiaye, Marie Nimier, Marie Redonnet* (Paris: L'Harmattan).
Sartre, Jean-Paul (1943) *L'Être et le néant: essai d'ontologie phénoménologique* (Paris: Gallimard).
Sauvage, Jérémi (1999) 'Interview: Marie Darrieussecq confesse à Jérémi Sauvage', *Ténèbres*, 8 (October), 61–6.
Scarry, Elaine (1985) *The Body in Pain: The Making and Unmaking of the World* (Oxford: Oxford University Press).
Schaeffer, Jean-Marie (1999) *Pourquoi la fiction?* (Paris: Seuil).
Schneider, Michel (2005) *Big Mother: psychopathologie de la vie politique* (Paris: Odile Jacob).

Sebbar, Leïla (1982) *Shérazade, 17 ans, brune, frisée, les yeux verts* (Paris: Stock).
Sebbar, Leïla (2004) *Mes Algéries en France: carnet de voyages* (Saint-Pourçain-sur-Sioule: Bleu Autour).
Selao, Ching (2005) 'Porter l'Algérie: *Garçon manqué* de Nina Bouraoui', *L'Esprit Créateur*, 45, 3 (fall), 74–84.
Seltzer, Mark (1997) 'Wound culture: trauma in the pathological public sphere', *October*, 80 (spring), 3–26.
Serrano Mañes, Montserrat (2007) 'Nina Bouraoui: *Poupée Bella*, secrets d'amour et d'écriture', *Expressions Maghrébines*, 6, 1 (summer), 167–82.
Smith, Sidonie (1993) *Subjectivity, Identity, and the Body: Women's Autobiographical Practices in the Twentieth Century* (Bloomington: Indiana University Press).
Smith, Sidonie and Julia Watson (2001) *Reading Autobiography: A Guide for Interpreting Life Narratives* (Minneapolis: University of Minnesota Press).
Sollors, Werner (1997) *Neither Black nor White Yet Both: Thematic Explorations of Interracial Literature* (Oxford: Oxford University Press).
Sontag, Susan (1978) *On Photography* (London: Allen Lane).
Spelman, Elizabeth (1982) 'Woman as body: ancient and contemporary view', *Feminist Studies*, 8, 1, 109–31.
Spender, Stephen (1980) 'Confessions and autobiography', in *Autobiography: Essays Theoretical and Critical*, ed. James Olney (Princeton: Princeton University Press), pp. 115–22.
Spiegelman, Art (2003) *The Complete Maus* (London: Penguin).
Stimpson, Catharine (2005) 'Do these deaths surpass understanding? The literary figure of the mother who murders', *TriQuarterly*, 25 (December), 45–62.
Stone, Martin (1997) *The Agony of Algeria* (New York: Columbia University Press).
Suleiman, Susan (2006) *Crises of Memory and the Second World War* (Cambridge, MA: Harvard University Press).
Surya, Michel (2004) *Humanimalités: matériologies 3* (Paris: Léo Scheer).
Susam-Sarajeva, Sebnem (2006) *Theories on the Move: Translation's Role in the Travels of Literary Theories* (Amsterdam and New York: Rodopi).
Tambling, Jeremy (1990) *Confession: Sexuality, Sin, the Subject* (Manchester: Manchester University Press).
Tardieu, Laurence (2002) *Comme un père* (Paris: Seuil).
Tardieu, Laurence (2004) *Le Jugement de Léa* (Paris: Arléa).
Taylor, Chloë (2009) *The Culture of Confession from Augustine to Foucault: A Genealogy of the 'Confessing Animal'* (New York and London: Routledge).
Terrasse, Jean-Marc (2003) '"Comment j'écris": entretien avec Marie Darrieussecq', in *La Création en acte*, ed. Paul Gifford and Marion Schmid (Amsterdam: Rodopi), pp. 253–68.
Thomas, Lynn (1999) *Annie Ernaux: An Introduction to the Writer and her Audience* (Oxford and New York: Berg).
Thumerel, Fabrice (ed.) (2004) *Annie Ernaux: une œuvre de l'entre-deux* (Arras: Artois Presses Université).
Tisseron, Serge (2005) 'Du désir d'intimité à celui d'extimité, et de leur protection respective', in *L'Intimité*, ed. Lila Ibrahim-Lamrous and

Séveryne Muller (Clermont-Ferrand: Presses Universitaires Blaise Pascal), pp. 271–81.
Todorov, Tzvetan (1998) *Les Abus de la mémoire* (Paris: Arléa).
Tombs, George (1992) 'Le père a-t-il un avenir?', *Cité libre*, 20, 1, 8–10.
Tort, Michel (2005) *Fin du dogme paternel* (Paris: Aubier).
Tran Huy, Minh (2001) 'Entretien avec Chloé Delaume', http://www.zone-litteraire.com/interviews/entretien-avec-chloe-delaume.
Valéry, Francis (1999) 'Un souffle de liberté insolente', *Ténèbres*, 8 (October), 67–76.
Vassallo, Helen (2007) 'Wounded storyteller: illness as life narrative in Nina Bouraoui's *Garçon manqué*', *The Forum for Modern Languages Studies*, 43, 1 (January), 46–56.
Vassallo, Helen (2009) 'Embodied memory: war and the remembrance of wounds in Nina Bouraoui's *Garçon manqué* and Leïla Sebbar's *Lettres parisiennes*', *Journal of War and Culture Studies*, 1, 2 (January), 189–200.
Vassallo, Helen (2012) *The Body Besieged: The Embodiment of Historical Memory in Nina Bouraoui and Leïla Sebbar* (Lanham, MA: Lexington Books).
Vegh, Claudine (1975) *Je ne lui ai pas dit au revoir: les enfants de déportés parlent* (Paris: Gallimard).
Vian, Boris (1947) *Les Morts ont tous la même peau* (Paris: Scorpion).
Vian, Boris (1997) [1947] *L'Écume des jours*, introduced Gilbert Pestureau and Michel Rybalka (Paris: Pauvert/Livre de Poche).
Vieux-Chauvet, Marie (2010) [1968] *Amour, colère et folie* (Paris: Zellige).
Vigan, Delphine de (2007) *Nô et moi* (Paris: J. C. Lattès).
Vigan, Delphine de (2009) [2001] *Jours sans faim* (Paris: J'ai lu).
Vilain, Philippe (2009) *L'Autofiction en théorie* (Paris: Transparence).
Ward Jouve, Nicole (1977) *Le Spectre du gris* (Paris: des femmes).
Wheelwright, Julie (2002) '"Nothing in between": modern cases of infanticide', in *Historical Perspectives on Child Murder and Concealment, 1550–2000*, ed. Mark Jackson (London: Ashgate), pp. 270–85.
Willging, Jennifer (2007) *Telling Anxiety: Anxious Narration in the Work of Marguerite Duras, Annie Ernaux, Nathalie Sarraute and Anne Hébert* (Toronto: University of Toronto Press).
Wilson, Elizabeth (2001) *The Contradictions of Culture: Cities, Culture, Women* (London: SAGE publications).
Wilson, Emma (1996) *Sexuality and the Reading Encounter: Identity and Desire in Proust, Duras, Tournier and Cixous* (Oxford: Clarendon Press).
Winders, James A. (2001) *European Culture since 1848: From Modern to Postmodern and Beyond* (London: Palgrave).
Winnicott, D. W. (1958) 'Primary maternal preoccupation', in *Collected Papers: Through Paediatrics to Psycho-Analysis* (London: Tavistock), pp. 300–5.
Winnicott, D. W. (1965) 'Ego distortion in terms of true and false self', in *The Maturational Processes and the Facilitating Environment: Studies in the Theory of Emotional Development* (London: Hogarth Press), pp. 140–52.
Wittig, Monique (1973) *Le Corps lesbien* (Paris: Minuit).
Wittig, Monique (1985) *Virgile, non* (Paris: Minuit).
Wittig, Monique (1992) 'The straight mind', in *The Straight Mind and Other Essays* (New York: Harvester Wheatsheaf), pp. 21–32.

Worton, Michael (2005) 'My name is white: Michael Worton is enthralled by Marie Darrieussecq's Antarctic meditations', *Guardian*, 28 May.
Yaeger, Patricia (1989) 'The father's breasts', in *Refiguring the Father: New Feminist Readings of Patriarchy*, ed. Beth Kowaleksi-Wallace and Patricia Yaeger (Carbondale and Edwardsville: Southern Illinois Press), pp. 8–21.
Young, James E. (2000) *At Memory's Edge: After-Images of the Holocaust in Contemporary Art and Architecture* (New Haven, CT: Yale University Press).
Zaidman, Annette (2002) *Mémoire d'une enfance volée (1938–1948)* (Paris: Ramsay).
Zalberg, Carole (2004) *Chez eux* (Paris: Phébus).
Zeif, Colette (2010) *La Grande s'occupera de la petite* (Brive: Monédières).
Zola, Émile (1885) *Germinal* (Paris: Charpentier).

Index

Abécassis, Éliette 26, 98
abjection 73, 115
abortion 8, 154
abuse 11, 85 n15, 132, 217
adoption 8, 16 n7
aesthetics
  anorexic 117, 118, 243
  decadent 237–50
  of crisis 15 n3
affect, affectivity 11, 77, 80, 82, 86 n19, 118, 122, 198, 205, 207, 208, 220
ageing 39, 198
agency 7, 8, 33, 36, 37, 39, 70–1
Algeria 5, 19, 60–72, 73, 141–53, 210 n1
Algerian War 5, 59 n26, 60–72, 142, 143, 148
alterity (see also difference) 53, 129–30, 134, 139, 139 n1
Amanieux, Laureline 117, 242
amorality (see also morality) 247–8
angels 132, 139 n11, 229, 235 n19, n20
Angelo, Adrienne 142
Angot, Christine 3, 11, 13, 26, 42 n12, 98, 154–67, 178 n10, 213, 215, 216
  Léonore, toujours 98
  L'Inceste 156–60, 165 n6
  Quitter la ville 156
  La Peur du lendemain 156, 158–9
  Rendez-Vous 156, 157, 159–61, 166 n17
  Le Marché des amants 178 n10
  Les Petits 178 n10
animals, animality 91, 96 n11, 127–40, 205–8

  domestic 134
  human-animal 127–40
anorexia (see also eating disorders) 10, 14, 65, 113–26, 243
anorexic
  aesthetic 117, 118, 243
  behaviour 114
  body 114–17, 123–4, 125
  logic 114
anti-semitism 49–51, 56
anxiety (of the author) 13, 168–79, 199–203
Arribert-Narce, Fabien 210 n6
artifice
  and aesthetics 238–9, 241
  and gender 152 n1, 228
  and language 184
  and race 79–80
Asibong, Andrew 9
audience 213, 215
author
  as character 120–1
  death of 120–1
  authorial anxiety 168–79, 199–203
  control 168–79, 199–203, 214–15, 246–8
  unavailability 201–2
autobiography 13, 42 n12, 48, 62, 75, 117, 141–4, 150, 154–6, 161, 168–79, 183, 196, 199, 202, 203, 209, 210 n1, 210 n2, 213, 215, 218, 223 n17, 246
autobiographical pact 142–3, 221, 224 n36
autobio-history 61
autoethnography 13

autofiction 11, 13–14, 141, 154, 156, 158, 159, 178 n10, 183, 202, 210 n1, 210 n2, 212–24, 231, 235 n28
  and gender 13–14
  interactive 218–19
autothanatography 199
autotopography 202

Badinter, Élisabeth 98–9
Baetens, Jan 16 n11, 196, 197
Bainbrigge, Susan 117
ballet 117–18, 243
Barbery, Muriel 27, 31
Barnet, Marie-Claire 9, 10
Barthes, Roland 16 n12, 24, 42–3 n20, 183–6, 193, 194 n7, 194 n8, 195 n33, 195 n34
beauty (see also monstrosity) 79, 115, 117, 237–50
Beauvoir, Simone de 17, 20, 22, 27, 203, 210 n8, 227
Beck, Béatrix 203, 204
Besnaci-Lancou, Fatima 60–2, 65–6, 68, 71
becoming
  becoming animal 130–2
  bodily becoming 113–26
belonging 52, 128, 130, 139, 145, 147, 151, 186, 194 n10
bereavement (see also death, grief, mourning) 53, 197, 198, 210 n8
betrayal 55
best-seller 4, 27, 30–43, 170, 173, 183
Bible 164
bilingual text 28
birth 85 n14, 89, 92, 100, 102, 104, 109 n5, 118, 120, 128, 219, 227
blackness 73–86
blankness 73–86, 150
blogging 15
body 10, 27, 66, 73, 113–26, 127–40, 141–53, 154–67, 189, 218–19, 222 n5, 227, 234 n5, 235–6 n31, 237–50
  and text 113–26, 141–53
  as territory 141–53
  as text 121–5
  Body without Organs 115
  female 10, 113–26, 130–2, 154–67, 222 n5, 227, 234 n5, 235–6 n31, 237–50
  female reproductive 227, 239, 241
  maternal 100, 227
  sexualised 154–67, 218–19
bodily
  conflict 113, 115
  experience 10, 117, 118, 122, 125
  image 10, 27, 116, 124
Bouraoui, Nina 3, 10, 13, 26, 84 n3, 114, 141–53
  La Voyeuse interdite 141
  Garçon manqué 141–53
  Poupée Bella 142–53
  Mes mauvaises pensées 142, 144, 147–53
  Appelez-moi par mon prénom 143, 149–53
Burko-Falcman, Berthe 57, 58, 59
Butler, Judith 7

Caine, Philippa 9
Cairns, Lucille 5, 11, 59 n24, 121, 225
Calle, Sophie 11, 197, 202, 203, 210 n3, 210 n8
camps
  concentration/death 48, 57 n9
  housing 60, 63
cancer 154, 172, 173, 174, 178 n12, 197, 199–203, 214, 223 n9
canon 4, 17, 19, 20, 213
capitalism 33, 114, 115, 118
Cardinal, Marie 5, 6, 21, 22, 28, 98, 235–6 n31
chastity 11
Chen, Ying 99
children 5, 8, 35, 47–59, 60–72, 79, 85 n16, 87–97, 98–110
  and fathers 87–97
  and mothers 98–110
  childbirth 85 n14, 89, 92, 100, 102, 104, 109 n5, 118, 120, 128, 219

children's literature 26
hidden children 5, 47–59
murder (see also infanticide) 98–110
childhood 5, 53, 55, 63, 65, 84 n5, 85 n16, 94, 101, 117, 118, 119, 122, 137, 145, 146, 148, 160, 168, 203, 205, 208, 241–3
aesthetics of 117–18, 241–2
city 146, 150–1
Cixous, Hélène 5, 10, 11, 12, 22, 23–4, 26, 83–4 n2, 96 n2, 98, 240, 248 n10
class 159, 170, 176, 197
clinamen 212–13, 219
collaboration
Vichy 5, 47–59
collective, collectivity
agency 52
creativity 222, 224
discourse 185
female collectivity 32, 37–8, 238–9, 247–8
(hi)story 71
memory 68, 173, 176, 178 n14, 179 n23
colonialism 66, 72 n16, 99
Colonna, Vincent 13, 223 n14
community 32, 38, 53, 70, 72 n16, 128, 145–6, 165, 233, 239
confession 154–67, 169
Christian 155
epistolary 160, 166
feminist 155–6
sexual 156, 161
Connan-Pintado, Christiane 210 n7
Connon, Daisy 9
consumerism 33–4, 176
contamination
anxiety 168–79
corporeality (see also body) 10, 113–26
practices 114, 115
Cotille-Foley, Nora 210
counter-narrative 66
creativity 3, 12–15, 19, 26, 29, 117, 119–21, 123–5, 143, 173, 184–5, 190–1, 196, 213–15,
219, 222, 238, 242–3, 246–8, 248 n4, 248 n7, 251
crime 31, 67, 90, 94, 99, 108, 200, 202, 245, 249 n22, 240 n25
fiction 31
crisis 4
and aesthetics 15 n3, 16 n11, 193, 194 n8
cruelty 244–5
Cruickshank, Ruth 15 n3
cure 142, 198, 209
talking 142
curse 66, 70, 72 n32
Cusset, Catherine 11, 13, 196, 197, 210 n1, 215
cyber
fiction 219
world 15
cyborgs 232

Damlé, Amaleena 9, 11, 16 n8
Darrieussecq, Marie 3, 12, 13, 14, 17, 26, 27, 29 n2, 42 n12, 42–3 n20, 73, 83–4 n2, 98, 99, 114, 128, 183–95, 223 n11
Truismes 73, 83–4 n2, 128, 183
Naissance des fantômes 184
Bref séjour chez les vivants 184
Le Bébé 98
White 99, 183–95
Le Pays 183–95
Tom est mort 184
daughters (see also fathers, mothers) 8, 9, 37, 50, 60–72, 75, 76, 87–97, 101, 118, 123, 129, 132–4, 138, 143, 152 n5, 158, 171, 176, 203, 206, 214, 227, 233, 234, 248 n15
Davis, Colin 5, 12
death 10, 11, 12, 27, 34, 38, 47–59, 67–8, 85 n16, 87, 88, 93, 96 n2, 106, 109 n5, 120, 122, 126 n12, 129, 183, 194 n6, 196–211, 222 n7, 223 n19, 227, 228–9, 234 n7, 235 n22, 241–2, 246, 251
and femininity 10, 11, 122, 227, 241–2

Index

camp 48, 57 n9
drive 234 n7
living-dead 76
of parent 27, 67–8, 87, 88, 93, 96 n2, 120, 203–11
of the author 12, 120
psychic 85 n16
Decadence 237–41, 247–8
deconstruction 12
Delaume, Chloé 3, 12, 13, 14, 15, 196, 197, 210 n1, 210 n3, 212–24
   Les Mouflettes d'Atropos 213, 216–18
   Le Cri du sablier 213, 215, 216–18, 220, 224 n28
   Corpus Simsi 218–19, 224 n25
   La Vanité des somnambules 218
   Certainement pas 218, 219
   Les Juins ont tous la même peau 214, 215, 216
   J'habite dans la télévision 218, 224 n34
   La Nuit je suis Buffy Summers 210, 219
   Dans ma maison sous terre 214, 219–21, 222 n7
   Éden matin midi et soir 223 n9
   La Règle du je 210, 213, 216, 221–2, 223 n12
   'S'écrire mode d'emploi' 14, 212, 214–15, 218
   Une femme avec personne dedans 213, 222
Deleuze, Gilles 115–19, 123, 125, 125 n3, 126 n16
Delvaux, Martine 210 n5
desire (see also passion) 10–12, 14, 37–8, 141–2, 145–7, 150–2, 154, 157, 161, 163–5, 225, 230–3, 234 n16, 235 n31, 236 n33
desirability 79
female 10–12, 154, 157, 161, 163–5
lesbian 11–12, 141–2, 145–7, 157, 225, 230–3, 234 n16, 235 n31, 236 n33
transgressive 11–12

Despentes, Virginie 3, 7, 11, 16 n8, 26, 87–97, 216, 225–36
   Baise-moi 226
   Teen spirit 87–97
   King Kong théorie 7, 227
   Apocalypse bébé 226, 232
detective fiction 25, 27
deterritorialisation 9–10, 124
Devi, Ananda 3, 10, 11, 15 n1, 26, 114, 127–40
   Rue la Poudrière 127
   Moi, l'interdite 127–40
   Ève de ses décombres 127
   Le Sari vert 127–40
diaries 144, 147, 156, 161, 169, 170–1, 174, 179 n23
difference (see also alterity) 6–7, 11, 50–1, 75–7, 84 n10, 116, 120, 121, 129, 130, 138–9, 143, 152 n8, 198, 227–9
   racial 6, 73–86, 143, 152 n8
   sexual 6–7, 11, 198, 227–9
discrimination 7, 77, 81
disembodiment 10
disfigurement 130, 244
displacement 9–10, 14, 61, 75, 144–5, 198
dispossession 48
divinity 77, 132, 133–5, 249 n32
divorce 8, 88
double 14, 75, 77, 91, 156, 159, 166 n17, 174, 178 n15, 206, 211 n9, 222, 246
Doubrovsky, Serge 13, 14, 178 n10, 215, 219–21
Dreyfus Affair 50
drowning 38, 70, 229, 248
Ducas, Sylvie 224 n25
Duras, Marguerite 17, 20, 21, 22, 27, 36, 41 n6, 73, 98, 183, 215, 222 n7

eating disorders (see also anorexia) 114
écriture féminine 12, 227, 240, 248 n10

Index 279

écriture genitale 227
écriture utérine 227, 234 n6
Edwards, Nathalie 9, 14, 210 n2
ekphrasis 197, 200, 205
embodiment (see also disembodiment) 10, 141–53, 165, 190, 193, 227, 240
empowerment 40, 71, 74, 247
enfant caché 5, 47–59
Enlightenment, the philosophy of 52
environment 10, 141–53
  artificial 238
  externalisation of 146–7, 148–9
  internalisation of 143–4, 148–9
  international 186
  social 144
equality (see also inequality) 6–7, 52, 69
  parité 6
Ernaux, Annie 5, 6, 11, 13, 14, 17, 21, 22, 26, 27, 29 n2, 38, 96 n2, 154, 168–79, 196–211, 215
  La Place 96 n2, 168, 171
  Une femme 168
  Passion simple 171, 172, 174, 175
  Journal du dehors 172
  La Honte 168, 171, 174
  'Je ne suis pas sortie de ma nuit' 169, 206, 207, 208
  L'Événement, 154, 170, 176
  La Vie extérieure 170
  Se perdre 154, 170, 171
  L'Occupation 169, 170, 172, 174
  Les Années 170, 173–7
  with Frédéric-Yves Jeannet, *L'Écriture comme un couteau* 170, 171, 175
  with Marc Marie, *L'Usage de la photo* 154, 172–3, 174, 197, 198, 199–203, 205, 208
Eros (see also *Thanatos*) 40, 199, 226
eroticism 161–5, 200, 210 n1, 216, 234 n8
escapism 30, 35
essentialism 7–8, 227, 233, 234 n6

biological 233
gender 233
ethics 8, 12, 15, 49, 53, 55–6, 57 n3, 74, 89, 108, 127–40, 196, 206, 238, 239, 240, 234–6, 248, 252
ethnicity 6, 47, 49
  ethnic marker 61
exclusion 5, 47, 49, 53, 55, 56, 57 n3, 67
exemplary memory 55, 59 n24
experiment 15, 28, 116, 119, 156, 161, 183–95, 196–211, 212–24, 251
  generic 161
  textual 15, 185–6, 193, 196, 199
exposure 11, 38, 154, 171, 199, 213, 215
externalisation (see also internalisation) 144–7, 149, 151–2
extreme contemporary 12, 154–67
evil 127, 129, 130, 134, 136, 164

fables 12, 28, 63, 206
Facebook 15, 32
facticity 238
Faerber, Johan 165 n6
Fairbairn, W. R. D. 85 n13
fairytale 118, 119, 121
Fallaize, Elizabeth 5, 12, 15 n2, 21–2, 27, 28, 29 n1, 29 n2
family 5–10, 15 n4, 39–40, 48, 60–72, 74, 84 n5, 88–9, 90, 92, 96, 103, 106, 122–4, 126 n10, 128, 130–1, 137, 138, 141, 143–4, 149, 153 n18, 165, 178 n8, 183, 184, 194 n5, 197, 205, 214, 216, 218–20, 223 n16, 244, 251
  drama 40, 214, 219
  relations 5, 8–9, 39, 123, 251
  as practice 9
  dysfunctional 39
  survival of 62
Fanon, Frantz 81, 85 n16
fantastic 12, 74, 75, 79, 218, 220

fantasy 31, 54, 80, 102, 154, 161, 172, 218, 220
fashion 247
fathers 8, 60–72, 74, 75, 77, 84 n5, 87–97, 102, 103, 109 n8, 118, 122–4, 133, 138, 141, 152 n6, 153 n14, 157–61, 166 nn9–15, 205, 214, 215, 217, 219, 223 n20
  absent/returning 74, 87–97
  as subject 8, 88–9
  figure 87, 159
  father-daughter relationship 87–97, 133, 138, 157–61, 166 nn9–15, 214, 215
fatherhood 87–9, 92, 93, 95, 96, 96 n5, 97 n23
Felman, Shoshana 5, 16 n12, 61
Felski, Rita 155–7, 161–4
feminine 9, 30, 32, 40, 235 n18, 237, 239, 240
femininity 8, 78, 113, 127, 134, 152 n1, 227
feminist 3, 7–8, 16 n8, 19, 21, 23–4, 31, 32–3, 70, 88, 113–14, 116, 132, 155–6, 157, 162–3, 164, 177, 209, 226, 233, 234 n8, 237–50
  activism 7
  theory 7, 16 n8, 19, 21, 23–4, 32–3, 88, 113–14, 116, 209, 226–8, 233, 234 n8, 237, 239, 243, 248
feminism 7–8, 15 n5, 16 n8, 33, 99, 115–16, 156, 225–36, 237–50
Fernandes, Martine 142
fiction (see also autofiction) 5, 8, 14, 15 n3, 21, 25, 27–8, 30–43, 75, 88, 89, 90, 95, 96, 96 n7, 116–17, 143, 150, 151, 161, 163, 168, 186, 187, 210 n1, 212–24, 228–31, 233 n1, 234 n16, 234–5 n17, 235 n30, 240, 244–7
  detective 25
  popular 30–43
film 17, 28, 58 n12, 99, 121, 175, 178 n17, 226, 232

fin de millénaire 4
fiction 15 n3
First World War 49
food 118, 119, 123, 124, 243
foreclosure 93
Foucault, Michel 155, 156
Fouque, Antoinette 225–36
friendship 77, 85 n17, 224–5
fundamentalism 7

Gallay, Claudie 3, 30–43
games 210, 212–24, 244
  literary 244
  textual 212–24
  virtual 210, 218
Garréta, Anne 8, 11, 22, 29 n2, 225–36
  Sphinx 225, 228–9, 230, 232
  Pour en finir avec le genre humain 226
  Ciels liquides 225, 228, 229
  La Décomposition 225, 228, 229–30, 231, 235 n27
  Pas un jour 226, 228, 230–3
Gaudet, Jeannette 186
Gavalda, Anna 3, 15, 31, 32, 39–40, 41 n7, 42 n8
gay (and lesbian) experience 7, 11, 16, 134, 141, 142, 146–8, 157, 225, 230–2
  identity 11, 141, 142, 146–8, 230–2
  rights 7, 16
gender 5–8, 10, 13–14, 30, 47, 60, 65, 69–70, 72 n27, 79, 88, 114, 120, 128–9, 132–3, 136, 142, 146, 152 n3, 156, 198, 225–36, 240, 248, 251
  as fiction 225–6
  binary 136, 146, 227
  gendered experience 79
  politics 7, 12
generation 3, 5, 6, 12, 15 n2, 15 n4, 61, 66, 71, 72 n24, 170, 174, 176
  interactive media generation 212
  new generation of women's writing 3, 5, 15

genocide 5, 47–8, 53, 56
Gervais-Marx, Danièle 47–59
ghosts, ghostliness 62, 69, 76, 83, 113, 159–60, 189, 192
Gladieu, Stéphan 62
globalisation 7, 9, 15, 25
God, gods, goddesses 127–40
Gorrara, Claire 240
graphic text 14, 184, 197, 203–11
Green, André 73, 80, 81, 83 n1, 85–6 n19, 86 n21
grief (see also bereavement, death, mourning) 34, 36, 198, 199, 208, 241
Grosz, Elizabeth 7, 133, 136
Guattari, Félix 115–17, 123, 125, 126 n16
guilt 54, 65, 79, 108, 143, 158, 164, 167 n27

hallucination
  negative 6, 73–86
haptic 200
harassment 7
Haraway, Donna J. 7, 232
harkis 5, 60–72
haunting 6, 78
Havercroft, Barbara 12, 13, 116, 165 n6, 167 n29, 210 n5
healing 5, 35, 60–1, 66–7, 69–70, 71 n4, 139 n19, 142–3, 149, 152 n4
health (see also illness) 78, 83, 116–17, 141
Henke, Suzette 71 n5, 149, 152 n4
Henric, Jacques 210 n1
heritage 62, 64, 70, 71 n7, 141, 145, 147, 148, 152 n3, 215, 247
  unwanted 70
Héritier, Françoise 98
hero, heroine 36–8, 66, 125 n5, 135, 139 n20, 238–9, 242, 248
  decadent 238–9, 242, 248
  romantic 36–8, 119, 125 n5
heterocentrism 11
heteronormativity 7, 11
heteropatriarchy 115, 134
heterosexism 148

heterosexual 33, 37, 150–1, 227, 234 n8
  couple 33, 37, 234 n8
  maleness 227
heterosexuality 11
highbrow 37
Hirsch, Marianne 15 n4, 88, 205, 206
historiography 47, 56
history 4–6, 49, 60–72, 88, 96 n3, 100, 103, 142, 143, 147, 148, 150, 152 n3, 170, 173, 175, 177, 178 n14, 179 n22, 185, 194, 251
  collective 5, 71
  colonial 66, 72, 141–3
  external 49
  familial 6, 60–72, 143–4
  national 61, 66
  oral 62
  personal 49, 103, 147, 175, 178 n14
  social 170, 173, 175, 179 n22
Hogarth, Chris 9
Holmes, Diana 11, 248 n5
Holocaust, the 55, 58–9 n23, 72 n24, 205
hologram 188
homosexuality (see also gay and lesbian) 11, 142, 227, 233, 234 n8
hope 4, 15, 35, 36, 71, 124
Humanities
  study of 24, 251
humour 213, 233, 247
husbands 62, 64, 75, 102, 134, 184, 216–17
Hutton, Margaret-Anne 9, 12
hybridity 8, 9, 10, 14, 49, 73–86, 127–40, 158, 163, 196–9, 212, 215, 222 n2, 226, 232
  genre 49, 158, 163, 196–9, 212, 215, 222 n2, 226, 232
  metaphors of 9
  moral 132–6, 136–9
  physical 128–32, 136–9
hyperreal 10, 115
hysteria 114

Hyvrard, Jeanne 21, 22, 235–6 n31
Hubbell, Amy 14, 210 n2

ideology 50, 52, 115–17, 118, 119, 124–5, 126 n16, 133, 156
identification 79, 89–93, 144–7, 150, 165, 177, 184, 206, 225, 227, 230
  reader's 177, 184
  visual 89–93
identity 6–10, 37, 38, 40, 42 n12, 48, 49, 50, 53, 54, 61, 64, 67, 69, 71 n10, 72 n18, 73–86, 88, 90, 94, 99, 128, 130–1, 138–9, 141–54, 165, 177, 183, 186, 187, 191–3, 197–8, 212–24, 226, 228–9, 230, 231, 233, 251
  autofictional 212–24
  change 54
  crisis 69
  cultural 141–53
  female 8, 9, 99, 127–40, 141–53, 183
  fractured 9, 42, 141, 148, 191–3, 198
  group 177, 186
  human 130–2
  hybrid 9, 73–86, 128, 127–40
  international 186
  local 186
  male 88, 231
  national 141, 186, 197
  postcolonial 197
  quest 142, 144, 147, 151
  racial 6, 73–86
  religious 6
  sexual 141–2, 144, 146, 228–9, 233 n1, 251
  split 9, 94
  transmittable 61
illegitimacy 88–90
illness (see also health) 7, 10, 11, 70, 95, 104, 106, 135, 142–5, 147, 149, 151, 198, 199–200, 203, 208
  mental 70, 104, 106
image 10, 14–15, 27, 35–7, 42 n19, 52, 61, 62, 64, 66, 67, 69, 70, 75, 81, 91–2, 94, 116, 124, 132–3, 166 n13, 174, 175, 178 n15, 179 n18, 187, 190–1, 196–211, 216, 220, 223 n7, 244
  making 205, 208, 209
  of thought 116, 124
  body 10, 27
  mirror 91–2, 94
  word and image 14–15, 187, 190–1, 196–211, 220, 223 n7
immigrant, immigration 6, 60, 70, 71 n2, 84 n6, 90
incest 11, 14, 73, 90, 154–61, 165
individualism 239–40, 246
inequality 70, 72, 73
infanticide (see also child murder) 8, 98–110
inheritance 61, 63, 67, 68, 71
installation art (see also multimedia) 15, 197, 202, 203, 210 n3
internalisation (see also externalisation) 6, 65, 143–4, 146, 151–2
intimacy 8, 10–11, 36, 82, 89, 92, 100, 101, 154–7, 159, 165, 166 n23, 169, 171, 198, 200–1, 202, 209, 252
Irigaray, Luce 9, 22, 88
irony 50, 91, 92, 94, 104, 135, 177, 247
Islam 6, 15, 55
  politicised 55
  face veils 6, 15
IVF (*in vitro* fertilisation) 8

jealousy 27, 147, 169–70, 174, 177
Jeannelle, Jean-Louis 13, 223
Jewish 5, 47–59
Jordan, Shirley 9, 10, 13, 15 n2, 16 n8, 42 n12, 81, 84 n10, 184, 194 n2, 203, 210 n2, n5, n7
jouissance 42–3 n22, 185–6, 193, 240, 243, 248 n7, 248 n10
journal extime 170
judgement 79, 90, 93, 101, 106, 108, 148, 155–6, 157, 162

Kawakami, Akane 210 n5
Kemp, Anna 15 n5, 121
Kemp, Simon 9, 12, 194 n2, 210 n6
Kerchouche, Dalila 60–5, 68–9
Kristeva, Julia 139 n1

Lacan, Jacques 85 n6, 93
landscape 35, 69, 144, 148, 151, 189
language 14, 17–29, 31, 33, 34, 40, 54–5, 81, 92, 116–17, 119–24, 128, 129, 130, 132–3, 138, 156, 162–3, 165, 166 n19, 183–95, 212–24, 225, 230–1, 235 n23, n27, 240, 249
  feminine 40
  insufficiency of 81, 92, 191, 193
  politics of 187
Lasserre, Audrey 9
Laub, Dori 5, 16 n12, 61
Lejeune, Philippe 142, 223 n14
lesbian (and gay) experience 7, 11, 16, 134, 141, 142, 146–8, 157, 225, 230–6
  identity 11, 141, 142, 146–8, 230–6
  rights 7, 16
Lévinas, Emmanuel 55
libidinal 233
life-writing 10, 13, 140–53, 161, 199, 202
  women's 13
linguistic sign 188, 191
literary prizes/prizewinners 30, 31, 34, 41 n3, n6, 42 n14, 47, 57 n3, 100, 127, 141, 218, 230
littérature-monde 15
loneliness 34, 39
love 30–43, 90–2, 102, 104, 119, 128, 131, 139 n6, 145–7, 153 nn11–12, 159, 163–4, 167 n24, 171–3, 178 n8, 183, 186, 208
  and writing 149
  parent-child 90–2, 102, 104, 208
  romantic 30–43, 119, 128, 131, 145–7, 153 nn11–12, 159, 163–4, 167 n24, 171–3, 178 n8
lowbrow 37

McIlvanney, Siobhán 116, 118, 120, 168–9, 174
madness 38, 82, 100, 103, 109, 127, 147, 188, 195 n19
Maghreb 60, 141
marginalisation, marginality 75, 76, 87, 90, 95, 127–30, 138
marriage 5, 7, 16 n7, 38, 70, 100, 102
Marson, Magali 130, 131
matricide 120
media 10, 62, 100, 105, 108, 114, 183, 196–7, 202, 209, 212, 218–19, 232
  interactive 212, 218–19
  intermediality 196
  multi- 212, 218–19
  visual 196–211
melodrama 31, 40
memoir 26, 56, 169, 170
memory 6, 14, 54–9, 60–72, 101, 103, 142, 147–8, 160–1, 166 n12, 173, 176, 178 n14, 179 n23, 183, 184, 188, 190–3, 194 n5, 205, 213, 231, 232, 235 n31
  exemplary 55, 59
  family 60–72
  post 205
menstruation 241
metamorphosis 130–2
  female 117
metanarrative 169
metaphor 9, 35, 42 n19, 48, 75, 91, 95, 217, 240, 241
metatextual 14, 161, 184, 193
métissage 73–86
middlebrow 4
migrant writers 4
migration (see also immigration) 25, 152
  textual 25
Miller, Ann 14, 210 n2
Miller, Nancy K. 199, 202
Millet, Catherine 11, 26, 154, 163, 196, 210 n1, 215
mimesis 12, 31–2, 35–6, 40, 42 n10, 117, 125, 188, 193

mirror, mirroring 14, 91–2, 94, 96 n12, 137, 140 n27, 206, 223 n9
misogyny 132–5, 138, 148, 237, 239–42, 246, 247, 248 n2
misrecognition (see also non-recognition, recognition) 76
mixed race 4, 73–86, 128, 143
writers 4
modernity 38
Morello, Nathalie 5, 15 n2, 16 n8, 41 n3, 42 n12, 109 n3
monsters 66, 127–31, 135–7, 139 n22, 140 n23–5
monstrosity 117, 129–30, 136–40
moral 129, 136–9
ordinary 136, 140 n25
morality 50, 51, 55, 164, 237–50
indifference to (see also amorality) 164, 237–50
monstrous 129, 136–40
mortality (see also death) 10, 208
mothers 5, 8, 9, 37, 49–50, 60–72, 74, 87–97, 98–110, 118–20, 123, 137–8, 141, 171, 178 n8, 190, 214, 220, 227, 229, 233, 234 n8
mother-child bond/relationship 8, 98–110, 118–20, 123, 137–8, 203, 205–8, 210 n8, 211 n10
mother-daughter bond/ relationship 8, 9, 37, 49–50, 60–72, 74, 87, 88, 118–20, 123, 126, 137–8, 171, 178, 190, 205–8, 210 n8, 211 n10, 227, 233, 234 n8
voice of 8, 62–4, 89, 95
motherhood 5, 8, 16 n9, 98–110, 233
homosexual 233
surrogate 16 n9
mothering 8, 98–91
narratives of 8, 101
Motte, Warren 12, 27, 28, 29 n2, 222 n1
mourning (see also bereavement, grief) 34, 38, 55, 59 n27, 184, 203, 205, 208, 248 n15
multicultural France 4

multimedia
installation 212–13, 218–19
murder 48, 53, 54, 91, 95, 99, 108, 118, 120, 138, 214, 217, 219, 220, 230, 241, 246
music 128, 131, 212, 216–21, 223 n22
mystery 34, 37, 38, 40, 219
myth, mythology 33, 134–5, 223 n17, 239
Hindu/Western 134–5
mythification
le mythe résistanciel 51–2, 58 n12
mythologisation 249

narcissism 156, 237, 239, 240, 241, 247
narrative
coherence 32, 37
coming-of-age 69
counter 66
illness 144, 151
life 142–4, 147
national 66
of mothering 8, 101
quest 142–3, 145, 149, 151
recovery 116
resolution (in form of narrative) 116, 117, 119, 121
resolution (within the narrative) 32, 33, 38, 39, 124, 145, 147, 149, 150, 151, 198
romance 34
self- 15, 203
voice 12, 93–5, 186, 191–3, 195 n30
naturalism 238
NDiaye, Marie 6, 73–86
  La Femme changé en bûche 85 n17, 99
  En famille 74, 85 n17
  La Sorcière 74–5
  Rosie Carpe 76, 81, 85 n15, 85 n17
  Papa doit manger 76, 84 n10
  Autoportrait en vert 85 n14, 197
  Mon cœur à l'étroit 85 n14
  'Les Sœurs' 74, 77–83, 85 n17

Trois femmes puissantes 31, 41 n6, 86 n23
Les Grandes Personnes 76
Ndiaye, Pap 74, 84 n4
Nietzsche, Friedrich 242
Nimier, Marie 3, 26, 96 n2, 154, 216
nomadism 9
non-recognition (see also recognition, misrecognition) 78, 85 n19, 89, 92, 94
Nothomb, Amélie 3, 12, 17, 26, 27, 29 n2, 31, 113, 117–21, 122, 125, 125 n1, 177 n1, 237–50, 251
  Hygiène de l'assassin 239–42, 246
  Mercure 243–6, 249–50 n33
  Métaphysique des tubes 246–7, 249 n30
  Robert des noms propres 113, 114, 117–21, 122, 125, 125 n1, 242–3, 249 n18, n31
  Biographie de la faim 117
  Une forme de vie 249 n16, n31
nouveau romanciers 12
novel, the 12, 30, 145
  best-selling 4, 27, 30–43, 100, 183
  contemporary 12, 90
  detective 25, 27
  French 9, 16 n11, 183
  graphic 14, 197
  popular 31–2, 33, 34 (see also romance)
  women's novel 31

Occupied France 48, 49, 52
Olmi, Véronique 3, 15 n1, 98–110
optimism 32, 34, 36, 37, 38, 40, 84 n4
organic 115
  an-organic 115, 121
origins 53, 58 n17, 75, 84 n5, 128, 147, 152 n3, n9, 247
other(s) 7, 9, 10, 12, 15, 29, 39, 54, 80, 81, 92, 105, 106, 107, 123, 124, 129–30, 135, 144, 145, 150, 158, 177, 209, 229, 230, 239, 240, 242, 246
otherness 139, 149, 151, 152 n3, n8, 193, 240
relations with 12, 15, 29, 106, 146, 200, 239
Oulipo 12, 213, 215, 216, 222 n1, 226, 228, 235 n17

PaCS (*Pacte civil de solidarité*) 6
pain 14, 35, 36, 37, 55, 61, 63, 65, 67, 69, 74, 80, 81, 83, 88, 102, 107, 158, 173, 192, 198, 203–9, 241
palliative
  image-making as 198, 208
parents 6, 27, 54, 64, 68, 77, 79, 102, 103, 143, 168, 176, 205, 207, 208, 214, 217
  single 8, 88, 106
  parent-child relationship 100, 208
parenting 27, 95
  group 8
  same-sex 8, 88
  single 8, 88
Paris 7, 39, 49, 53, 144–7, 148, 150, 186, 189, 214, 232
parité 6, 7
passion (see also desire) 38, 133, 134, 167 n29, 170, 171, 172, 200
past, the 4–6, 21, 37, 55, 59, 61, 63, 65, 66, 67, 68, 69, 101, 121, 124, 129, 144, 150, 174, 186, 189, 252
  recovery of 66, 68
pathology 7, 78, 115, 116, 119, 120, 124, 149
patriarchy 100, 133
  authority 88, 134
  discourse 248
  ideals 115
  power 88
  prejudice 127
  society 89, 115, 132, 138
  demise of 9
patricide 91
pedagogy 18

performance 14, 80, 114, 116, 118, 164, 213, 216, 218–19, 222, 224 n33
perpetrator (see also victim) 130, 202
photography 14, 54, 55, 170, 173, 176, 197, 198, 199–203, 208, 210 n1, n3, n6, 232
  analogue 197, 199, 203
  digital 197, 199, 203
phototext 199–203, 208
pieds noirs 71
place 10, 34, 39, 64, 68, 69, 90, 96, 144, 146, 148, 150, 186–7, 188–9
pleasure 11, 30, 31, 73, 200, 208, 240
  sexual 154, 161–4, 165, 240, 248 n7
  textual 15, 30–43, 185, 193, 194, 200
poems 28, 127, 161, 216
poetry 26, 28, 189, 223 n9
politics 5, 6, 7, 15, 40, 55, 56, 70, 74, 75, 83, 89, 114, 115, 119, 152 n3, 156, 187, 197, 213, 221, 237–9, 240, 245
  feminist 237, 239, 243, 247, 248, 251
  gender 7, 10, 132, 157
  sexual 7, 12
popular literature 4, 20, 27, 30–43, 117, 174, 197
pornography 11, 78, 154
postcolonialism 9, 78, 99, 152 n3
  postcolonial identities/relationships 197
post-human 233
postmemory 6, 15 n4, 205
postmodernism 7, 9, 33, 40, 73, 74, 114, 115, 120
poststructuralism 7, 9, 16 n8
poverty 39, 82, 104
Prébois, Sigolène 197, 198, 203–9
pregnancy 102, 118, 128
psyche 76, 83, 85 n13, 136
psychiatry, psychiatric 103, 104, 106, 115, 147, 150, 217, 219

psychoanalysis 5, 9, 74, 78, 80, 81, 88, 96 n3, 114, 115, 118, 120, 122, 124, 139 n1, 200, 220
  object relations 85 n13, 115
publishers 17, 19, 20, 21, 24, 27, 28, 41 n4, 75, 171, 197
publishing 28, 220

queer 7, 8, 12, 232

Rabaté, Dominque 86
race 4, 6, 74, 75, 76, 78, 83, 84 n4, n6, n10, 85 n17, 197
  post-race 75, 77
racialising discourse 73, 74, 76, 79
racialised identity 6, 74, 75, 76, 77, 80, 81, 82, 83, 84 n10, 85 n17, 152 n3, 214, 251
Radway, Janice 32, 33, 35, 43 n25
Rahmani, Zahia 60, 63, 64, 65, 66, 67, 72 n27
rape 11, 14
readers 4, 12, 15, 17, 22, 23, 26, 27, 42 n11, 52, 53, 69, 74, 76, 79, 81, 82, 83, 101, 103, 104, 105, 106, 107, 108, 124, 135, 138, 155, 157, 158, 162, 168, 169, 170, 175, 177, 184, 185, 188, 189, 190, 191, 193, 198, 208, 209, 212, 213, 216, 222, 230, 240, 244, 252
  active 5, 33, 101, 108, 157, 184, 199, 218, 219, 220, 221, 222, 231
  as interlocutor 108, 157, 158, 161–2, 166 n17
  author-reader relationship 157, 162, 174, 219, 222
  birth of 12
  feminist 243, 251
  readerly hesitation 13
  women 27, 30–43, 156, 162
readership 4, 17, 21, 28, 31, 35, 36, 41 n6, 42 n14, 177
reading 4, 13, 15, 33, 34, 37, 41 n1, 42 n9, 43 n20, 85 n14, 108, 119, 120, 169, 184, 185, 186,

193, 199, 208, 239, 240, 243, 248, 251, 252
  as dynamic process 16 n12
  collective dimension of 32, 42 n9
  feminisation of 30, 32, 41 n2
  fiction 30, 31, 39
  pleasure 13, 31, 32, 34, 35, 41 n6, 185, 194, 251
  revisionary 33
reality 4, 6, 9, 17, 30, 33, 35, 36, 40, 48, 54, 82, 83, 100, 104, 109, 114, 120, 127, 129, 135, 152 n10, 184, 185, 188, 189, 229, 232, 238, 240, 248 n3
realism 32, 35, 40, 238
reason (see also unreason) 131, 133, 134
recognition (see also misrecognition, non-recognition) 6, 39, 64, 67, 68, 74, 87–97, 146, 150
  self-recognition 82, 146
redemption 38, 51, 93, 135, 154, 155, 158
Redonnet, Marie 10, 21, 22, 28
referentiality 156, 184, 191–2, 216
  self-referentiality 209
relationality 239
relations 5, 8, 11, 15, 37, 39, 60, 100, 122, 123, 143, 155, 157, 163, 190, 228, 233, 251
relationships
  and the self 78, 187, 188
  between concepts 6, 8, 14, 31, 35, 73, 113, 116, 117, 118, 119, 121, 122, 124, 125, 127, 128, 137, 152, 165, 184, 186, 191, 197, 251
  between people 7, 27, 33, 40, 49, 82, 100, 101, 106, 119, 122, 143, 147, 151, 155, 158, 160, 162, 172, 184, 192, 198, 200, 216, 233
  family 79, 100, 101, 102, 120, 183, 208
  father-daughter 65, 68, 87–97, 122

mother-daughter 9, 171, 227, 234 n8
  sexual 134, 150, 157, 159–60
religion 6, 89, 236 n37
reparation 68, 80
representation (see also self-representation) 6, 10, 12, 14, 33, 56, 74, 77, 81, 100, 109, 115–21, 122, 124, 125, 187, 190, 205, 217, 228, 230
repression 60
reproduction 14, 198
  artistic 198, 239
  sexual 239, 241
reproductive technologies 8
republic, republican 6, 49, 50, 52, 58 n11, 59 n26
  Third Republic 50, 58 n11
Resistance, the 51, 58 n12
Reyes, Alina 11, 154, 156, 161–4, 165, 166 n23, 167 n29
  Le Boucher 163
  Derrière la porte 163
  Ma vie douce 154, 161–4, 165
rhizome 117
Robson, Kathryn 10
Rodgers, Catherine 5, 15 n2, 16 n8, 41 n3, 42 n12, 183, 194 n2, 243, 248 n1
romance 11, 31, 32–40, 42 n8, 172, 226
  danger of 38
  hero 36–7
  heroine 37
  mass-market 37
  narrative 33, 34
  return to 11
  script 32, 37, 39
  tropes 36
roman-feuilleton 34, 39
Roudinesco, Élisabeth 8, 9
Rousso, Henry 58 n12
Rye, Gill 8, 9, 15 n2, 16 n12, 42 n12, 101, 157, 194 n2, 195 n30

Saint-Martin, Lori 88, 90, 95
same-sex marriage 16 n7
same-sex families 16 n7, 88

Sarrey-Strack, Colette 15 n2
Scarry, Elaine 143, 148, 151
schizophrenia 77, 219, 220
scopophilia 200
scriptotherapy 142, 152 n4
Sebbar, Leïla 6, 26, 73, 152 n3, 196, 210 n1
Second World War 5, 47–59, 66, 245
secularity 6, 158
Selao, Ching 142
self 10, 13, 14, 15, 33, 37, 38, 39, 52, 55, 67, 76, 78, 79, 80, 84 n10, 85 n13, n16, 92, 114, 116, 129, 137, 141–53, 168, 176, 177, 186, 188, 189, 192, 201, 202, 203, 209, 233, 235 n17, 240, 242–3, 246, 247
  -consciousness 12, 14, 74, 121, 170, 203, 229
  -denigration 158
  -destruction 38, 65, 230, 243, 247
  embodied 10, 189
  -erasure 77, 232
  -exaggeration 77
  -exhibition 118
  -exposure 38, 213
  false 74, 78–82, 86 n23
  -fulfilment 38
  -identification 79, 145–6, 232
  -interrogation 145
  narrated 170
  narrating 170
  -narrative 15
  -negation 6, 73–86
  -protection 38, 77, 79
  -recognition 82, 146
  -recovery 145
  -re-creation 215
  -reinvention 141–53, 213
  -representation 164, 165, 212–24, 246
  -signification 120, 121, 123, 124
  writerly 13, 173
Serrano Mañes, Montserrat 142
sex 11, 155, 156, 157, 161–4, 165 n2, 200, 227
  agency 37
  ambiguity 225, 226, 227, 229, 232
  difference 6, 227, 228, 229
  identity 141, 142, 144, 146, 164, 228, 251
  indeterminacy 228, 233
  pleasure 154
  politics 7, 12
  relationship 134, 150, 157, 159–60
  revelations 163
  sexual acts 11, 154, 162, 163
sexual difference 6, 227, 228, 229
sexuality 5, 7, 142, 146, 147, 155, 165, 166 n23, 200, 227, 234 n6
  ambiguous 225, 226, 227, 229, 232
  women's 11, 142, 154, 164, 237
shame 57 n7, 63, 65, 67, 68, 91, 102, 154, 155, 164, 165, 167 n30, 168, 202, 219
  legacy of 61, 63, 70
Shoah 49, 55
short story 6, 74, 77, 100, 127, 183, 226
siblings 78, 80, 205
signification 13, 48, 115, 117, 119, 120, 121, 125
  processes of 10
  self-signification 120, 121, 123, 124
signifying practices 118, 125 n2
silence 5, 19, 55, 63, 64, 65, 66, 67, 75, 83, 106, 108, 123, 146, 147, 148, 151, 157, 174
Simon, Anne 9
sisters 69, 70, 74, 77–83, 85 n17, 122, 126 n10, 131
Smith, Sidonie 142, 155, 165
society 6, 10, 21, 74, 76, 88, 89, 98, 101, 105, 107, 109, 114, 128, 129, 132, 135, 136, 138, 142, 155, 176, 177, 228, 239
solipsism 240, 246, 247
Sontag, Susan 200
space 9, 10, 11, 13, 15, 34, 40, 81, 100, 117, 138, 143, 147, 148, 149, 150, 151, 158, 186, 189, 199, 208, 219, 230, 240, 248

species 132, 133, 134
  speciesism 132
Sphinx 225–36
starvation 35, 116, 122
story (see also life story, love story, short story, war story) 12, 63, 65, 68, 69, 71, 81, 87, 88, 93, 94, 100, 101, 106, 108, 119, 120, 121, 122, 123, 124, 128, 142, 143, 144, 147, 149, 157, 167 n29, 174, 203, 205, 206, 219, 231, 241, 242, 243, 244, 245, 246, 247
  untold 61
storyteller 63
storytelling 12, 30, 36, 41 n6, 64, 183
subject 32, 42 n12, 69, 71 n5, 74, 75, 78, 80, 81, 83, 101, 114, 115, 116, 128, 144, 151, 154, 155, 157, 158, 159, 161, 184, 199, 209
  becoming 9
  female 11, 165
  in-between 9
  mixed (hybrid) 9, 74, 75, 76, 78, 79, 84 n4
  shifting 9
  split 13–14
  uncanny 9
subjectivity 9, 10, 11, 14, 33, 49, 74, 76, 85, 103, 114, 141, 144, 156, 164–5, 197
  dissolution of 114–15
  of fathers 88–9
  female 5, 13, 37
  fictionalised 14
  plural 14
  schizoid 76, 85 n17
  sexual 11
  suppression of 173
suffering 11, 32, 53, 57 n9, 62, 67, 68, 78, 113, 123, 124, 143, 148, 160, 161, 199, 243
suicide 65, 68, 70, 91, 94, 118, 178 n10, 217, 220, 221, 222
Suleiman, Susan 71 n3
surrogacy 8

surrogate motherhood 16 n9
survivors 48, 49, 53, 56, 57 n9, 61, 68, 70
  survivor's guilt 54

Tardieu, Laurence 3, 26, 87–97, 98, 101–10
technology 9, 10, 15, 19, 197, 198, 203, 210 n1, 232, 247
  reproductive 8
Tel Quel 12
television 18, 28, 58 n12, 92, 219
territory 26, 148
  deterritorialisation 9, 10, 123, 124
  reterritorialisation 10, 150, 152 n9
testimony 5, 15 n4, 47, 48, 49, 54, 60, 62, 104, 108, 116, 117, 121, 124, 152 n4, 158, 169, 205
Thanatos (see also *Eros*) 199
theatre 23, 26, 28, 83, 94
therapy 83, 142, 149, 158, 220
theriomorphosis 130
thinness 114, 118
Thomas, Lynn 170
Thumerel, Fabrice 9, 170
Todorov, Tzvetan 55, 59 n24
tolerance 50
Toonder, Jeanette den 117
tragedy 53, 108
traitor 61, 66, 70
transcultural 47, 114, 198
  journeys 24
transformation 6, 49, 127, 128, 130–2, 137
transgender 230
transgression 8
translation 4, 17–29
  history of 18
  translated authors 17, 20, 22, 23, 26, 27, 41 n5
  texts 7, 17, 18, 20, 21, 23, 24, 27, 34, 100, 183, 214
  studies 18, 22
  theory 22–5
transsexuality 7

trauma 5, 10, 14, 15 n4, 49, 53, 54, 55, 60, 61, 62, 65, 66, 68, 70, 74, 78, 79, 85 n18, 101, 115, 116, 118, 137, 154, 155, 168, 198, 213, 216, 217, 252
  collective 68
twins 75
Twitter 15

Uncanny, the 9, 77, 136, 201
universalism 6, 50
unreason (see also reason) 134, 136

Vassallo, Helen 142, 144
Vichy France 5, 47–59
victim (see also perpetrator) 40, 52, 54, 56, 71, 77, 82, 108, 115, 116, 130, 160, 161, 165, 200, 202, 220, 222, 230, 231
video games 218
Vigan, Delphine de 113, 114, 117, 121–4, 125
Vilain, Philippe 223 n14
violence 7, 11, 34, 35, 36, 55, 62, 70, 90, 93–5, 113, 120, 122, 133, 168, 171, 174, 200, 251
  bodily 118
  female 100
virginity 38, 102
virtual, the 10, 15, 218
visual, the 10, 14, 15, 62, 90, 114, 116, 177 n1, 196–211
voice 8, 61, 62, 64, 67, 68, 69, 71, 89, 96, 101–5, 105–7, 108, 147, 157, 170, 191, 193, 215, 216, 217, 218, 220, 221, 246
  female 5, 62, 89, 96, 238
  narrative 12, 93–5, 101–5, 186, 191, 193, 195 n30
vulnerability 10, 38, 39, 47, 54, 88, 94, 207

war 5, 49, 59 n26, 95, 214
  Algerian War 5, 59 n26, 60–72, 142, 143, 148
  Second World War 5, 47–59, 66, 245
war story 61, 67, 69, 71
Watson, Julia 142, 155
whiteness 80
wife, wives 60–5, 71, 76, 89, 91, 106, 129, 133, 134, 176, 178 n10
Wilson, Emma 16 n12
Winnicott, D. W. 78, 82, 85 n16
witch 74–5
witchcraft 75
witness, witnessing 6, 10, 61, 66, 77, 105, 108, 196, 200, 201, 202, 220, 221
  bearing witness 5, 6, 61, 121, 155, 251–2
  irresponsible witness 108
Wittig, Monique 21, 22, 27, 232, 235 n20, n24
wound culture 10
wounds 5, 35, 60, 61, 62, 66, 67, 69, 82, 143, 148, 149, 151, 159
Worton, Michael 15, 42, 186
writing 23, 36, 66, 67, 68, 69, 71, 76, 77, 81, 83, 85 n18, 94, 114, 116, 121, 124, 144, 145, 149, 158, 163, 170–9, 184, 191, 196, 210 n1, 213, 218, 219, 221, 230, 231, 239, 240, 251
  as healing 69, 142
  as reparative 61
  creative 29

Zaidman, Annette 56, 57 n2, n7, n11, 58 n13, n19
Zalberg, Carole 57 n2, n11, 58 n13, n15, n19, n21
Zeif, Colette 57 n2, n5, 58 n13, n19, n22, 59 n31